BED & BREAKFASTS
IN QUÉBEC 1999

AGRICOTOURS

ULYSSES
TRAVEL PUBLICATIONS
Travel better... enjoy more

Project coordinators	*Page layout*	*Illustrations of houses*
Odette Chaput	Judith Lefebvre	Marie-Annick Viatour
(Féd. Agricotours)	Isabelle Lalonde	Lorette Pierson
Claude Morneau		Sandrine Delbaen
Pascale Couture	*Collaboration*	Myriam Gagné
(Ulysses)	Odile Bélanger	
	Diane Drapeau	*Cartography*
Translation	Isabelle Larocque	André Duchesne
Danielle Gauthier	Andrée Lyne Allaire	Patrick Thivierge
Tara Salman	Carole Chevalier	
		Photo
Correction		Bullaty / Lomeo (Image Bank)
Tara Salman		

Distributors

Canada : Ulysses Books & Maps, 4176, St-Denis, Montréal (Québec) H2W 2M5
☎ (514) 843-9882, poste 2232, ☎ (800) 748-9171, fax : 514-843-9448 www.ulysse.ca, guiduly@ulysse.ca

États-Unis : Distribooks, 820 N. Ridgeway, Skokie, IL 60076-2911
☎ (847) 676-1596, fax : (847) 676-1195

Belgique-Luxembourg : Vander, 321 av. des Volontaires, B-1150 Bruxelles
☎ (02) 762 98 04, fax : (02) 762 06 62

France : Vilo, 25, rue Ginoux, 75737 Paris, cedex 15
☎ 01 45 77 08 05, fax : 01 45 79 97 15

Espagne : Altaïr, Balmes 69, E-08007 Barcelona
☎ (3) 323-3062, fax : (3) 451-2559

Italie : Centro cartografico Del Riccio, Via di Soffiano 164/A, 50143 Firenze
☎ (055) 71 33 33, fax : (055) 71 63 50

Suisse : Diffusion Payot SA, p.a. OLF S.A., C.P. 1061, CH-1701 Fribourg
☎(26) 467 51 11, fax : (26) 467 54 66

Other countries, contact Ulysses Books & Maps (Montréal), Fax: (514) 843-9448

For information on the Fédération des Agricotours network:

Fédération des Agricotours du Québec
4545, av. Pierre de Coubertin
C.P. 1000, Succursale M.
Montréal, Québec
H1V 3R2
(514) 252-3138
fax (514) 252-3173
internet http://www.agricotours.qc.ca
E-mail agricotours-q@sympatico.ca

Issued also in French under title: Gîtes du passant au Québec 1999

c Éditions Ulysse
All rights reserved
Bibliothèque nationale du Québec
Legal deposit - Premier trimestre 1999
ISBN 2-89464-199-8

TABLE OF CONTENTS

INTRODUCTION

Here, finally, is a guide offering more than 600 different establishments, giving you the opportunity to get to know Québec's regions, its countryside, its cities and its people.

- A little jaunt to Île d'Orléans?
- A week's vacation on the Côte-Nord?
- A ski weekend in the Laurentides?
- A delicious meal with a group of friends at a Table Champêtre in the Townships?
- An afternoon family outing on a farm in Montérégie?

The Fédération des Agricotours of Québec offers six different choices for your vacation and leisure time:

- **Gîte du Passant** ^{MD}* (Bed & Breakfast)
- **Auberge du Passant**^{MC}* (Country Inn)
- Farm stays
- Country and city home
- **Table Champêtre** ^{MC}* (Country-Style Dining)
- Farm excursions

FARM ACTIVITIES

At the end of each region, in the "B&B and Inns" section of the guide, you'll find a list of farm activities. Enjoy a gourmet excursion with some country-style dining on delicious meals prepared with farm-fresh ingredients... Stay in the cosy ambiance of a farm and experience all that goes into a well-run agricultural operation... Or how about a farm excursion, explore and relax in forests and fields with the animals... Whatever your preference, rich and memorable adventures on the farm await!

QUALITY CONTROL

Each establishment in the nerwork is inspected regularly by the federation, and must conform to precise standards of security, cleanliness, comfort and quality of service. On site, a sign indicating Agricotours membership is your assurance that the owners belong to the Fédération des Agricotours du Québec. To further assure guests a quality stay, each establishment offering accommodation must display a certificate in each room stating that it has been verified Agricotours and is in compliance with their quality standards.

Do not hesitate to complete the "We want Your Opinion" sheets at the end of the book as well as those available in the rooms or dining rooms to let us know how you enjoyed your Agricotours experience. We need your feedback, suggestions and criticism to continue to improve the quality of the network and the services provided.

PRACTICAL INFORMATION

Though the guide is revised each year, all information contained herein is subject to change without notice. However, the prices listed for each establishment are valid until the publication of the next edition, expected in Febuary 2000.

TAXES

As per federal and provincial laws, customers may have to pay federal Goods and Services tax (7%) and the provincial tax (6.5%). Establishments where taxe is not included are marked "Taxes extra". Foreign visitors can be refund upon presentation of their receipts.

According to provincial law, some tourist regions (Montréal, Laval) must charge an additional tax of $2 per night for each unit rented. This tax goes toward a partnership fund which is used to promote the region's tourist offerings.

TELEPHONE NUMBER

Since June 13, 1998, the 514 area code as been reserved for the island of Montréal. Those establishments off the island that used the 514 area code now use 450.

---

* Mark of certification and trademarks registered to the Fédération des Agricotours du Québec. Only members may use this designation.

INTERNET

Visit the Fédération des Agricotours on internet at:
www.agricotours.qc.ca
or write to us :
agricotours-q@sympatico.ca

COMPLETE A COMMENT CARD AND YOU MIGHT WIN
A STAY IN AN ACCREDITED AGRICOTOURS ESTABLISHMENT

Each year Agricotours awards Excellence Prizes to its members. These prizes are awarded based on the feedback on comment cards that we receive from clients. You are therefore invited to show your appreciation by filling out one of the comment cards found in each Agricoutours establishment.

Excellence Prize 1998

«Congratulations to the these hosts and hostesses for the consistently remarkable service and welcome they offered their guests»

AGRICOTOURS

24 years of hospitality
1975-1999

Provincial Winner

CANTONS-DE-L'EST
Au Chant du Huard
Françoise et Gérald Périnet
Lac Mégantic

Régional Winners 1998

BAS-ST-LAURENT
Le Terroir des Basques
Marguerite et Pierre-Paul Belzile
Trois-Pistoles

CANTONS-DE-L'EST
Au Chant du Huard
Françoise et Gérald Périnet
Lac-Mégantic

CHARLEVOIX
La Riveraine
Lise Dufour
Isle-aux-Coudres

CHAUDIÈRE-APPALACHES
Au Gré du Vent
Michèle Fournier et Jean L'Heureux
Beaumont

CÔTE-NORD
Le Gîte Fleuri
Marianne Roussel
Les Escoumins

GASPÉSIE
Le Panorama
Marie-Jeanne et Hector Fortin
St-Luc-de-Matane

LANAUDIÈRE
Gîte aux p'tits Oiseaux
Céline Coutu
Joliette

LAURENTIDES
La Chant'Oiseau
Martine et Marc Sabourin
Val-Morin

MAURICIE-BOIS-FRANCS
Le Soleil Levant
Léonie Lavoie et Yves Pilon
Pointe-du-Lac

MONTÉRÉGIE
Aux Deux Lucarnes
Ginette et Jean-Marie Laplante
St-Hubert

MONTRÉAL
Manoir Harvard
Robert et Lyne Bertrand
Notre-Dame-de-Grâce

OUTAOUAIS
Au Charme de la Montagne
Thérèse André et Armand Ducharme
Pontiac

QUÉBEC
La Maison Ancestrale Thomassin
Madeleine Guay
Beauport

SAGUENAY-LAC-SAINT-JEAN
Gîte le Merleau
Andrée Côté et Léo April
Jonquière

TABLE CHAMPÊTRE
Aux Douceurs de la Ruche
Danielle Rochon et Mario Morrissette
Ste-Scholastique

6.

TABLE OF SYMBOLS

F French spoken fluently

f Some French spoken

E English spoken fluently (50% of establishments)

e Some English spoken

Guests are requested to refrain from smoking

Wheelchair access

P Private parking

Swimming on premises

Pick-up from public transportation with or without additional charge

Pets on the premises

Restaurant on site

R4 Distance (km) to nearest restaurant

M4 Distance (km) to nearest grocery store

TA Establishment that accepts travel agency reservations

ACTIVITIES

Art gallery, museum

Summer theatre

Boat cruise

Swimming

Golf

Hiking

Cycling path

Horseback riding

Snowmobile

Downhill skiing

Cross-country skiing

Dog sled

METHOD OF PAYMENT

VS	Visa	ER	En Route
MC	MasterCard	IT	Direct payment
AM	American Express		

FOUR HOLIDAY PACKAGES

BED AND BREAKFASTS

This option, known as the **Gîte du Passant***, offers bed and breakfast in a private residence in the country, on a farm, in a village, in the suburbs or in the city. There are as many different kinds of lodgings and friendly hosts as there are warm welcomes and varieties of facilities and comforts... and flexible price. The Gîte du Passant offers up to five rooms per residence. For a long or short stay, choose one of the 421 Gîte du Passant throughout the regions of Québec.

COUNTRY INNS

Bed and breakfast in a small country inn with a relaxed atmosphere. These 72 establishments offer up to 12 rooms in the main residence or adjoining buildings, some also provide additional meals in a dining room. Known as **Auberge du Passant***, these inns distinguish themselves from traditional hotels by the uniqueness and their personalized attention to detail. Though inns accommodate more guests that B&Bs, you'll find the same friendly welcome. See complete list p 13.

* Mark of certification and trademarks registered to the fédération des Agricotours du Québec. Only members of the federation may use this designation.

FARM STAYS

This fun-filled holiday package consists of bed and full board or half board in a farm house, where hosts invite you to discover the life on a farm. The activities on each farm differ according to the type of animals and farming. Certain farms will allow children without adults. 21 Farm Stays in the province ensure a fun and unique holiday in natural settings for the whole family. **See complete list p 35.**

COUNTRY AND CITY HOMES

This may take the form of a fully equipped house, cottage, apartment or studio, and is ideal for an independent holiday in the city or country. Wheter you want to enjoy the beauty of nature or lose yourself in the city, you'll be warmly welcomed into one of the 68 country or city homes to ensure a perfect stay. Monthly, weekly, weekend and even daily rates are available. **See complete list p 43.**

In the guide, a descriptive text is provided along with a drawing of the house. The hosts briefly describe the unique characteristics of their home, its decor and surroundings. Information is also given on the activities available in the region.

You will notice above the illustration either B&B, INN, COUNTRY HOME, or CITY HOME, this indicates the type of accommodation offered.

For your ingormation, specifics are also provided concerning the rooms and washrooms facilities reserved for guests.

Please note that all bed linen and towels are included in the price indicated in the guide.

RESERVATIONS AND METHOD OF PAYMENT

It is always advisable to reserve in advance to be sure of getting the size and type of accommodation you want especially in high season (July and August). For reservations, contact the establishment directly, either by mail or by telephone. Since each place is different, it is usually a good idea to confirm details with your host: the type of room, the number of beds per room, wheter single or double beds, what restaurant facilities are nearby, what time you plan to arrive, up until what time your reservation should be held in case of delay, what forms of payment are accepted, etc. Generally, expect to pay with traveller's cheques or cash. The establishments which accept credit have VS, MC, AM, ER, IT written under their rate charts. As well, if you have any conditions which might prove pertinent (example is you are allergic to pets), you are strongly encouraged to check with your hosts before making reservations.

INTERNET

Surf on our site:
www.agricotours.qc.ca
or write to us at the following adress:
agricotours-q@sympatico.ca

DEPOSIT AND CANCELLATION

For B&Bs and Inns:

A deposit of 40% or a minimum of $20 may be required to confirm a reservation. The balance of the fee will be paid during your stay. If you cannot honour your reservation, flexible cancellation rules may apply. It is a good idea to get these specifications in writting. However, if no written agreement is produced, the money foreseen and received as a deposit will be kept by the host for damages according to the following rules:
16 to 21 day's notice: $10 is retained; 8 to 15 day's notice: 50% of deposit (minimum $20) is retained; 7 or fewer days' notice: entire deposit is retained. If your stay must be cut short before the end, 40% of the unused portion of the stay may be retained. When cancelling, it is advisable to postpone the reservation to avoid losing your deposit.
N.B.: In accordance with provincial and federal laws, all establishments must charge taxes on the deposit.

For country and city homes:

Check with owners of country houses for their individual deposit and cancellation policies.

FOR EUROPEAN CUSTOMERS

You can reserve your stay in advance in several ways: either contact the establishment directly, use a travel agent or contact Tourisme Chez l'Habitant in France or Hospitality Canada.

TOURISME CHEZ L'HABITANT: Reservations can be made by mail or by telephone with a credit card. All the arrangements and payment are made in advance and you head for Québec with address in hand! An additional charge is added to the price for all reservation services. Information is sent free of charge.

Tourisme chez l'habitant
15 rue des Pas Perdus, B.P. 8338
95 804 - Cergy St-Christophe cedex
Tél: (1) 34.25.44.44,
Fax (1) 34.25.44.45

HOSPITALITY CANADA: For a stay of 2 nights or more, you can reserve through the Hospitality Canada network. There is no charge for these reservations from France, Belgium or Switzerland by calling 0-800-90-3355.

You can also make your reservations by telephone after you arrive or by visiting their offices located in the tourist offices in Montréal and Québec City:

By telephone: **(514) 393-1528 ou 393-9049**

In person:

Centre Infotouriste
1001 Square Dorchester
Montréal
(Coin Ste-Catherine & Peel)

Maison du tourisme
12, rue Sainte-Anne
Vieux-Québec
Opposite the Château Frontenac

Bed & Breakfasts and Country Inns are presented as follows:

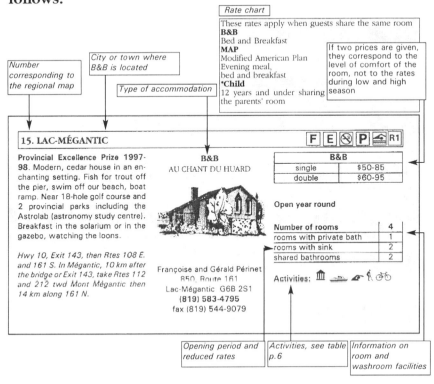

Country and City Homes are presented as follows:

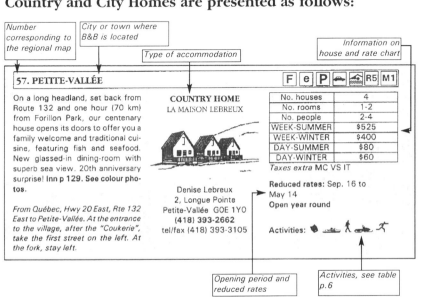

Country-Style Dining

COUNTRY-STYLE DINING

11.

MANICOUAGAN

BAS-ST-LAURENT

CHARLEVOIX

QUÉBEC CITY (REGION)

SAGUENAY - LAC-ST-JEAN

CHAUDIÈRE - APPALACHES

MAINE (UNITED STATES)

MAURICIE - BOIS-FRANCS

CANTONS-DE-L'EST

MAURICIE - BOIS-FRANCS

MONTÉRÉGIE

LANAUDIÈRE

LAURENTIDES

OUTAOUAIS

ONTARIO

ABITIBI-TÉMISCAMINGUE

© ULYSSES

1. Dunham
2. Magog
3. Sainte-Anne-de-la-Rochelle
4. Saint-Léon-de-Standon
5. Saint-Ambroise-de-Kildare
6. Saint-Jacques-de-Montcalm
7. L'Annonciation
8. Lachute, Argenteuil
9. Mirabel, Lachute
10. Mirabel, Sainte-Scholastique
11. Saint-André-Est
12. Saint-Eustache
13. Sainte-Anne-des-Plaines
14. Louiseville
15. Huntingdon
16. Huntingdon
17. Saint-David, Yamaska
18. Saint-Paul-d'Abbostsford
19. Saint-Rémi-de-Napierville
20. Saint-Urbain
21. Saint-Valérien
22. Sainte-Justine-de-Newton
23. Saint-Sixte

TABLES CHAMPÊTRES ^{MC}* (COUNTRY-STYLE DINING)

For getting together with family or friends, to celebrate a special event or anniversary, or to commemorate a reunion, the Tables Champêtres hosts offer meals carefully prepared in their own kitchens and served the intimacy of the dining room of their farmhouse or an adjoining building, all year round. The 25 Tables Champêtres offer a unique opportunity to relax and talk with friends. Sometimes, the hosts will also share the pleasure of country life with their guests, taking you on a tour of the grounds, a walk in the woods, or other activities.

PRACTICAL INFORMATION

In the guide, owners describe briefly the characteristics of their home, the decor, the surroundings, the animals or their crops. A meal with several courses is also proposed, with ingredient from their own farm. The suggested price for the menu is included in the description. Precise directions will help you find your way.

THE MENUS

The menus given in this guide are but examples of the type of meals served. In addition to the menu presented, the hosts may offer you a variety of other menus at various prices. These new menus are always made with fresh farm products.

At the request of the hosts, the menus have been left in their original French to preserve their authenticity.

BRING YOUR OWN WINE because it is not available on site.

NUMBER OF PEOPLE

The number of people welcomed during the week and on weekends is given for each establishment. The minimum may vary depending on the season. Note that some hosts can accommodate more than one group at a time. In these cases, depending on the minimum number of people set out by the owners, it is possible to reserve the whole establishment for your group.

RESERVATIONS

You must reserve with the hosts directly. It is always advisable to book several weeks in advance. A maximum deposit of 50% of the total price may be required to confirm a reservation.

If you cannot honour your reservation, flexible cancellation rules may apply. It is a good idea to get these specifications in writting. However, if no written agreement is produced, the cancellation policy is as follows: 30 days or less before the reservation date, the entire deposit is retained.

When cancelling, it is advisable to postpone the reservation to avoid losing the deposit.

RATES

Certain places offer reduced rates for children 12 years and under. Hosts may reserve the right to charge for the number of places reserved even if the actual number of guests is less. Service charge are not included in the prices, this is left to the discretion of the patrons.

*Registered trademark. Only members of the Fédération des Agricotours du Québec may use this designation.

1. DUNHAM

LA CHÈVRERIE DES ACACIAS
Renée Ducharme and Gérard Landry
356, chemin Bruce (route 202)
Dunham J0E 1M0
(450) 295-2548

On the road to the vineyards, our homestead is a major goat-breeding, fodder-crop and poultry farm. The originality of the food served in the ambiance of a 19th-century house will charm you. Our menu constitutes a gastronomic adventure orchestrated around our farm products combined with those of our neighbours. Our home is just the place to end an unforgettable day in the region.

Located 1 hour from the Champlain bridge. From Montreal or Sherbrooke: Hwy 10, Exit 68 for Cowansville Rte 139. Then take Rte 202 to Dunham. In the village, turn on Chemin Bruce (Rte 202) at the corner of "Estrie Gaz". The goat farm is 1.2 km from the village.

Open year round

Activities:

Jus de légumes frais
Canapés et Bruschetta
Mosaïque de légumes
au fromage frais de chèvre
Potage croustillant aux amandes
Chabrot, surprise à découvrir
Complet de chevreau au cary
Sorbet aux deux melons
Salade verte à la bûche de chèvre
Variations des Cantons

Meal : $33 taxes extra	
week:12 to 30 people	w/e: 12 to 30 people
Min. nb. of guests may vary depending on the season	
Able to accommodate more than one group / 2 dining rooms available	
(exclusive use depends on season, nb. of people)	

Includes: visit of the farm

---

2. MAGOG (Canton de)

AUX JARDINS CHAMPÊTRES
Monique Dubuc
1575, chemin des Pères, R.R.4
Canton de Magog J1X 5R9
(819) 868-0665
fax (819) 868-6744

Just steps from Magog and Orford in the magnificent Eastern Townships region, you'll give in to the charming countryside, the warmth of our hundred-year-old house as well as the "pure delights" that we will serve you. Our dishes are concocted from our various farm animals, organic vegetables and edible flowers. Do not resist, rather enjoy it with your friends and while staying at our B&B. One and two-day packages starting at $68 per person, double occupancy. Bring your own wine. **B&B p 71.**

From Montréal, Hwy 10 East, Exit 115 South-Magog/St-Benoît-du-Lac, drive 1.8 km. Turn right on Chemin des Pères twd St-Benoît-du-Lac/Austin. Drive 6.1 km, look for sign on your right. We are waiting for you!

Open year round

Activities:

Salade au confit de canard et vinaigrette tiède balsamique ou
rillettes de lapin aux pistaches
Potage aux poires et cresson
Aumônière de poireaux sauce cheddar
et coulis de poivrons rouges ou
foie de lapereau sauté aux champignons sauce porto
Granité au calvados
Canard de barbarie sauce genièvre et caribou ou râble de lapin aux pruneaux et armagnac ou scalopini de volaille aux cerises de terre
Fromages de St-Benoit-du-Lac
Crêpes glacées aux pommes et figues ou gâteau à la pâte d'amande ou soufflé aux marrons et sabayon au Grand Marnier

---

Meal : $36 taxes extra / VS MC IT	
week: 1 to 50 people	w/e: 1 to 50 people
Able to accommodate more than one group/ 3 dining rooms	
(exclusive use depends on season, nb of people)	

Includes: visit of the farm (in season)

3. STE-ANNE-DE-LA-ROCHELLE

At Les Ancêtres, life flows to the rhythm of the seasons, in harmony with nature. The house is just over 120 years old and once housed Rosée, Ovide and their "little family"! They had sixteen children including Réginald, my grandfather. To find out the whole story come visit us, right at the top of the hill in Ste-Anne-de-la-Rochelle.
See you soon, Marjolaine and Paul.
Nearby: bike path, Bombardier museum, Cristal Kébec mine, Safari Tour and ski resorts.

From Montréal, Hwy 10 E., Exit 90. Rte 243 N. to Ste-Anne. Left on Chemin Ste-Anne North for 2.5 km, go right on Rang 9 for 2.3 km. From Sherbrooke and Granby: 30 min. From Champlain Bridge: 75 min.

Open year round

Activities:

FERME DES ANCÊTRES
Marjolaine Martin and Paul Brien
601, Rang 9
Ste-Anne-de-la-Rochelle J0E 2B0
(450) 539-0191
www.geocities.com/napavalley/9669/

Hors-d'œuvre de la maison
Pâté de chevreau ou rillettes de chevreau
Crème de poires, carottes et thym
Pains maison aux herbes de Provence
Aumônière de champignons
Granité de romarin
Gigot et côtelettes de chevreau
Pomme de terre en croûte
Petites carottes à l'érable
Purée de navets à la menthe
Gelées et chutneys maison
Salade verte moutardée à l'érable
Assiette de fromages
Parfait glacé à l'érable, café, chocolat, sur crème anglaise, garni d'une tuile à l'orange
Thé, café, infusions

Meal : $30-35 taxes extra
week: 8 to 20 people   w/e: 10 to 20 people
Min. nb. of guests may vary depending on the season
Able to accommodate more than one group/ 2 dining rooms available
(exclusive use depends on season, nb. of people)

Includes : visit of the farm (in season)

4. ST-LÉON-DE-STANDON

Tourism Grand Prize 1997. One hour from Québec City in the heart of the Appalachians, come and experience the gourmet adventure of the Ferme La Colombe. You'll relish every moment in our cosy hewn-timber dining room, made all the more charming by the crackling fireplace and the beautiful panoramic view from the window. You will be won over by our regional cuisine, made of wild turkey, guinea fowl, rabbit and trout, while enjoying the lovely view. Horse-drawn carriage rides. B&B and dining packages available. **Farm excursion p 29, farm Stay p 37 and B&B p 98.**

From Québec City, Hwy 20 E., Exit 325 twd Lac-Etchemin, Rtes 173 S. and 277 S. to Saint-Léon-de-Standon, Rue Principale. Go 0.9 km beyond the church, cross the 277 at the stop sign, left on the Village road and drive 4 km. Turn right on rang Ste-Anne and drive 2 km.

Open : Sep. 1 to June 30

Activities:

FERME LA COLOMBE
Rita Grégoire and Jean-Yves Marleau
104, rang Sainte-Anne
St-Léon-de-Standon G0R 4L0
(418) 642-5152
fax (418) 642-2991

Cocktail de bienvenue
Bouchées au fromage de chèvre,
canard mariné et œufs de caille
Truite du lac en gelée
Velouté de rutabaga façon érablière
Aumônière de pintade ou
poitrine de dindon sauvage farcie à l'abricot
Riz basmati et riz sauvage ou
couscous citronné
Carottes glacées et
betteraves au tapioca
Salade Colombine
Gâteau de fromage marbré au chocolat
sur coulis de framboises
Thé, café, tisane

Meal: $30-32 taxes extra	
week: 8 to 20 people	w/e: 8 to 20 people
Only one group at a time	

Includes: visit of the farm

5. ST-AMBROISE-DE-KILDARE

BERGERIE DES NEIGES
Desneiges Pepin and Pierre Juillet
1401, Rang 5
St-Ambroise-de-Kildare J0K 1C0
tel/fax (450) 756-8395

A life's dream... Goodbye law practice, so long teacher's summer holidays... Desneiges Pepin and Pierre Juillet (two "dyed in the wool" city dwellers...) Took over this farm and settled with 11 ewes in 1985. What do they do for fun? They share their experience and show guests the daily renewed life of the farm. How? Over a good meal. More than 10 years and 400 ewes later, they have retained that "city kid" enthusiasm for the country. They offer you a gastronomic adventure at La Bergerie des Neiges. **B&B p 142.**

From Montréal, Hwy 40 E., Exit 122, Hwy 31 N. Rte 158, 1 km, left on Rte 343 N., drive for 15 km to St-Ambroise. At the flashing yellow light, go left on Rang 5 for 2 km. The farm is white and pink, on the left!

Open year round

Activities:

Merguez maison et mayonnaise harissa
Potage de carottes du rang 5
Rillettes d'agneau et compote d'oignons
Duo d'agneau, sauce ricaneuse
Légumes de Lanaudière
Salade de fromage feta de brebis
Tulipe et glace maison sur coulis de fruits
Thé, café, tisanes
Other menus upon request

Meal: $35 taxes extra / MC
week:12 to 36 people   w/e: 12 to 36 people
Min. nb. of guests may
vary depending on the season
Only one group at a time

Includes: visit of the farm

6. ST-JACQUES-DE-MONTCALM

BERGERIE VOYNE
Lise Savard and Mario Gagnon
2795, rang St-Jacques, route 341
St-Jacques-de-Montcalm J0K 2R0
(450) 839-6583

In the beautiful Lanaudière region, we raise lambs and produce our own maple syrup. The ancestral home of the Venne family, also known as "Voyne", in green and white cedar, is ready for your visit. Lamb is featured in our cuisine, and the shepherd knows all the secrets of its preparation. You can see the herd on a tour of the farm.

From Montréal, Hwy 25 North to St-Esprit (40 km). Rte 158 East to St-Jacques, left on Rte 341 North. It's 4.8 km from the intersection with Rte 158.

Open: May 1 to Feb. 28

Activities:

Terrine de campagne et feuilles de
vigne farcies au veau et aux pignons
Tourte aux poireaux ou
feuilleté de canard, sauce poivrade
Potage saisonnier
Gigot d'agneau sauce au porto blanc ou
rôti de veau forestière
Salade du potager
Plateau de fromages de la région
Fondue à l'érable ou
parfait aux bleuets et chocolat blanc
Café, thé, infusion

Meal: $35-36
week: 8 to 20 people   w/e: 10 to 20 people
Only one group at a time

Includes : visit of the farm

7. L'ANNONCIATION

LA CLAIRIÈRE DE LA CÔTE
Monique Lanthier and Yves Bégin
16, chemin Laliberté
L'Annonciation JOT 1T0
(819) 275-2877

In the Hautes Laurentiennes, you are invited to our table to spend some peaceful hours in the clearing of a forest of varied species. We live in harmony with nature amongst a variety of small animals (lambs, rabbits, grain-fed chickens, calves and deer), which become succulent dishes accompanied by fresh vegetables from our organic gardens. **Farm stay p 38 and B&B p 150.**

From Montréal, Hwy 15 North and Rte 117 to L'Annonciation. Drive 4.3 km beyond the hospital. Turn left on Chemin Laliberté. First house on right (almond Canadian-style house).

Open : Dec. 1 to Mar. 31, May 1 to Oct. 31

Activities:

Rougette crémière
Foie gras poulette
Pesto en pâte
Velouté de saison
Tournedos dindonneau au fouillis jardinier
Verdoyant potager, crémerie de fines herbes
Fromagerie raisinet
Fruiterie sauvagine en velours
Pouding paysan sirop d'érable
Thé, café, tisane
Other menus upon request

Meal : $30	
week: 6 to 20 people	w/e: 6 to 20 people
Only one group at a time	

Includes: **visit of the farm**

8. LACHUTE, ARGENTEUIL

AU PIED DE LA CHUTE
Deschênes family
273, Route 329 Nord
Lachute J8H 3W9
(450) 562-3147
fax (450) 562-1056

In the calm of the country, our wood house offers charm, comfort and the delicacies of reputed country-style dining, where poultry and lamb are the specialties. Family-style welcome is both warm and personalized. Pastoral walks near our pond and at the foot of the falls will add to the magic of the countryside and the pleasures of dining. Welcome to our place!

From Montréal, Hwy 15 N., Exit 35. Hwy 50 to Côte St-Louis, go right to Rte 158 W., left to Rte 329 N. At the flashing yellow light, go right for exactly 1.5 km. It's on your left.

Open year round

Activities:

Bouchées miniatures de bienvenue
Salade tiède au confit de pintade ou
Terrine de volaille au Vermouth et pistaches
ou Crêpe farcie aux épinards, sauce mornay ou
Nid de pâtes aux herbes et saucisson d'agneau
Potage deux saveurs
Granité au cidre Du Minot
Gigot d'agneau, sauce aux herbes fraîches ou
Feuilleté d'agneau au curry ou
Roulade de lapereau, ciboulette et dijonnaise
ou Suprême de chapon, vanille et cinq baies
ou Pintadeau aux poires et canneberges
ou Duo de daim aux pommes et groseilles
Salade campagnarde à l'érable
Raclette d'Argenteuil à la gelée de Sauternes
Duo de desserts «surprise» sur coulis
Also: Whole spit-roasted-lamb-méchoui, holiday and Easter menus, among others.

Meal: $33-43 taxes extra/VS MC IT	
Reduced rates: Mar. 1 to Apr. 15	
week: 6 to 27 people	w/e: 14 to 27 people
Only one group at a time	

Includes: **visit of the farm**

9. MIRABEL, LACHUTE

LES RONDINS
Lorraine Douesnard and François Bernard
3015, Sir Wilfrid Laurier, route 158
Mirabel (Lachute) J8H 3W7
(450) 562-7215
(450) 258-2467
fax (450) 562-5209

45 minutes from Montréal, come share the intimacy of our house built in 1860. The Victorian decor, the fireplaces, the piano and the furnishings will send you gently back in time. Dishes are made from our own veal, grain-fed chickens and Muscovy ducks. The old stove cooks country-style bread and products from our own maple grove.

From Montréal: Hwy 15 North, Exit 35. Follow Hwy 50 West, take Chemin Louis Exit 272. Turn right, continue to traffic light. Turn left onto Rte 158 West, drive 1 km, 3rd farmhouse on the right. Or: Hwy 15 North, Exit 39, Lachute-bound Rte 158 Ouest, drive 20.7 km.

Bouchées d'avant
Roulade de chapon farcie
Potage «Mirabel»
Salade tiède au confit de canard
Canard de barbarie à la framboise ou mijoton de veau au basilic ou pavé de veau pomme d'érable
Fromage «La Longeraie »
Gâteau rhubarbe et sirop d'érable
Parfait maison
Mimi-gourmandise
Other menus available

Open year round

Activities:

Meal: $35-37
week:10 to 26 people   w/e: 14 to 26 people
Min. nb. of guests may
vary depending on the season
Only one group at a time

Includes: visit of the farm (in season)

10. MIRABEL, STE-SCHOLASTIQUE

AUX DOUCEURS DE LA RUCHE
Danielle Rochon and Mario Morrissette
10351, St-Vincent
Mirabel, Ste-Scholastique J0N 1S0
tel/fax (514) 990-2450
(450) 258-3122

Excellence Prize 1997-98. In the lovely Basses-Laurentides region, only 40 min from Montréal, come rediscover the calm of the countryside. A majestic drive lined by spruce trees leads to a home that has witnessed Québec's history. It is here that we await you. In the kitchen, our fowl is slowly being roasted and the sweet scent of warm honey house fills the room. A visit of the honey-house will reveal the secret world of bees you'll also taste "beehive sweets". A wood fire is already warming the dining room; the only thing missing is you.

From Montréal, Hwy 15 North, Exit 20 West, Hwy 640 West, Exit 11 Boul Arthur-Sauvé, towards Lachute. Drive 17.5 km. After Belle-Rivière Restaurant turn right on St-Vincent. 5 km to 10351. We await your arrival at the end of the spruce drive.

Open year round

Activities:

Mousse de foies de volaille au cognac
Jus de légumes frais
Oeufs de caille dans leur nid et terrine de volaille
Velouté de navet aux pommes
Perdrix rôtie, sauce moutarde au miel
Riz sauvage aux fines herbes ou pommes de terre
Petits légumes de saison
Salade «Miramiel»
Fromages de chèvre frais
La ruche et ses ouvrières
Thé, tisanes, café
Pain maison, douceur «chocomiel»
Other menus available

Meal: $37 taxes extra
week: 4 to 24 people   w/e: 4 to 24 people
Min. nb. of guests may vary depending on the season
Able to accommodate more than one group (exclusive use depends on season, nb. of people)

Includes: visit of the farm

11. ST-ANDRÉ EST

LA FERME CATHERINE
Marie Marchand and Robert Dorais
2045, Route 344
St-André Est J0V 1X0
tel/fax (450) 537-3704

Crémant de pomme
Saucisse deux viandes sur
tombée de tomates ou
tourte aux marinades fruitées
Terrine de bison au confit d'oignons
Potage fermière
Rôti de bison ou
de bœuf braisé aux fines herbes
Salade trois feuilles
Assiette de fromages assortis et fruits
Délices de la saison
Thé, café ou infusion
Other menus are available upon request
with or without buffalo meat

Marie, Catherine and Robert invite you to come enjoy family ambience and country cooking close to the old wood stove whose warmth mixes with the warmth of the hosts. Robert will take you around the farm and you can admire a superb view of Lake of Two Mountains and surroundings. If you love good food, have a seat and let the feast begin.

From Montréal, Hwy 13 or 15 to Hwy 640 twd of Oka. From Oka, take Hwy 344 for 19 km. On the 344 it's 6 km after St-Placide. The road gets narrower and winding as you arrive at La Ferme Catherine.

Open year round

Activities:

Meal: $38	
week:12 to 32 people	w/e: 12 to 32 people
Only one group at a time	

Includes: visit of the farm

12. ST-EUSTACHE

LE RÉGALIN
Alain Latour and Réjean Brouillard
991, boul. Arthur-Sauvé,
route 148 ouest
St-Eustache J7R 4K3
tel/fax (450) 623-9668
toll free 1-877-523-9668

Mousse de foies de lapereau et pain maison
Feuilleté de faisan au poivre vert ou
aumônières de pintade à l'érable
Potage de saison
Lapin aux abricots, au cidre ou à l'érable ou
médaillon d'autruche à l'hydromel ou
suprême de faisan au poivre rose
Salade verdurette
Plateau de fromages fins
Profiteroles au chocolat ou
gâteau mousse aux abricots
Café, thé, infusions
Other menus upon request

Less than 30 minutes from Montréal, in the maple area of St-Eustache, a beautiful, typical old house with dormer windows overlooking a large orchard extending as far as the eye can see. Farm animals (rabbits, pheasants, guinea fowl, geese, ducks and ostriches) inspire the planning of our menus. One weekend a month, we offer dinner concerts for one and all.

From Montréal, Hwy 15 North, Exit 20 West, Hwy 640 West, Exit 11. Boul. Arthur-Sauvé twd Lachute. 5 km from the exit, 8 houses after the Pépinière Eco-Verdure (tree nursery) on the right side.

Open year round

Activities:

Meal: $38-43	
week:15 to 50 people	w/e: 15 to 50 people
Min. nb. of guests may vary depending on the season	
Only one group at a time	

Includes: visit of the farm

13. STE-ANNE-DES-PLAINES

We chanced upon this place on the way back from a great family adventure, and were won over by the warmth of this large B.C.-pine house and its solarium in the undergrowth. For us, this enchanting spot represented the conclusion of a wonderful trip and a new challenge. We have been sharing our life in the country with a growing clientele ever since. Winter, spring, summer, winter or fall, we invite you to explore our grounds, savour our fresh farm products and enjoy a warm welcome.

From Montréal or the north, Hwy 15, Exit 31, east on Rue Victor, drive 13.9 km (Rue Victor becomes Rang Lepage; you'll pass a flashing light at Rte 335). Right on Boulevard Normandie, drive 0.5 km. Or from Montréal or Laval, Hwy 640, Exit 28, drive 9.3 km north on Rte 335. Turn right at the flashing light on Rang Lepage, drive 3.2 km Right on Boulevard Normandie, drive 0.5 km.

Open year round

Activities: 🐚 ⚘ 🚶 🏇 🏕

LA CONCLUSION
Chantal and Gilles Fournier
12, boul. Normandie
Ste-Anne-des-Plaines J0N 1H0
(450) 478-2598 ou (514) 990-7085
fax (450) 478-0209
www.web-solut.com/laconclusion

Potage ou crème du jardin
Pain maison aux cinq grains
Caille glacée au vinaigre de framboises ou
gâteau de lapin au vin blanc ou
aumônière de foies de lapin à la crème
Assortiment de pâtés, gelée Jalapenoise
Lapin aux pommes et raisins ou
lapin farci aux abricots ou
lapin chasseur aux olives ou
cailles rôties, sauce porto et raisins verts
Salade de saison
Tarte aux framboises glacée au sirop d'érable
ou gâteau mousse aux fraises et à rhubarbe ou
crêpes de blé au Cointreau et bleuets ou
gâteau moka et mousse d'amandes
Crème glacée maison et gourmandises
Goat cheese available upon request

Meal: $25-42
week: 2 to 24 people   w/e: 2 to 24 people
Min. nb. of guests may
vary depending on the season
Able to accommodate more than one group
(exclusive use depends on seasons, nb.
of people)

Includes: visit of the farm

14. LOUISEVILLE

60 min from Montréal, La Seigneurie looks forward to spoiling you in its cosy home! You'll delight in our 9-course meal composed of produce from our small traditional farm. The vegetable garden, flower beds and herb garden make our food healthy, while the colours make for an attractive presentation. After a feast complemented by wine what could be better than joining Morpheus in one of our B&B's 5 cosy rooms! **Farm excursion (tour of the gardens) p 32, farm stay p 38, B&B p 175 and country home (La Maison du Jardinier) p 184. See colour photos and advertisement end of Mauricie-Bois-Francs region, accommodation section.**

From Montréal or Québec City, Hwy 40 Exit 166, Rte 138 E., 2.4 km to Rte 348 W. At the lights, left twd Ste-Ursule, 1.5 km, 1st road on the right, 1st house tucked away behind the trees.

Open year round

Activities: 🏛 ⚘ 🏃 ᧞ 🐎

LA TABLE DE LA SEIGNEURIE
Michel Gilbert
480, chemin du Golf
Louiseville J5V 2L4
tel/fax (819) 228-8224

Bouchées cordiales à l'apéritif
Feuilleté de filet de perchaude
du Lac Saint-Pierre
Soupière de Bortsch québécois
Granité Bienfaisant
Le porc, le veau, le lapin ou
l'agneau de la Seigneurie sont à l'honneur
Légumes potagers
Laitue, vinaigrette «Fin Palais»
Éphémère triangle de fromages
Bagatelle «Seigneuriale» au sherry
Douceurs inoubliables
We also suggest other menus
Exceptional menus inspired from Monet and
Colette's cuisine

Meal: $39 taxes extra
week: 8 to 26 people   w/e: 10 to 26 people
Min. nb. of guests may vary depending on the season
Able to accommodate more than one group (exclusive use depends on season, nb. of people)

Includes: visit of the farm (in season)

15. HUNTINGDON

DOMAINE DE LA TEMPLERIE
Chantale Legault et Roland Guillon
312, chemin New Erin
Godmanchester (Huntingdon) JOS 1H0
tel/fax (450) 264-9405

Nestled in fields and woods, our ancestral home awaits you. Walking in the forest, visiting the sugar shack, outdoor activities. At your discretion: soccer field, volleyball court, bowling green and horseshoes space. Our farm-bred geese, guinea fowl, pheasants and ducks will treat you to an unforgettable concert. You will enjoy succulent dishes prepared by your host, who has some thirty years' cooking experience, in a relaxed ambiance.

From Montréal, Rte 138 West twd Huntingdon. 9 km after the stop in Ormstown, turn right at the Montée Seigneuriale, drive 4.7 km, turn left and you're at New Erin. Drive 1.3 km.

Open year round

Activities: 🐷 ⛵ 🚶 🏃 🚴

Petits fours apéritif, velouté en cachette
Plateau de trois charcuteries
Au choix : Escargots façon du Domaine,
ris de veau aux poires, truite farcie en croûte,
flan de pétoncles
Selon votre goût : Suprême de faisan,
filet d'oie au roquefort, médaillon d'autruche,
confit de canard,
fricassée de veau à l'ancienne
Également nous vous offrons :
Chapon, agneau, lapin, pintadeau et porc
Pommes noisette, jardinière de légumes
Salade de cœurs et de gésiers confits
Plateau de fromages
Coupe de la Templerie
Soufflé glacé à l'érable et au calvados
Café, thé, infusion

Meal: $30-38 taxes extra
week:10 to 38 people   w/e: 12 to 38 people Min. nb. of guests may vary depending on the season
Only one group at a time

Includes: visit of the farm (in season)

16. HUNTINGDON

FERME RHÉA
Susan Ostrovsky and Robert Wilson
1503, 1ʳᵉ Concession
Huntingdon JOS 1A0
tel/fax (450) 264-2089
www.rocler.qc.ca/rhea
rhea@rocler.qc.ca

In the words of Brillat-Savarin: "Inviting someone is to cater to their happiness for as long as they are under your roof." We agree, and therefore invite you to our stone-built house erected in 1832. You will visit our farm-bred animal: Angora, Boer and alpine goats, ducks and Chantecler cocks, as well as our large organic vegetable garden and our shop, where we sell our hand-made mohair products.

From the Mercier bridge in Montréal: Rte 138 West twd Huntingdon. At the Huntingdon Exit, turn right at the Rte 138 U.S.-border sign, drive 14.7 km. Turn left at the 1st concession Rd. and drive 5.8 km. Red-roofed house on the left.

Open year round

Activities: ⛵ 🚶 🚴 🏇 🎿

Saucisses de chevreau ou
mousse de foie de volaille ou
poireaux vinaigrette
Terrine de chevreau à l'échalotte ou
pâté de campagne
Potage maison
Bourguignon de chevreau ou
lapin à la forestière ou
coq au vin ou
confit de canard ou
magret de canard, sauce aigre-douce
Salade du potager
Fromage de chèvre
Crème renversée au caramel ou
tarte aux pommes ou
gâteau maison
Café, thé, infusion

Meal: $32-36 taxes extra / VS MC
week:10 to 25 people   w/e: 10 to 25 people
Able to accommodate more than one group/ 2 dining rooms available (exclusive use depends on seasons, nb. of people)

Includes: visit of the farm (in season)

17. ST-DAVID, YAMASKA

On the little farm where we raise suckling pig and draft horses, the table is set with many little side dishes, tastes of the quality meal to come. As well as suckling pig, we offer horse meat served in a Chinese or Burgundy fondue. Year-round carriage rides with the horses are available if reserved ahead of time. Welcome to the country where life is good.

45 min from St-Hyacinthe, 30 min from Drummondville. From Montréal, Hwy 20 East, Exit 170 Yamaska-Sorel, Rte 122 West. Drive 24 km to St-David. At the end of the village, turn right, drive 2 km.

Open year round

Activities:

LA TABLÉE
Carolle and Normand Lavallée
130, rang Rivière David
St-David, Yamaska J0G 1L0
(450) 789-2305
fax (450) 789-0930

Charcuteries maison :
tête fromagée, cretons,
saucissons
Soupe de saison
Porcelet farci de «La Tablée»
Légumes variés
Salade santé amandine
Tarte au suif Marie-Claire
Gâteau au fromage chocolaté

Horse meat, pheasant and rabbit
also available on the menu.

Meal: $28-30 taxes extra	
week: 8 to 20 people	w/e: 8 to 20 people
Min. nb. of guests may	
vary depending on the season	
Only one group at a time	

Includes: visit of the farm

18. ST-PAUL-D'ABBOTSFORD

For those who have heartfund memories have memory of an aunt and uncle living on the farm, in a peaceful setting. An uncle who harvests his hay, milks his cows, picks his apples and makes delicious maple syrup. An aunt who offers you her loveliest flowers in her little shop and prepares meals from the fruits of the earth for you. Savour dishes by the warmth of a wood fire. Don't think twice, we are here for you! **Farm excursion p 33.**

Hwy 10, Exit 55, Rte 235 North, drive 5 km, turn right on 2nd road. Or from Hwy 20, St-Hyacinthe Exit, Rte 235 South. Cross Rte 112, turn left on 1st road.

Open year round

Activities:

LA PETITE BERGERIE
Pierrette and Michel Scott
1460, rang Papineau
St-Paul-d'Abbotsford J0E 1A0
tel/fax (450) 379-5842

Pâté campagnard au veau et agneau
Salade et vinaigrette au sirop d'érable
La soupe à ma tante
Au choix : agneau-veau-bœuf ou
porc et sa sauce
Riz aux fines herbes ou
croûté aux pommes de terre
Légumes de saison
Plateau de fromages et pomme
Délice à l'érable ou
choix du chef et son coulis
Thé, café, tisanes

Meal: $35	
week:10 to 26 people	w/e: 12 to 26 people
Only one group at a time	

Includes: visit of the farm

19. ST-RÉMI-DE-NAPIERVILLE

On the wide expanses of the Rive-Sud, only 15 minutes from Montréal, come experience true gastronomy. A charming entrance, lined with apple trees and forest, a dining room redolent with the wonderful smell of well-browned chicken at the edge of a property near a pond provide a warm and soothing ambiance. While we prepare a feast for you, what could be better than an early evening drink on the terrace whose charm is only enhanced by your presence.

From the Champlain bridge, Hwy 15 twd the U.S.A., Exit 42 (Rte 132). Rte 209 South, to St-Rémi. From the church, drive 2.2 km, 1st road on the right is Rang St-Antoine. Or from the Mercier bridge, Rte 207 South and 221 South until Rte 209 South, to St-Rémi.

Open year round

Activities:

FERME KOSA
Ada and Lajos Kosa
1845, rang St-Antoine
St-Rémi-de-Napierville JOL 2L0
(450) 454-4490

Cocktail de bienvenue
Amuse-gueule
Crème de légumes de saison
Tomate à l'antiboise
Tagliatelle aux asperges ou aux poivrons
Magrets de canard au vinaigre balsamique et aux navets confits
Légumes du potager
Salade de saison
Quelques fromages fermiers (chèvre)
Couronne de pommes caramélisée au jus de cidre
Café, thé, infusion
Other menus upon request

Meal: $35
week:10 to 40 people   w/e: 14 to 40 people
Min. nb. of guests may vary depending on the season
Only one group at a time

Includes: visit of the farm (in season)

20. ST-URBAIN-PREMIER

A country house set back from the road, nestled in the midst of a perennial-flower garden and hilly fields. In season, outdoor games let you appreciate the setting. Inside, the fire crackles in the woodstove, the table sports its Sunday tablecloth with place settings from the pine cupboard. We'll share with you little details on lamb breeding, growing mixed herbs and edible flowers. Welcoming you to our home is both a pleasure and a passion.

From the Champlain bridge: Hwy 15 S., Exit 42 (Rte 132). At 5th light, take Rte 209 S. twd St-Rémi. Drive 26.6 km. Then take Rte 205 for 2.4 km. From the Mercier bridge: toward Rte 138 W., 1st exit right on Rte 221 to St-Rémi for 7 km. Rte 207 S. Drive twd St-Isidore for 16 km. Rte 205 S. for 3,4 km.

Open year round

Activities:

LA BERGERIE DU SUROÎT
Nathalie Laberge and Stéphane Couture
440, rang Double
St-Urbain-Premier JOS 1Y0
(450) 427-1235

Pâté de foie et son confit d'oignons
Potage de cresson et champignons ou du jardin
Feuilles de vignes farcies sur coulis d'abricots ou papillottes d'agneau sauce au yogourt
Carré d'agneau aux herbes de Provence ou gigot d'agneau aux trois parfums
Brunoise de légumes croquants ou brochette de légumes marinés
Verdure aux herbes fraîches ou salade de mer et d'agrumes
Aumônière de pommes et fromage
Douceur glacée aux fruits de la saison ou surprise chocolatée

Meal: $36
week:10 to 24 people   w/e: 10 to 24 people
Only one group at a time

Includes: visit of the farm

21. ST-VALÉRIEN

Depending on the season, you will be welcomed either by our gardens or a fire in the hearth. Rabbit is on the menu, as well as lamb and farm birds including delicious young pigeon, our new dish. Edible flowers cheer up and flavour our dishes. Arrive early, as there is a lot to see. **Farm Excursion p 33.**

20 minutes from St-Hyacinthe or from Granby. From Montréal, Hwy 20 East, Exit 141 to St-Valérien. In the village, take Chemin Milton and the 1st road on the right (2nd flashing light). Or Hwy 10, Exit 68, Rte 139 towards Granby. Rte 112 and Rte 137 North to Ste-Cécile. After Ste-Cécile, right on Chemin St-Valérien to the first flashing light, turn left.

Open year round

LA RABOUILLÈRE
Pierre Pilon
1073, rang de l'Égypte
St-Valérien J0H 2B0
(450) 793-4998
fax (450) 793-2529

*Cocktail de fruits et légumes
et assiette de canapés
Terrine de pintadeau aux avelines ou
foies de lapin au porto
Potage provençal (tomates, ail,
pesto, chèvre frais)
Cuisseau de lapin farci à l'estragon ou
pigeonneau à la niçoise ou suprême de pintade
aux pommes et au cidre ou magret
de canard au miel ou au vinaigre de framboises
ou gigot d'agneau au miel et au romarin
Salade mille fleurs (in season)
Fromages de chèvre
Gâteau au fromage, amande et
fruits sur crème anglaise*
Other menus upon request (brunch, méchoui, etc.)

Meal: $35-45	
week:12 to 45people w/e: 15 to 45 people	
Min. nb. of guests may vary depending on the season	

Able to accommodate more than one group/ 2 dining rooms available (exclusive use depends on seasons, nb. of people)

Includes: visit of the farm

---

22. STE-JUSTINE-DE-NEWTON

At the heart of a farming region, share the intimacy of our hundred-year-old house with Victorian decor. Enjoy meals with fresh bread baked daily in our authentic bread oven. The piano is always at your disposal. Full range of products from our maple grove. Visit the pheasants, horses, chickens and other animals at our farm. Percheron horses can take you for a carriage or sleigh ride (reservation). Our windmill pumps water for the garden. Welcome! **See colour photos.**

From Montréal, Hwy 40 W., twd Ottawa, Exit 17 (Montée Lavigne). Left on Rte 201 S. for 9.6 km to Rang Ste-Marie-de-Ste-Marthe. Take this for 4.6 km, at the first stop, go left for 5.1 km

Open year round

Activities: 🐷 🦌 🚶 🚲 🎿

LA SEIGNEURIE DE NEWTON
Lucille F. Lavallée
750, 3e Rang
Ste-Justine-de-Newton J0P 1T0
(450) 764-3420

*Spécialité faisan :
Terrine de foies de faisan et
rillettes au poivre vert
Potage saisonnier
Feuilleté aux épinards
Faisan au cognac
Carottes persillées ou légumes saisonniers
Riz aux fines herbes
Salade de la maison centennaire
Fins fromages régionaux
Crêpes divines to l'érable ou
tartelettes paysannes au sirop d'érable
Café, thé, infusions*
2nd menu: Festin d'agneau

Meal: $35-40	
week:10 to 24 people w/e: 10 to 24 people	
Only one group at a time	

Includes: visit of the farm

23. ST-SIXTE

FERME CAVALIER
Gertie and Marc Cavalier
39, montée St-André
St-Sixte J0X 3B0
(819) 985-2490
fax (819) 985-1411
marc.cavalier@sympatico.ca

In our beautiful valley, beside the Rivière St-Sixte, lamb and poultry from our farm are served in the two traditions: the richness of French gastronomy and the exotism of Moroccan cuisine. Give in to temptation with our changing menu, depending on the seasons and available products and the vision of your hosts. And don't forget our package including accommodation in a cosy and comfortable B&B.

One hour from Hull, 2 from Montréal. From Hull, Hwy 50 to Masson, then Rte 148 to Thurso. Route 317 North for 18 km to Montée Paquette. Turn and continue to Montée St-André. Turn left, the farm is 800 m away.

Open year round

Activities: 🐚 🎿 🚶 🛷 🐎

Velouté de saison
Filet de truite et sa crème de persil
Noisettes d'agneau marinées aux herbes
Raviole aux champignons des bois
Flan de courgettes et tomates
Bouquet de fraîcheur du jardin
Fromages de la Petite Nation avec pain
aux noix et au miel
Mille-feuille à la mousse d'érable
Café, thé, tisanes, pain maison
Ask about our Moroccan
spreads and other specialties.
We can assist you in
planning your special occasions.

Meal : $23-33 taxes extra
week: 6 to 25 people   w/e: 14 to 25 people
Min. nb. of guests may vary depending on the season
Able to accommodate more than one group/ 2 dining rooms available
(exclusive use depends selon saison, nbre de people)

Includes: visit of the farm (in season)

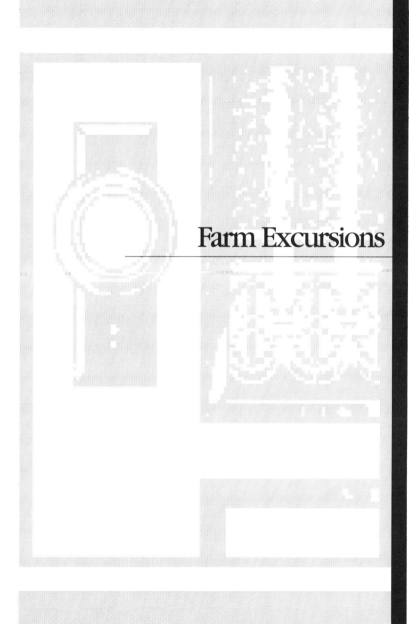

Farm Excursions

FARM EXCURSIONS

Farmers offer fun and educational activities as a means of enjoying a few hours in the great outdoors, or a whole day on a farm, and of experiencing life on the farm. These excursions are designed for both small and large groups, upon reservation.

Whether for a school trip, a get-together for members of an association, a family reunion, a picnic among friends, a bicycle trip, a longer hike or a car rally, the participating farmers offer children, families, friends, and people of all ages a range of activities limited only by the imagination. These excursions offer the opportunity to see facets of the country such as milking the cows, rabbit breeding, market gardening, the upkeep of horses, collecting eggs and raising chicks, the world of bees, as well as many other aspects of daily life on a farm. Visitors will learn to identify garden vegetables and wild plants, as well as a number of farm animals such as cows, goats, horses, sheep, geese, ducks, rabbits... And also some more exotic animals like llamas, peacocks, wild boars, ostriches, deer...

Pony rides, sleigh rides, campfires, corn on the cob are just some of the suggestions your hosts may provide to make your visit even more pleasant.

RESERVATIONS

Reservations should be made directly at the selected farm. A 40% deposit (minimum $20) may be required to confirm the reservation.

If you cannot honour your reservation, flexible cancellation rules may apply. It is a good idea to get these specifications in writing. However, if no written agreement is produced, the money foreseen and received as a deposit will be kept by the host for damages according to the following rules:

- 16 to 21 days' notice, a sum of $10 will be retained;

- 8 to 15 days' notice, 50% of the deposit will be retained (minimum $20);

- 7 days or less before the reservation date, the entire deposit will be retained.

When cancelling, it is advisable to postpone the reservation to avoid losing your deposit.

1. ST-LÉON-DE-STANDON

JARDINS DES TOURTEREAUX
DE LA FERME LA COLOMBE
Jean-Yves Marleau
104, rang Ste-Anne
St-Léon-de-Standon
G0R 4L0
(418) 883-5833
(418) 642-5152
fax (418) 642-2991
www.fermelacolombe.qc.ca

A booklet enables you to discover the great number of plants laid out in 10 thematic gardens. Trails, a pergola, swings, little bridges spanning ponds are graced with aviaries and an animal park. Come enjoy a relaxing picnic by the gently babbling brook. These unique gardens, situated in the heart of the mountains, will fill your everyday life with romanticism and reverie. A stay or country-style dining at La Colombe farm B&B will allow you to further enjoy our gardens. **Country-style dining p 15, farm stay p 37 and B&B p 98.**

90km from St-Georges de Beauce
100 km from Québec
70 km from Lévis

FOR FAMILIES AND SMALL GROUPS : mid-June to beginning of September
(Tuesday to Sunday 9 am to 4 pm)
For groups of 20 to 80 personnes : May to November (with reservation)

- horticultural farm: tending and reproducing plants
- Visiting the various theme gardens:
- edible flowers (40 varieties)
- fragrant flowers (rose gardens, lilacs, etc.)
- gardens of colours or garden of Eden
- garden of birds and hummingbirds
- secret garden
- garden of indigenous plants
- berry garden
- lovers' garden
- water garden (6 ponds and a lake)
- nature-interpretation relay

- Dinner on the farm and feeding the animals*
- For school groups: "Tour of Noah's ark"*
- guided visit of the animals (20 species)
- treasure hunt
- horse-drawn carriage rides
- plant arrangements
- tour of gardens

Rates:
$3.50 per person
$3.00 Senior citizens
$2.50 students
$1.00 children from 2 to 6

*additional charge

2. RAWDON

ARCHE DE NOÉ
Bernard Boucher
4117, ch. Greene
Rawdon
JOK 1SO
(450) 834-7874
(450) 834-3934

55 km from Montréal
80 km from Longueuil
30 km from Joliette

You can begin your stroll immediately upon your arrival by visiting the different animals. This guided tour through the property introduce you to more than 15 animal species, some of which run free. The flower gardens and the different landscapes are sure to make your visit most enchanting. You may make reservations to take part in the daily tasks of farm life. Moreover, pleasant footpaths lead you through our valleys to peaceful picnic and rest stops. We can organize a party*, a spit-roasted-lamb barbecue* or other event* for you: just contact us!

From Montréal: Aut 25 Nord to Rawdon. Rte 337 Nord, left on Rue Queen (at the IGA). Cross the village to 16e Avenue, then turn left at the Chemin Morgan intersection. We are 6 km farther.

FOR FAMILIES AND SMALL GROUPS: May 1 to October 31
For groups of 2 to 200 personnes: May 1 to October 31

- The Arche de Noé is 1 hour from Montréal!
- Ostriches, boars, Vietnamese pot-bellied pigs, miniature goats, horses, (Limousin) cattle, birds, cats and dog.
- Footpaths and picnic areas able to accommodate up to 200 people..
- Landscaped volleyball court and horseshoes space.
- Unforgettable scenery and family ambiance that will brighten up your day!
  Rates :
  $6 per person
  $20 for groups of 4 people or more
  groups on reservation

FARM EXCURSIONS

3. ST-BENOIT, MIRABEL

INTERMIEL
Viviane and Christian Macle
10291, La Fresnière
St-Benoît, Mirabel JON 1K0
(450) 258-2713
fax (450) 258-2708
www.cloxt.com/intermiel
intermiel@sympatico.ca

15 km from St-Eustache
45 km from Montréal
25 km from Mirabel airport

In St-Benoît, come to the largest beekeeping area in Québec. The guided tour includes a visit to the mead cellar, a video, demonstrations of our various products and a "Bee Safari" in season. Free entrance to the educational games room and our "honey boutique".

From Montréal, Hwy 15 North, Exit 20, Hwy 640 West, Exit 8. Follow the blue tourist information signs (18 km).

Open year round
Schools and groups: with reservations
Hour-long guided tours including honey/mead sampling. **Free admission.**
School package: 2-hour educational visit.
Price: $5.50 (includes snack and a pot of honey)

- Movie on the beekeeping activities of the farm
- Learn about the bee
- Observation of living hives
- Handling of an active hive by the beekeeper (in summer)
- Demonstration of production techniques
- Visit the mead cellar

- Mead tasting and sale of mead and all the beehive products
- Educational games room
- Marionette theatre
- Exhibition shop (candles, crafts, gifts, cosmetics, etc.)
- Picnic area
- Mini-barn, potting smaller animals (goat, lambs, rabbits, etc...)

4. LOUISEVILLE

LES JARDINS
DE LA SEIGNEURIE
Michel Gilbert
480, chemin du Golf
Louiseville J5V 2L4
tel/fax (819) 228-8224

26 km from Trois-Rivières
160 km from Québec
120 km from Montréal

All around a traditional little farm, these gardens have been restored and enlarged, taking inspiration from 19th-century bourgeois farm life. You'll get an inside look at Québec's natural farming heritage, raising animals and ecological farming, and the art of country living. Your five senses will be charmed. "One of 20 gardens to visit in Quebec" (l'Essentiel, July 98; La Semaine Verte, August 98). The **Gîte de La Seigneurie p 175** at the **Maison du Jardinier p 184**, and the **Table Champêtre p 21**, are the best places to stay to take advantage of these romantic gardens. **Advertisement end of Mauricie-Bois-Francs region, accommodation section.**

From Montréal or Québec City, Hwy 40 Exit 166, Rte 138 E., 2.4 km to Rte 348 W. At the lights, left twd Ste-Ursule, 1.5 km, 1st road on the right, 1st house tucked away behind the trees.

FOR FAMILIES AND SMALL GROUPS : June 15 to September 15 (with reservations)
For groups of 10 to 40 personnes : June 15 to September 15 (with reservations)

- Identification of old flower varieties, fruits and vegetables in flower beds, a rose garden, groves and vegetable gardens
- Enclosed herb garden and an exhibition on their medicinal properties
- Buckwheat fields
- Composting and complementary gardening
- The advantages of a greenhouse
- Visit sheep, goat and horse pastures
- Demonstration on how to use some old gardening tools
- Identification of 60 tree varieties
- Visit the farmyard (turkeys, geese, chickens, ducks, guinea-fowl)

- Iroquois vegetable garden
- Cut-flower garden (900 gladiola)
- Visit heritage buildings and their "residents": pigs, calves, rabbits and cats

Price: $6 per person including tasting of farm products in the garden.

Schedule: guided tour (90 min) every day at 3 pm or otherwise with reservations.

Supper on the farm (5 courses, $20) is available after the tour, with reservations. The tour is free for those staying at the Seigneurie.

FARM EXCURSIONS

5. ST-PAUL-D'ABBOTSFORD

LA PETITE BERGERIE
Pierrette and Michel Scott
1460, rang Papineau
St-Paul-d'Abbotsford,
JOE 1A0
tel/fax (450) 379-5842

15 km from Granby
55 km from Montréal
25 km from St-Hyacinthe

Here, on a little country road, at the foot of a mountain, where you wouldn't expect to see anything, live Annabelle the cow, Églantine the ewe, Charlotte the goat and their friends. They invite you to come and learn while having fun with them and discovering the thousand and one marvels of the farm. See you soon! *Calin* **Country-Style Dining p 23.**

Hwy 10, Exit 55, Rte 235 North. From the exit, drive 5 km, 2nd road on your right. Or Hwy 20, St-Hyacinthe Exit, Rte 235 South, cross Rte 112, 1st road on your left.

> **FOR FAMILIES AND SMALL GROUPS** : May 15 to September 1(with reservations)
> **For groups of 30 to 75 personnes** : May 15 to September 15 (with reservations)

- Contact with smaller animals (lambs, goats, rabbits, ducks, chickens, etc.)
- Hay ride
- Pony rides
- Petting the soft rabbits
- Leaping in the hay

- Touring the flower greenhouse
- Ferreting about in the "Petite Fleur" shop
- Visiting the dairy cows
- Cheese sampling*
Rates : $5.00 per person
*additional charge

6. ST-VALÉRIEN

LA RABOUILLÈRE
Pierre Pilon
1073, rang de l'Égypte
St-Valérien J0H 2B0
(450) 793-4998
fax (450) 793-2529

80 km from Montréal
20 km from St-Hyacinthe
20 from de Granby

La Rabouillère, a unique farm. Your host, a veterinarian, has an infectious enthusiasm for animals and flowers... A unique collection of many animal species and breeds in magnificent countryside. (Ideal site for family parties, anniversaries, weddings, etc.). **Country-Style Dining** also available see p. 25.

From Montréal, Hwy 20 East, Exit 141, twd St-Valérien. In the village, take Chemin Milton, and the first road on the right (2nd flashing light). Or from Hwy 10, Exit 68, Rte 139 twd Granby, then Rte 112 and 137 North twd St-Hyacinthe. After Ste-Cécile, Chemin St-Valérien to the right, to the next flashing light turn left.

> Our farm is now open from May to October, weather permitting,
> for families and small or large groups.
> RESERVATIONS ALWAYS REQUIRED
> Snacks available upon request*

- The garden: large varieties of perennials and herbs (flowers in the kitchen, composting, water garden, the flora and fauna)
- The rabbit hutch: rabbits of different breeds (giant, dwarf, Angora...)
- Goats: care of the different breeds (milk, Angora, dwarf)
- Horse breeding: visit the stables, care and training of foals
- The farmyard: more than 50 types of birds
- The sheepfold (rare breeds): four-horned Jacob Sheep, Barbarian sheep and katadin (wool-less)

- Curiosities: llamas, donkeys, miniature horses...
- Other activities: pony rides, pool, volleyball, musical shows (folksinger or classical)*, campfire*, spit-roasted lamb (méchoui)*, corn on the cob*, brunch*, snack of terrines, pâtés and brochettes*
Price: $5 per person
* additional charge

7. ST-PIE

FERME JEAN DUCHESNE
Diane Authier and Jean Duchesne
1981-84, Haut-de-la-Rivière Sud
St-Pie J0H 1W0
(450) 772-6512

60 km from Montréal
20 km from St-Hyacinthe
15 km from Granby

For families and groups... Turn your children into little farmers by having them take part in our many farm activities. Everything is planned out for them! At the end of their exciting day, make them proud to receive their "Farmer For A Day" certificate of merit, officially presented by the "Big Farmer". For close and heart-warming contact with the animals, an educational, recreational and, above all, experimental outing, our huge farm is everyone's dream — for young and old alike!!

Hwy 20 Exit 123 St-Hyacinthe. Left at the stop sign on Rte 235 S. to St-Pie. At the flashing light after the bridge, turn left on Rue Emilleville then left on 2e Rang. Aut 10, Granby Exit 68. Turn right on Rte 139 Nord, left on Rte 112 to Grand Rang St-Charles to St-Paul and right on 2e Rang.

FOR FAMILIES AND SMALL GROUPS : 1 to 30 people April to October (with reservations)
For groups of 2 to 150 personnes : April 9 to October 11 (with reservations)

- Guided 5-hour tour, namely from 10 am to 3pm (times can be changed for groups)
- Guided tour: educational/recreational program adapted for different age groups
- "Smart" barn, kitten house, hay games, etc.
- "Big surprises" building!
- Introduction to several farm-bred animals, such as rabbits and their warren, the cow and its dairy, the birds and egg hatching, goat milking, etc.
- Feeding the many animals
- Hay rides to the sheepfold
- Presentation of "Farmer For A Day" certificate of merit with the farmer's handshake
- Indoor and outdoor games and picnic areas

- Indoor facilities in case of rain
- Children's birthday parties, anniversaries of all kinds (private reception available)

*Extra option including tour of the farm: family barouche ride, corn-husking party, apple picking in a hay wagon, hot/cold buffet with or without caterer, spit-roasted-lamb barbecue, farm products

Rates :
    $6 per person
    $5 For groups of 25 to 150 people
* additional charge

Farm Stays

		RATES* per day per person (double occ.)		ANIMALS	ACTIVITIES
		2 meals	3 meals		
BAS-ST-LAURENT					
St-Jean-de-Dieu Ferme Paysagée ☎ (418) 963-3315 (page 55)	adult	---	35	Deer, lamas, ponies, lambs, sheeps, goats, cows, peacocks, golden ducks, chickens, rabbits, pheasant.	Milking a cow, bringing the cows in from pasture, gathering eggs from chickens and quails. Feeding the small animals. Trout fishing. Walking along our trails and through our fields. **See advertisement end of Bas-St-Laurent region** (accommodation section).
	child	---	depends on age		
	child alone	---			
CANTONS-DE-L'EST					
Courcelles Ferme Auberge d'Andromède ☎ (418) 483-5442 (418) 486-7135 (page 64)	adult	45-60	48-65	French and Canadian percheron horses, pony, duck, goose, quail, hens, rabbits, pigs, Labrador and Irish setter.	In summer and winter alike, come take part in our farm activities. Children will love it, spending hours petting the animals. We provide an educational program for them, and they are free to play on our extensive grounds. Enjoy picking raspberries and flowers as well as a good farm meal made from eggs you have gathered. Come swimming, cycling and play with my children, William and Jordan. Welcome.
	child	25	30		
	child alone	25	30		
Danville Le Clos des Pins ☎ (819) 839-3521 (page 64)	adult	45-52^{50}	---	Cows, calves, horses, pigs, cats, sheep, rabbits, ducks, chickens, quail, guinea-fowl, Bernese bouvier dogs and cats.	Walks (135 acres), horse-drawn carriage rides, animal care, swimming, campfires, outdoor games, fruit picking, maintaining the organic vegetable garden, swing, children's playground. Daycare available for a small fee.
	child	20-25	---		
	child alone	---	---		
Ste-Anne-de-la-Rochelle Gîte En Effeuillant la Marguerite ☎ (450) 539-2943 (page 73)	adult	45-58	---	Sheeps, horses, cows, goats, rabbits, ducks, chickens, roosters, geese, peacocks, emus, guinea-pigs.	Observe, feed and hold the animals, possibility of participation in the farm activities. Playground, rest and picnic area. Walking in the fields and woods (100 acres). Bicycles, snowshoes and toboggan available. Cross-country skiing trail, site accessible by skidoo. Also: holiday menu, saphouse and birthday-party menu. Group rates.
	child	17	---		
	child alone	---	---		

* The price indicated is for one person, double occupancy. An additional charge may be added for a single person or for a child not sharing the parent's room.

		RATES * per day per person (double occ.)		ANIMALS	ACTIVITIES
		2 meals	3 meals		
CHAUDIÈRES-APPALACHES					
St-Léon-de-Standon Ferme la Colombe ☎ (418) 642-5152 (page 98)	adult child child alone	42-50 15-30 ...	... ...	Horse, goat, sheep, rabbits, various fowl, guinea-fowl, wild turkeys, quails, ducks, dog and cats.	Informative visit of the animals. Feed the animals, collect eggs. Visit the greenhouse where ornamental shrubs are produced. Trout fishing, swimming, canoeing, hebertism course, cycling, camp fires, indoor games, natural path near a stream, fruit picking, rest, bird-watching, winter sports, ski packages. Skating rink on site. **Country-style dining p 15 and farm excursion p 29.**
CÔTE-NORD					
Sacré-Cœur Ferme -5- Étoiles ☎ (418) 236-4551 (418) 236-4833 (page 106)	adult child child alone	49 45 ...	... ... 	Buffalo, deer, boar, peacocks, cows, horses, more than 32 species of farm birds...	Guided tour of the farm and its animals, the daily care of the animals, tractor and horse rides, excursions: hiking, all-terrain vehicles, kayaking, sailing or boat trips on the Saguenay Fjord, whale-watching cruises, backcountry camping. **Country home p 112. For activities: see advertisement in Côte-Nord and Saguenay-Lac-St-Jean regions.**
GASPÉSIE					
St-René-de-Matane Gîte des Sommets ☎ (418) 224-3497 (page 124)	adult child	29⁵⁰ 14	... ...	Cattle breeding, goat farm, chickens, rabbits and Ti- Lou, our friendly dog.	Guided tours of the farm, hikes on the well-marked and maintained trails. Fishing in the brook, mountain biking, picnics, campfires, mushroom picking, wild-berry picking, photo safari. Mountain climbing, visit to beaver pond. In winter season: snowshoeing, cross-country skiing, sliding, skidooing (equipment not provided).

*The price indicated is for one person, double occupancy. An additional charge may be added for a single person or for a child not sharing the parent's room.

		RATES* per day per person (double occ.)		ANIMALS	ACTIVITIES
		2 meals	3 meals		
LAURENTIDES					
L'Annonciation La Clairière de la Côte ☎ (819) 275-2877 (page 150)	adult child child alone	--- --- ---	40 20 ---	Cows, calves, goats, sheeps, rabbits, grain-fed chickens, turkeys, gooses, dogs and cats.	Visit of the farm. Forest walks (300 acres). Organic gardens, fine herbs, flowers, greenhouse. See chicks hatch. Transformation of farm products. Smoking of meat and fish. Rest areas. Campfires. Games. Life on the farm is busy. **Country-Style Dining p 17.**
St-Faustin Ferme de la Butte Magique ☎ (819) 425-5688 (page 155)	adult child child alone	45 28 ---	--- --- ---	Ewes and lambs for milk and wool, laying hens and broiler cocks, pigs in the forest, Collie dogs and cats.	Come discover why the Butte is magical! From daily animal care seasonal farming: the birthing of lambs, hand-milking the ewes, making cheese, maple syrup, shearing and spinning wool, gardening... All this interspersed with swimming, hikes, picnics, games in the shepherds' hut, campfires or sliding and skating on the lake. "Simple conviviality at its best" for 10 years now!
MAURICIE-BOIS-FRANCS					
Hérouxville Accueil les Semailles ☎ (418) 365-5190 (418) 365-5590 (page 175)	adult child child alone	28 13-15 ---	36 16-20 ---	Bullocks, horses, rabbits, chickens, ducks, goats, sheep, pigs, cats.	Visit the farm, feed the animals, pool, swing set, volleyball court, horseshoes, bicycles, outdoor fireplace.
Louiseville Ferme de la Seigneurie ☎ (819) 228-8224 (page 175)	adult child child alone	52-65 30 ---	--- --- ---	Goats, calves, sheep, horses, rabbits, ducks, turkeys, chickens, geese, guinea-fowl, dogs, cats.	Get close to nature at this small traditional farm: observe and feed fowl and other animals, identify birds. 40 varieties of trees, 86 varieties of flowers and medicinal herbs. Learn about the organic farming of the large vegetable garden and go all the way to the river through the fields. The guided tour of the farm and its gardens, at 3pm, is free. Winter: dogsledding, excursions. **Country Home p 184. Country-Style Dining p 21. Farm excursion p 32. See colour photos and advertisement end of the accommodation section in Mauricie-Bois-Francs region.**

* *The price indicated is for one person, double occupancy. An additional charge may be added for a single person or for a child not sharing the parent's room.*

	RATES * per day per person (double occ.)		ANIMALS	ACTIVITIES
	2 meals	3 meals		
MAURICIE-BOIS-FRANCS				
Tingwick Les Douces Heures d'Antan ☎ (819) 359-2813 (page 180)			Rabbits, chickens, ducks, turkeys, quails, sheep, peacocks, pigs, calves, dogs, cats.	Farm tour: sheep pen, rabbit warren, farmyard... Participate in the care and upkeep of animals, gather eggs, garden in our huge organic vegetable garden and our aromatic-herb and edible-flower garden. Go berry picking, fish in the stream or the pond. Swimming (heated outdoor spa), swing sets, bikes, indoor and outdoor games, campfires. Horse-drawn carriage rides possible.
adult	45	---		
child	25	---		
child alone	---	---		
MONTÉRÉGIE				
Howick (Riverfield) Auberge La Chaumière ☎ (450) 825-0702 (page 190)			Horses, sheep, donkey, dogs and cats.	Walks, cycling, swimming, canoeing, fishing, cross-country skiing, skating, snowshoeing, horseback riding, golfing, dogsledding, ornithology. **Country house p 196.**
Adult	37	43		
child	18	23		
child alone	37	43		
Howick Hazelbrae Farm ☎ (450) 825-2390 (page 191)			Cows and variety of small animals.	Campfire, carriage ride, pool, bikes, fruit picking, farm activities. Observe the milking of the cows, haymaking.
adult	---	45		
child	---	12-		
child alone	---	20-30		
Ste-Agnès-de-Dundee Chez Mimi ☎ (450) 264-4115 (page 194)			Horses, ponies, cows, chickens, rabbits, goats, ducks, cats, dogs.	Taking care of the garden and flowers. Feed the rabbits, collect eggs, make hay, pick vegetables. Bird-watching, river fishing, golf courses, snowmobile stopovers, horseback riding, country walks, bike paths.
adult	45	---		
child	20	---		
child alone	---	---		

* The price indicated is for one person, double occupancy. An additional charge may be added for a single person or for a child not sharing the parent's room.

| | | RATES *
per day
per person
(double occ.) | | ANIMALS | ACTIVITIES |
		2 meals	3 meals		
OUTAOUAIS					
Vinoy, **Chénéville** Les Jardins de Vinoy ☎ (819) 428-3774 (page 218)	adult child child alone	48 19 ---	55⁵⁰ 22⁷⁵ ---	Goats, pigs, sheep, wild boar, rabbits, guinea-fowl, ducks, geese, chickens, hens, dog, cats.	Yesteryear's charm, modern comforts. Animal husbandry, old-time sugaring off, sleigh rides (dogs, horses), soap-making, preserves, bread making, spinning, medicinal plants, forest trekking, cross-country skiing, snowshoeing, playground, campfire, organic garden, regional table d'hôte. **See colour photos.**
QUÉBEC (RÉGION DE)					
St-Gabriel-de- **Valcartier** Le Gîte des Equerres ☎ (418) 844-2424 toll free : 1-877-844-2424 (page 240)	adult child child alone	55-60 --- ---	--- --- ---	Forestry and horticultural farm, greenhouse garden. Dogs, cats, small farmyard animals (summer only).	Large property in the Jacques-Cartier Valley. Lake, river, forest, orchards, fields and gardens. Kilometres of walking trails, cycling, cross-country skiing, snowshoeing. Campfires, pool, tennis, library and music. Depending on the season, courses on tending of gardens, orchards and trails, drying and arranging fresh-cut flowers, game and bird watching.

The price indicated is for one person, double occupancy. An additional charge may be added for a single person or for a child not sharing the parent's room.

		RATES * per day per person (double occ.)		ANIMALS	ACTIVITIES
		2 meals	3 meals		
SAGUENAY - LAC-SAINT-JEAN					
Hébertville Jacques et Carole Martel ☎ (418) 344-1323 (page 250)	Adult child child alone	35 15 ---	--- ---	Cows, heifers, calves, dogs, cats, fowl.	Tour of the farm and observation of farm activities (milking, maintenance, etc.) Grain farming square and round hay baling. Capacity: 5 people.
La Baie Chez Grand-Maman ☎ (418) 544-7396 (page 253)	adult single occ. child child alone	50 60 15-20 ---	--- --- ---	Cows, calves, chickens, hens, turkeys, cats, dogs.	Try milking a cow. Feed the animals and see to their care. Walk along the shores of the Baie des HA! HA!. Outdoor fireplace, pool, and ice-fishing during winter.
Lac-à-la-Croix Céline et Georges Martin ☎ (418) 349-2583 (page 256)	adult child child alone	34 16 ---	--- ---	Cows, heifers, calves, dog.	Visit of the farm.
St-Félix-d'Otis Gîte de la Basse-Cour ☎ (418) 544-8766 (page 261)	Adult child child alone	45 20 ---	--- ---	Sheep, chickens, ducks, rabbits, partridges, pigeons, quails, dog.	Observing and feeding the animals, collecting eggs, feeding trout, bird watching and identification, tending of organic vegetable garden, vegetable and berry picking, preparing and baking bread in the outdoor bread oven, hiking, campfires, regional table d'hôte. Winter: cross-country skiing, snowshoeing, walking, skidooing (local trail 383 only 3 kilometres away). Available with reservation: kayaking on the fjord, dogsledding, ice fishing and skidoo rental.

FARM STAYS

* The price indicated is for one person, double occupancy. An additional charge may be added for a single person or for a child not sharing the parent's room.

Bed and Breakfasts

Country Inns

Country Homes

City Homes

Where to find the...

COUNTRY INNS			

COUNTRY HOMES

CITY HOMES (APARTMENTS & STUDIOS)

ABITIBI-TÉMISCAMINGUE

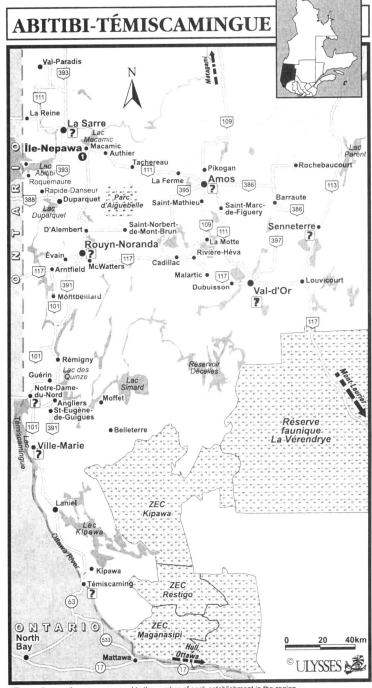

Val-Paradis
393
111
La Reine
La Sarre
?
Lac Macamic
Île-Nepawa Macamic
Authier
Tachereau
111
La Ferme
395
Saint-Mathieu
Lac Abitibi 393
Roquemaure
Rapide-Danseur
388 Duparquet
Parc d'Aiguebelle
Lac Duparquet
D'Alembert
Saint-Norbert-de-Mont-Brun
Rouyn-Noranda
?
Évain
McWatters
117
Cadillac
117 Arntfield
391
Montbeillard
101

Matagami

N

109
Lac Parent
Rochebaucourt
Pikogan
Amos
?
Barraute
386
Saint-Marc-de-Figuery
386 113
109
111 Senneterre
La Motte 397 ?
Rivière-Héva
Malartic 117
Dubuisson Louvicourt
Val-d'Or
?

117

101
Rémigny
Guérin Lac des Quinze
Notre-Dame-du-Nord
? Angliers Moffet
St-Eugène-de-Guigues
101 391
Ville-Marie
?

Lac Simard

Belleterre

Réservoir Décelles

Mont-Laurier

Réserve faunique La Vérendrye

Témiscamingue

Laniel

ZEC Kipawa

Lac Kipawa

Ottawa River

Kipawa

Témiscaming
?
63

ZEC Restigo

ONTARIO
North Bay
533

ZEC Maganasipi

Hull
Ottawa

Mattawa
17
17

0 20 40km

© ULYSSES

*The numbers on the map correspond to the number of each establishment in the region.

1. ÎLE-NEPAWA

F E 🐕 🚗 P ⛵ R30 M10

Three comfortable chalets in the wilderness on the shores of Lac Abitibi, including a Swiss-style with fireplace as well as two bungalows. We raise cattle, goats and horses. Water sports, hunting and fishing. Near the Aiguebelle conservation park. Come and enjoy a visit with Quebecers of German descent.

From Rouyn, Rte 101 to La Sarre. 3 km past La Sarre, follow the signs for Ste-Hélène and Île Nepawa (half-paved gravel road). 1st house on the right after the bridge to the island.

COUNTRY HOUSES
FERME VACANCES

Hélène and Hermann Wille
695 Île-Nepawa, R.R. # 1
Ste-Hélène-de-Mancebourg
J0Z 2T0
(819) 333-6103

No. houses	3
No. rooms	2-3
No. people	6-8
WEEK-SUMMER	$250
W/E-SUMMER	$125
DAY-SUMMER	$50

Open: May 1 to Oct. 31

Activities: ⛵ 🧍 🐎

COUNTRY HOMES

BAS-SAINT-LAURENT

GASPÉSIE

NEW BRUNSWICK

MANICOUAGAN

CHARLEVOIX

MAINE (UNITED STATES)

CHAUDIÈRE-APPALACHES

Mont-Joli

Saint-Donat
Saint-Marcellin
Sainte-Blandine
Sainte-Odile
Saint-Eugène-de-Ladrivère
Saint-Mathieu

Sainte-Luce-sur-Mer
Pointe-au-Père
Rimouski
Luceville
Le Bic
Pointe-aux-Anglais
Parc du Bic
Île Du Bic
Saint-Fabien
Saint-Simon
Saint-Narcisse-de-Rimouski
Réserve Duchénier
Trinité-des-Monts
ZEC Bas-Saint-Laurent
Réserve faunique de Rimouski
Esprit-Saint
Biencourt
ZEC Owen
Lejeune
Lac-des-Aigles
Squatec
Lots-Renversés
Rivière Madawaska
Saint-Jean-de-la-Lande
Packington
Dégelis
Saint-Eusèbe
Rivière-Bleue

Trois-Pistoles
Île aux Basques
Saint-Éloi
Saint-Jean-de-Dieu
Sainte-Françoise
Saint-Paul-de-la-Croix
Sainte-Rita
Saint-Cyprien
Saint-Clément
St-Clément
St-Hubert
Saint-Honoré
Saint-Pierre-de-Lamy
Lac Témiscouata
Cabano
Notre-Dame-du-Lac
Lac de l'Est

L'Isle-Verte
Île Verte
Phare de l'Île Verte
Cacouna
Rivière-du-Loup
Saint-Épiphane
Saint-Modeste
Saint-Antonin
Saint-Louis-du-Ha! Ha!
Saint-Elzéar
Saint-Éleuthère
Estcourt
Sully
Pohénégamook

Saint-Patrice
Saint-Alexandre
Withworth
Sainte-Hélène
Réserve de Parke

Saint-André
Kamouraska
Saint-Pascal
Saint-Bruno
Saint-Gabriel
Lac de l'Est

Saint-Siméon
Saint-Denis
St-Philippe-de-Néri
La Pocatière
Saint-Onésime
ZEC Chapais

La Malbaie
Québec

Les Escoumins
Grandes-Bergeronnes
Baie-Sainte-Catherine
Tadoussac
Rivière Saguenay
St. Lawrence River

© ULYSSES

N

0   15   30km

*The numbers on the map correspond to the number of each establishment in the region.

1. BIC

F E 🚭 P 🚗 🐕 R2 TA

On the shore of the St. Lawrence, in Bic Harbour, our century-old house awaits you in its calm setting with its old-fashioned decor and ambiance. Idyllically situated hugging the seashore. From the porch, a spectacle of sea birds follows the eternal movement of the tides.

From Québec City, Hwy 20 East, Rte 132 to Bic. Take the Aux Cormorans and Club de Golf exit. Drive 2 km. On the point, «Aux Cormorans» is the last house on the left, on the seashore.

B&B
AUX CORMORANS

Judy Parceaud
213, chemin du Golf
Pointe-aux-Anglais
Bic G0L 1B0
(418) 736-8113
fax (418) 736-4216
cormoran@globetrotter.qc.ca

B&B	
single	$40-75
double	$50-75
triple	$60

VS

Open year round

Number of rooms	5
rooms with private bath	1
shared bathrooms	2

Activities: 🦆 ⚓ 🎿 🚴 🏃

2. BIC

F e 🐕 🍴 P R1 TA

Quintessential Québec house dating from 1830. Aux 5 Lucarnes offers you 4 large rooms with sink, a "table d'hôte" prepared with local products, sea-kayak packages and access to the sea... Lunchbox service for your hikes. And so much more...

From Québec City, Hwy 20 East and Rte 132 East. At Bic exit, left at flashing light, about 3 km along Rte 132.

B&B
AUX 5 LUCARNES

Johanne Desjardins
2175, Route 132 Est
Bic G0L 1B0
tel/fax (418) 736-5435
www.cam.org/~bsl/lucarnes/
polyfilm@cgocable.ca

	B&B	PAM
single	$40	$60-65
double	$50	$90-100
triple	$60	$120-135
quad.	$70	$150-170
child	$10	$20-32,⁵⁰

Taxes extra VS ER

Open year round

Number of rooms	4
rooms with sink	4
shared bathrooms	2

Activities: 🦆 ⚓ 🎿 🏃 🚴

3. BIC

F e 🚭 🚗 P R.5

Hundred-year-old house deep in the country. Great sunsets on Rivière-Hâtée cove. Ambiance where flowers meet the magic of Christmas. King-sized beds, private bathrooms. Old-fashioned or healthy lunches, tea time, outdoor barbecues. Patio, balcony, family garden. Enjoy seaside solitude.

From Québec City, Hwy 20 E., Rte 132 E. At East Bic exit, left at flashing light on Rte 132, about 2 km. From Ste-Flavie or Mont-Joli, Rte 132 W. twd Bic. Marie-Roses on right.

INN
CHEZ MARIE-ROSES

Jacqueline and Jean-Guy Caron
2322, Route 132 Est
Bic G0L 1B0
(418) 736-5311
(418) 736-4954
fax (418) 736-5955
www.philsar.com/caron/jc.htm

B&B	
single	$50-60
double	$60-70
triple	$75-85
child	$10

Taxes extra VS MC IT

Reduced rates: Oct. 1 to May 31
Open: Feb. 1 to Dec. 31

Number of rooms	7
rooms with private bath	5
rooms in basement	1
shared wc	1
shared bathrooms	1

Activities: 🦆 🏃 🎿 🚴 🏃

4. BIC

F e 🐕 P R3 TA

A charming Norman-style house with antique furniture, this B&B overlooks the river and offers you a magnificent view of islands and mountains. Two rooms have their own bathroom and private entrance with view over the river. In a secluded setting, discover the wide expanses...

3 hours from Québec City, Hwy 20 East, Rte 132 East to Bic. First exit turn right on Rue Ste-Cécile. Turn right on the first small cross street, Rue Voyer. Voyer becomes 2e Rang Ouest. Drive 4 km.

B&B
LA PETITE NORMANDE

Claire Beaudoin
456, Rang 2 Ouest
C. P. 553
Bic G0L 1B0
(418) 736-5897
www.destinationQuébec.
com/ftpdocs/normande/
normande.htm

B&B	
single	$50-55
double	$55-65

Reduced rates: Oct. 20 to May 1
Open year round

Number of rooms	4
rooms with private bath	2
shared bathrooms	1
rooms in semi-basement	2

Activities: 🦆 ⛱ 👤 🚶 🚲

---

5. BIC, ST-FABIEN

F E 🚫 🐟 P R3 TA

At the gates of Parc du Bic, I invite you to share with me the charm of yesteryear, modern comfort, tranquillity (away from Rte 132) and a hearty breakfast of home-made bread and jam. Warm welcome. I love company!

Rte 132 from Gaspé or Montréal. In St-Simon, 11 km from Petro Canada. Left on Rang 1 for 2 km (white house, red roof). In St-Fabien, 3 km from art mill. Right on Rang 1.

B&B
CLAIREVALLÉE

Marguerite Voyer
178, Rang 1 Ouest
St-Fabien G0L 2Z0
tel/fax (418) 869-3582
from Nov.1 to May 1
(418) 862-7889
www.cam.org/
~bsl/clairevallee/

B&B	
single	$40-45
double	$55 60
triple	$70-75
quad.	$85-90
child	$0-15

VS

Open: May 15 to Oct. 15

Number of rooms	5
rooms with private bath	2
shared bathrooms	3

Activities: 🏛 🦆 ⛱ 👤 🚲

---

6. BIC, ST-FABIEN

F E 🐕 P R1 TA

A stone's throw from Parc du Bic, the old cobbler's house invites you into the warmth of its turn-of-the-century decor redolent with good bread and the joy of living. Nature, the mountain and the sea are within your reach, offering you an abundance of health and beauty. Welcome to our home.

From Québec City, Hwy 20 East, Rte 132 East to St-Fabien. Yellow Québec-style house near the caisse populaire in the centre of the village.

B&B
LA MAISON DU
CORDONNIER

Thérèse Gagné
26, 7e Avenue, C.P. 488
St-Fabien G0L 2Z0
(418) 869-2002

B&B	
single	$38
double	$50
triple	$62
child	$12

Taxes extra

Open year round

Number of rooms	3
shared bathrooms	1

Activities: 🦆 👤 🚶 🚲 🏇

B&Bs AND INNS

7. DÉGELIS

F E 🚭 🐕 🚗 P 🏊 R1.5

Located in a forest by Lac Témiscouata. Great comfort, clear panoramic view of the lake, famous à-la-carte breakfast. Come nightfall, around a fire on the beach, the song of the loon and golden sparks meeting the stars make up nature's sound and light show. Reserve from Oct. 15 to May 15.

Hwy 20, Exit 499, Rte 185 South. In Dégelis, Rte 295 North twd Auclair, for 6 km. By bike, cross the Dégelis dam and follow the 295 North, turn left and ride 2.5 km.

B&B
GÎTE AU TOIT ROUGE

Dominique Lagarde and
André Demers
441, Route 295
Dégelis G5T 1R2
(418) 853-3036
(418) 853-2294

B&B	
single	$40-50
double	$55-65
triple	$70-80
quad.	$80-95
child	$5-12

Reduced rates: Oct. 15 to Apr. 15
Open: Jan. 6 to Dec. 20

Number of rooms	4
rooms with private bath	1
rooms with sink	3
shared bathrooms	1

Activities: 🚣 🎿 🚴 🐎 🚶

8. DÉGELIS

F e P 🚗 R.13

Welcome to our welcoming B&B: water garden and falls, fragrant with flowers. Private entrance, big parking lot. Direct access to "Le Petit Témis" bike path; bike storage. Balcony, lounge, TV, fridge. Lavish breakfast in sunroom. Family picnics in gazebo. Restaurant nearby. Children welcome. See you soon!

From Québec City, Hwy 20 E. to Riv.-du-Loup, Rte 185 S. In Dégelis, 1st exit on left on Ave Principale. From New Brunswick Rte 185 N. In Dégelis, 1st exit on right, Ave Principale.

B&B
LA BELLE MAISON BLANCHE

Monique and André Lavoie
513, av. Principale
Dégelis G5T 1L8
(418) 853-3324
fax (418) 853-5507
www.destinationQuébec.com

B&B	
single	$40
double	$40-60
triple	$70-75
quad.	$80-90
child	$15

Reduced rates: Nov. 1 to May 31
Open year round

Number of rooms	5
shared wc	1
shared showers	1
shared bathrooms	1

Activities: 🎿 🚶 🚴 🐎 🛷

9. KAMOURASKA

F e 🚭 P 🚗 R.5 TA

This beautiful century-old house will leave you with unforgettable memories, marked by the rhythm of the wind and the tide. Comfort, cleanliness, and *joie de vivre* await. Close to the sea, with a 2 km-long promenade: what memories are made of. The sea air will whet your appetite for the gourmet breakfast to come. Bas-St-Laurent Excellence Prize 1995-96.

From Québec City, Hwy 20 East, Exit 465. Drive 5 km to Kamouraska. Once in the village, left on Ave. Morel (Rte 132). The second house after the church.

B&B
CHEZ JEAN ET NICOLE

Nicole and Jean Bossé
81, av. Morel, route 132
Kamouraska G0L 1M0
(418) 492-2921
www.total.net/
~stefnat/gite.html

B&B	
single	$40
double	$50-60
triple	$80
child	$10

VS

Reduced rates: Oct. 15 to May 15
Open year round

Number of rooms	3
rooms with private bath	1
shared wc	1
shared bathrooms	1

Activities: 🛶 🎿 🚶 🚴 🐎

10. L'ISLE-VERTE

F e ⊗ P R1 TA

Would you like to relive a page of our history, while admiring the accomplishments of our ancestors? We would like to share our large 150-year-old seigneurial house with you. Interior decor inspired by the highlights of the Victorian era: flowers, lace... You'll find charm, warm, old-fashioned hospitality and copious breakfasts. **Country home p 59.**

From Québec City, Hwy 20, Rte 132 East. Turn right before the bridge at the flashing light. Or from Rimouski, Rte 132 West, turn left after the bridge at the flashing light. 1st house on the right on a hill.

B&B
AUX BERGES DE LA RIVIÈRE

Eve and Noëlla Caron
24, rue Villeray
L'Isle-Verte GOL 1L0
(418) 898-2501
(418) 862-8547
noella@icrdl.net

B&B	
single	$45
double	$55
triple	$70
quad.	$80
child	$10

Open: June 15 to Sep. 15

Number of rooms	5
shared bathrooms	2

Activities: 🦞 ⛱ 🛥 🎿 🚲

---

11. L'ISLE-VERTE

F e 🐕 P R.5

A Victorian-style house with centenary charm that extends a warm and genuine welcome. Large tree-lined property. In the early morning wake up to the crowing of the cock and birdsong mingled with the aroma of a hearty breakfast. View of the river and access to nearby leisure activities. Make yourselves at home.

From Québec City: Hwy 20 East, Rte 132 East. In the village, turn right at the Caisse populaire, house on the left, on the hill. From Rimouski: Rte 132 West, turn left at the Caisse populaire.

B&B
LA MAISON ANCESTRALE

Diane Lévesque and
Joseph-Marie Fraser
5, rue Béland, C.P. 245
L'Isle-Verte GOL 1K0
(418) 898-2633
(418) 898-2053

B&B	
single	$40
double	$50
triple	$65
child	$10

Open: June to Sep. 15

Number of rooms	4
shared wc	1
shared bathrooms	2

Activities: 🏛 🦞 ⛱ 🎿 🚶

---

12. L'ISLE-VERTE

F 🛥 P R.5 TA

On the road to Gaspésie. Family ambiance and warm reception just for you! View of the St-Laurent River. Near the ferry to the island, the bus, restaurants. Spectacular sunsets. Rest and relaxation guaranteed. Let us treat you, after all, you are one of the family! See you soon!

From Québec City, Hwy 20 East, Rte 132 East. At flashing light, 0.5 km along Rte 132. Left on Rue Louise-Bertrand. From Gaspé, Rte 132 to L'Isle-Verte, right on 2nd street. 1 km from the ferry.

B&B
LES CAPUCINES

Marie-Anna and Yvon Lafrance
31, Louis-Bertrand, C.P. 105
L'Isle-Verte GOL 1K0
(418) 898-3276

B&B	
single	$35
double	$50
triple	$65
quad.	$75
child	$10

Reduced rates: Nov. 1to Apr. 30
Open year round

Number of rooms	3
rooms in basement	1
shared bathrooms	2

Activities: 🏛 🦞 ⛱ 🎿 ⛷

B&Bs AND INNS

13. LA POCATIÈRE

F | e | 👤 | ✂ | 🚗 | P | 🏔 | TA

More than an inn, this is a place where we get to know our guests. A place whose charm and landscape inspires peace and love, where the aromas of regional dishes mingle with the fragrances of the ancient woods. Packages available, home-made meals, discounts for longer stays. Children welcome; 3 kilometres from various attractions...

One hour from Québec City, Hwy 20 East, Exit 436, turn right (west) at the stop, continue for 500 metres and you're here. From Gaspé, Exit 436...

INN
AUBERGE AU DIABLO-VERT

Manon Brochu and Luc Gagnon
72, route 132 Ouest B.P.9
La Pocatière G0R 1Z0
(418) 856-4117
fax (418) 856-5161
www.Québecweb.com
/diablovert
diablove@globetrotter.net

	B&B	PAM
single	$55	$80
double	$65	$115
triple	$75	$150

Taxes extra VS MC AM IT

Reduced rates: Oct. 15 to June 1
Open year round

Number of rooms	4
shared wc	1
shared bathrooms	2

Activities: 🏛 🍷 🛶 🎿 🛷

14. POINTE-AU-PÈRE

F | e | ✂ | P

Come to our Victorian home, built around 1860 and dream of travelling. Former property of Sieur Louis-Marie Lavoie, known as "Louis XVI", who was master-pilot on the St. Lawrence for the city of Québec and upriver. This charming home has since become an inn where you'll be spoiled by serenity and a warm welcome. **See colour photos.**

From Québec City, Hwy 20 East, Rte 132 to Rimouski, Rte 132 to Pointe-au-Père, drive 1 km past the church.

INN
AUBERGE LA MARÉE DOUCE

Marguerite Lévesque
1329, boul. Ste-Anne
Pointe-au-Père, Rimouski
G5M 1W2
(418) 722-0822
(418) 723-4512
fax (418) 736-5167

	B&B
single	$70-80
double	$75-85
triple	$100
quad.	$110
child	$15

Taxes extra VS MC

Reduced rates: May,
Oct 1 to Dec 23
Open: May 1 to Dec 23

Number of rooms	9
rooms with private bath	9

Activities: 🏛 🍷 🎣 🏃 🚴

15. POINTE-AU-PÈRE

F | E | 🚭 | P | 🚗 | R.5 | TA

Magnificent location, panoramic view, warm welcome, comfortable bed, affable host, nearby restaurant, quiet walks, sunsets, beach campfires, starry nights, northern lights, lapping waves, deep sleep. Quiet mornings, fragrant coffee, talks... Activities: kayaking, museum, cycling, hiking... Enjoy your stay, *Sonia & André.*

Drop anchor at the end of the 20! Past Rimouski, Rte 132 East, between Bic and Métis, below the Pointe-au-Père lighthouse, 'twixtsky and sea (Rue du Phare), for a delightful time, unforgettable memories.

B&B
GÎTE DE LA POINTE

Sonia Soucy and
André Gamache
1046, rue du Phare
Pointe-au-Père G5M 1L8
(418) 724-6614
(418) 750-3332

	B&B
single	$40
double	$50
triple	$60

Taxes extra VS

Reduced rates: Sep. 15 to
June 15
Open: Jan. 15 to Dec. 15

Number of rooms	5
rooms in semi-basement	4
shared wc	3
shared bathrooms	1

Activities: 🏛 🛶 🎣 🚴 🏊

16. RIMOUSKI

F e 🐕 🛏 P R6 TA

An ancestral home
A family farm
A friendly ambiance
Amazing breakfasts
Enticing eggs, crepes
That young and old alike will enjoy
The house, the rooms, the stay
Are lovingly decorated
So that you will always remember
That at La Maison Bérubé
You are like family
Who visit us yearly

3 hours from Québec City, Hwy 20 East, Rte 132 East. At the Eastern Bic exit, at the flashing light turn left to return to Rte 132. Drive for 6.4 km to the left. 11.5 km from Rimouski.

B&B
LA MAISON BÉRUBÉ

Louise Brunet and Marcel Bérubé
1216, boul. St-Germain Ouest,
route 132
Rimouski G5L 8Y9
tel/fax (418) 723-1578

B&B	
single	$45
double	$55
triple	$70
quad.	$85
child	$5-15

Reduced rates: Oct. 1 to Apr. 30
Open year round

Number of rooms	5
rooms with sink	1
shared wc	1
shared bathrooms	2

Activities: 🏛 ☙ 🚣 ⚲ 🐎

17. RIMOUSKI, ST-NARCISSE

F e ♿ P 🏄 R4

For romantic dreamers, nature lovers. Rural family place. View of private lake. Indoor and outdoor fireplaces. Small farm animals. Swimming, canoeing. Dogsled to maple grove. Free activities. Ten minutes from Canyon des Portes de l'Enfer, waterfall, highest footbridge in Québec. A real vacation...

From Québec City, Hwy 20 East, Exit 610, 16 km along Rte 232 W., past St-Narcisse intersection. After 1 km, left on Rang 1, drive 1 km.

B&B
DOMAINE DU BON
VIEUX TEMPS

Hélène Rioux
89-1, chemin de l'Écluse
Rimouski-St-Narcisse G0K 1S0
(418) 735-5646
www.chez.com/
bonvieuxtemps

B&B	
single	$45
double	$45-55
child	$10

Open year round

Number of rooms	3
rooms with private wc	2
shared bathrooms	1

Activities:

18. RIVIÈRE-DU-LOUP

F E 🚭 P R1

A superb 1895 Victorian house. Admire the sunsets from the solarium while breathing in the salty air. Rest in the shade of hundred-year-old trees. Two lounges suitable for relaxation. Prime Ministers John A. MacDonald and Louis St-Laurent once stayed here. Magnificent surroundings!

Via Hwy 20, Exit 503, turn left at the stop, 11th house on the left. Located on Rte 132 between Notre-Dame-du-Portage and Rivière-du-Loup.

B&B
AUBERGE LA SABLINE

Monique Gaudet and
Jean Cousineau
343, Fraser Ouest
Rivière-du-Loup G5R 3Y4
(418) 867-4890

B&B	
single	$60-70
double	$65-75
triple	$80-90
quad.	$95-105
child	$10

VS MC IT

Reduced rates: Sep. 15 to June 15
Open year round

Number of rooms	3
rooms with private bath	1
shared wc	1
shared bathrooms	1

Activities: 🚣 🚲 ⚲ 🏃 🚲

B&Bs AND INNS

19. RIVIÈRE-DU-LOUP, ST-ANTONIN

F e P R.5 TA

Located less than 5 kilometres from Rivière-du-Loup, on the road to Edmunston, "La Maison de Mon Enfance" awaits you. For your relaxation: books, photos and old artifacts. For your leisure: cruise packages, museums, theatre, Petit Témis cycling path 1 kilometre away. See you soon, *Roseline*.

Rte 185: In St-Antonin, at the flashing light turn toward the Trans Canadien restaurant; it's at the stop. From Riv.-du-Loup: twd Edmunston, Jct. 185 for 4 km. On the right.

B&B
LA MAISON DE MON ENFANCE

Roseline Desrosiers
718, ch. Rivière-Verte
St-Antonin G0L 2J0
(418) 862-3624
fax (418) 862-8969

B&B	
single	$40-50
double	$50-60
triple	$60-70
quad.	$80

VS IT

Open: May 1 to 31 Oct.

Number of rooms	5
shared wc	1
shared bathrooms	2

Activities: 🐚 ⚓ 🎣 🚶 🚲

---

20. ST-ALEXANDRE, KAMOURASKA

F e P 🚗 R.3 TA

Spend your holidays in the beautiful ancestral home of Marie-Alice Dumont, first professional photographer in Eastern Québec. Mouthwatering breakfasts served by the stained-glass window of the former photography studio. The warmest of welcomes awaits. Bas St-Laurent Excellence Prize 1994-95.

From Québec City, Hwy 20 East, Exit 488 to St-Alexandre. The "Maison au Toit Bleu" is in the village, at the intersection of Rtes 230 and 289, near the large cross.

B&B
LA MAISON AU TOIT BLEU

Madame Daria Dumont
490, av. St-Clovis
St-Alexandre G0L 2G0
tel/fax (418) 495-2701
(418) 495-2368

B&B	
single	$40
double	$50
child	$10

Open year round

Number of rooms	3
shared bathrooms	2

Activities: 🏛 🐚 ⚓ 🚤 🎣

---

21. ST-ANDRÉ, KAMOURASKA

F e P ☒ TA

Renew ties with the inn traditions of long ago. A historic home, authentic period decor, sumptuous rooms with sink and clawfooted bathtub, a view of the St. Lawrence, a refined and delicious table d'hôte... everything you dreamed of, everything to spoil you. **See colour photos.**

From Hwy 20, Exit 480, to St-André. At the village, turn right, Rue Principale. The house is next to the post office. Direct access by Rte 132.

INN
AUBERGE LA SOLAILLERIE

Isabelle Poyau and Yvon Robert
112, rue Principale
St-André-de-Kamouraska
G0L 2H0
(418) 493-2914
fax (418) 493-2243

B&B	
single	$45-80
double	$54-89
child	$15-20

Taxes extra VS MC

Reduced rates: spring and fall
Open: Apr. 15 to Oct. 31

Number of rooms	11
rooms with private bath	6
rooms with bath and sink	3
rooms with sink	2
shared wc	2
shared bathrooms	1

Activities: 🐚 ⚓ 🎣 🚶 🚲

22. ST-ÉLOI

F P TA

Come and share the comfort and tranquillity of a more-than-hundred-year-old presbytery near l'Isle-Verte. Breathe in the fresh air in this peaceful village, explore the building and admire the view of the St. Lawrence. Copious breakfasts. Children welcome. Visits to the family farm also possible. **Advertisement end of this region.**

From Québec City, Hwy 20 East, Rte 132 East for 19 km to the Rte St-Éloi Exit. Drive 5 km twd the town of St-Éloi. Turn left on Rue Principale. House next to church.

INN

AU VIEUX PRESBYTÈRE

Raymonde and Yvon Pettigrew
350, rue Principale Est
St-Éloi G0L 2V0
(418) 898-6147

B&B	
single	$38-40
double	$53-55
triple	$68-70
quad.	$85
child	$10

Taxes extra VS, IT

Reduced rates: Nov. 1 to Dec. 20 and Jan. 15 to Apr. 30

Open year round

Number of rooms	4
rooms with sink	4
shared bathrooms	3

Activities:

23. ST-JEAN-DE-DIEU

F P R4

Family with children, all happy to have you as guests. Dairy farm. Fishing and small animals: peacocks, ducks, rabbits, sheep, goats, deer, llamas... Crepes with maple syrup for breakfast. A warm atmosphere and healthy food. 20 min from the river. Families welcome. **Farm stay p 36. Advertisement end of this region.**

From Québec City, Hwy 20 East, Rte 132 East to Trois-Pistoles. Rte 293 South to St-Jean-de-Dieu. Drive 4 km past the church.

B&B

LA FERME PAYSAGÉE

Gabrielle and Régis Rouleau
121, Route 293 Sud
St-Jean-de-Dieu G0L 3M0
(418) 963-3315
rouls@globetrotter.net

B&B	
single	$30
double	$40
child	$10

Open year round

Number of rooms	3
shared bathrooms	2

Activities:

24. ST-LOUIS-DU-HA! HA!

F e P R6 TA

Why stay with us? For the great welcome, the cleanliness, peacefulness and comfort of our B&B. Family house from the 1920s in the heart of the Témis mountains. Magnificent view. Lavish home-made breakfasts Family-size room. Bike shed. Packages. Off-season rates.

From Québec City: Hwy 20 to Rivière-du-Loup. 60 km along Rte 185 Sud to the only flashing light, turn right, drive 1.6 km. Left onto Rang Beauséjour, continue for 5 km.

B&B

GÎTE BEAU-SÉJOUR

Louiselle Ouellet and
Paul Gauvin
145, rang Beauséjour
St-Louis-du-Ha! Ha! G0L 3S0
tel/fax (418) 854-0559
lgauvin@sympatico.ca

B&B	
single	$40
double	$50
triple	$60
quad.	$70
child	free

Reduced rates: Oct. 15 to Jan. 1and Mar. 15 to June

Open year round

Number of rooms	4
shared bathrooms	2

Activities:

B&Bs AND INNS

25. ST-LOUIS-DU-HA! HA!

F E P R3

Country house and farm in an enchanting location in vast wilderness typical of the Temiscamingue countryside. Warm welcome, excellent all-you-can-eat gourmet breakfast. Come experience a stay in a comfortable bedroom of our house or in a studio built in the farm's old dairy.

From Québec City, Hwy 20 to Rivière-du-Loup. Rte 185 South to the second flashing light, turn right, drive 1.6 km. Turn right onto Chemin Bellevue, drive 1.7 km.

B&B
GÎTE DE LA GIBECIÈRE

Marc Laperrière and
Mathieu M. Laperrière (fils)
58, chemin Bellevue
St-Louis-du-Ha! Ha! G0L 3S0
tel/fax (418) 854-6151

B&B	
single	$38
double	$48
child	$8

Taxes extra

Open: May 1 to Oct. 31

Number of rooms	3
shared bathrooms	2

Activities:

26. ST-LOUIS-DU-HA! HA!

F E P R2 TA

Located right on the "Petit Témis" cycling path, Le Doux Repaire's name suits it well. Deep in the country, this former post office offers peace and comfort in an original setting. A living room next to the rooms is reserved for guests. The terrace with view of the mountains will enchant you.

From Québec City: Hwy 20, Exit 499. On Rte 185 South, 7 km from the St-Honoré entrance. Right on Rte Vauban. Right on Rte Bossé. From the south, 5.2 km from St-Louis-du-Ha! Ha!

B&B
LE DOUX REPAIRE

Elyse Cossette and
Gilles Gagné
26, route Bossé
St-Louis-du-Ha!Ha! G0L 3S0
(418) 854-9851

B&B	
single	$35
double	$50
triple	$60
child	$5

Reduced rates: Oct. 15 to Jan. 1 and Mar. 15 to June 15
Open year round

Number of rooms	4
shared bathrooms	2

Activities:

27. ST-PATRICE-DE-RIVIÈRE-DU-LOUP

F E P

"Who sleeps, eats" at Au Bonheur du Jour, a rural B&B between the road and the sea in L'Anse-au-Persil. As night falls the dining room offers 6-course meals to guests whith reservations. The next morning there will be fresh bread toasted on the wood stove. Bring your own wine and binoculars. Io parlo più che meno l'italiano.

L'Anse-au-Persil is between Rivière-du-Loup and Cacouna. From Riv.-du-Loup, Rte 132 East to #284. A short, private marked road leads to the B&B hidden from the road.

B&B
AU BONHEUR DU JOUR

Marie Anne Rainville
284, Anse-au-Persil, rte 132
St-Patrice-de-Rivière-du-Loup
G5R 3Y5
tel/fax (418) 862-3670

	B&B	PAM
single	$40	$60
double	$55	$100
triple	$70	$140
child	$10	$35

Open: June 20 to Sep. 1

Number of rooms	3
shared bathrooms	1

Activities:

28. ST-PATRICE-DE-RIVIÈRE-DU-LOUP

F E 🚫 ⛵ P R3

Summer residence of Canada's first Prime Minister, Sir John A. Macdonald from 1872 to 1890. Magnificient heritage house which gives visitors a splendid view across the St. Lawrence River to the mountainous north shore. Enjoy your stay in a quiet and peaceful environment as well as our delicious home-made breakfast. Many activities and day trips nearby. **Country home in Percé, Gaspésie region, p 134, no 56.**

Hwy 20 to Rivière-du-Loup then west on Hwy 132 to St-Patrice (civic number 336 Rue Fraser).

B&B
LES ROCHERS

L'Héritage Canadien du Québec
336, rue Fraser
St-Patrice, Rivière-du-Loup
G5R 3Y4
(514) 393-1417
(418) 868-1435
fax (514) 393-9444
www.total.net/~chq
chq@total.net

B&B	
single	$65-75
double	$70-85
triple	$80-95
child	$10

VS MC

Open: June 1to Sep. 1

Number of rooms	5
rooms with private bath	2
rooms with sink	3
shared bathrooms	3

Activities:

---

29. ST-SIMON, TROIS-PISTOLES

F E 🚗 P 🐕 R4 TA

Lovely home (1820). Bucolic setting. Farmhouse. Rooms with old baths. Private beach. Packages: excursions (whale-watching, Île aux Basques), theatre. Footpaths: Trois-Pistoles river, Parc du Bic... Skiing. Skidoo. Hearty breakfasts. Outdoor cooking available. Senior citizens, 15% discount off-season. **Advertisement end of this region.**

Directly accessible via Rte 132. Eastbound : 7 km east of Trois-Pistoles. Westbound : 4 km west of St-Simon. 10 min from the ferry.

B&B
CHEZ CHOINIÈRE

Alain Choinière
71, rue Principale Ouest
St-Simon G0L 4C0
(418) 738-2245
chezchoiniere@hotmail.com

B&B	
single	$40
double	$55
triple	$70
quad.	$85
child	$10

Reduced rates: Oct. 15 to June 1, and 10% for 3 nights and more
Open year round

Number of rooms	5
rooms with sink and bath	2
rooms with private bath	3
shared bathrooms	1

Activities:

---

30. STE-LUCE-SUR-MER

F E ♿ 🍽 P 🏊 TA

Right on the beach and just a few kilometres from the Jardins de Métis, we offer an oasis of peace in harmony with the rhythm of the seas. In concert with the setting sun and our fine regional cuisine (included in the menu), you will experience a magical sound and light show.

From Québec City, Hwy 20 East, Rte 132 twd Ste-Flavie. After Pte-au-Père, watch for "Camping La Luciole", drive 500 ft. and turn left, then right on Route du Fleuve.

INN
AUBERGE DE L'EIDER

Johanne Cloutier
and Maurice Gendron
90, route du Fleuve Est
Ste-Luce-sur-Mer G0K 1P0
tel/fax (450) 448-5110
(418) 739-3535

B&B	
single	$53
double	$60-75
triple	$75-85
quad.	$95
child	$10

Taxes extra VS MC ER

Open: June 15 to Sep. 30

Number of rooms	12
rooms with private bath	12

Activities:

B&Bs AND INNS

31. STE-LUCE-SUR-MER

F E P 🛏 🐕 🏄R.1 TA

On the banks of the St. Lawrence, charming 1920 house with country colours, landscaped grounds and private beach. Creative "eye-catching" breakfast will whet your appetite. Relaxing gazebo. Unforgettable evening show as the fiery sun kisses the sea. Cocktail hour. 15 minutes from Jardins de Métis, Parc du Bic, Côte-Nord ferry.

Mid-way between Rimouski and Mont-Joli via Rte 132. Enter the picturesque village of Ste-Luce along the river; we are 0.2 km west of the church, near the river.

B&B
MAISON DES GALLANT

Nicole Dumont and
Jean Gallant
40, du Fleuve Ouest, C.P. 52
Ste-Luce-sur-Mer G0K 1P0
(418) 739-3512
toll free 1-888-739-3512
jean.gallant@cgocable.ca
www.bbcanada.
com/1992.html

B&B	
single	$45
double	$55
triple	$70
child	$10

Open year round

Number of rooms	3
shared wc	1
shared bathrooms	1

Activities: 🏛 🌊 ⚲ 🚴 🎿

---

32. TROIS-PISTOLES

F E 🐕 🛏 P R1

Let the river, excursions to Îles aux Basques, the whales, the museums, the summer theatre and other activities cast their spells on you. You will return home on the ferry, just 5 min away, having experienced the unique charm and fine dining of our B&B. **Advertisement end of this region.**

Halfway between Montréal and Percé, and 0.5 km from the western edge of the town of Trois-Pistoles, on the north bank looking over the river, and 2 km from the Les Escoumins ferry.

B&B
AU GRÉ DES MARÉES

Jeanne Riverin and
Marcel Hardy
525, Notre-Dame Ouest
Trois-Pistoles G0L 4K0
(418) 851-3819

B&B	
single	$40
double	$50
triple	$65
child	$10

VS

Reduced rates: Nov. 1 to May 31
Open year round

Number of rooms	3
shared bathrooms	2

Activities: 🏛 🍷 ⛴ 🌊 ⚲

---

33. TROIS-PISTOLES

F 🛏 P R4

Bas-St-Laurent Excellence Prize 1997-98. It's so good to be home! Enjoy a stay on our farm in the quiet countryside, in a hundred-year-old house furnished with antiques, surrounded by flowers, trees and birds. Hearty breakfasts, home-made jams and bread. Near the ferry to the north bank. Come share in our joy; the only thing missing here is you. **Advertisement end of this region.**

From Québec City, Hwy 20 East, Rte 132 East to Trois-Pistoles. Rte 293 South, 1 km, right on Rang 2 West, 2.7 km. From ferry, 1st street on left, Rte 293 South, 1 km, turn right, 2.7 km.

B&B
FERME LE TERROIR
DES BASQUES

Marguerite and
Pierre-Paul Belzile
65, Rang 2 Ouest
Trois-Pistoles G0L 4K0
tel/fax (418) 851-2001

B&B	
single	$40
double	$50
triple	$70
quad.	$90
child	$10

Open: May 1 to Oct. 30

Number of rooms	4
rooms with sink	2
shared bathrooms	2

Activities: 🏛 🍷 ⛴ 🚶 🚴

34. L'ISLE-VERTE

F e 🚭 P R1 M1 TA

On ground level, part of our house can accommodate 4 people (2 rooms, kitchen, etc.) for an autonomous stay. Modest, clean and convenient, the place is pleasant and advantageous. Located in an enchanting spot halfway between Rivière-du-Loup and Trois-Pistoles, near several activities. We look forward to seeing you. **B&B p 51.**

From Québec City: Hwy 20, Rte 132 East. Before the bridge, right at the flashing light. From Rimouski: Rte 132, after the bridge, left at flashing light. 1st house on the right on the hill.

COUNTRY HOMES
AUX BERGES DE LA RIVIÈRE

Ève and Noëlla Caron
24, rue Villeray
Isle-Verte G0L 1L0
(418) 898-2501
(418) 862-8547
noella@icrdl.net

No. houses	2
No. rooms	2
No. people	4
WEEK-SUMMER	$235
W/E-SUMMER	$95

Open: Apr. 1 to Nov. 1

Activities: 🐚 ⛵ 🚣 ⚜ 🚲

35. ST-ALEXANDRE, KAMOURASKA

F e ♿ 🐕 P 🚗 🏊 🍴 M19 TA

Unique outdoor experiences on our forested farm: 3 lakes, 2 rivers, fauna flora, 11.4 km of trails, lookouts, cycling, snowshoeing, X-country skiing, snowmobiling, winter camping, rides on horse sleighs and carriages... Meals upon request. Free farm tour. You'll feel at home in the beautiful Québec country side. **See colour photos.**

From Montréal, Hwy 20 East, Exit 488. Rte 289 turn right, drive 20 km (15 minutes from Hwy 20). Or, from Gaspésie, Hwy 20, Exit 488, Rte 289 turn left, drive 20 km.

COUNTRY HOMES
LE REFUGE FORESTIER

Réal Sorel
Havre du Parke,
Route 289, C.P. 220
St-Alexandre G0L 2G0
(418) 495-2333
toll free 1-888-495-2333
fax (418) 495-2509

No. houses	2
No. rooms	3-34
No. people	12-60
WEEK-SUMMER	$495-1995
WEEK-WINTER	$495-1995
W/E-SUMMER	$295-1195
W/E-WINTER	$295-1195
DAY-SUMMER	$125-495
DAY-WINTER	$125-495
Taxes extra VS IT	

Open year round

Activities: ⛵ ⚜ 🚲 ⛷ 🐕 🚩

36. ST-MATHIEU-DE-RIOUX

F E 🚭 🐕 🚗 P 🏊 R6 M6 TA

Magnificent spot, large plot of land, tranquillity, panoramic view, mountains, St-Laurent River; 2-kilometre-long wild private lake, with clear unpolluted water, surrounded by a forest. Large, renovated 2-story house with cachet, 4-sided porch, veranda, cathedral roof, equipped kitchen, fireplace, 2 bathrooms. **City house, Québec region p 244, no 70.**

From St-Simon (on Rte 132 East of Rivière-du-Loup) take 1st road on right, east of the village towards St-Mathieu. From St-Mathieu, 1st road on right, east of the village, to rang 4 then Rang 5 East.

COUNTRY HOMES
MAISON BRISSON

Chantal Brisson and
Serge Thibaudeau
307, rang 5 Est
St-Mathieu-de-Rioux G0L 3T0
(418) 640-9255
fax (418) 640-0795
www.craph.org/mti
sthibau@globetrotter.net

No. houses	1
No. rooms	4
No. people	8
WEEK-SUMMER	$800
WEEK-WINTER	$800
W/E-SUMMER	$400
W/E-WINTER	$400

Open year round

Activities: 🐚 🎿 ⚜ 🚲 ⛷

FARM ACTIVITIES

Farm Stay:

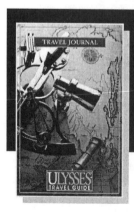

CANTONS-DE-L'EST

CHAUDIÈRE-APPALACHES

201
Saint-Théophile
Saint-Martin
Saint-Ludger
108
Saint-Gédéon
Saint-Sébastien
Lac-Mégantic 13 14 17
Saint-Augustin-de-Woburn
204
Sainte-Cécile-de-Whitton
Lac Mégantic
Courcelles 4
Lambton
Stratford
108
Stornoway
Nantes
Milan
Notre-Dame-des-Bois
212
Gould 9
Scotstown
Chartierville
257
Beaulac
Saint-Gérard
Bishopton
108
Brookbury
214
La Patrie
West Ditton
Coleraine
112
Disraëli
Saint-Camille
112
255
Saint-Malo
253
Paquette
Beacher Falls
263
N.-D.-de-Ham
St-Adrien-de-Ham 31
Wotton 30
Saint-Camille
255
Stoke-Centre
East-Angus
Cookshire
212
Martinville
Sainte-Edwidge-de-Clifton
Coaticook
Stanhope
147
Norton
161
Warwick
Tingwick
Asbestos
255
Richmond
249
Windsor
Bromptonville
Ascot Corner
Eaton Corner
Rock Forest
Sherbrooke 35 36
Compton
North Hatley 29 32
Ayer's Cliff 1 2
Way's Mills
Stanstead
143
116
Danville 6
116
Maricourt
243
St-Élie-d'Orford
St-Étienne-de-Bohan
Orford 28
Magog 25 18 à 24
Austin
Georgeville
55
MAURICE-BOIS-FRANCS
255
Saint-Lucien
Saint-Nicéphore
L'Avenir
Lefebvre
55
243
Roxton Falls
222
220
Eastman
Bolton Centre
Bolton Sud
Mansonville
Highwater
North Troy
20
Drummondville
Saint-Germain
143
Sainte-Hélène-de-Bagot
Upton
116
Valcourt 45
Sainte-Anne-de-la-Rochelle
Waterloo
Warden
32 33
Foster
7
245
Bolton
10
Brome
Glen Sutton
Sutton
139
Richford
143
Saint-Edmond-de-Grantham
Saint-Eugène-de-Grantham
Acton Vale
Saint-Dominique
137
Granby 10 11 12
Bromont 5
Lac-Brome (Knowlton) 8
Dunham 7 37
7
2
Saint-Simon
Saint-Pie
Rougemont
Ange-Gardien
Farnham
St-Alexandre
Cowansville
Mystic
Bedford
Freighsburg
7
2
20
Marieville
Saint-Hyacinthe
MONTÉRÉGIE
Pike River 29 30
UNITED STATES

N

© ULYSSES

0   15   30km

*The numbers on the map correspond to the number of each establishment in the region.

1. AYER'S CLIFF

F E P R10

Lovers of peace, vastness and harmony, "La Chevrière" welcomes you into its newly built country house. One luxurious room with grand piano, stone fireplace and balcony. Angora-goat breeding. Mohair-processing demonstration. Coaticook Gorge, North Hatley Mine.

Hwy 10, Exit 121, Hwy 55, Exit 21, Rte 141 South. 3 km after "Hatley-Kingscroft-way's mills" sign, turn left (Chemin Roy N.), drive 4 km. Field stone and wood house on the right.

B&B
FERME «LA CHEVRIÈRE»

Monique Marchand and
Serge Paradis
3238, chemin Roy Nord
Ayer's Cliff (Kingscroft)
J0B 1C0
tel/fax (819) 838-5292

B&B	
single	$45-100
double	$65-100
child	$20

Taxes extra VS

Open year round

Number of rooms	3
rooms with private bath	1
shared wc	1
shared bathrooms	1

Activities:

---

2. AYER'S CLIFF

F P R5 TA

Hundred-year-old house in the country, panoramic view, quiet place. Home cooking. Swimming in Lake Massawippi 3 km away, summer theatre, Coaticook Gorge, cross-country skiing, downhill skiing 15 min. away, 8 min. from golf, 200 ft. from skidooing. Near North Hatley, Mont Orford and Magog. Horseback riding 15 min. away. Ideal for hiking and cycling.

From Montréal: Hwy 10 Est, Exit 121. Hwy 55 South, Exit 21, Rte 141 South. About 2.5 km. after intersection of Rte 143, left on Chemin Audet. Big white house on the hill.

B&B

Cécile Lauzier
3119 ch. Audet, Kingscroft
Ayer's Cliff J0B 1C0
(819) 838-4433

B&B	
single	$45-50
double	$55-65
triple	$75

Open year round

Number of rooms	3
shared bathrooms	2

Activities:

---

3. BROMONT

F E P   R1 TA

Spacious residence on a hillside where lace and silverware combine with modern comforts. High-quality B&B, tennis, pool, fireplace, 5-course breakfasts, warm welcome and special touches make your stay a memorable experience. Gift certificate, ski packages, golf, theatre, spa, biking, restaurant.

30 min from the U.S., 15 min from Lac Brome and 45 min from Montréal. Hwy 10, Exit 74 to Bromont. From the stop take Boul. Pierre-Laporte (Rte 241) for 6.5 km. Left on des Verrières, 1st street on right is De La Rigole.

B&B
Ô MÛRES MURES

Ginette Lambert and
Jean-Guy Tremblay
5, rue de la Rigole
Bromont J2L 1T2
(450) 534-5242
fax (450) 534-5409
www.virtuel.qc.ca/omurmur
maurice@virtuel.qc.ca

B&B	
single	$55-75
double	$70-95
triple	$90-115
child	$15

VS

Reduced rates: April and Nov.
Open year round

Number of rooms	3
rooms with private bath	1
shared bathrooms	1

Activities:

B&Bs AND INNS

4. COURCELLES

F E P 🐕 ✂ TA

Our farm-inn offers you fine regional cuisine. Savour our dishes in a magnificent sunroom looking over flowers, horses and fawns. Enjoy the period decor with your hosts Gina and Gilles, who will introduce you to fine food and attractions. Delicious and rejuvenating holiday. **Farm Stay p 36.**

From Montréal, Hwy 10 E. twd Sherbrooke. Exit Boul Université to Lennoxville, Rte 108 twd Beauceville. From Québec City, Pierre-Laporte bridge twd St-Georges, St-Joseph Exit. In Beauceville, 108 W. twd Courcelles.

B&B
L'AUBERGE D'ANDROMÈDE

Gina Hallé and Gilles Leclerc
495, Rang 6
Courcelles G0M 1C0
tel/fax (418) 483-5442
(418) 486-7135

	B&B	PAM
single	$35	$60
double	$60	$120
child	$15	$25

Taxes extra

Reduced rates : Jan. 1to Apr. 1
Open year round

Number of rooms	2
rooms with private bath	2

Activities: 🏛 🚲 🛷 🎿 🥢

---

5. COWANSVILLE

F E 🚤 P 🏊 R.5 TA

Enchanting site near Bromont and Lac Brome. Discover our paradise on a 10-acre hill, overlooking Lac d'Avignon with view over the mountains. Flowery expanses, pond, footpaths, in-ground pool, VIP suites, hearty and varied breakfasts. Near cultural and sports activities. Gift certificates and "golf" packages available. "Sheer bliss."

From Montréal or Sherbrooke, Hwy 10, Exit 74, Boul Pierre Laporte twd Cowansville. At BMP hospital, left on Rue Principale drive 0.5 km.

B&B
DOMAINE SUR LA COLLINE B&B

Nicole and Gilles Deslauriers
1221, rue Principale
Cowansville J2K 1K7
(450) 266-1910
cell. (450) 531-1416
fax (450) 266-4320
www.surlacolline.qc.ca
info@surlacolline.qc.ca

	B&B
single	$70-100
double	$75-110
triple	$120-130
quad.	$140-150
child	$10-20

VS MC

Reduced rates : Oct. 16 to Dec. 10 and Jan. 15 to May 13
Open year round

Number of rooms	4
rooms with private bath	2
shared wc	1
shared bathrooms	1

Activities: 🥢 🍷 🚲 🎿 🐎

---

6. DANVILLE

F e 🚭 🚤 P 🏊 ✂ R3 TA

Nature lovers: spacious estate with forest, trails and animals, where only the beauty of the landscapes rivals the peace and quiet. Table d'hôte served by the fire or on the terrace in summer. Hiking, cycling (path), swimming, X-country skiing. Packages: theatre, golf, cycling, riding. **Farm Stay p 36.**

From Montréal, Hwy 20, Exit 147, Rte 116 East. In Richmond, at lights, drive 13.9 km, left on Demers drive 2.5 km. From Québec City, Hwy 20, Exit 253, Rte 116 W. In Danville at lights 3 km Demers.

B&B
LE CLOS DES PINS

Josée Brouillette and
Daniel Godbout
60, chemin Boisvert
Danville J0A 1A0
tel/fax (819) 839-3521

	B&B	PAM
single	$40-55	$55-70
double	$55-70	$85-100
triple	$85	$130
4 pers.	$100	$160
child	$10-15	$20-25

Taxes extra

Reduced rates: Nov. 15 to Dec. 15 and Jan. 15 to May 15
Open year round

Number of rooms	4
shared bathrooms	2

Activities: 🍷 🥢 🚲 🐎 🛷

7. DUNHAM

F e P R.25

After touring the vineyards, unwind at our magnificent Victorian manor. Terrace, living room with fireplace, air-conditioned suites and private bathrooms. Relax to soft music in our spa or enjoy a game of pool. We look forward to seeing you soon.

Take Cantons-de-l'Est Hwy 10 to Exit 68, Rte 139 to Cowansville (18 km). At second traffic light, take Rte 202 to Dunham (8 km). 200 metres past the corner store, Rue du Collège (left).

B&B
AUX DOUCES HEURES

Lyette Leroux Dumoulin and André Dumoulin
110, rue du Collège C.P. 40
Dunham J0E 1M0
(450) 295-2476
toll free 1-877-295-2476

B&B	
single	$50
double	$75
child	$15

Taxes extra

Open: Mar. 1to Nov. 30

Number of rooms	5
rooms with private bath	5
shared wc	1

Activities:

8. DUNHAM

F E P R5 TA

Pierre Foglia of La Presse newspaper called it a "a great find, with a lovely name... A superb house run by a young couple. The stately trees along the path here form a leafy tunnel... just like being in Vermont... lavish breakfast...".

Hwy 10, Exit 68, Rte 139 South twd Cowansville (about 20 km). At the 2nd traffic lights in Cowansville, turn right, Rte 202 South to Dunham about 2 km. Left Rang Fitchett, (about 2 km) left Rang Vail (2 km). The house at end of tunnel of trees on the left.

B&B
LE TEMPS DES MÛRES

Marie-Josée Potvin and Pierre Cormier
2024, chemin Vail
Dunham J0E 1M0
(450) 266-1319
fax (450) 266-1303
toll free 1-888-708-8050

B&B	
single	$45-60
double	$60-75
child	$5-25

VS MC

Reduced rates: Nov. 1to Apr. 1
Open year round

Number of rooms	5
rooms with private bath	1
shared bathrooms	2

Activities:

9. GOULD

F E P R.15 TA

Built in 1913 in the heart of a Scottish village settled in 1837, our B&B retains the style and cachets of those first settlers. Large house with fireplace, original woodwork and antiques. Traditional regional cuisine. 150 metres from first general store.

50 km to Lac Mégantic and Sherbrooke. From Montréal, Hwy 10, Exit 150 twd East Angus, Rte 112. At East Angus, Rte 214 to junction with Rte 108 east to Gould. From U.S.A., Rte 3, at the border, Rte 257 to Gould.

B&B
LA MAISON McAULEY

Daniel Audet and Jacques Cloutier
26, Route 257 Sud
Gould J0B 2Z0
tel/fax (819) 877-3446
toll free 1-888-305-3526

	B&B	PAM
single	$50	$75
double	$55	$105

Taxes extra VS MC ER IT

Open year round

Number of rooms	4
rooms with sink	2
shared bathrooms	2

Activities:

B&Bs AND INNS

10. GRANBY

F E ⊗ ♿ 🚗 P 🏊 R.5

Right near the zoo, a unique concept ideal for families & groups (12 people): three 2-room units (suites) with private bathroom. Children's game room, private entrance, modern kitchen for your stay. Special packages for the Granby Zoo.

From Hwy 10, follow directions to Zoo. On Boul. David Bouchard at traffic light, south St-Hubert. 2 stops. Turn left on Bourget Ouest. 100 ft. to # 347 on the left.

B&B
AUBERGE DU ZOO

Ginette Marcoux and
Claude Gladu
347, Bourget Ouest
Granby J2G 1E8
(450) 378-6161
toll free 1-888-882-5252

B&B	
single	$55
double	$65
triple	$80
quad.	$95
child	$10

Taxes extra VS IT

Open: May 15 to Oct. 3

Number of rooms	3
rooms with private bath	3

Activities: 🏛 🍂 🛶 🎣 🚲

---

11. GRANBY

F E 🚗 P ⊗ R1

Located on the shores of Lac Boivin, a short bike ride away from l'Estriade, we offer guests stunning sunsets in an enchanting setting. Private lounge with fireplace, terrace and barbecue in season, skiing, skating, hiking, horseback riding: everything for your comfort and relaxation.

Hwy 10, Exit 74 twd Granby. At end of Pierre Laporte, left on Rte 112, right from L'Iris, left from the Potentille and left from Nénuphar.

B&B
LA MAISON DUCLAS

Ginette Canuel and
Camil Duchesne
213, du Nénuphar
Granby J2H 2J9
(450) 360-0641

B&B	
single	$50
double	$65
triple	$85
child	$10

Reduced rates: Oct. 15 to May 1
Open year round

Number of rooms	2
rooms with private bath	2
rooms in basement	2

Activities: 🍂 🎣 🚲 🏊 ⛷

---

12. GRANBY

F E ⊗ P R.5 TA

Carole and Michel welcome you to their charming raspberry-coloured house. Let us pamper you in this relaxing setting on Lac Boivin located near a park. Enjoy coffee on the waterfront among flowers and facing the Estriade cycling path. Close to the downtown shops and restaurants. Rooms with air conditionning. **See colour photos.**

From Montréal, Hwy 10 East. Exit 74, Rte 112 West to Granby. Right at the 1st traffic lights on Rue Church, right on Drummond to #90.

B&B
UNE FLEUR AU BORD DE L'EAU

Carole Bélanger and
Michel Iannantuono
90, Drummond
Granby J2G 2S6
tel/fax (450) 776-1141
1-888-375-1747
busines hours - toll free
www.clubtrs.ca/fleurvtg
fleurvtg@login.net

B&B	
single	$50-65
double	$55-70
child	$10

VS MC AM

Reduced rates: Jan. 6 to Apr. 15,
Oct. 30 to Dec. 15
Open year round

Number of rooms	4
rooms with private bath	2
shared bathrooms	1

Activities: 🍂 🎣 🚲 ⛷ 🚶

13. LAC-BROME, FULFORD

F E P R5 TA

A warm welcome in our English "tudor" house, located between Bromont and Knowlton. Enjoy a stroll on our property where dogs and ducks live side by side. You'll find a brook, a wooded countryside, a pool and patio. Snowshoeing, snowmobile trail in winter. Discounts for long stays.

Exit 78 on Hwy 10 to Bromont. Straight ahead for 7 km, turn right at red flashing light (Brome road). We are 1 km further on your left.

B&B
LE TU-DOR

Ghislaine Lemay and
Jean-Guy Laforce
394, chemin Brome
Fulford, Lac-Brome
JOE 1S0
(450) 534-3947
fax (450) 534-5543

B&B	
single	$55-65
double	$70-80
triple	$90-100
quad.	$110-120
child	$15

VS MC

Open year round

Number of rooms	4
rooms with private bath	4

Activities:

---

14. LAC-BROME, KNOWLTON

F E P R.5 TA

Take a much needed rest in the peaceful tranquillity of our charming B&B, the only one located within walking distance from the village. We'll welcome you like one of our own! Our specialty: fruit-filled crepes, a recipe passed down by our great-grandmother.

From Montréal: Hwy 10, exit 90, Rte 243 to Knowlton, 2nd stop, right 0.8 km. From Québec: Hwy 20, Hwy 55 Sud, Hwy 10, Exit 90, Rte 243 to Knowlton, 2nd stop, right 0.8 km.

B&B
LA DORMANCE

Jocelyne Rollin and
Normand Faubert
402, ch. Knowlton, C.P. 795
Lac-Brome, Knowlton JOE 1V0
(450) 242-1217
www3.sympatico.ca/
ladormance
ladormance@sympatico.ca

B&B	
single	$50
double	$65
triple	$75
quad.	$85

Reduced rates : 3 nights or more
Open year round

Number of rooms	3
rooms with sink	2
shared wc	1
shared bathrooms	1

Activities:

---

15. LAC-MÉGANTIC

F E P R1

Provincial Excellence Prize 1997-98. Modern, cedar house in an enchanting setting. Fish for trout off the pier, swim off our beach, boat ramp. Near 18-hole golf course and 2 provincial parks including the Astrolab (astronomy study centre). Breakfast in the solarium or in the gazebo, watching the loons.

Hwy 10, Exit 143, then Rtes 108 East and 161 South In Mégantic, 10 km after the bridge or Exit 143, take Rtes 112 and 212 twd Mont Mégantic then 14 km along 161 North.

B&B
AU CHANT DU HUARD

Françoise and Gérald Périnet
850, Route 161
Lac-Mégantic G6B 2S1
(819) 583-4795
fax (819) 544-9079

B&B	
single	$50-85
double	$60-95

Open year round

Number of rooms	4
rooms with private bath	1
rooms with sink	2
shared bathrooms	2

Activities:

16. LAC-MÉGANTIC   F E P R1

Visit our B&B perched on a hill overlooking the lake, located 1 km. from the golf course. Near the Observatoire & Astrolab. Peaceful setting. 34 hectares of woodlands. Ponds and trails leading to the beaver dam. Panoramic view, ideal for fall colours. Private beach nearby. 2 large rooms with queen-size beds. Breakfast on solarium overlooking the lake.

From Montréal or Sherbrooke, Hwy 10, Rtes 143 S., 108 E., 161 S. From Mégantic, 8 km twd golf club. From N.D. des Bois, Rtes 212 E., 161 N., 1 km after golf course.

B&B
AU SOLEIL COUCHANT

Nicole and Gérard Théberge
1137, Route 161
Lac-Mégantic G6B 2S1
(819) 583-4900
www.destinationquebec.com

B&B	
single	$45-60
double	$55-75

Open: May to Oct. 31

Number of rooms	4
rooms in basement	2
rooms with private bath	2
shared bathrooms	1

Activities: 🏛 ⚓ 🎣 🎿 🚴

---

17. LAC-MÉGANTIC   F E P 🚫 🐕 R4

Tastefully decorated warm and cosy house, located in the town centre in a quiet residential neighbourhood near the lake, marina and restaurants. Our breakfasts are also very generous; guests benefit from air conditioning in summer.

From Sherbrooke Rte 161. Left at 2nd light, Rue Maisonneuve, right on Rue Dollard. From Québec City or Woburn, cross downtown after railway, right on Rue Villeneuve, left on Dollard.

B&B
LA MAISON BLANCHE

Noreen Kavanagh Legendre
4850, rue Dollard
Lac-Mégantic G6B 1G8
(819) 583-2665

B&B	
single	$45
double	$55

Reduced rates : after Thanksgiving
Open year round

Number of rooms	2
rooms with private bath	2

Activities: 🏊 ⚓ 🎣 🚴 🏃

---

18. MAGOG   F E 🚗 P 🐕 R.1 TA

Awaiting you is our elegant Victorian home, its yard, a warm welcome and our gourmet breakfast with international fine cuisine menus. Lounge, fireplace, sunroom. By the lake with its walking/bike paths, near restaurants and shops, close to Mont Orford park, ski packages, bikes to lend. Assured comfort and relaxation! **Ad on back cover.**

From Montréal or Sherbrooke, Hwy 10, Exit 118 to Magog. After the Magog River, turn left at the McDonald's. Third house on the right.

B&B
À TOUT VENANT

Margaret McCulloch and
Marc Grenier
624, Bellevue Ouest
Magog J1X 3H4
(819) 868-0419
toll free 1-888-611-5577
www.bbcanada.
com/1553.html

B&B	
single	$55-64
double	$65-74
triple	$85-94
quad.	$105-114
child	$0-15

Taxes extra

Reduced rates: sep. 15 to june 15
Open year round

Number of rooms	5
rooms with private bath	5

Activities: 🏛 🚤 🛶 ⚓ 🎣

19. MAGOG

F E ⊗ P ♿ R.1

Charming good spirits and the comfort of a hundred-year-old house (fireplace, terrace). Located near restaurants and the beach, on the wine route and the road to Mont Orford. Gourmet lunch made by a French pastrychef. Cultural and summer/winter outdoor activities (hiking, skiing, snowshoeing, skidoo, skating, fishing...) Packages. See you soon.

From Montréal or Sherbrooke, Hwy 10, Exit 118 for Magog. Rte 141, Rue Merry North. From Québec City, Hwy 20 West, Hwy 55 South, 10 West, Exit 118 for Magog.

B&B
AU SAUT DU LIT

Lydia Paraskéva and
Patrick Bonnot
224, rue Merry Nord
Magog J1X 2E8
tel/fax (819) 847-3074
ausaudulit@qc.aira.com

B&B	
single	$65
double	$85
triple	$115
child	$10-20

VS MC IT

Reduced rates: Oct. 15 to May 15
Open year round

Number of rooms	5
rooms with private bath	5

Activities: ● ⅋ ☁ ⚡ 🐎

---

20. MAGOG

F E 🚗 P 🏊 R.5 TA

We invite you to discover the charm of our lovely city and our hundred-year-old house (1878) with our large and welcoming country-style rooms with queen-size beds and whirlpool bath. Two minutes from the town centre and Lake Memphrémagog, with its park, beaches and cycling path. Explore Mont-Orford and the Centre d'Arts. A region "par excellence".

Hwy 10, Exit 118, Rte 141 South to Magog. At the McDonald's, turn left on Chemin Hatley. Keep left (1st house on the headland).

B&B
AMOUR ET AMITIÉ

Gysèle Tremblay and
Jean-Guy Gendron
600, ch. Hatley Ouest
Magog J1X 3G4
(819) 868-1945

B&B	
single	$50-95
double	$55-105
triple	$125
quad.	$145
child	$0-20

Reduced rates: Oct. 15 to Dec. 15 and Jan. 15 to May 15
Open year round

Number of rooms	5
rooms with sink	2
rooms with private bath	3
shared wc	1
shared bathrooms	1

Activities: ● ☁ ⚓ ☁ ⚡

---

21. MAGOG

F E P R.1 TA

Escape to the Eastern Townships! This warm 1880 house will delight you with its creature comforts, guaranteed peace and quiet and sublime breakfasts. Take a nap beneath the apple trees or discover the peacefulness of Lake Memphrémagog or, again, the bustle of the Main Street. **See colour photos.**

From Montréal or Sherbrooke: Hwy 10, Exit 118, toward Magog (Rte 141), for 3 km. At traffic light, turn left on St-Patrice West, then 1st left on Abbott.

B&B
LA BELLE ÉCHAPPÉE

Louise Fournier
145, rue Abbott
Magog J1X 2H4
tel/fax (819) 843-8061
toll free 1-877-843-8061

B&B	
single	$45-60
double	$60-85
child	$15

VS MC

Reduced rates : Nov. 1 to June 1
Open year round

Number of rooms	5
room with sink	3
shared bathrooms	2

Activities: ● ⚓ ⅋ ☁ ⚡

B&Bs AND INNS

22. MAGOG

F E 🚭 🚗 P R.1 TA

Steps from downtown and Memphrémagog Lake, Victorian residence from 19th century surrounded by splendid gardens. Exquisite interior decorated with unique hand-painted objects. Painting workshop session packages. Ski, water sports, vineyards, horse-back riding.

From Montréal, Hwy 10 East, exit 118, dir. Magog (3 km) on Rte 141/Rue Merry Nord. From Québec City, Hwys 20 West, 55 South, 10 West, exit 118, dir. Magog (3 km) on Rte 141/Rue Merry Nord

B&B
LA BELLE VICTORIENNE

Louise Côté and Réal Viens
142, rue Merry Nord
Magog J1X 2E8
tel/fax (819) 847-0476

B&B	
single	$65-85
double	$70-90
triple	$105
child	$10

Taxes extra MC

Reduced rates : mid-Oct. to mid-May
Open year round

Number of rooms	5
rooms with private bath	3
shared bathrooms	2

Activities: 🏛 🍷 🚣 ⚲ 🚲

23. MAGOG

F E P 🚗 R.1 TA

Hike, cycle, bird watch or let us take you on our sailboat to discover one of our best kept secrets, Lake Mempremagog. In winter enjoy the Mt. Orford region in a sleigh, a dog sled or on skis. A warm welcome and all the comforts of home await you at La Maison Campbell. We hope our attractive rooms, our cozy fireplace, our café au lait and lovely home cooked breakfasts will make your stay here a memorable one. **Ad on back cover.**

From Mtl or Sherbrooke, Hwy 10, Exit 118 twd Magog. Pass over the Magog river turn left at the flashing yellow light, dir. Ayer's Cliff, keep to the right (becomes Bellevue Street).

B&B
LA MAISON CAMPBELL

Francine Guérin and
Louise Hodder
584, rue Bellevue Ouest
Magog J1X 3H2
(819) 843-9000
fax (819) 843-3352
www3.sympatico.ca/
maisoncampbell
maisoncampbell@sympatico.ca

B&B	
single	$50-70
double	$55-75
child	$0-20

Taxes extra

Reduced rates: Oct. 13 to June 15
Open year round

Number of rooms	5
rooms with private bath	3
shared bathrooms	1

Activities: 🛶 🚶 🚲 ⛷ 🐎

24. MAGOG

F e 🚭 P 🏊 R.1 TA

An oasis of peace in the heart of Magog. Between the pool's clear refreshing water and the cosy fireplace, you will be pleasantly surprised by your attentive hosts' warm welcome. We will turn your dreams of such moments into reality. Package deals available (sports and culture). Near Lake Magog, bike path, mountain. **Ad on back cover.**

Hwy 10, Exit 118 twd Magog. You are then on Rue Merry Nord. After crossing the main street, you are on Rue Merry Sud. We are steps from McDonald's.

B&B
LE MANOIR DE
LA RUE MERRY

Jocelyne Gobeil and
Alain Tremblay
92, rue Merry Sud
Magog J1X 3L3
toll free 1-800-450-1860
(819) 868-1860

B&B	
single	$75
double	$80
triple	$100
quad.	$120
child	$20

Taxes extra VS MC IT

Reduced rates: mid-Sep. to mid-May
Open year round

Number of rooms	5
rooms with private bath	5

Activities: 🍷 🚣 ⚲ 🚲 ⛷

25. MAGOG (Canton de)

F E 🐕 P 🏊 ✕ R6 TA

Enjoy a change of scenery and breathe in the fresh country air. Savour an unforgettable 5-course breakfast by the fireside or a country dinner on our terrace near the pool. After a walk through our flowered gardens, to the small farm or stream, you will have but one desire: to come back! **Country-style dining p 13.**

From Montréal, Hwy 10, Exit 115 South-Magog/St-Benoît-de-Lac, drive 1.8 km. Right on Chemin des Pères, twd St-Benoît-du-Lac/Austin. Drive 6.1 km. Watch for the sign on your right. We're waiting for you.

B&B
AUX JARDINS CHAMPÊTRES

Monique Dubuc
1575, ch. des Pères, R.R. 4
Magog (Canton de) J1X 5R9
(819) 868-0665
fax (819) 868-6744

	B&B	PAM
single	$65-85	$93-113
double	$70-90	$126-150
triple	$90-110	$179-203
child	$20	$40

Taxes extra VS MC IT

Open year round

Number of rooms	5
rooms with private bath	1
shared wc	1
shared bathrooms	1

Activities: 🏊 🚣 🚴 🎿 🏃

---

26. NORTH HATLEY

F E 🚗 P 🏊 R.2 TA

Right by the water: small manor uniting the charm of a Loyalist home with the tranquil and relaxing panoramic view of Lac Massawipi. Lovely, spacious and comfortable rooms. Excellent "brunch-style" breakfast. On site: swimming, pedal boat, snowshoeing, ice fishing. Possibilities: snowmobiling and dogsledding.

From Montréal, Hwy 10, Exit 121. Hwy 55 S., Exit 29. Rte 108 E. to North Hatley. Lili Morgane stands 400 m on the right, lakeside.

B&B
LILI MORGANE

Valérie Thomas and
André Gervais
4215, chemin Magog
North Hatley J0B 2C0
(819) 842-4208
fax (819) 842-1132
agervais@courrier.usherb.ca

	B&B
single	$90
double	$110
child	$15

Reduced rates: Nov. 1 to May 31
Open year round

Number of rooms	2
shared bathrooms	1

Activities: 🎿 🚴 🐎 🎿 🏃

---

27. NORTH HATLEY

F E 🚫 🚗 P R.3 TA

Charming Victorain home described by Montréal's La Presse as "A delight!" 1997 Award of Excellence in Hospitality. First B&B in Canada to be featured on the 1998 *Kellogg's*® *Müslix*®(1998) cereal box. Artist studio on location. B&B and craft workshops offered in fall and spring. Non-smoking.

From Montréal, Hwy 10, exit 121. Hwy 55 south, exit 29. Rte 108 East. In the village, cross the bridge and go straight ahead 0.3 km. Entrance on right at 50 m. past Tapioca sign.

B&B
TAPIOCA

Dominique Lavigueur and
Robert Chiasson
680, ch Sherbrooke, C.P. 496
North Hatley J0B 2C0
tel/fax (819) 842-2743
www.tapioca.qc.ca
tapioca@tapioca.qc.ca

	B&B
single	$82-102
double	$90-110
triple	$128
quad.	$146

Taxes extra VS MC AM

Open year round

Number of rooms	5
rooms with private bath	5
shared wc	1

Activities: 🚣 🎿 🚴 🐎 🏃

28. ORFORD

Lovely neocolonial residence with rural cachet, barn, wooden silo and large property including a golf course. Warm and welcoming interior with fireplaces, gleaming pine decor, parquet floors and French doors. Well-kept rooms. Terrace and gardens. We are located in Orford, between the lake and the mountain, in a world-class resort. Exquisite breakfasts.

From Montréal or Sherbrooke: Hwy 10, Exit 118 to Orford. At the village exit, follow the golf course by turning on Alfred-Desrochers or follow the signs. Third house on the right.

B&B
AUBERGE DE LA TOUR

Francine Gouin and
André Taillefer
1837, chemin
Alfred-Desrochers
Orford J1X 3W3
(819) 868-0763
fax (819) 868-4091
pages.infinit.net/tradat
franny@videotron.ca

B&B	
single	$65-105
double	$75-115
triple	$100-135
child	$10

Taxes extra

Open year round

Number of rooms	5
rooms with private bath	5
shared wc	1

Activities: 🚣 ⛵ 🚴 ⛷ 🎿

29. PIKE-RIVER

Located in the heart of farming country. We are a Swiss family that has lived here for 30 years. In our small restaurant we serve Swiss home-cooked meals and produce home made breads, jams and sauces. Take long quiet walks on the 100 acres of land surrounding our inn. We look forward to meeting you.

From Montréal, Champlain bridge, Hwy 10 East, Exit 22 St-Jean-sur-Richelieu. Hwy 35 South to Rte 133 South (30 min), brown house on left. Or from US, Interstate 89 North to Philipsburg, then Rte 133 North, about 13 km on the right.

INN
AUBERGE LA SUISSE

Dora and Roger Baertschi
119, Route 133
St-Pierre-de-Véronne-à-
Pike-River J0J 1P0
(450) 244-5870
fax (450) 244-5181
www.bbcanada.com
/1899.html

B&B	
single	$55-60
double	$65-75
child	$25

Taxes extra VS MC AM IT

Reduced rates: Feb. 1 to Apr. 30, Dec.
Open: Feb. 1 to Dec. 31

Number of rooms	4
rooms with private bath	4

Activities: 🏛 ⛵ ⛄ 🚴 🐎

30. PIKE-RIVER

One hour from Montréal and 10 min from Vermont: on the riverbank, an opulent, flowery B&B invites you for a restful break in a cosy atmosphere. Hearty Swiss breakfast with home-made bread and goods from our farm. Bicycling tours. Near the wildlife reserve, the Musée Missisquoi and the vineyards.

From Montréal, Champlain bridge. Hwy 10 East, Exit 22 twd St-Jean, Rte 35 South then Rte 133 twd St-Pierre-de-Vérone-à-Pike-River. In the curve, turn left on Chemin des Rivières. Drive 1.5 km.

B&B
LA VILLA DES CHÊNES

Noëlle and Rolf Gasser
300, Desrivières
Pike-River J0J 1P0
(450) 296-8848
fax (450) 296-4990

B&B	
single	$40-45
double	$60-65
child	$10

Open : Feb. 1 to Nov. 30

Number of rooms	4
rooms with private bath	1
rooms in basement	1
shared bathrooms	2

Activities: 🏛 🚣 ⛵ 🚴 🎿

31. ST-ADRIEN-DE-HAM

F E 🐕 🚗 P R15 TA

Overlooking the village, our French cottage-style house warmly welcomes you with its gardens and stretches of water over 119 acres of land. Located 8 kilometres from Mont-Ham. On site: footpaths, cross-country skiing, snowshoeing and massage. Nearby: cycling path, golf, summer theatre, downhill skiing, skidooing and fishing.

From Montréal: Hwy 20, Exit 147, Rte 116 to Danville, Rte 255 South, Rte 216 East, about 8 km from St-Adrien.

B&B
EAU SOLEIL LE VENT

Jacqueline Sauriol and
Yves Castonguay
1200, Route 216
St-Adrien-de-Ham J0A 1C0
(819) 828-0919

B&B	
single	$40-60
double	$50-70
triple	$70-80
child	$10

VS MC

Open year round

Number of rooms	3
shared wc	1
shared bathrooms	1

Activities: 🛶 ⛷ 🏃 🚲 🎿

---

32. STE-ANNE-DE-LA-ROCHELLE

F E 🐕 ❌🍴 R1 P TA

Wooded valleys and a river dotted with fields and pastures: a typical township setting near Waterloo and Valcourt. Genuine and generous hospitality whether you visit for a farm excursion, a stop-over or longer. Hearty home-cooked food, gardens in bloom, variety of animals... Packages available. **Farm Stay p 36.**

Hwy 10, Exit 88 to Waterloo, Rte 243 North to Lawrenceville. At the "La Licorne" restaurant, turn left on Chemin Yamaska, then left on Rang 9 to the top of the hill.

B&B
EN EFFEUILLANT
LA MARGUERITE

Nathalie Carbonneau
1393, Rang 9
Ste-Anne-de-la-Rochelle
J0E 2B0
(450) 539-2943

	B&B	PAM
single	$50-75	$65-90
double	$60-85	$90-115
triple	$90-105	$135-150
quad.	$110-125	$170-185
child	$10	$17

Taxes extra

Reduced rates: off season
Open year round

Number of rooms	5
rooms with private bath	2
shared bathrooms	2

Activities: 🚜 ⛷ 🚲 ⛷ 🏃

---

33. SHERBROOKE

F e 🚭 🚗 P R.4 TA

In the heart of a 19th-c. residential district, this superb Second Empire-style house transports you to Provence. A setting of warm coulours with soothing lavender scents. Pastis and olives offered as cokctails on the sun terrace in summer, by the fire in winter. Discover "the charms of the country in the city, the attractions of the city in the country".

From Montréal: Hwy 10. From Québec City: Hwy 20 and 55; Exit 140, Hwy 410 to Boul. Portland, then follow it for 4 km. After the Domaine Howard park, turn left on Rue Québec.

B&B
CHARMES DE PROVENCE

Céline Desrosiers and
Alexis Rampin
350, rue du Québec
Sherbrooke J1H 3L8
(819) 348-1147

B&B	
single	$50
double	$65
triple	$80
quad.	$95
child	$10

Taxes extra

Open year round

Number of rooms	3
shared wc	1
shared bathrooms	1

Activities: 🏛 ⛷ 🏃 🚲 ⛷

B&Bs AND INNS

34. SHERBROOKE

F E 🚫 🐕 P R1 TA

Imbued with the spirit of a former pastor, this old presbytery with old-fashioned woodwork, thematic rooms and private lounge promotes relaxation. Piano, fireplace and a delicious, lavish morning feast will rouse your 5 senses. A special meeting place in the heart of the historic district, a stone's throw from outdoor activities.

From Montréal: Hwy 10 (from Québec City, Hwy 55), Exit 140, then Rte 410 to Boul. Portland. Drive 3 km past the Carrefour de l'Estrie. On the right after Parc Howard. Welcome!

B&B
COUETTE ET CAFÉ
LE VIEUX PRESBYTÈRE

Flore Béland and Carl Thibeault
1162, boul. de Portland
Sherbrooke J1H 1H9
(819) 346-1665

B&B	
single	$45-60
double	$60-75
triple	$80-90
child	$10

Open: May 1 to Sep. 30

Number of rooms	5
rooms with private bath	1
shared bathrooms	2

Activities: 🏛 🦆 🧑 🚶 🚲

35. VALCOURT

F E 🚗 P 🏊 R10 TA

In the calm and tranquillity of the Township countryside, the Auberge Boscobel offers you 120 acres of nature in all its forms: forest, maple grove, stream, lake, fields... and spectacular wildlife. You'll savour home-made goods. 10 km from the Musée Bombardier.

Hwy 10, Exit 78. Rte 241 North to Warden, then Rte 243 North. Or Hwy 20, Exit 147, Rtes 116 East, 139 South, 222 East. In Valcourt at the stop sign, Ch. de la Montagne twd Roxton Falls, 2.8 km. Ch. Boscobel, 5.3 km. At the fork, left on 10e Rang, 2 km.

B&B
AUBERGE BOSCOBEL

Sandra and Jean-Pierre Simon
6387, 10ᵉ Rang Nord
Valcourt J0E 2L0
tel/fax (450) 548-2442
www.bbcanada.com/
2108.html
www.destinationquebec.
com/ftpdocs/bosco/bosco.htm
jpsimon@total.net

B&B	
single	$35
double	$60
child	$10

Open year round

Number of rooms	3
rooms with private bath	1
shared bathrooms	2

Activities: 🦆 🛶 🚲 ⛷ 🏃

B&Bs AND INNS

36. WOTTON F P R5 M4

Cosy cottage with old-fashioned charm and magnificent view of the lakes. Activities include pedal-boats, canoeing, snowmobiling, hiking through forests and fields. Cross-country skiing, snowshoeing, golf and swimming close by. 4 km from Asbestos.

From Montréal, Hwy 20 East, Exit 147. Rte 116 East to Danville, Rte 255 South to Wotton. 4 km after crossing Rte 249, turn left on Route des Lacs, drive 2 km on the gravel road.

COUNTRY HOME
LA MAISON DES LACS

Monique and Jean Mercier
28, chemin des Lacs
Wotton J0A 1N0
(819) 346-3575
pager (819) 573-9478

No.houses	1
No. rooms	5
No. people	10
WEEK-SUMMER	$500
W/E-SUMMER	$250
W/E-WINTER	$250
DAY-SUMMER	$150
DAY-WINTER	$150

Open: weekends only from Sep. 1 to June 30, anytime during July and Aug.

Activities: 🏛 🖼 👤 🛷 🎿

FARM ACTIVITIES

Farm Stays :

4 FERME AUBERGE D'ANDROMÈDE, Courcelles 36

32 B&B EN EFFEUILLANT LA MARGUERITE, Ste-Anne-de-la-Rochelle 36

6 LE CLOS DES PINS, Danville 36

Country-style dining * :*

25 AUX JARDINS CHAMPÊTRES, Canton de Magog 13

37 LA CHÈVRERIE DES ACACIAS, Dunham 13

38 FERME DES ANCÊTRES, Ste-Anne-de-la-Rochelle 14

* Registered trademark.

COUNTRY HOMES

CHARLEVOIX

0   10   20km

Chicoutimi

170

SAGUENAY–
LAC-SAINT-JEAN

N

381

Chicoutimi

138

Baie-Sainte-Catherine
8 9

Sagard

Baie-des-
Rochers

170

29

Port-aux-
Quilles

Parc régional
des Hautes-Gorges-
de-la-rivière-Malbaie

Réserve
faunique
des Laurentides

ZEC
du
Lac-au-Sable

Saint-Siméon

Port-au-
Persil

Rivière-du-Loup

Lac des
Martres

Mont
Grand-Fonds

Port-au-
Saumon

Parc des
Grands-Jardins

ZEC
des
Martres

Saint-Fidèle

26

Saint-Aimé-des-Lacs

Clermont
10

Cap-à-l'Aigle

Notre-Dame-
des-Monts

Sainte-Agnès

La Malbaie
14 15

381

31

Pointe-au-Pic
23 24 25

Réserve
faunique
des Laurentides

Saint-Urbain
30

138

Saint-Hilarion

Saint-Irénée
27 28 32

132

Les Éboulements
? 16 à 20

20

Baie-Saint-Paul
? 1 à 7

362

Saint-Joseph-
de-la-Rive

St-Bernard

?

La Baleine

Saint-Placide-
de-Charlevoix

Cap-à-la-
Branche

?

Île aux
Coudres
11 12 13

St. Lawrence River

Saint-Cassien-
des-Caps

Saint-Louis

Petite-Rivière-
Saint-François
21 22

138

Le Massif

BAS-SAINT-LAURENT

20

ENVIRONS
DE QUÉBEC

360

Saint-Tite-des-Caps

Île aux
Oies

132

Saint-Ferréol-les-Neiges

Québec

Cap-Tourmente

Saint-Joachim

Beaupré

© ULYSSES

Île
d'Orléans

Saint-François

Montmagny

*The numbers on the map correspond to the number of each establishment in the region.

1. BAIE-ST-PAUL

F E P 🚗 ⛴ R.2 TA

An old and colourful house in the heart of artistic Baie-St-Paul. Woodwork, lace, duvet. Wood-burning stove to warm up chilly mornings. Piano, reading room. Terraces and flowery gardens looking on to the countryside and its mountains. Local and home-made products at breakfast. Access to kitchen. Ski packages. **See colour photos.**

From Québec City, Rte 138 East. In Baie-St-Paul, Rte 362 East (Boul. Fafard). At the church, turn right on Rue Ste-Anne turn right on Rue Leblanc, 1st blue house.

B&B
À LA CHOUETTE

Ginette Guérette and François Rivard
2, rue Leblanc
Baie-St-Paul G3Z 1W9
(418) 435-3217

B&B	
single	$70
double	$75
triple	$90
child	$5-10

Reduced rates: Apr. 5 to May 15, Oct. 11 to Dec. 23
Open year round

Number of rooms	4
rooms with private bath	4

Activities: 🏛 ⛵ 🧍 🎿 🏃

---

2. BAIE-ST-PAUL

F E 🚗 P R.5 TA

At the historic heart of the village, come enjoy the comfort of our Victorian home, with the warm fireplace and the terrace overlooking the mountains. Home-made jams and pastries. Discover good restaurants, art galleries, exhibits and shops just a few steps away. "Whale" packages. "Ski at the Massif" in Petite Rivière St-François (15 min. away) package.

100 km from Québec City, twd Ste-Anne-De-Beaupré, Rte 138 E. At Baie-St-Paul, Rte 362 E. At the church, cross the bridge, 1st street on the right.

B&B
AU CLOCHETON

Johanne Robin
50, rue St-Joseph,
Baie-St-Paul G3Z 1H7
tel/fax (418) 435-3393

B&B	
single	$45-65
double	$50-70
triple	$70-85
quad.	$100
child	$5-10

MC

Reduced rates: Apr. 6 to June 18, Oct.12 to Jan. 31
Open year round

Number of rooms	4
rooms with sink	3
rooms with private bath	1
shared bathrooms	1

Activities: ⛵ 🎣 🐎 🏃 🐴

---

3. BAIE-ST-PAUL

F E 🚗 P 🐕 R3.5 TA

Come discover one of the loveliest places in Charlevoix! Exceptional view of the river. Peaceful environment. Picturesque house built on the mountainside. Rooms with panoramic view, private entrance and terrace. Lounge. Therapeutic massage on the premises. Massif ski package. 5 minutes from downtown.

From Québec, Rte 138 E. twd Ste-Anne-de-Beaupré for 100 km. At the Baie-St-Paul church, Rte 362 E. for 2 km. At the sign for "Les Encadrements du Cap" turn right on Chemin Cap-aux-Rets. 2nd house on the left, after the cross.

B&B
AU PERCHOIR

Jacinthe Tremblay and Réjean Thériault
443, Cap-aux-Rets
Baie-St-Paul G3Z 1C1
(418) 435-6955

B&B	
single	$70-95
double	$75-100
triple	$90-115
quad.	$105-130
child	$5-15

Reduced rates: Apr.12 to June 18, Oct. 12 to 23 Dec.

Open year round

Number of rooms	3
rooms with private bath	3

Activities: 🏛 🎣 🧍 🚴 🎿

B&Bs AND INNS

4. BAIE-ST-PAUL

F | E | 🐕 | P | 🚗 | ✕ | R5 | TA

Our century-old house, 5 km from Baie-St-Paul, in the Charlevoix countryside, has been renovated to its original style. Relax in front of the fire and enjoy a generous breakfast after a night in a charming room. View of the river. Ski packages available. Evening meal offered from October 1st to May 1st.

100 km from Québec City twd Ste-Anne-de-Beaupré, Rte 138 E. to Baie-St-Paul. Rte 362 E., cross the bridge at the church and continue on Rte 362 for 5 km. Green and white house on the left.

INN
AUBERGE LA CORBIÈRE

Carole Bédard and
Jean Roch Provencher
188, Cap-aux-Corbeaux Nord
Baie-St-Paul G3Z 1A7
(418) 435-2533
toll free 1-800-471-2533
fax (418) 435-3186
quebecweb.com./lacorbiere
corbiere@charlevoix.net

B&B	
single	$50-70
double	$55-85
triple	$70-100
child	$10

Taxes extra VS MC ER IT

Reduced rates: Oct. 15 to Dec. 15 and Apr. 5 to June 5 except holidays
Open year round

Number of rooms	10
rooms with private bath	7
rooms with sink	3
shared bathrooms	2

Activities: 🏛 ⚶ 🚶 ⛷ 🐎

5. BAIE-ST-PAUL

F | e | 🚭 | 🐕 | P | 🚗 | ✕ | TA

Peace, serenity, soft music, hospitality and fine food. A Victorian house with centenary charm nestled beneath the maples in the heart of the village. Fireplace, terrace and garden. Near shops, the Massif and a host of activities, parks, golf, casino, cruise... In summer, MAP plan only. **See colour photos.**

100 km from Québec City twd Ste-Anne-de-Beaupré, Rte 138 E. At Baie-St-Paul, Rte 362 E. At church, left on Rue St-Jean-Baptiste. Or from La Malbaie, Rtes 138 or 362 West.

INN
AUBERGE LA MUSE

Evelyne Tremblay and
Robert Arsenault
39, rue St-Jean-Baptiste
Baie-St-Paul, G3Z 1M3
(418) 435-6839
fax (418) 435-6289
toll free 1-800-841-6839
www.lamuse.com
lamuse@charlevoix.net

	B&B	MAP
single	$70	$92.50
double	$80-90	$125-135
triple	$112.50	$180
quad.	$135	$225
child	$10-20	$15-40

Taxes extra VS MC ER IT

Reduced rates: Apr. 5 to June 18, Oct.11 to Dec 23. Also during week (off season only).
Open year round

Number of rooms	10
rooms with private bath	10

Activities: 🏛 ⚶ 👤 🚶 ⛷

6. BAIE-ST-PAUL

F | e | 🚗 | P | R.25 | TA

In the heart of tourist activities, near galleries and restaurants, 15 minutes from the Massif, our house has successfully kept its charm of yesteryear, with its high ceilings and large balcony. Rooms decorated in art-related themes. Queen-size beds. Gourmet lunch. Flowery garden. Recommended by *La Presse.* **See colour photos.**

From Québec City, Rte 138 E. In Baie-St-Paul, Rte 362 E. Located across from the Franciscan convent. In the village, Rte 362 turns into Boul. Fafard.

INN
AUX PETITS OISEAUX

Danielle Trussart and
Jacques Roussel
30, boul. Fafard
Baie-St-Paul G3Z 2J4
(418) 435-3888
(450) 433-2296
fax (418) 435-0465

B&B	
single	$60
double	$65-85
triple	$85-100
quad.	$115
child	$10-15

Taxes extra

Reduced rates: Oct. 15 to Dec. 15 Apr. 15 to June 15.
Open year round

Number of rooms	7
rooms with sink	2
rooms with private bath	5
shared bathrooms	2

Activities: 🏛 🚲 ⚶ 🚶 ⛷

7. BAIE-ST-PAUL

F E P 🐕 R.1 TA

This turn-of-the-century former rooming house has found its calling again with the arrival of your hosts Marcelle and Jean, who will help make your stay here an unforgettable one. Savour the greatest variety of home-made jams, jellies, marmalades and *cretons* in Charlevoix.

Located a stone's throw from the Baie-St-Paul church on Rue Ste-Anne (street where the pier is). Red-brick Québec-style house on your right.

B&B
L'ARTOÎT

Marcelle Rodrigue and
Jean Perron
50, rue Ste-Anne
Baie-St-Paul G3Z 1P2
(418) 435-4091

B&B	
single	$50
double	$55
triple	$70
quad.	$110
child	$5-10

Reduced rates: Oct.15 to May 15
Open year round

Number of rooms	3
shared wc	1
shared bathrooms	1

Activities: 🏛 🧍 ⛷ 🎿 🐎

---

8. BAIE-STE-CATHERINE

F e 🚫 🚗 P 🐕 ✕ R1 TA

Now swept away by the fury of the waves, now enchanted by the tranquility of the woods, N.-D. de l'Espace watches over the secret world of whales and our village. Anne-Marie's table d'hôte, regional home cooking. Dogsled, cruise tickets. Charlevoix Excellence Prize 1994-95.

From Québec City, Rte 138 East twd La Malbaie. At bridge, twd Tadoussac. At Baie-Ste-Catherine sign, 2.8 km. From Tadoussac, 4 km after the ferry.

B&B
ENTRE MER ET MONTS

Anne-Marie and Réal Savard
476, Route 138
Baie-Ste-Catherine G0T 1A0
(418) 237-4391
fax (418) 237-4252

	B&B	MAP
single	$35-40	$50-55
double	$45-50	$75-80
triple	$65-70	$110-115
child	$15-20	$22.⁵⁰30

VS MC

Reduced rates: Nov. 1 to May 31
Open year round

Number of rooms	5
rooms with sink	3
rooms in basement	3
shared wc	1
shared bathrooms	2

Activities: 🚤 🧍 🚶 🛷 🐎

---

9. BAIE-STE-CATHERINE

F 🚗 P 🚢 R.5 TA

Beautifully located in a magnificent bay, near a little church at the heart of a peaceful village, come and immerse yourself in the beautiful countryside. Discover the beauty of the sea. Far from the noise of Rte 138 for peaceful and restful nights. Rooms on the main floor or in the basement. Boat cruise tickets for sale.

From Québec City, Rte 138 E. twd Tadoussac. From the Baie-Ste-Catherine "Bienvenue" (welcome) sign, drive 4 km. First road on the left. Watch for the provincial sign on Rte 138.

B&B
GÎTE DU CAPITAINE

Etiennette and Benoit Imbeault
343, rue Leclerc
Baie-Ste-Catherine G0T 1A0
(418) 237-4320
(418) 237-4359

B&B	
single	$40
double	$45
triple	$60
quad.	$80
child	$15

VS

Open: May 1 to Oct. 31

Number of rooms	5
rooms in basement	2
shared bathrooms	2

Activities: 🚤 🧍 🏇 🏛 🎣

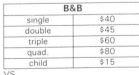

B&Bs AND INNS

10. CLERMONT F e P R1

In the heart of Charlevoix, you will experience a personal warmth and hospitality, as well as our fondness for this country. In the comfort of our large home, your history will fascinate us while ours will enchant you. Come and relax in the gentle warmth of our company.

From Québec City, Rte 138 E. drive 130 km to Clermont. Or from La Malbaie, Rte 138 W., drive 7 km to Clermont.

B&B
LA MAISON GAUDREAULT

Jeannine and Antonio
230, boul. Notre-Dame
Route 138
Clermont G4A 1E9
(418) 439-4149
antonio.gaudreault
@sympatico.ca

B&B	
single	$40
double	$50
child	$0-15

Open year round

Number of rooms	5
shared bathrooms	2

Activities: 🏛 🎿 🚶 ⛵ 🐎

---

11. ISLE-AUX-COUDRES F e 🚗 P R2

Large, peaceful beautiful and welcoming house where your hosts Rita and Vincent offer you warm hearts and good food. Steps from the river and near cultural and tourist activities. Let yourself be soothed and pampered to the rhythm of the tides in a unique setting.

From Québec City, Rte 138 E. twd Baie-St-Paul. Rte 362 to St-Joseph-de-la-Rive ferry. On the island, left at stop sign, drive 3 km.

B&B
GÎTE LA MAISON BLANCHE

Rita and Vincent Laurin
232, Royale Est, C.P. 238
Isle-aux-Coudres G0A 3J0
(418) 438-2883

B&B	
single	$50
double	$70

Reduced rates: Oct. 15 to June 15
Open year round

Number of rooms	5
rooms with private bath	1
rooms with sink	4
shared wc	2
shared bathrooms	2

Activities: 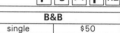 ⛴ 🦆 🚶 🚴 🏃

---

12. ISLE-AUX-COUDRES F 🚗 P R2 TA

Excellence Prize Charlevoix 1997-98. Let yourselves be pampered and charmed by Uncle Wilfrid's house, where we can chit-chat in a setting redolent of yesteryear. Cycling, walks, prowling handicraft shops and other activities... will help you digest Isle-aux-Coudriers' typical charm.

From Québec City, Rte 138 E. twd Baie-St-Paul. Rte 362 to the ferry. On the island, straight ahead after the stop for 3 km, turn right at the 2nd stop, drive 2 km.

B&B
GÎTE LA RIVERAINE

Lise Dufour
6, rue Principale
La Baleine, Isle-aux-Coudres
G0A 2A0
(418) 438-2831

B&B	
single	$40
double	$55
child	$10

Open year round

Number of rooms	3
rooms with sink	3
shared bathrooms	2

Activities: 🦆 ⛵ 🚴 ⛵ 🏃

13. ISLE-AUX-COUDRES

F e ♿ P 🚗 🐕 TA

Away from the bustle of the city, on an enchanting island. As if time had stopped. Wake up to birds chirping and breakfast on the terrace. Relaxing, large, sunny and flowered living-room. For a unique holiday: bring your hat, I'll supply the brushes, and together we'll do a painting.

From Québec City, Rte 138 E. twd Baie-St-Paul. Rte 362 to St-Joseph-de-la-Rive ferry. On the island, right at flashing light, drive 10 km. 500 m after St-Louis church.

B&B
VILLA DU MOULIN

Louise F. Belley
252, chemin des Moulins
Isle-aux-Coudres G0A 1X0
(418) 438-2649
(418) 665-6126

B&B	
single	$40
double	$60
triple	$75
quad.	$90
child	$10

Open: Apr. 1 to Oct. 31

Number of rooms	5
shared bathrooms	2

Activities: 🏛 🍷 ⛵ 🏊 🚴

14. LA MALBAIE

F E P 🏊 R.5

In the mood to hit the casino? It's only 130 seconds away! How about mountains, lakes and attractions? They are all near our residence where guests are always warmly greeted in a quiet, enchanting setting. Welcome.

Whether you're coming from Rtes 138 or 362, by the river, the exit before or after traffic light at the shopping centre, turn and it's the 3rd house on the right.

B&B
GÎTE E.T. HARVEY

Etudienne Tremblay Harvey
19, rue Laure-Conan
La Malbaie G5A 1H8
tel/fax (418) 665-2779

B&B	
single	$40
double	$45-50
child	$15

Reduced rates: Oct. 30 to Apr. 30, three nights or more

Open year round

Number of rooms	4
rooms in basement	1
shared wc	1
shared bathrooms	1

Activities: 🏛 🚴 🏃 🏊 🐎

15. LA MALBAIE

F e 🚗 P 🏊 R.7 TA

Our B&B offers rest and relaxation, with its flowery garden, indoor and outdoor fireplaces, outdoor spa, 2-person therapeutic bath, sound-proof rooms, TV, small lounge, front and back balconies with view over the river. Not to mention the delicious breakfasts, from orange crepes to Yvonne's brioches.

Two km from the casino. Rte 138 E. twd La Malbaie 1st street on your right after the tourist office then left on Rue Laure-Conan. Or Rte 362 to La Malbaie, 2nd street after shopping centre.

B&B
LA MAISON
DUFOUR-BOUCHARD

Micheline Dufour
18, rue Laure-Conan
La Malbaie G5A 1H8
(418) 665-4002

B&B	
single	$35-45
double	$45-55
triple	$60-70
quad.	$80-85
child	$5-15

Open year round

Number of rooms	4
shared bathrooms	2

Activities: 🍷 🏊 🏃 🐎 ⛵

B&Bs AND INNS

16. LES ÉBOULEMENTS

F E ♿ 🚗 P 🐕 R.5

Up in the heights of Les Éboulements, overlooking the St. Lawrence and Isle-aux-Coudres and centred among the marvels of Charlevoix, the inn la Bouclée is haven of peace for your vacation. Fall in love... An old-fashioned charm that thrills many a heart. For groups, families or sweethearts, young and old, our family welcomes you into its home.

From Baie St-Paul, Rte 362 E. twd La Malbaie/ Isle-aux-Coudres, drive about 16 km. Right at the flashing light. Left after 500 m. Welcome.

INN
AUBERGE LA BOUCLÉE

Ginette and Mario Ouellet
6, route du Port
Les Éboulements G0A 2M0
(418) 635-2531
toll free 1-888-635-2531
www.quebecweb.com/
labouclee

B&B	
single	$52
double	$69-89
triple	$104
quad.	$119
child	$0-15

Taxes extra VS MC ER IT

Reduced rates: Oct. 20 to June 20
Open year round

Number of rooms	9
rooms with sink	9
shared wc	1
shared bathrooms	4

Activities: 🏛 🎿 🛷 🏊 🏃

17. LES ÉBOULEMENTS

F e P 🚗 ✂ TA

Amidst cultural and sports activities, inn Le Surouêt (southwest wind) offers an unobstructed view of Île-aux-Coudres, a grand decor, luxury rooms with balcony and fireplace, dining room, terrace, tea room, fine cuisine, art gallery and gift shop. All under the same roof for an unforgettable stay.

From Baie-St-Paul. Rte 362 E. for 16 km. 700 m from flashing light. We are on the right. Welcome.

INN
AUBERGE LE SUROUÊT

Micheline and Rhéaume Gélinas
195, rue Principale
Les Éboulements G0A 2M0
(418) 635-1401
(418) 635-1402
fax (418) 635-1404

	B&B	PAM
single	$82,50- $102,50	$110-130
double	$105-125	$160-180
triple	$140	$215
child	$17,50	$27,50

Taxes extra VS MC AM ER IT

Reduced rates: 10 % from Sep. 15 to June 15
Open year round

Number of rooms	5
rooms with private bath	5

Activities: 🏛 🍷 ⛷ 🏃 🐎

18. LES ÉBOULEMENTS

F e ♿ P 🐕 R2

Experience an extraordinary holiday with me in my ancestral home, located in the middle of Charlevoix. In the mountains with a view of the St. Lawrence, in the great outdoors yet close to all the great tourist attractions: whales, casino, Île-aux-Coudres, Baie-St-Paul, etc.

From Québec City, via Rte 138, enter Baie-St-Paul, twd the church, straight to Les Éboulements, Rte 362 E., for about 14 km.

B&B
GÎTE DU VACANCIER

Jacqueline Audet
104, Route 362
Rang St-Joseph
Les Éboulements G0A 2M0
(418) 635-2736
(418) 653-2851

B&B	
single	$35-45
double	$45-60
triple	$60-75
quad.	$65-80
child	$10-15

Open: June 15 to Oct. 15

Number of rooms	5
rooms with private bath	1
rooms with sink	4
shared bathrooms	2

Activities: 🏛 🚣 ⛷ 🏃 🚴

19. LES ÉBOULEMENTS

F e ✕ 🚗 P R2

Ancestral house facing Île-aux-Coudres. The village's first hotel in 1930. Decor in the style of yester-year. Relax on the big porch and admire the mountains and the river that runs between the houses. A paradise to discover, amidst the region's tourist attractions. Varied all-you-can-eat breakfast complemented by little treats lovingly prepared by your hosts.

From Québec City: Rte 138 East to Baie-St-Paul. From Baie-St-Paul: Rte 362 East to Les Éboulements.

B&B
GÎTE VILLA DES ROSES

Pierrette Simard and
Leonce Tremblay
290, rue Principale, C.P. 28
Les Éboulements G0A 2M0
(418) 635-2733

B&B	
single	$40
double	$50
triple	$65
child	$0-15

Reduced rates: Oct. 15 to June 15
Open year round

Number of rooms	5
rooms with sink	4
shared wc	3
shared bathrooms	2

Activities: 🏛 🚶 🚲 🎿 🐎

20. LES ÉBOULEMENTS

F e P R1.5 TA

Nestled between the mountains and the river, this two-hundred-year-old house offers, calm, reverie and peace of mind. Comfortable rooms with private bathrooms, antique furniture, a smiling welcome and the delight of home-made pastries and jams make for a veritable Nid-Chouette, or cute little nest!

From Québec City, twd Ste-Anne-de-Beaupré, Rte 138 E. to Baie-St-Paul (about 100 km). From Baie-St-Paul, Rte 362 E. to Les Éboulements, drive 20 km. Or from La Malbaie, Rte 362 W. for 25 km.

B&B
LE NICHOUETTE

Gilberte Tremblay
216, rue Principale
Les Éboulements G0A 2M0
(418) 635-2458
www.chouette.freeservers.
com/nichouette.html
chouette@cite.net

B&B	
single	$40
double	$50
triple	$70
quad.	$85
child	$0-16

VS MC

Open: May 1 to Oct. 31

Number of rooms	3
rooms with private bath	3

Activities: 🏛 🍷 ⛴ 🚶

21. PETITE-RIVIÈRE-ST-FRANÇOIS

F e 🚗 P 🏊 ✕ R15 TA

Located by the majestic St-Laurent river and near the "Le Massif" ski resort, our house is a haven of peace. Enjoy an exhilarating holiday, a good chat, a delicious meal and the luxury of a cosy *courte-pointe* or quilt. Come and get to know us. "Bonnes Tables du Québec" directory, 3-star hotel. Panoramic view.
Your hosts,
Alice and Maurice.

From Québec City twd Baie-St-Paul, 90 km. Right at Petite-Rivière-St-François sign, for 8 km, left on Rue Racine.

INN
AUBERGE LA COURTEPOINTE

Alice and Maurice Bouchard
8, rue Racine
Petite-Rivière-St-François
G0A 2L0
(418) 632-5858
fax (418) 632-5786
www.aubergecourtepointe
qbc.net

	B&B	PAM
single	$50	$70
double	$90	$130

Taxes extra VS MC AM ER IT

Open year round

Number of rooms	8
rooms with private bath	8

Activities: 🏛 🚶 🎿 🌊 🎿

B&Bs AND INNS

22. PETITE-RIVIÈRE-ST-FRANÇOIS   F E ⊗ P R4 TA

Charlevoix Excellence Prize 1996-97. Mountain B&B in the Rivière-du-Sot valley near the Massif ski resort and Baie-St-Paul. Balcony overlooking the river with a view of Charlevoix's "extravagant" landscape. And of course... the VIP treatment... See colour photos.

From Québec City, drive 90 km twd Baie-St-Paul. At the Petite-Rivière-St-François sign turn right. Drive 3 km, our house is 200 metres back on the left-hand side of the road.

B&B
TOURLOGNON

Lise Archambault and
Irénée Marier
279, rue Principale
Petite-Rivière-St-François
G0A 2L0
tel/fax (418) 632-5708
toll free 1-888-868-7564
www.quebecweb.
com/tourlognon

B&B	
single	$60-70
double	$70-80
triple	$100
child	$15-20

Taxes extra MC

Open year round

Number of rooms	5
rooms with private bath	5

Activities: 🏛 ⛷ 🚶 🎿 🏃

---

23. POINTE-AU-PIC   F e P R1 TA

My ready smile and Charlevoix's down-to-earth people bid you a warm welcome. Clean, spacious rooms with antique decor and copious breakfasts. We have been told: "your warm welcome makes us feel right at home". Near major tourist attractions: casino, museum, golf, etc. Let yourselves be pampered!

From Québec City, Rte 138 E. twd La Malbaie. At Manoir Richelieu, straight for about 1 km, left from the hill. Or Rte 362 twd Pointe-au-Pic, 2 km from Golf du Manoir, right from the hill.

B&B
GÎTE BELLEVUE

Juliette and Louise Forgues
107, côte Bellevue
Pointe-au-Pic G0T 1M0
(418) 665-6126
(418) 438-2649

B&B	
single	$40
double	$55
triple	$70
quad.	$90
child	$10

Reduced rates: Feb. 1 to Avr. 1
Open year round

Number of rooms	2
shared bathrooms	2

Activities: 🏛 🚲 🎣 🚣 🎿

---

24. POINTE-AU-PIC   F E 🚗 P R1 TA

The ancestral Eau Berge house faces the river and welcomes you with its unique decor. The rooms are particularly comfortable and inviting. Choice of healthy breakfast, or otherwise! Come and be refreshed. Close to the casino and other activities. See you soon.

From Québec City, Rte 138 E. to La Malbaie. At the traffic lights of the bridge, continue straight. 500 m from the shopping centre on the right across from the "Irving". Or Rte 362 to Pointe-au-Pic, beside the river, on the boulevard. At the "Irving" on the left.

INN
L'EAU BERGE

Claudette Dessureault
1220, boul. De Comporte,
C.P. 152
Pointe-au-Pic G0T 1M0
(418) 665-3003
fax (418) 665-2480

B&B	
single	$60-100
double	$65-105
triple	$90-125
quad.	$145
child	$15-20

Taxes extra VS MC

Open: Feb. 1 to Oct. 1

Number of rooms	7
rooms with sink	1
rooms with private bath	2
shared wc	1
shared bathrooms	2

Activities: 🏛 🛶 🚣  🎿 🚶

25. POINTE-AU-PIC

F E P R.5 TA

A warm and cosy Austrian house overlooking the river and Manoir Richelieu awaits you here. Come discover: peace and comfort, private entrance, fireplace and balcony, terraces and flowery gardens, delicious breakfasts. All year round, in the midst of activities, 5 minutes from the casino. Charlevoix Excellence Prize 1995-96.

From Québec City, Rte 138 E. to Baie-St-Paul. Rte 362 E. twd Pointe-au-Pic. From the "Golf du Manoir Richelieu", drive 2 km and turn right. Or from La Malbaie, Rte 138 E. From the bridge, Rte 362 West, drive 4.4 km and turn left.

B&B
LA MAISON FRIZZI

Raymonde Vermette
8, Côteau-sur-Mer, C.P. 526
La Malbaie, Pointe-au-Pic
GOT 1M0
(418) 665-4668
fax (418) 665-1143

B&B	
single	$50-60
double	$60-70
triple	$85-95
child	$0-15

Reduced rates: Oct. 15 to Dec. 20, Apr. 1 to June 1
Open year round

Number of rooms	4
rooms with sink	4
shared bathrooms	2

Activities:

---

26. ST-AIMÉ-DES-LACS

F E P X TA

A large property in mountains, combines modern comfort and the calm of the boreal forest. As a member of the Route des Saveurs, the Relais offers tasty, creative and colourful cuisine from products of our terroir. Under the gazebo, at the camp fire, plan all season activities either at the Parc, in a glacial valley or near-by in the back country.

Rte 138 between St-Hilarion and Clermont, St-Aimé Exit, follow blue tourist signs. We are 13 km from the start, passed a little white bridge, on your right, at 23 km from the Parc des Hautes-Gorges.

INN
AUBERGE LE RELAIS DES HAUTES GORGES

Lucille Dazé and Rhéal Séguin
317, rue Principale
St-Aimé-des-Lacs GOT 1S0
tel/fax (418) 439-5110
toll free 1-800-889-7655
www.quebecweb.com/relais

	B&B	MAP
single	$55	$85
double	$68	$110
triple	$93	$152.50
quad.	$118	$195
child	$0-12.50	$0-25

Taxes extra VS MC

Reduced rates: Nov. and Apr.
Open year round

Number of rooms	8
rooms with private bath	8
shared wc	2

Activities:

---

27. ST-IRÉNÉE

F e P R1 TA

After 35 years of living in Saint-Irénée, I had the chance to purchase a classic Charlevoix house set on the edge of a one-of-a-kind beach on the St. Lawrence. Come get away from it all in this extremely relaxing setting.
Lucie Tremblay.

From Québec City: Route 138, about 120 km. Route 362 across from the Baie-St-Paul church. Scenic highway to Saint-Irénée, 25 km. From La Malbaie: Route 362 West for about 15 km.

INN
LA LUCIOLE

Lucie Tremblay
178, chemin Des Bains
St-Irénée GOT 1V0
(418) 452-8283
www.clic.
net/~maxinfo/luciole.htm

B&B	
single	$50
double	$55
triple	$75
child	$10

VS

Reduced rates: Sep. 15 to May 31
Open year round

Number of rooms	6
rooms with private bath	1
rooms with sink	1
shared bathrooms	2
shared wc	1

Activities:

B&Bs AND INNS

28. ST-IRÉNÉE

F E P R3

Perched on the high cliffs of St-Irénée and next to the Domaine Forget concert hall, the Manoir offers spacious rooms and a breathtaking view of the St. Lawrence and Charlevoix mountains. Two-km-long seaside promenade in La Malbaie. Superb terrace for breakfast. Packages change with the seasons.

From Québec City, Rte 138 to Baie-St-Paul, then Rte 362 (La Panoramique) to St-Irénée, 25 km. Or from La Malbaie, Rte 362 W., 15 km.

B&B

MANOIR HORTENSIA

Alida Landry
320, chemin les Bains
St-Irénée G0T 1V0
(418) 452-8180
tel/fax (418) 452-3357
hortensia@cite.net

B&B	
single	$60-90
double	$80-115
triple	$100-135
child	$15

Taxes extra VS MC IT

Reduced rates: Oct. 15 to May 15
Open year round

Number of rooms	5
rooms with private bath	4
shared wc	1
shared bathrooms	1

Activities:

29. ST-SIMÉON, BAIE-DES-ROCHERS

F e P R1 TA

You are invited to stop over in the hamlet of Baie-des-Rochers where warmth, peace and comfort come together. Nature awaits with the river flowing behind the house. The bay is 3 km away, as is the network of hiking trails offering staggering panoramic views of the surroundings.

From Québec City, Rte 138 E. twd Tadoussac. 15 km from St-Siméon at the corner store, sign indicating "Gîte de la Baie", turn right.

B&B

GÎTE DE LA BAIE

Judith Savard and
Maurice Morneau
68, rue de la Chapelle
(Baie-des-Rochers)
St-Siméon G0T 1X0
(418) 638-2821

B&B	
single	$30
double	$55
triple	$70
quad.	$80
child	$10

Open: June 1 to Oct. 13

Number of rooms	5
rooms with private bath	2
rooms with sink	2
shared bathrooms	2

Activities:

30. ST-URBAIN

F e P R1.3 TA

Cosy, peaceful B&B in business for almost 20 years. Located in the heart of Charlevoix, 10 minutes from Parc des Grands Jardins, Mont du Lac des Cygnes and Baie-St-Paul. Bordered by a salmon river. Emu farm on site. Various outdoor activities. Big lounge with TV; picnic areas. Homemade breakfast with varied regional products. Welcome to Gertrude's. **See colour photos.**

From Québec City, Rte 138 E. After Baie-St-Paul, drive 10 km on Rte 381 N. From the intersection of Rtes 138 and 381, drive 3 km.

B&B

CHEZ GERTRUDE

Gertrude and
RaymondeTremblay
706, St-Édouard,(rte 381)
C.P 293
St-Urbain G0A 4K0
(418) 639-2205
fax (418) 639-2467

B&B	
single	$32-37
double	$45-50
triple	$60-65
quad.	$70-75
child	$10-15

Open year round

Number of rooms	5
rooms with sink	1
shared wc	4
shared bathrooms	2

Activities:

31. STE-AGNÈS

F | e | P |  R4 | TA

Warm welcome, Canadian house (1858) nestled amidst mountains in the back country. Three-kilometre property. Farm: ratite (emus and rheas) study centre. Overnight stay includes a tour. Boutique, pool. Gatherings in an unforgettable family ambiance. Twenty minutes from Baie-St-Paul and the casino.

From Québec City, La Malbaie-bound Rte 138 to St-Hilarion. From Ultramar station, continue along Rte 138 for 4.6 km. Left at crossroads of Rang 4, 1 km.

B&B
LE GÎTE DU MARAIS

Diane D. Tremblay
131, rang St-Jean-Baptiste
Ste-Agnès G0T 1R0
tel/fax **(418) 439-3719**
pager (418) 665-0200

B&B	
single	$40
double	$50
triple	$60
quad.	$70
child	$10

VS MC

Open year round

Number of rooms	2
shared bathrooms	2

Activities: 🏛 ♨ 🚶 🚶 🐎

B&Bs AND INNS

32. ST-IRÉNÉE

Small, two-star family-run hotel complex comprising two cottages, the whole located on the edge of the forest at an altitude of 225 metres. View of more than 100 kilometres over both banks of the St-Lawrence, 2 kilometres from the river and Domaine Forget, in the midst of Charlevoix's tourist activities.

From Québec City, Rte 138 E. to Baie-St-Paul. Rte 362 to St-Irénée. 100 m from the pier, follow Chemin St-Antoine for 2 km. Or from La Malbaie, take Rte 362 West...

COUNTRY HOME
VILLA GRANDE VUE

Irène Desroches and
Gilles Girard
360, chemin St-Antoine
St-Irénée G0T 1V0
(418) 452-3209

No. houses	2
No. rooms	1
No. people	2
WEEK-SUMMER	$220-320
W/E-SUMMER	$120-150
DAY-SUMMER	$50-60

Reduced rates: May 1 to June 19, Sep. 15 to Nov 1
Open: May 1 to Nov.1

Activities:

COUNTRY HOMES

CHAUDIÈRE-APPALACHES

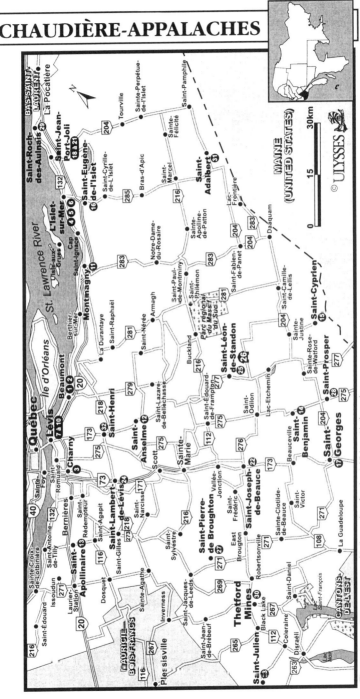

*The numbers on the map correspond to the number of each establishment in the region.

1. BEAUMONT

F | E | ⊗ | P | 🐾 | R5 | TA

Chaudière Appalaches Excellence Prize 1997-1998. Warm and friendly hospitality in bicentenary Québec-style home with country decor and period furnishing. Snuggle up by the ancient fireplace or wood burning stove. Just 15 min from ferry boat to the heart of old Québec city and Irish Mem. Nat. Hist. Site. Ideal stop between Ontario and the Maritimes.

From Mtl, Québec city or Riv.-du-Loup, Rte 132 to Beaumont, turn on Rte 279 S. (Shell) towards St-Charles. Pass the highway, 1st road right (Ch. St-Roch for 1.8 km).

B&B
AU GRÉ DU VENT

Michèle Fournier and
Jean L'Heureux
220, chemin St-Roch
Beaumont G0R 1C0
(418) 838-9020
fax (418) 838-9074
www.bbcanada.
com/2487.html
augreduvent@msn.com

B&B	
single	$50-60
double	$55-65
triple	$70-80
quad.	$90
child	$0-15

VS

Open: May 1 to Sep. 30,
Oct. 1 to 30 Apr. (with reservation)

Number of rooms	3
rooms with sink	2
shared bathrooms	1

Activities: 🍂 🏛 ↑ ↑ 🚲

2. BEAUMONT

F | E | P | 🏊 | R1 | TA

110-acre property overlooking the St-Laurent. 15 minutes from the bridges and the Lévis/Québec ferry. Charming, restored 30-room mansion. Sumptuous and comfortable rooms. Antique decor, peaceful and romantic ambiance, breakfast with fine silver, view of more than 20 church steeples, heated pool, sleigh or carriage rides. German spoken. Chateau living! 20% low-season discounts.

From Québec City, Hwy 20 E., Exit 330 N., Rte 132 E. for 4 km. Or from Riv.-du-Loup, Hwy 20 W., Exit 337 N., Rte 132 West for 1 km.

B&B
MANOIR DE BEAUMONT

Denis Vézina
485, du Fleuve, route 132
Beaumont G0R 1C0
(418) 833-5635
fax (418) 833-7891
www.manoir
debeaumont.qbc.net
manoirbeaumont
@sympatico.ca

B&B	
single	$85-115
double	$90-120
triple	$105

Taxes extra VS MC AM IT

Reduced rates: Feb. to June 17
Sep. 6 to Dec. 30
Open year round

Number of rooms	5
rooms with private bath	3
shared bathrooms	2

Activities: 🍂 🚣 ↑ 🚲 ⛷

3. CHARNY

F | E | P | 🚗 | ⊗ | R.2

A place where one feels in the country while only 5 kilometres from Quebec City and the Chaudière falls. One kilometre from Gaspésie-bound Aut. 20. At the gateway to the Beauce Rte 73. Quiet neighbourhood near many services. Relax and enjoy breakfast on the flowery terrace. Kitchen garden with several varieties of mixed herbs. Health menu.

From Mtl., Hwy 20, or from Québec City, Pierre-Laporte bridge twd. Riv.-du-Loup, Exit 175 S. Charny. Turn right at 1st light (facing McDonald's), then right on Ave. Sous le Vent. Left of the Mistral, about 400 m.

B&B
LE GÎTE DE LA
CHUTE CHAUDIÈRE

Yvette McIntyre
and Normand Beaudin
8069, du Mistral
Charny G6X 1G1
(418) 832-0728

B&B	
single	$40
double	$50
child	$10

Open year round

Number of rooms	3
rooms with sink	2
rooms in basement	2
shared bathrooms	2

Activities: 🏛 🍂 🚡 ↑ ⛷

4. L'ISLET-SUR-MER

F E 🚫 ✕ 🚗 P R1 TA

This old country house dating from the French regime has delighted many visitors since 1986. We as experienced hosts, we know how to make your stay here a most pleasant one. Refined local cuisine, open to all. Packages available. A stay with us is an unexpected pleasure. 3-star hotel.

100 km from Québec City, on the south shore. Hwy 20, Exit 400, Rte 285 N. for 2.5 km, Rte 132 East on right for 1 km, 150 metres east of the Maritime Museum.

INN
AUBERGE LA MARGUERITE

Marguerite and Denis Caron
88, Des Pionniers Est (rte 132)
L'Islet-sur-Mer G0R 2B0
(418) 247-5454
www.quebecweb.
com/lamarguerite

	B&B	PAM
single	$59-120	$82-150
double	$75-130	$121-190
child	$10-18	

Taxes extra VS MC IT

Reduced rates: Nov. 1 to May 15
Open year round

Number of rooms	8
rooms with private bath	8
shared wc	1

Activities: 🏛 ⛵ 🎣 🚴 🏃

5. L'ISLET-SUR-MER

F E P 🚫 R1 TA

Luxurious, monumental English residence from 1867. Entirely renovated with pine, fireplace and solarium. Right on the St Laurent River, just steps from the Musée Maritime Bernier, enchanting setting, pond, fountains, patios, spa... Panoramic room with balcony. Complete all-you-can-eat breakfast. Cruise packages to Grosse-Île, gourmet, golf, relaxation... **See colour photos.**

100 km (1 hour) from Québec City or Riv.-du-Loup, Hwy 20, Exit 400. Follow the signs to the Musée Maritime: 2.5 km North (twd the river), turn right, 1 km East on Rte 132.

B&B
LE GÎTE DU DOCTEUR B&B

Nicole, Simon
and Sébastien Toussaint
81, des Pionniers, route 132
L'Islet-sur-Mer G0R 2B0
tel/fax (418) 247-3112
www.qbc.clic.net/~gitedoc
gitedoc@qbc.clic.net

	B&B
single	$65-80
double	$65-90
triple	$85-110
quad.	$105-130
child	$15

VS MC

Reduced rates: May 1 to May 31
Open: May 1 to Oct. 30

Number of rooms	4
rooms with sink	2
rooms with private bath	2
shared wc	1
shared bathrooms	1

Activities: 🏛 🐎 ⛵ 🎣 🚴

6. L'ISLET-SUR-MER

F e 🚫 P 🐕 R.5 TA

A privileged place for relaxing to the sound of the waves where a charming, very comfortable hundred-year-old house decorated for you. Dreamy rooms and dining room on the river. Fancy health/delicacy breakfast. Snow geese in the fall, relaxation, photography, fresh air, music and hospitality. **Advertisement end of this region.**

One hour from Quebec City or Riv.-du-Loup (100 km), Hwy 20, Exit Islet North, Rte 132 East (Chemin des Pionniers Est) for 5 km, or Exit St-Jean-Port-Joli North, Rte 132 West, 10 km.

B&B
LES PIEDS DANS L'EAU

Solange Tremblay
549, des Pionniers Est
L'Islet-sur-Mer G0R 2B0
(418) 247-5575
fax (418) 247-7772
seul@globetrotter.net

	B&B
single	$45
double	$60-75
quad.	$110-130
child	$20

Open: all year except Nov.

Number of rooms	4
rooms in basement	1
rooms with private bath	3
shared wc	1
shared bathrooms	1

Activities: 🏛 ⛵ 🏇 🛶 🏃

7. LÉVIS | F | E | 🚗 | P | R.5 | TA |

Overlooking the St-Laurent, facing Old Québec. Near the ferry. Scenic tours. Enchanting light show, from the residence or terrace. Comfort. Relax by the fire. Central air conditioning. Welcome.

From Québec City or Riv.-du-Loup Hwy 20 Exit 327 right on Mgr-Bourget. After 2nd light, drive 1 km, left on Champagnat. At 2nd stop right on Des Bosquets. From ferry, in Lévis, right on Côte du Passage, after 1st light left on Champagnat, after 6 stops, left on Des Bosquets.

B&B
GÎTE DES BOSQUETS

Véronique and Émile Pelletier
162, rue des Bosquets
Lévis G6V 6V7
(418) 835-3494
fax (418) 835-0563
toll free with reservation only
1-888-335-3959

B&B	
single	$35-40
double	$50-60
triple	$70
quad.	$85

VS MC

Open year round

Number of rooms	3
rooms with private bath	2
shared bathrooms	1

Activities: 🏛 ⛵ 👤 ⛷ 🚴

8. LÉVIS | F | e | P | 🚗 | R1 |

Two kilometres from the 10-minute ferry to the very heart of Old Québec. Come gaze upon the exceptionally beautiful panorama of Québec City. In winter, we offer snowmobile trips and dogsledding.

Hwy 20, Exit 325 N., keep right. Left on Côte du Passage, drive 3.5 km, right on Wolfe, drive 1.5 km. From Québec City-Lévis ferry, turn left, drive 1.5 km, right on Bienville, left on De l'Entente.

B&B
GÎTE LA LIVAUDIÈRE

Cécile Demers and
Jocelyn Bernard
129, de l'Entente
Lévis G6V 1S2
tel/fax (418) 833-0898

B&B	
single	$50-65
double	$60-75
triple	$75-90
child	$10

VS

Open year round

Number of rooms	5
rooms with private bath	1
rooms with sink	2
shared bathrooms	2

Activities: 🏛 ⛵ 🚴 🐟 ⛷

9. LÉVIS | F | e | 🚭 | P | 🚗 | R2 |

Welcoming B&B in a peaceful, quiet area, ideal for rest and relaxation. View of the river and Québec City. 3 km from the ferry that leads to the charms of old Québec City. Close to public transportation. 1 km from golf course, 2 km from shopping centres, restaurants, river cruises, etc. Terrace from which to admire Québec City.

From Québec City or Riv.-du-Loup, Hwy 20, Exit 321, Chemin des Îles. Turn left to the north 2.2 km straight ahead, at the traffic lights, take St-Georges for 0.3 km. At the stop sign, left on Rue Robitaille for 280 m, left on Rue Papineau.

B&B
LA MAISON BLANCHE
AU TOIT VERT

Irène Carrier and
A. Thiboutôt
13, Papineau
Lévis G6W 1J9
(418) 833-8904

B&B	
single	$30
double	$45

Open year round

Number of rooms	2
shared bathrooms	1

Activities: 🏛 ⛵ 👤 🚴 ⛷

10. LÉVIS

F E P R2

A peaceful place, 10 minutes from Vieux-Québec by ferry, in the heart of scenic routes. The magic of a warm Victorian house. View of the river, Île d'Orléans and the Montmorency Falls. A restful dream home all year round. Family welcome, attentive hosts. We speak German.

From Montreal or Rivière-du-Loup: Hwy 20, Exit 327, Mgr. Bourget to the end and right on Rue St-Joseph. Or from Québec City-Lévis ferry: left, 3.5 km. White house with black roof.

B&B
LE ROSIER

Diane Boucher and
Jean-Louis Fricker
473, rue St-Joseph
Lévis G6V 1G9
(418) 833-6233

B&B	
single	$45
double	$60
triple	$75
quad.	$90
child	$10

Taxes extra VS

Open year round

Number of rooms	5
rooms with sink	1
shared bathrooms	2

Activities: 🐾 ⚓ 🚣 ♦ 🚲

---

11. MONTMAGNY

F e ⊗ 🚗 P R1 TA

Only 40 min from Québec City, discover the Snow Goose capital, nature, a superb woodland, a calm and inviting home. Comfortable rooms with fans. Wake up to the birds singing and enjoy a generous breakfast "à la Cécilienne". Golf, cruises to the national historic site of Grosse-Île and to Île-aux-Grues. World Accordion Jamboree festival and goose hunting. Welcome: make yourselves at home.

From Québec city, Hwy 20, Exit 376, ch. des Poirier, rte 132 East, cross the bridge of Rivière-du-Sud, continue for 0. 5 km. The B&B is on the right.

B&B
LA CÉCILIENNE

Doris and Cécile Boudreau
340, boul. Taché Est
Montmagny G5V 1E1
(418) 248-0165
www.bbcanada.com/
2853.html

B&B	
single	$40
double	$50-55
child	$15

VS

Open year round

Number of rooms	4
shared bathrooms	2

Activities: 🏛 🐾 ⚓ 🚶 🚲

---

12. ST-ANSELME

F e ⊗ P 🏊 R.5

In the heart of Chaudière-Appalaches, on the doorstep of the Beauce, a dreamy spot decorated to ensure comfort, escape relaxation. Soundproofed rooms, boudoirs, livingroom, fireplace, hot tub, etc. Outdoor enthusiasts: outdoor fireplace, 40' heated pool, patio, terrace, flowery wooded property. Golf, cycling, skiing. Staying at Douces Évasions is energizing, enriching. Welcome!

20 min from Québec City. Hwy 20, Exit 325 S. twd Lac Etchemin, right at the entrance of St-Anselme, burgundy sign, house with red-tile roof.

B&B
DOUCES ÉVASIONS

Gabrielle Corriveau and
Gérard Bilodeau
1043, boul. Bégin (rte 277)
St-Anselme G0R 2N0
tel/fax (418) 885-9033
www.québecweb.
com/evasions

B&B	
single	$45-50
double	$65-70
child	$10-15

Reduced rates: 10% for 5 nights and more
Open year round

Number of rooms	3
rooms with private bath	1
rooms in basement	1
shared bathrooms	3

Activities: 🐾 🚣 🚲 🏃 ⛷

13. ST-APOLLINAIRE

F | e | P | 🚗 R3 | TA

Twenty minutes from Québec City, mid-way between Niagara Falls and Gaspésie, the charm of yesteryear in our bicentenary house. Cuisine appreciated by gourmands! On site: museum, farm activities, snowmobile, sleigh. Nearby: river, Domaine Joly, Chaudière river falls, snowmobile trail.

From Montréal or Rivière-du-Loup, Hwy 20, Exit 291, Rte 273 N., twd St-Antoine-de-Tilly, drive 2.5 km. On right, 1.7 km. White and green shingled house on the left.

B&B
NOTRE CAMPAGNE D'ANTAN

Marie-Claude Roux and Donald Foster
412, rang Bois-Franc Est
St-Apollinaire G0S 2E0
(418) 881-3418

B&B	
single	$40
double	$50
child	$15

Open year round

Number of rooms	2
shared bathrooms	1

Activities: 🎿 🚲 🐎 🛷 🎣

14. ST-BENJAMIN, BEAUCE

F | e | P | R.5 | TA

In the heart of this lovely back-country village stands L'Antiquaille, filled with an atmosphere of yesteryear. Come admire our collection of antiques: wood-burning stoves, clawfoot baths, old curios, lace... Breakfast is the hostess' secret! Health package: massotherapy, Swedish massage, reflexology.

Hwy 20, Exit Hwy 73 South twd St-Georges, Exit 173 South. In St-Odilon, turn right on Rte 275 South twd St-Benjamin.

B&B
L'ANTIQUAILLE

Jacqueline and Catherine
218, rue Principale
St-Benjamin G0M 1N0
(418) 594-8693

B&B	
single	$30
double	$45
child	$12

Open: Mar. 1 to Nov. 30

Number of rooms	3
shared wc	1
shared bathrooms	2

Activities: 🏛 🍂 🚶 🎿 🚲

15. ST-CYPRIEN

F | e | 🚭 | P | R6

Our B&B is located in the heart of a luxuriant landscape in maple country. Discover: mini farm, organic garden, birds, etc. Healthy breakfast and treats: home-made jams and maple products. Cycling path and skidoo trail right nearby. Packages: health, exploring the maple grove and its saphouse. We are pleased to welcome you.

From Québec City: Hwy 20 East, twd Lac-Etchemin Exit 325, Rte 277 South to Rte 204. Twd Ste-Justine for 7.8 km, then right toward St-Cyprien.

B&B
LE JARDIN DES MÉSANGES

Hélène Couture
482, route Fortier
St-Cyprien, Barré G0R1B0
tel/fax (418) 383-5777

B&B	
single	$40
double	$55
triple	$70
quad.	$85
child	$5-15

Taxes extra

Open year round

Number of rooms	4
shared bathrooms	3

Activities: 🏛 🍂 🎿 🚶 🎿

16. ST-EUGÈNE-DE-L'ISLET

F e P 🛶 ✕ TA

Delightful former seigneurial mill will seduce you with its warm ambiance, country decor, gastronomic cuisine. In the heart of a vast estate, the inn boasts remarkable surroundings: river, swimming lake, bird-watching trails. Various packages (golf, cycling, cruise, massage, skiing) also offered. Very romantic! **See colour photos.**

On the south shore, 1 hour from Québec City. At Exit 400 off Hwy 20 E., turn left twd St-Eugène-de-L'Islet, left on Rang Lamartine and left on Route Tortue.

INN
AUBERGE DES GLACIS

Micheline Sibuet and
Pierre Walters
46, route Tortue
St-Eugène-de-l'Islet G0R 1X0
(418) 247-7486
1-877-245-2247 (toll free)
fax (418) 247-7182

	B&B	PAM
single	$84	$127-149
double	$94	$164-209

Taxes extra VS MC AM IT

Reduced rates: Oct. 31 to June 15
Open year round

Number of rooms	10
rooms with private bath	10

Activities: ⛵ 🛶 🏕 🚶 🎿

17. ST-GEORGES, BEAUCE

F e P R3 TA

Dream decor you will fall in love with. Large house with antiques. Sleep on a 125-year-old canopy bed... Romantic decor of old lamps and lace... Period photos of ancestors... Flowery countryside in beautiful region. Hearty breakfast, china wear and table lace. Golf, museum, warm welcome.

From Québec City, Rte 73 S. In Vallée-Jonction, Rte 173 S. twd St-Georges. After McDonald's, left on 90e Rue, drive 3 km, left on 35e Ave, 9th house on the right.

B&B
GÎTE LA SÉRÉNADE

Berthe and Bernard Bisson
8835, 35th Av. (by the 90th street)
St-Georges-de-Beauce Est
G5Y 5C2
(418) 228-1059

	B&B
single	$45
double	$55-59
triple	$70-74
child	$15

VS

Open year round

Number of rooms	4
shared bathrooms	2

Activities: 🏛 🍴 🛶 🎿

18. ST-JEAN-PORT-JOLI

F E P R.1 TA

Authentic 200-year-old Canadian home located in the heart of the sculpture capital of Québec and by the St-Laurent River. In our house it is our pleasure to receive you as a friend. Year-round package to maple grove visits and tastings. **Advertisement end of this region.**

From Montréal or Québec, Hwy 20 East, Exit 414, turn right, to Rte 132. At Rte 132 turn right, turn right 0.5 km. Large white house with red roof, a hundred meters past the church.

B&B
AU BOISÉ JOLI

Michelle Bélanger and
Hermann Jalbert
41, de Gaspé Est
St-Jean-Port-Joli G0R 3G0
tel/fax (418) 598-0774

	B&B
single	$45
double	$50-55
triple	$65
child	$10

Taxes extra VS MC

Reduced rates: Sep. 7 to June 15
Open year round

Number of rooms	5
shared bathrooms	3
shared wc	1

Activities: 🏛 🍴 🛶 🚶 🚲

19. ST-JEAN-PORT-JOLI

F | e | 🚗 | P | ⛵ R.5 | TA

Bungalow 30 metres from the marina. Relax to the sound of the tide while breathing in the salt air. A hearty home-made breakfast is prepared for you. Summer: hiking, cycling, sailboarding, sea kayaking. Winter: cross-country and downhill skiing, snowshoeing, dogsledding. Equipment is provided. Recounting your day's adventures by the fire at night will make your stay with us even more memorable.

Hwy 20, Exit 414, twd 204 North to Rte 132. Turn left, follow "Marina Quai" sign on right. On Rue du Quai, at the Des Pionniers junction, turn left.

B&B
GÎTE AUX VENTS ET MARÉES

Francine Bernier and
Henri Bélanger
15, rue Des Pionniers Ouest,
C.P. 764
St-Jean-Port-Joli G0R 3G0
(418) 598-3112

B&B	
single	$40
double	$60
triple	$85
quad.	$110
child	$10

VS

Reduced rates: Sep. 15 to Dec. 15, Jan. 15 to May 15
Open year round

Number of rooms	4
shared bathrooms	2

Activities: 🚣 🎿 🚶 🛶 ⛷

20. ST-JEAN-PORT-JOLI

F | E | 🚭 | 🐕 | 🚗 | P | ⛵ R1 | TA

Ancestral bicentennial house in the heart of the sculpture capital. Today's comforts meet those of yesteryear in a friendly and cordial atmosphere. Garden, flowers, woods, fireplace, pool and striking view of the Appalachians and the St. Lawrence River. Located in quiet countryside near various sites of artistic interest. Packages available. **Pub at the end of this section**

1 h from Québec, or from Riv.-du-Loup Aut 20 Exit 414. Right until the 132. Then 132 Ouest 2.7 km. Red-roofed house on the left.

B&B
LA MAISON AUX LILAS

Joan Dubreuil and
Normand Brisebois
315, De Gaspé Ouest
St-Jean-Port-Joli G0R 3G0
(418) 598-6844
norbrise@globetrotter.net
www.cam.org/~bblilas

B&B	
single	$45
double	$50-55
triple	$65
child	$10

VS MC

Reduced rates: Sep. 15 to June 15
Open year round (with reservations from Jan. 15 to Mar. 15)

Number of rooms	3
shared wc	1
shared bathrooms	1

Activities: 🏛 🍴 ⛴ 🎿 🚲

21. ST-JEAN-PORT-JOLI

F | E | 🚭 | 🐕 | P | 🚗 | R.3

Located in the village, a lovely Victorian home of yesteryear set back from the main road. Large plot of land by the river, next to the marina. A peaceful place in an intimate setting. Charming rooms and a lavish breakfast will enhance your stay. Welcome to our home. **Advertisement end of this region. See colour photos.**

From Montréal or Québec City, Aut. 20 E., right on Exit 414 to Rte 132. Left on Rte 132 W. for 0.4 km, right on Rue de l'Ermitage.

B&B
LA MAISON DE L'ERMITAGE

Johanne Grenier and
Adrien Gagnon
56, de l'Ermitage
St-Jean-Port-Joli G0R 3G0
(418) 598-7553
fax (418) 598-7667
ermitage@globetrotter.net

B&B	
single	$48-70
double	$58-80
child	$15

Taxes extra VS MC

Reduced rates: Sep. 15 to June 15
Open year round

Number of rooms	5
rooms with private bath	1
shared bathrooms	2

Activities: 🏛 🍴 🚶 🛶

22. ST-JOSEPH-DE-BEAUCE

F e P R.5 TA

Discover the changeable aspects of the valley and the architecture of hundred-year-old houses, overlooking the mad course of the capricious Chaudière river toward the St-Laurent. A stunning panorama for every season... Play area, bike shed, pool. Welcoming you would be a great pleasure.

From Québec City, Hwy 73 S. In St-Joseph, south on Ave. du Palais to shopping centre. Rue St-Luc, house facing the curve.

B&B
«LES RÊVERIES»

Louise and Roland Doyon
1003, rue St-Luc
St-Joseph-de-Beauce G0S 2V0
(418) 397-4814
fax (418) 397-6439
reverie@microtec.net

B&B	
single	$30
double	$45
triple	$60
child	$5-10

VS

Open year round

Number of rooms	2
rooms in basement	2
shared wc	1
shared bathrooms	1

Activities:

23. ST-JULIEN

F e P R15

Chaudière-Appalaches Excellence Prize 1996-97. Nature-lovers, hikers, skiers and bikers, our cedar-shingled home awaits you in the Appalachians. Enjoy calm, views, armchair bird-watching and walks. After a good meal (available upon request), dream in front of the fireplace or on the terrace. Treat yourself! O'P'tits Oignons, the B&B difference.

Hwy 20, from Montréal Exit 228 or from Québec City Exit 253 twd Thetford-Mines. After the detour to Bernierville (St-Ferdinand) turn right on Rte 216 West to St-Julien. Turn right, before the village, to reach O' P'tits Oignons.

B&B
O' P'TITS OIGNONS

Brigitte and Gérard Marti
917, chemin Gosford,
route 216
St-Julien G0N 1B0
tel/fax (418) 423-2512
www.minfo.net/ptits-oignons/
bgmarti@megantic.net

	B&B	PAM
single	$40-50	$55-65
double	$50-60	$80-90

Open year round

Number of rooms	3
rooms with private bath	1
shared wc	1
shared bathrooms	1

Activities:

24. ST-LAMBERT-DE-LÉVIS

F E P R2.5 TA

20 min from Old Québec City, enjoy the warm, welcoming atmosphere of a country setting. Large landscaped grounds, outdoor pool and flowery patio overlooking the Rivière Chaudière. In winter, relax by a cosy fire. Nearby: cycling, golf, swimming, horseback riding, cross-country skiing, skidoo and skating. Dogsledding package available upon request.

From Montréal Hwy 20 East; from Québec City Pierre-Laporte bridge; from Riv.-du-Loup Hwy 20 West, Hwy 73 South, Exit 115 St-Lambert. Right on Dupont 1 km. Left on des Érables at the church, 1.5 km.

B&B
LA MAISON BLEUE

Francine and Yvon Arsenault
122, rue Dufour
St-Lambert-de-Lévis G0S 2W0
(418) 889-0545
fax (418) 889-5122
www.total.net/~asor
pages.infinit.net/bleue/
lamaisonbleue@videotron.ca

B&B	
single	$40
double	$50
child	$10

Open year round

Number of rooms	2
shared wc	1
shared bathrooms	1

Activities:

25. ST-LÉON-DE-STANDON

F E ♿ P ⛵ ✖ R4 TA

Discover our inn, an ancestral house, which can accommodate up to 26 guests with 3 private and 2 family-sized rooms with bunk beds. 1.3 km² of land offering hiking, swimming (lake/river), cycling and fishing in summer, snowshoeing and skating in winter, or just simple tranquillity.

Hwy 20, Exit 325 Pintendre-Lac Etchemin. Rtes 173 S. and 277 S. In St-Léon, from Rte de l'Église, right on Rang St-François, drive 3.6 km.

INN
AUBERGE TERRE DE RÊVE

Jean Comeau
65, rang St-François
St-Léon-de-Standon G0R 4L0
(418) 642-5559
fax (418) 642-2764

B&B	
single	$40
double	$50
triple	$70
quad.	$90
child	$0-15

VS

Open year round

Number of rooms	5
rooms with private bath	1
rooms with sink	2
shared wc	4
shared bathrooms	2

Activities: 🚲 🎣 🛷 ⛷ 🐴

26. ST-LÉON-DE-STANDON

F e 🐾 P 🚗 ✖ ⛵ R7

Tourism Grand Prize 1997. Familial paradise 1 hr from Québec City. 100 yr-old house nestled in the Appalachians. Spacious rooms in the B&B or the log pavilion. Patio near private lake, beach, cascading river, trails. Ski & winter sports packages. Private dining and sitting rooms. Chaudière-Appalaches Excellence Prize 1995-96. **Country-style dining p15, farm excursion p 29 farm stay p 37.**
From Québec City, Hwy 20 E., Exit 325 twd Lac-Etchemin, Rtes 173 S. and 277 S. to St-Léon-de-Standon, Rue Principale. 0.9 km after the church, at stop, cross Rte 277, left Rte du Village, 4 km. Right Rang Ste-Anne, 2 km.

B&B
FERME LA COLOMBE

Rita Grégoire and
Jean-Yves Marleau
104, rang Ste-Anne,
route 277
St-Léon-de-Standon G0R 4L0
(418) 642-5152
fax (418) 642-2991

	B&B	PAM
single	$40	$50
double	$55-60	$84-90
triple	$75	$120
quad.	$85	$145
child	$5-10	

Taxes extra

Open year round

Number of rooms	2
rooms with private bath	2

Activities: 🚲 🎣 🐾 ⛷ 🏃

27. ST-PIERRE-DE-BROUGHTON

F e P 🐕 ⛵ ✖ R5 TA

Chateau life in a little corner of paradise! Have tea in the gazebo, learn the history of this large Victorian-style house, discover the "soapstone", swim in the pond, visit the farmyard, feed the deer/goats/rabbits/ponies, walk the trails! Make yourselves at home.

From Mtl, Hwy 20 E., Exit 228 Princeville, Rte 165 twd Black-Lake, Rte 112 to Québec City, drive 24 km. Left, drive 2 km. From Québec City Rte 173 Vallée-Jct Exit, Rte 112 to St-Pierre-de-Broughton, right, drive 2 km.

B&B
AUBERGE DE LA
PIERRE FLEURIE

Pierrette Gagné and Pierre Cyr
193, Rang 11
St-Pierre-de-Broughton
G0N 1T0
(418) 424-3024

	B&B	PAM
single	$40	$55
double	$45	$75

Taxes extra

Open year round

Number of rooms	4
shared bathrooms	2

Activities: 🏛 🍎 🎣 🛷 🐴 🐴

28. ST-PROSPER

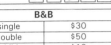

Monique invites you to a warm house with 2 quiet rooms; children welcome, daycare. Varied breakfasts, "home-made" jellies, jams, maple products, breads. Picnic area, trails through maple grove. Restaurant 3 kilometres away. Two kilometres from summer theatre and museum.

From Québec City: Hwy 20, Hwy De Beauce, St-Georges Exit. From St-Georges: take Rte 204 East for about 24 km. At red light, 3 km East. Address: 3390 8e Rue or Rte 204 Est.

B&B
À L'ABRI

Monique Poirier Samson
3390, 8e rue route 204
St-Prosper G0M 1Y0
(418) 594-8009

B&B	
single	$30
double	$50
child	$10

Open year round

Number of rooms	2
shared bathrooms	1

Activities: 🏛 🍴 👤 🚶 🛶

---

29. ST-ROCH-DES-AULNAIES

Ｆ Ｐ 🚗 ✕ R.5 TA

A perfect dream! Fall under the charm of a 200-year-old house on an immense property bordering the St Laurent. Dining room, view of the river, home cooking. Let time drift by slowly. Marvel at the return of the snow geese, the sunsets, the tides, the winter storms, while keeping warm inside by the fireplace. Meal with reservations. **Advertisement end of region.**

1 hour from Québec City, 45 min from Riv.-du-Loup, Hwy 20 Exit 430, left twd Seigneurie des Aulnaies. From Québec City, Rte 132, 15.5 km from the St-Jean-Port-Joli church.

B&B
AU SOIR QUI PENCHE

Guy Gilbert
800, ch. de la Seigneurie
St-Roch-des-Aulnaies G0R 4E0
tel/fax (418) 354-7744
www.quebecweb.com/
ausoirquipenche

B&B	
single	$40
double	$45
triple	$55
quad.	$60

Open year round

Number of rooms	4
rooms with private bath	1
rooms with sink	1
shared wc	1
shared bathrooms	2

Activities: 🍴 🚣 👤 🚶 ⛷

---

30. THETFORD MINES

Ｆ Ｅ Ｐ 🚗 R.5

For a royal stay, little manor dating from 1930. Its yesteryear bourgeois look and charm invite to a "halt" in time. The surrounding wooded grounds bordering a river contribute to the peaceful atmosphere. Near services and attractions. Complete breakfasts. Little extras included. Ski/golf package deals.

From Montréal (240 km), Hwy Jean-Lesage (20 East), Exit 228, Rte 165 in Black Lake, Rte 112 East to downtown Thetford Mines. Or from Québec City (105 km), Hwy Robert-Cliche (73 S.), Exit 81, in Vallée-Jonction Rte 112 West to downtown Thetford Mines.

B&B
LE KINGSVILLE

Thérèse Donovan
Rock Vachon
609, Notre-Dame Nord
Thetford Mines G6G 2S6
(418) 338-0638

B&B	
single	$45-55
double	$60-70
triple	$75-85
child	$15

Taxes extra VS MC

Open year round

Number of rooms	3
rooms with private bath	1
shared bathrooms	1

Activities: 🏛 👤 🚲 🛶 ⛷

B&Bs AND INNS

31. ST-ADALBERT

F e 🐕 ✖ 🚗 P 🏊 M10 TA

Experience a vacation in harmony with nature in a house located near our rare-animal (17 varieties) breeding farm. One-day farmer packages: caring for animals, shearing, spinning, bread-making, etc. Various workshops on request. Forest walks. Visit to maple grove. 20 kilometres from St-Pamphile golf course.

From Québec City: Hwy 20, Exit 400 for St-Eugène. Rte 285 South toward St-Marcel. Drive 41.5 km, turn right at the "Rang 3, Rang 4" sign and continue for 2 km.

COUNTRY HOUSE
FERME JOUVENCE

Nicole Bélanger and
Raymond Raby
36 rang 4
St-Adalbert G0R 2M0
(418) 356-5060
fax (418) 356-2355
www.quebecweb.com/
jouvence
raby@globetrotter.qc.ca

No. houses	1
No. rooms	5
No. people	10
WEEK-SUMMER	$350-550
WEEK-WINTER	$350-550
W/E-SUMMER	$120-200
W/E-WINTER	$120-200
DAY-SUMMER	$60-100
DAY-WINTER	$60-100

Taxes extra

Open year round

Activities: 🚣 🎣 🚶 🐎 🎿

32. ST-HENRI

F e P R6 M8 TA

This spacious and well-lit cottage with cathedral roof and stone fireplace welcomes you to a quiet place. Located at the end of a country road, between fields and forest, it offers you the peace of its woodlands. Ambiance inspired by the seasons. Local tours, agrotourism, maple groves...

30 minutes from Vieux-Québec. Hwy 20, Exit 325 S. for Rivière-du-Loup, toward Pintendre, Lac Etchemin, Rte 173 South drive 10 km, turn left on Chemin de la Tourbière, 2.5 km, turn right, 2 km.

COUNTRY HOME
TEMPÉRAMENT SAUVAGE

Sylvie Bouthillette and
Pier Grenier
523, chemin St-Jean-Baptiste
St-Henri G0R 3E0
(418) 882-0558

No. houses	1
No. rooms	2
No. people	4
WEEK-SUMMER	$535-715
WEEK-WINTER	$535-715
W/E-SUMMER	on request
W/E-WINTER	$195-255

MC

Open year round

Activities: 🏛 🚴 🐎 🛷 🎿

COUNTRY HOMES

FARM ACTIVITIES

Farm stays:

26 FERME LA COLOMBE, St-Léon-de-Standon 37

Country-style dining*:

26 FERME LA COLOMBE, St-Léon-de-Standon 15

Farm excursions:

26 JARDINS DES TOURTEREAUX DE LA FERME LA COLOMBE, St-Léon- de-Standon 29

* Registered trademark.

CÔTE-NORD

© ULYSSES

N

Gulf of St. Lawrence

Îles-de-la-Madeleine

0   50   100km

Musquaro

La Romaine

Kegaska

Natashquan

Aguanish

Baie-Johan-Beetz

Havre-Saint-Pierre

Saint-Pierre

Mingan

Parc national de l'Archipel-de-Mingan

Magpie

Sheldrake

Longue-Pointe-de-Mingan

Rivière-au-Tonnerre

Rivière-Saint-Jean

Manitou

Île d'Anticosti

Détroit de Jacques-Cartier

Détroit d'Honguedo

Port-Menier

L'Anse-au-Griffon

Parc national Forillon

Percé

Parc de l'Île-Bonaventure-et-du-Rocher-Percé

Newport

Bonaventure

Chandler

New Richmond

Réserve faunique de Port-Daniel

Carleton

NEW BRUNSWICK

Grande-Vallée

Gaspé

La Mattre

Cap-Chat

Parc de la Gaspésie

GASPÉSIE

Matane

Causapscal

BAS-SAINT-LAURENT

132

132

132

132

Molise

Moisie

Parc régional de l'archipel des Sept-Îles

Sept-Îles

Réserve faunique de Sept-Îles–Port-Cartier

Port-Cartier

Rivière-Pentecôte

Pointe-aux-Anglais

Les Îlets-Caribou

Baie-Trinité

Pointe-des-Monts

Godbout

Baie-Comeau

Pointe-Lebel

Parc régional de Pointe-aux-Outardes

Chute-aux-Outardes

Betsiamites

Forestville

Sainte-Anne-de-Portneuf

Les Escoumins

Bergeronnes

Sacré-Coeur

Tadoussac

Trois-Pistoles

Le Bic

Rimouski

Ste-Flavie

Métis-sur-Mer

St-Lawrence River

DUPLESSIS

MANICOUAGAN

Fermont

Île René-Levasseur

Mont Babel

Réservoir Manicouagan

Barrage Daniel-Johnson (Manic-5)

Lac Sainte-Anne

Réservoir Manic-3

Réservoir Manic-2

Réservoir Outardes-4

Charleville

389

385

138

138

138

132

172

*The numbers on the map correspond to the number of each establishment in the region.

1. BAIE-COMEAU, POINTE-LEBEL

F | e | P |  R2

Calm, cosy and comfortable B&B to discover. Warm family welcome. Nature lovers will cherish the grandeur and beauty of our beach, where the St-Laurent meets the Manicouagan; swimming, walks and pool await you. Lavish home-made breakfast. Package deals upon reservation, from November to May.

From Québec City, Rte 138 E. to Baie-Comeau. 7.5 km after Chute-aux-Outardes turn right at the traffic lights. Drive 15 km to Pointe-Lebel.

B&B
AU PETIT BONHEUR

Carmen Poitras
and Mario Lévesque
1099, rue Granier
Pointe-Lebel G0H 1N0
(418) 589-6476
(418) 295-3419
fax (418) 589-9243

B&B	
single	$35
double	$45-55
triple	$65
quad.	$75
child	$10

Reduced rates: Nov. 1 to Apr 30
Open year round

Nombre de chambres	4
rooms in basement	4
shared wc	1
shared bathrooms	2

Activities: 🦪 ⛵ 🎣 🚴 🛶

2. BAIE-COMEAU, POINTE-LEBEL

F | E | 🚗 | 🐕 | P | 🛶 | R1 | TA

Côte-Nord Excellence Prize 1996-97. 14 km from Baie-Comeau, 200 m from an immense beach, between the St-Laurent and the Rivière Manicouagan, discover a swimming, cycling, hiking and horseback riding paradise. Big and cosy house with Victorian charm. Stylish rooms, quiet stay and hearty breakfast.

From Québec City, Rte 138 E. to Baie-Comeau. After Chute-aux-Outardes, drive 7.5 km, right at the traffic lights and drive 11.5 km. After the church, turn left on the 1st street.

B&B
LES TOURNE-PIERRES

Bernadette Vincent
and Jean-Yves Landry
18, rue Chouinard
Pointe-Lebel G0H 1N0
(418) 589-5432
fax (418) 589-1430
gite.tourne-pierres@
enter-net.com

B&B	
single	$40
double	$55
triple	$75
child	$15

Reduced rates: Oct. 1 to May 31
Open year round

Nombre de chambres	5
shared wc	1
shared bathrooms	2

Activities: 🛶 🎣 🚶 🚴 🐎

3. BAIE-TRINITÉ

F | E | ✖ | P | TA

Old lighthouse keeper's house: rooms upstairs. 2nd bathroom outside. Also, 7 cottages with bathrooms, by the sea, some of which are log houses. Breakfast service in the main house. Whale-, sea perch- and gannet-watching. Museum, excursion and fine-cuisine restaurant on site, from mid-June to late August. **Country home p 112. Advertisement end of this region.**

From Québec City or from the Matane-Godbout ferry, Rte 138 E., right at the entrance to Pointe-des-Monts, drive 11 km. For reception cross footbridge.

INN
LE GÎTE DU PHARE DE
POINTE-DES-MONTS

Jean-Louis Frenette
Route du Vieux Phare
Baie-Trinité G0H 1A0
(418) 939-2332
(418) 589-8408
pointe-des-monts@
globetrotter.net

	B&B	PAM
single	$40	$69
double	$48	$106
triple	$56	$143
child	$8	

Taxes extra VS MC IT

Open: June 12 to Sep. 28
Reduced rates: Sep. 6 to Sep. 28

Number of rooms	9
rooms with private bath	5
shared wc	1
shared bathrooms	1

Activities: ⛵ 🛶 🚶 🚴 🛶

B&Bs AND INNS

4. BERGERONNES

F E P 🚗 R.1 TA

Quiet family house recommended by a French guide. Unlimited home-made jams. Lots of information about the region available. Whale-watching from shore. Numerous interpretation centres. Swimming. We look forward to meeting you.

3 hours from Québec City, Rte 138 E. 20 min from Tadoussac and 10 min from Escoumins from Trois-Pistoles (ferry). Kitty-corner from the church.

B&B
BIENVENUE
CHEZ LES PETIT

Janet Harvey
and Jean-Claude Petit
56, rue Principale
Bergeronnes G0T 1G0
(418) 232-6338
fax (418) 232-1171
gitepetit@ihcn.qc.ca

B&B	
single	$40
double	$48
triple	$60
quad.	$80
child	$15

Reduced rates: Oct. 15 to May 15
Open year round

Number of rooms	5
rooms with sink	1
shared bathrooms	2

Activities: 🏛 ⚓ 🎣 🚴 🛶

5. BERGERONNES

F e 🚗 P R.1

Rock and chat on Petite Baleine's green veranda. The sloping hills unfold in front. Ducks and locals chat on Côte-à-Bouleau hill. One river flows by, then another and another. A smile invites you in. A spirit flows from room to room, breathing the perfumes of yester-day. A piano. A *catalogne* in bed inspires dreams. Sun beams dance across the crystal jam pots as if this were a ball, with Cinderella on the throne. Chicoutai charms our morning table! **See colour photos.**

Near the church.

B&B
LA P'TITE BALEINE

Geneviève Ross
50, rue Principale
Bergeronnes G0T 1G0
(418) 232-6756
(418) 232-6653

B&B	
single	$40
double	$50
triple	$65
child	$15

VS

Reduced rates: Sep. 15 to May 15
Open year round

Number of rooms	5
rooms with private bath	1
rooms with sink	2
rooms in basement	1
shared wc	2
shared bathrooms	2

Activities: 🏛 ⚓ 🚣 🚶 🚴

6. BERGERONNES

F E ♿ P 🚗 ❌

For a real holiday in whale country, come to the pink granite inn, in the heart of the village. Whale-watching cruises, skidoo, sea kayaking, scuba diving. 5 km from Cap Bon-Désir, a whale-watching viewpoint, and only 2 km to a prehistory inter-pretive centre. Bike rental on the premises. Regional menu between 6pm and 10pm. Whale watching packages $89 double occ. Tx and service extra.

24 km from Tadoussac on Rte 138 E. Turn left 0.5 km after the Ber-geronnes tourist information booth. Follow the signs.

INN
LA ROSEPIERRE

Diane Gagnon
and Richard Bouchard
66, rue Principale, C.P. 116
Bergeronnes G0T 1G0
(418) 232-6543
toll free 1-888-264-6543
fax (418) 232-6215
rosepierre@mail.fjord-best.com

B&B	
single	$55-65
double	$65-75
triple	$75-85
quad.	$85-95
child	$10

Taxes extra VS MC IT

Reduced rates: Oct. 1to May 31
Open year round

Number of rooms	10
rooms with private bath	8
shared bathrooms	1

Activities: 🏛 ⚓ 🚶 🚴 ⛷

7. GODBOUT

Stay by the sea, near the ferry. Breakfast served in our restaurant "Aux Berges". Dinner with reservations. Calm and beautiful landscape, beaches, fishing, excursions at sea. Check out waterfalls full of jumping salmon!

From Québec City, Rte 138 E. to Godbout. Located near the ferry.

INN
AUX BERGES

Lucie Cordeau and
Eric Deschênes
180, rue Pascal Comeau
Godbout G0H 1G0
(418) 568-7748
(418) 568-7816
fax (418) 568-7833

B&B	
single	$35
double	$45
triple	$55
child	$8-15

Taxes extra VS MC AM ER IT

Open: May 1 to Oct. 31

Number of rooms	3
rooms with sink	3
shared bathrooms	1
shared wc	1

Activities: 🏛 ⛴ 🚣 🧍

---

8. LES ESCOUMINS

F E ⛴ P ⊠ R.5 TA

"A stop along the way to discovering the Côte-Nord..." Good beds, good cooking (meals with reservation). Personalized service whether you prefer to relax or explore: the sea, the river or the forest. Whales, salmon and trout are plentiful. Wonderful places for scuba-diving, snowmobiling. The inn is a cosy stop between the river and forest.

From Tadoussac, Rte 138 E., 40 km. From Baie-Comeau, Rte 138 West 150 km. 2 km from the Les Escoumins-Trois-Pistoles ferry.

INN
AUBERGE DE LA BAIE

Esther Gagné
267, Route 138, C.P. 818
Les Escoumins G0T 1K0
(418) 233-2010
toll free 1-800-287-2010
fax (418) 233-3378

B&B	
single	$45-75
double	$55-75
triple	$65-85
quad.	$76-95
child	$10

Taxes extra VS MC AM ER

Reduced rates: Oct. 1to May 31
Open year round

Number of rooms	12
rooms with private bath	12

Activities: ⛴ 🚣 🧍 🧍 🛥

---

9. LES ESCOUMINS

F E P 🚗 🐕 R4

"Located right next to the ISSIPIT Indian reserve, come discover the sea, kayaking, sailing, scuba-diving, and in the winter, ice-fishing and snowmobile excursions. The shoreline follows the edge of Parc Saguenay-St-Laurent, the first marine park in Canada where you can see whales from the shore or from a boat. Quiet mornings and breakfasts."

30 km east of Tadoussac (Rte 138), we are located on the edge of the ISSIPIT reserve. Follow the signs for the reserve, a flowery field on the left shows the way.

B&B
GÎTE DES GIROUETTES

Lucie Baillargeon
2, rue Roussel
Les Escoumins G0T 1K0
(418) 233-3297
paquette@mail.fjord-best.com

B&B	
single	$40
double	$50

Taxes extra

Open year round
Nov. 1 to May 1, on reservation

Number of rooms	3
shared bathrooms	2

Activities: ⛴ 🚣 🐎 🛥 🎿

B&Bs AND INNS

10. LES ESCOUMINS

 F e 🚗 P R.5

Côte-Nord Excellence Prize 1997-98. 1998 Award of Excellence in Hospitality from the Ass. Tour. Rég. Manicouagan. House located in the heart of the village, with view over the river. Charm, character and a warm ambiance. Rooms offering cosy comfort. All-you-can-eat breakfast in a laid-back, convivial atmosphere.

From Québec City, Rte 138 to Escoumins, go up to the church, turn left, 4th house.

B&B
LE GÎTE FLEURI

Marianne Roussel
21, de l'Église
Les Escoumins G0T 1K0
(418) 233-3155

B&B	
single	$40
double	$50
triple	$70

Open year round

Number of rooms	4
shared bathrooms	2

Activities: 🛶 🚣 🏃 🚴 🚤

11. NATASHQUAN

F e ♿ 🚗 ✕ P 🏊 R1

20 feet from the sea, this inn offers its guests relaxation, a warm welcome and personalized service. Minibus, guided tours, bike rental, river rafting, hiking and the beach. Let's meet in Natashquan, the "Port d'Attache" inn awaits.

Rte 138 to Natashquan.

INN
LE PORT D'ATTACHE

Nathalie Lapierre and
Magella Landry
70, du Pré
Natashquan G0G 2E0
(418) 726-3569
(418) 726-3440
fax (418) 726-3767

B&B	
single	$50
double	$65

Taxes extra VS

Open year round

Number of rooms	8
shared bathrooms	3

Activities: 🚣 🏃 🚴 🚤 🤸

12. SACRÉ-COEUR

F E P 🚗 ✕ 🏊 R1 TA

Share in our family ambiance. "4-season" activities and packages. Québec cuisine also served to our customers staying in our country homes. No charge: visit or care of animals, sugar shack, tennis, pool, hiking trails, game park. Info and reservation service. **Farm stay p 37, country home p 112. For activities, see ads in Côte-Nord and Saguenay-Lac-St-Jean.**

From Tadoussac, twd Chicoutimi, 17 km from the intersection of Rtes 138 and 172, and 6 km from the Sacré-Coeur church. Or from Chicoutimi-north, Rte 172 S. to the right, 60 m. before the rest area.

B&B
FERME 5 ÉTOILES

Stéphanie and
Claude Deschênes
465, Route 172 Nord
Sacré-Cœur G0T 1Y0
(418) 236-4833
toll free 1- 877-236-4551
tel/fax (418) 236-4551
ferme5etoile@ihcn.qc.ca

	B&B	MAP
single	$40	$53
double	$45	$69
triple	$55	$90
child	$10	$16-18

Taxes extra VS MC AM IT

Open year round

Number of rooms	4
rooms with sink	2
shared bathrooms	2

Activities: 🛶 🚣 🏃 🚤 🐎

13. SACRÉ-COEUR F e P R2 TA

Modern house known for its large spaces, its cleanliness, the warmth and cheer of its residents. Breakfast served in the large solarium with a view of the lake, the geese, the ducks and the other farm animals.

From Tadoussac, Rtes 138 E. and 172 N. Or from Chicoutimi North: Rte 172 S. Watch for our sign: "Ferme Camil and Ghislaine".

B&B
GÎTE GHISLAINE

Ghislaine Gauthier
243, Route 172
Sacré-Coeur GOT 1Y0
(418) 236-4372

B&B	
single	$40
double	$45
triple	$60
quad.	$65
child	$10-15

Open: June 1 to Oct 31

Number of rooms	3
rooms in basement	3
shared bathrooms	2

Activities: 🚣 🧍 🛷 🎿 🐎

14. STE-ANNE-DE-PORTNEUF F 🚭 P 🚗 R.1 TA

A warm welcome; Dreamy rooms; A well-earned sleep; A generous breakfast; Fresh fruit and vegetables; Tides to behold; A beach for strolling; Birds to observe; An enchanted forest; Endless trails; Friendship assured. Tickets for boat cruises. Provincial Excellence Prize 94-95.

From Québec City, Rte 138 E. to Ste-Anne-de-Portneuf, 288 km and 84 km from Tadoussac. Or from Matane/Baie Comeau ferry, Rte 138 West. Drive 135 km. From Les Escoumins: 33 km. From Forestville: 17 km.

B&B
GÎTE LA NICHÉE

Camille and Joachim Tremblay
46, rue Principale, route 138
Ste-Anne-de-Portneuf
GOT 1P0
(418) 238-2825
fax (418) 238-5513

B&B	
single	$35
double	$45
triple	$60
child	$10

VS

Reduced rates: Nov 1 to Apr. 30
Open year round

Number of rooms	5
rooms with sink	5
shared wc	1
shared bathrooms	2

Activities: 🏛 🚣 🚤 🛷 🧍

15. STE-ANNE-DE-PORTNEUF F e P 🚗 R2 TA

Going to Germina's is like visiting your grandmother. Crepes, jams and giggling fits await you here. Stroll along the sandbank, see the birds, marina, blue whales and a centenary house with coloured past from the times of cinema and grocer's. Welcome to a region as big as the wind, sea and forest.

From Québec City, Rte 138 E., 288 km. 4 houses from church. 84 km from Tadoussac. Ferries: Escoumins: 33 km, Forestville: 17 km, Baie-Comeau: 135 km, Godbout: 189 km, Havre: 505 km.

B&B
LA MAISON FLEURIE

Germina Fournier
193, Route 138, C.P. 40
Ste-Anne-de-Portneuf
GOT 1P0
(418) 238-2153
fax (418) 238-2793

B&B	
single	$35
double	$45-50
triple	$60
child	$10

Reduced rates: Nov. 1 to Apr. 30
Open year round

Number of rooms	3
shared bathrooms	2

Activities: 🏛 🚣 🚤 🛷 🎿

B&Bs AND INNS

16. SEPT-ÎLES

F e P R1 TA

Sept-Îles welcomes you. House located near the entrance of the town. Nearby: walking paths along the sea, bike paths and bikes available, horseback riding, snowmobiling trail, cross-country and downhill skiing. Large livingroom pool table. Simple and friendly hospitality. Breakfast served in a family atmosphere with home-made jam. Welcome!

In Sept-Îles head east, left on Rue Desmeules in front of the tourist information centre, turn right on Rue Fiset, 3 streets to Rue Thibault.

B&B
GÎTE DES ÎLES

Réjeanne and André Lemieux
50, rue Thibault
Sept-Îles G4S 1M7
(418) 962-6116

B&B	
single	$40
double	$50
triple	$65
child	$10

Reduced rates: Oct. 1 to May 31
Open year round

Number of rooms	2
rooms in basement	1
shared bathrooms	2

Activities: 🏛 ⛴ 🧍 🚶 🚴

17. TADOUSSAC

F E P 🚗 AV R.01

Right next to the Saguenay fjord, the Maison Gagné inn welcomes you into an ambiance of warmth and friendship. Lovers of nature and the great outdoors, the seasons welcome you to our house. At the foot of one of the prettiest hiking trails in the province, you will spot whales, and will leave with precious memories of your stay.

From Québec City, Rte 138 E. Left once off the ferry, you'll see the Maison Gagné. Ferry (400 m).

INN
AUBERGE «MAISON GAGNÉ»

Claire Gagné
139, rue Bateau-Passeur
Tadoussac G0T 2A0
(418) 235-4526
fax (418) 235-4832

B&B	
single	$59
double	$69-79
triple	$79-89
quad.	$89-99
child	$10

Taxes extra VS MC ER

Reduced rates: Sep. 15 to June 15
Open year round

Number of rooms	10
rooms in basement	2
rooms with private bath	10
shared wc	1

Activities: ⛴ 🚤 🧍 ⛵ 🎿

18. TADOUSSAC

F e 🚫 🚗 P R.3

Peaceful place at the edge of the forest. Ocean view. Our golden rules: friendship and availability. No nearby road traffic. For 2-, 3- or 4-day stay, your hosts organize whale-watching cruises, hikes, excursions, wildlife observation (bears, moose, beavers), dogsledding, skiing, snowmobiling. In-house tickets sales.

From Québec, Rte 138 E. At Tadoussac turn right on the 1st street. Turn right at the big church, follow the water, turn right at 1st street, turn left at "cul de sac" (dead-end) sign, drive 100 metres.

B&B
AUX SENTIERS DU FJORD

Elisabeth Mercier and
Xavier Abelé
148, Coupe de l'Islet
Tadoussac G0T 2A0
(418) 235-4934
fax (418) 235-4252
www.dreamcite.com/
harveylessard

B&B	
single	$55
double	$60
triple	$90
child	$10-15

Taxes extra MC

Reduced rates: Sep. 15 to May 31
Open year round

Number of rooms	5
rooms with sink	5
shared bathrooms	2

Activities: 🏛 ⛴ 🚶 🎿 🐴

19. TADOUSSAC

F 🚗 P 🚭 R.1 TA

Comfortable and intimate rooms in our home. Enjoy magnificent views of the St-Laurent and of the Saguenay Fjord from our solarium where buffet breakfast awaits you in the morning. Rest in harmony with nature throughout the day. Tickets for cruises available.

From Québec City, Rte 138 E. Drive 0.5 km from the Saguenay ferry. Right on Rue Des Pionniers, drive 0.3 km, left on Rue de Forgerons, drive 0.3 km. Right on de la Falaise, drive 0.1 km.

B&B
GÎTE DE LA FALAISE

Émilienne and Fernand Simard
264, de la Falaise
Tadoussac, G0T 2A0
tel/fax (418) 235-4344

B&B	
single	$45
double	$55
triple	$65
quad.	$75
child	$10

VS MC

Reduced rates: Feb. 1 to May 31, Oct., Nov.
Open: Feb. 1 to Nov. 30

Number of rooms	5
rooms with sink	5
rooms in basement	1
shared bathrooms	2

Activities: 🏛 ⛵ 🚶 ⛷ 🚲

---

20. TADOUSSAC

F e 🚗 P R.25 TA

A simple and warm welcome conducive to rest. A tranquil hideaway close to amenities. We will regale you with our generous home made breakfasts. Whale-watching cruises. We have extensive knowledge of marine mammals. Tickets for sale here.

From Québec City, Rte 138 E. Drive 1.5 km along road from Saguenay ferry. Right on Rue Bois-Franc, 300 ft, left on Rue des Bouleaux. We're waiting for you.

B&B
GÎTE DU BOULEAU

Claire-Hélène Boivin and
Jean-Yves Harvey
102, rue des Bouleaux,
C.P. 384
Tadoussac G0T 2A0
tel/fax (418) 235-4601

B&B	
single	$45
double	$50-60
triple	$65
quad.	$85

VS MC

Reduced rates: Apr. 1 to June 30 and Sep. 3 to Nov. 30
Open: Apr. 1 to Nov. 30

Number of rooms	5
shared bathrooms	3

Activities: 🏛 ⛵ 🚶 ⛷ 🚲

---

21. TADOUSSAC

F E 🚭 P 🚗 R1

Welcome to our large, peaceful restored house, a little outside the village. Biologist and guide, we enjoy acquainting guests with our region. Trails, kayaking, whales, bears, beavers, birds, good advice and tickets on premises. In winter, dogsledding, X-country skiing, snowmobiling, cosy fireplace...

From Québec City, after getting off ferry, 1st street on right, Rue des Pionniers, 1 km from church, on the left (200 m after golf course).

B&B
GÎTE DU MOULIN BAUDE

Virginie Chadenet and
Charles Breton
381, rue des Pionniers,
C.P. 411
Tadoussac G0T 2A0
(418) 235-4765
www.ihcn.qc.ca
/moulinbaude/gite/
moulinbaude@ihcn.qc.ca

B&B	
single	$60
double	$65-75
triple	$90
quad.	$100
child	$10-15

VS MC

Reduced rates: Sep. 7 to July 9 or 3 nights and more
Open year round

Number of rooms	4
rooms with private bath	4

Activities: ⛵ 🚶 ⛷ 🐕

22. TADOUSSAC

F E 🚭 P 🚗 🐕 R.5

Perched at the village summit, a house where every room offers a breathtaking view of the river, fjord, lake and flower garden. "Warm welcome and intimacy" perfectly describes the ambiance here. Private balcony, tastefully and romantically appointed soundproof rooms, 60" bed. Luxury suite (therapeutic bath, king-size bed, TV, air conditioning).

From the ferry, Rte 138 (1 km). Half-way up the hill, under the signs, turn left, take the next right. Continue and watch for the Harvey Lessard sign.

B&B
LA MAISON
HARVEY-LESSARD

Sabine Lessard and Luc Harvey
16, Rue Bellevue
Tadoussac G0T 2A0
in Tadoussac (418) 235-4802
in Québec (418) 827-5505
www.dreamcite.
com/harveylessard/

B&B	
single	$75-80
double	$80-85
doublesuite	$135
child	$10-15

Reduced rates: Sep. 7 to June 30
Open: May 1 to Oct. 31

Number of rooms	4
rooms with private bath	4
shared wc	1

Activities: ⚓ 🚣 👤 🏃 🚴

23. TADOUSSAC

F P 🚗 R.1

We are happy to welcome you into our home. Seen from Tadoussac, the Saguenay is breathtaking. Cruises with whale watching. Bus service at one kilometre. Welcome to our home.

From Québec City, Rte 138 E. to the ferry across the Saguenay. Once off the ferry, take the first road on the right.

B&B
MAISON FORTIER

Madeleine B. Fortier
176, rue des Pionniers
Tadoussac G0T 2A0
(418) 235-4215
fax (418) 235-1029

B&B	
single	42 $
double	52 $
triple	67 $
child	10 $

Taxes extra VS

Reduced rates: Nov.
Open year round

Number of rooms	5
rooms with sink	5
shared wc	1
shared bathrooms	3

Activities: 🐚 ⚓ 🚣 👤 🏃

24. TADOUSSAC

F E ♿ P 🚗 R.4 TA

Cosy, comfortable hundred-year-old house with view of the Saguenay, on the shores of the lake, in the heart of the village of Tadoussac. 5 rooms with private bathrooms. Rooms with private baths also available in the annex the "Suites de l'Anse". Buffet breakfast served in the Maison Gauthier or in your room. Exceptional off-season rates.

From Québec City, Rte 138 East to the Saguenay ferry at Baie Ste-Catherine. Once off the ferry, 250 m on your left.

INN
MAISON GAUTHIER ET LES
SUITES DE L'ANSE

Lise and Paulin Hovington
159, du Bateau-Passeur
Tadoussac G0T 2A0
(418) 235-4525
(450) 671-4656
fax (418) 235-4897
fax (450) 671-7586

B&B	
single	$60
double	$60-80
triple	$85-95
quad.	$100-110
child	$10-15

Taxes extra VS MC IT

Reduced rates: May, June
Open: May 1 to Oct 31

Number of rooms	12
rooms with private bath	12

Activities: ⚓ 🚣 👤 🏃 🚴

25. TADOUSSAC

F E P R.4

Century-old house with a view of the St-Laurent River. Rooms with private bathroom. Buffet breakfast. Whale-watching. Near the bus station and restaurants. The Hovington family is proud to welcome you into their home. **See colour photos.**

From Québec City, Rte 138 East to Baie Ste-Catherine. Take the ferry. In Tadoussac take the first street on your right, Rue des Pionniers.

B&B
MAISON HOVINGTON

Lise and Paulin Hovington
285, rue des Pionniers
Tadoussac G0T 2A0
(450) 671-4656
(418) 235-4466
fax (450) 671-7586
fax (418) 235-4897

B&B	
single	$55
double	$55-70
child	$15

Taxes extra VS MC IT

Open: May to Oct 31

Number of rooms	5
rooms with private bath	5

Activities:

B&Bs AND INNS

26. BAIE-TRINITÉ

7 comfortable chalets right by the sea, most of them loghouses, with kitchenette, bathroom and t.v. The Pointe-des-Monts headland juts out 11 km into the Gulf of St-Laurent. Right on the high seas! You'll see whales, seals and gannets from your kitchen window. Old lighthouse museum, excursions and gourmet restaurant all on site from mid-June to late August. **See ad end of this section and Inn p 103.**

From Québec, Rte 138 East. Exit at the entrance to Pointe-des-Monts, 4 km before Baie-Trinité (to the west), then follow the secondary road that ends at the old lighthouse.

COUNTRY HOME
LE GÎTE DU PHARE DE POINTE-DES-MONTS

Jean-Louis Frenette
Route du Vieux Phare
de Pointe-des-Monts
Baie-Trinité G0H 1A0
(418) 589-8408
(418) 939-2332

No. house	7
No. rooms	35885
No. people	36100
WEEK-SUMMER	$390-750
DAY-SUMMER	$62-150

Taxes extra VS MC IT

Reduced rates: May 1to June 12 and ⅓ of the price from Sep. 6 to Oct. 31
Open: May 1 to Oct. 31

Activities: ⚊ 🏊 🧍 🚴 🚤

27. SACRÉ-COEUR

Share our family ambiance, our 700 acres of farm and forest, access to the fjord, our choice of activities and accommodations with bedding, kitchen and amenities, t.v. and services free of charge.Near Tadoussac and Sainte-Rose-du-Nord. **Farm stay p 37, B&Bs p 106. For activities: see ads in Côte-Nord and Saguenay-Lac-St-Jean sections.**

From Tadoussac, twd Chicoutimi, 17 km from the intersection of Rtes 138 and 172, and 6 km from the Sacré-Coeur church. Or from Chicoutimi-north, Rte 172 South to the right, 60 metres before the rest area.

COUNTRY HOME
FERME 5 ÉTOILES

Stéphanie and Claude Deschênes
465, Route 172 Nord
Sacré-Cœur G0T 1Y0
(418) 236-4833
tel/fax (418) 236-4551
toll free 1-877-236-4551
ferme5etoile@ihcn.qc.ca

No. houses	9
No. rooms	1-3
No. people	2-8
WEEK-SUMMER	$410-1125
WEEK-WINTER	$285-910
W/E-SUMMER	$130-370
W/E-WINTER	$90-290
DAY-SUMMER	$40-55
DAY-WINTER	$40-50

Taxes extra VS MC AM IT

Reduced rates: Sep. 10 to June 10
Open year round

Activities: ⚊ 🏊 🧍 🛷 🐴

FARM ACTIVITIES

Farm stay:

COUNTRY HOMES

Welcome to the Québec North Shore
10 minutes from Tadoussac

Ferme 5 étoiles

4 seasons
Rental activities
duration : between 2 and 3 hours

Spring-Summer-Fall
★ Beluga, seal and whale watching cruises
★ 4 wheel carts mountain excursions
★ Canoeing on lakes and rivers
★ Sea kayaking on the Saguenay fjord
★ Fishing (gear supplied)
★ Mountain bike and hiking trails
★ Bear and beaver watching
★ Hydroplane
★ Horseriding
★ The life of today's lumberjacks (4 saisons)
★ Museum

Winter
★ Ice fishing
★ Igloo lodging
★ Sliding on air tubes
★ Truckdriver journey (4 seasons)
★ Dogsleding and snowmobile : Initiation and
  excursion (possibility of many days packages)
★ Sugar shack, maple taffy tasting and traditions
★ Snowshoeing and cross country skiing trails
  along the Saguenay fjord

Packages

1. «Wild discoveries»
(2 days - 1 night)
One rental activity included (your choice)
according to the season :
★ «Goodies» of the farm
★ One night
★ One copious breakfast
★ One traditionnal supper

79 $ /pers./bed & breakfast

95 $ /pers./country home

2. «Wild exploration»
(3 days - 2 nights)
Two rental activities included (your choice)
according to the season :
★ «Goodies» of the farm
★ Two night
★ Two copious breakfast
★ Two traditionnal supper

154 $ /pers./bed & breakfast

185 $ /pers./country home

3. «A la carte» (3 days and up)
Ask us exactly what you want and we will make
your «wilderness» dream come true!

Côte-Nord region
★ B&B's and Inns No.**12**
★ Country homes No. **27**

«Goodies» of the farm free for our clientele :
Guided tours of the farm and the sugar shack, animals
daily care (for kids), hiking and cross country skiing
trails, outdoor swiming pool, tennis, playground,
outdoor fireplace, B.B.Q.

★ Children under 12 with adults :
  save 20% on adult rates
★ Lodging rates for 2 pers.
★ Taxes are not included with prices
★ Group rates (11 pers. and up)

Informations - reservations
Phone : (418) **236-4833** • Toll free : 1 877 **236-4551** • Fax : (418) 236-4551
FERME 5 ÉTOILES, 465, route 172 Nord, Sacré-Coeur (Québec) G0T 1Y0 • E-mail : ferme5etoile@ihcn.qc.ca

GASPÉSIE

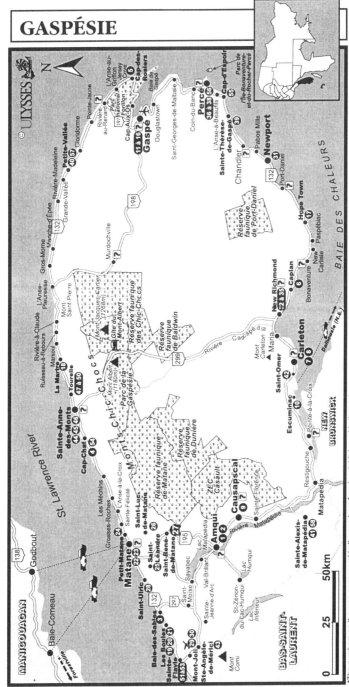

*The numbers on the map correspond to the number of each establishment in the region.

1. AMQUI

F | e | ⊗ | P | R4

House located on an old farm close to Lac Matapédia (5-min walk), private beach, a rest stop. Admire the green or colourful landscapes. Midway between Québec City and Percé or New-Brunswick. 4 km away: summer theatre, fishing, canoe, golf, park with bike paths and hiking. The generous home-made breakfast and friendly welcome will make you want to come again.

From Mont-Joli, Rte 132 East, watch for "Limites de la ville d'Amqui" sign and drive 2 km. From Percé, Rte 132 West through Amqui. 4 km past the 2nd light. On your right, after the camping site.

B&B
DOMAINE DU
LAC MATAPÉDIA

Carmelle and Roland Charest
780, Route 132 Ouest
Amqui G0J 1B0
(418) 629-5004

B&B	
single	$45-55
double	$55-65
triple	$75-80
quad.	$80-95
child	$10-15

Reduced rates: June 15 to June 24, Sep. 1 to Oct. 5
Open: June 15to Oct. 5

Number of rooms	5
rooms with private bath	1
rooms with sink	4
shared wc	1
shared bathrooms	2

Activities: ● ☞ ⌇ ⋏ ⬲

2. AMQUI

F | e | ⊗ | P | 🚗 | R.25 | TA

Welcome to Amqui! House in the heart of downtown. Magnificent landscape with flower beds and vegetable garden. Walking distance from restaurants and activities (tennis, pool, etc.). Sincere, friendly hospitality. Home-made breakfast served in family ambiance. Welcome to our home.

From Mont-Joli, Rte 132 East. In Amqui, right at CN train station, across railway, straight ahead. From Gaspé, Rte 132 West, through Amqui, left at railway, then straight ahead.

B&B
GÎTE DE LA VIEILLE MAISON

Anita Guénette and
Roland Roy
21, rue Proulx, C.P. 179
Amqui G0J 1B0
(418) 629-8184

B&B	
single	$45
double	$52
child	$10

Reduced rates: Oct. 1 to Oct. 31 Jan. 15 to Apr. 30 with reservations
Open: May 1 to Oct. 31, Jan. 15 to Apr. 30 with reservations

Number of rooms	3
shared wc	1
shared bathrooms	1

Activities: ● ☞ ⌇ 🐎 ⛷

3. BAIE-DES-SABLES

F | E | ⊗ | 🏊 | 🐕 | P | ✕ | R3 | TA

Enjoy the pace of life at Le Sablier. Discover the charms of this hundred-year-old house, located a few kilometres from Jardins de Métis, to the sound of the waves. The B&B also offers a golf package for golfing enthusiasts. It will be our pleasure to receive you in our lovely yellow house.

From Québec City, Hwy 20 East, Rte 132 East. Left on Rue de la Mer, 20 km past Sainte-Flavie. From Gaspé, Rte 132 West. Right on Rue de la Mer, 20 km past Matane.

B&B
LE SABLIER

Stéphane Lévesque
40, rue de la Mer, C.P. 255
Baie-des-Sables G0J 1C0
(418) 772-6333
www.bbcanada.com/
1143.html
caboche@quebectel.com

	B&B	PAM
single	$35	$55
double	$50	$90
triple	$65	$125
child	$10	$20

VS IT

Open: May 15 to Oct. 31

Number of rooms	5
shared wc	2
shared bathrooms	2

Activities: 🏛 ● ☞ ⌇ 🐎

4. CAP-CHAT

F | E | ⊘ | 🏊 | P | 🚗 | ✕ | R.4 | TA

Gaspésie Excellence Prize 1996-97. Come join us to the sound of the waves and the cries of the gulls. From our beach watch the whales disappear over the horizon into the gentle waves. Close your eyes at sunset and you'll feel the very soul of Gaspésie. You can visit the Parc de la Gaspésie and the Wind and Sea Interpretive Centre. Evening meal: delicious seafood au gratin. **Country Home p 134, no 54.**

From Québec City, Hwy 20 East and Rte 132 East to Cap-Chat. At the western edge of Cap-Chat, 3 km from the "éolienne", and 2 km from the Centre d'Interprétation du Vent et de la Mer on your right.

INN
AUBERGE «AU CRÉPUSCULE»

Monette Dion and Jean Ouellet
239, Notre-Dame Ouest,
route 132
Cap-Chat GOJ 1EO
tel/fax (418) 786-5751
www.bbcanada.com/323.html

	B&B	MAP
single	$40	$60
double	$55	$95
triple	$70	$130
quad.	$85	$165
child	$15	$30

VS MC IT

Open year round

Number of rooms	5
rooms with sink	3
rooms with private bath	1
rooms in basement	2
shared bathrooms	3

Activities: 🚣 🎿 🎿 🐎 🎿

---

5. CAP-DES-ROSIERS, FORILLON

F | e | P | 🚗 | 🐕 | R.5

Friendly, welcoming B&B near Forillon Park, with its enchanting landscape and animal life. Visit the tallest lighthouse in the country and go on one of our cruises (whale-, seal- and bird-watching). While savouring a copious breakfast, you'll be dazzled by a magnificent view out onto the sea. Welcome to our home.

From Québec City: Hwy 20 East and Rte 132 East to Cap-des-Rosiers. From Gaspé: Rte 132 to Cap-des-Rosiers; 3 km from the entrance to the north part of Forillon Park.

B&B
AUX PÉTALES DE ROSE

Alvine Lebrun
1184, Cap-des-Rosiers
Gaspé GOE 1EO
(418) 892-5031

	B&B
single	$40
double	$55
triple	$70
child	$10

Reduced rates: May 15 to June 15 and Oct. 1 to Oct. 31
Open: May 15 to Oct. 31

Number of rooms	5
rooms in basement	2
shared bathrooms	2

Activities: 🐚 ⛴ 🚣 🚲 🐎

---

6. CAPLAN

F | E | P | 🚗 | R1 | TA

Located between Bonaventure and Carleton, a memorable B&B overlooking Baie des Chaleurs - one you'll find hard to leave. Trails, beach, flowery gardens, farm animals. 10 minutes from Acadian Museum, Bioparc, adventure boats, golf, 2 salmon rivers, horseback riding. 20 minutes from St-Elzéar cave, British Heritage Centre. Lavish home-made breakfast.

In the heart of Baie-des-Chaleurs. From Percé, Rte 132, look for the "Municipalité de Caplan" sign after the bridge, 3 km. In Caplan west side, 1.5 km after the church.

B&B
L'AUBERGE DE LA FERME

Rose-Aline Landry and
Jocelyn Brière
185, boul. Perron Est
Caplan GOC 1HO
(418) 388-5603
fax (418) 388-2366
aubferme@globetrotter.net
www.bbcanada.com/2931.html

	B&B
single	$30-35
double	$50
triple	$60-65
quad.	$80
child	$0-10

Reduced rates: Oct. 1 to June 1
Open year round

Number of rooms	5
shared wc	1
shared bathrooms	2

Activities: 🏛 ⛴ 🚣 🎿 🐎

B&Bs AND INNS

7. CARLETON

F e P 🚗 R.1 TA

Located downtown, amidst all the activities. We can accommodate up to 16 guests. Tea time at 4 pm. It will be our pleasure to pick you up at train or bus station. Free laundry service and bicycles. Packages available. Something for every season. Copious breakfast.

From Ste-Flavie, Rte 132 East. At entrance to town, right at 1st light, Rte du Quai. From Percé, at entrance to town, left at 2nd light, Rte du Quai. At corner of Rte 132 and Rte du Quai.

INN
AUBERGE LA VISITE SURPRISE

Isabelle Quinn and Lise Leblanc
527, boul. Perron
Carleton G0C 1J0
(418) 364-6553
fax (418) 364-6890

B&B	
single	$35
double	$48
triple	$60
quad.	$72
child	$5-12

Taxes extra VS MC ER AM

Reduced rates: Oct. 1 to June 30
Open year round

Number of rooms	7
rooms in semi-basement	4
rooms with sink	5
shared bathrooms	3

Activities: 🦆 🚲 🚶 🎿 🛷

8. CARLETON

F E 🚫 P 🚗 R1 TA

Two Acadians welcome you to their granite Canadian-style house. Spacious rooms, country decor. Large veranda with view of Mont St-Joseph, a few kilometres from the B&B. Children welcome. Near playground, beach, hiking trails, bird-watching tower. 25 km from Parc de Miguasha.

From Québec City, Hwy 20 East, Rte 132 East. At the entrance to Carleton, next to "Optique Chaleurs". Entrance on Rue des Érables, 1st house on right. Or from Percé, drive 3 km from the church, next to Motel l'Abri.

B&B
GÎTE LES LEBLANC

Jocelyne and Rosaire LeBlanc
346, boul. Perron C.P. 143
Carleton G0C 1J0
(418) 364-7601
(418) 364-3208
fax (418) 364-6333
indleb@globetrotter.com

B&B	
single	$40
double	$50
triple	$60
quad.	$70
child	$10

VS MC

Open: May 1 to Oct. 31

Number of rooms	4
rooms with sink	2
shared bathrooms	2

Activities: 🏛 🦆 🚲 🚶 🚶

9. CAUSAPSCAL

F P R.2

B&B right in the heart of the village of Causapscal. Come relax in a setting typical of the Matapédia valley; it's just like being in a Swiss village. Enjoy a view of the Rivière Matapédia, where you'll see fishermen trying to catch salmon. Just the place for a pleasant stay!

Rte 132 West, Rue d'Anjou (first street on the right after the traffic lights), left on Rue Belzile. Or Rte 132 East, Rue d'Anjou (by the Caisse Populaire), left on Rue Belzile.

B&B
LE GÎTE DE LA VALLÉE

Gilberte Barriault
71, rue Belzile
Causapscal G0J 1J0
(418) 756-5226
(418) 756-3072

B&B	
single	$35
double	$45
triple	$60
child	$10

Reduced rates: Nov. 1 to Apr. 30
Open: Jan. 16 to Dec. 14

Number of rooms	3
shared bathrooms	1

Activities: 🦆 🚶 🚶 🛷 🎿

10. ESCUMINAC, MIGUASHA

F E 🚭 ♿ 🏊 P 🐕 R5 TA

Wanta-Qo-Ti, an experience worthy of its name: serenity. Located between the red cliffs of Miguasha and Baie des Chaleurs, facing the sea, this B&B was once a farm. Come discover this enchanting place. Right next to Parc de Miguasha, the ferry to the Îles-de-la-Madeleine, the ski hill and other activities.

From Carleton Rte 132 West to Nouvelle, twd Miguasha-Dalhousie ferry. At the ferry turn right on Rte Miguasha (becomes Pte-à-Fleurant) for 3.2 km. From Matapédia Rte 132 East to Escuminac. Right at Parc Miguasha sign, 6.2 km.

INN
AUBERGE WANTA-QO-TÍ

Bruce Wafer
77, chemin Pointe-Fleurant
Escuminac G0C 1N0
tel/fax (418) 788-5686
www.bbcanada.com/595.html

B&B	
single	$40-43
double	$57-66
triple	$81
quad.	$96
child	$0-12

Taxes extra VS MC IT

Reduced rates: Sep. 15 to June 15
Open year round

Number of rooms	8
rooms with private bath	4
shared bathrooms	2

Activities: 🏛 🚴 🎣 🚣 🎿

11. GASPÉ

F e ♿ 🚭 P 🚗 🐕 R1

Located close to Forillon Park, the Gîte Baie Jolie welcomes you to the cradle of Canada. The view of the Baie de Gaspé will thrill your senses. Rediscover history at the Musée de la Gaspésie. Numerous tourist activities are suggested by your welcoming hosts. A smile awaits. Generous breakfasts.

From Québec City, Hwy. 20 East, Rte 132 East. At the Gaspé bridge, do not take the bridge, but straight ahead for 1.5 km along the bay. Rte 198 West, at the corner of Rue Boulay. Or from Percé, Rte 132 West, turn left after the Gaspé bridge. Drive 1.5 km. Rte 198 West.

B&B
GÎTE BAIE JOLIE

Blanche A. Blanchette and Roland Fortin
270, Montée Wakeham
Gaspé G4X 1V5
(418) 368-2149

B&B	
single	$40-45
double	$45-55
triple	$55-65
child	$10

VS

Reduced rates: May 1 au May 31 and Oct 1 to Oct. 31
Open: May 1 to Oct. 31

Number of rooms	4
rooms with private bath	1
rooms with sink	3
rooms in basement	1
shared bathrooms	1

Activities: 🏛 🚣 🚴 🎣 🚶

12. GASPÉ

F e 🚭 ♿ 🚗 P R.2

You will feel right at home upon entering the Gîte de Gaspé with Louisette and Gaétan's warm welcome. Enjoy a restful night and breakfast served with products from the family maple grove. Unforgettable! Panoramic view of Parc Forillon and the Gaspé bay from the terrace. Suggested activities.

From Québec City: Hwy 20 East, Rte 132 to Gaspé, toward town centre and Rue Jacques-Cartier up to Rue Wakeham. Turn right, continue for 75 metres. Left on Rue Guignion.

B&B
GÎTE DE GASPÉ

Louisette Tapp and Gaétan Poirier
201, rue Guignion
Gaspé
(418) 368-5273
fax (418) 368-0119

B&B	
single	$45
double	$60
triple	$75
child	$10

Reduced rates: Sep. 15 to Oct. 31 and Apr. 1 to June 1
Open: Apr. 1 to Oct. 31

Number of rooms	3
rooms with private bath	3
rooms in basement	3

Activities: 🏛 🚣 🚴 🎣 🚶

B&Bs AND INNS

13. GASPÉ

F | E | 🐕 | ✕ | 🚗 | P

Across from the town of Gaspé, discover a lovely, welcoming period house, with its carved staircase, panoramic view and rich history. Come sample delicious cuisine where seafood holds pride of place. Fresh lobster from the fish tank, terrace, fireplace.

Rte 132 to Gaspé. Located on Boul. York East or Rte 198, across from the town, on the bay, right near the tourist office.

INN
GÎTE DE L'ANCÊTRE

Diane Lauzon and
Ronald Chevalier
55, boul. York Est, C.P. 2496
Gaspé G4X 2L1
(418) 368-4358
fax (418) 368-4054

B&B	
single	$55-60
double	$60-65
triple	$75
quad.	$85
child	$10

Open: May 1 to Oct. 31

Number of rooms	2
shared wc	2
shared bathrooms	1

Activities: 🦞 ⚜ 🚶 🚲 🐎

---

14. GASPÉ

F | E | 🚭 | 🐕 | 🚗 | P | R1

A large wooden house from 1922 with period furniture, Honeys' took in sailors during World War II. Enjoy a cocktail on the big porches facing the bay while admiring the superb sunsets. Next to the marina. Gaspé breakfasts. Picnic on the grounds.

From Percé: right at flashing light after the tourist office. From Forillon: left at Gaspé bridge, left at flashing light. From Murdochville: right at the bridge, left at flashing light.

B&B
GÎTE HONEYS

Françoise Lambert Kruse
4, de la Marina
Gaspé G4X 3B1
tel/fax (418) 368-3294
www.gaspesie.qc.ca/honeys
honeys@cablog.net

B&B	
single	$50
double	$50-60
child	$10

VS

Open: June 1 to Oct. 31

Number of rooms	5
shared bathrooms	2

Activities: 🏛 ⛴ 🤿 ⚜ 🚶

---

15. GASPÉ

F | E | 🚭 | P | 🐕 | R.5 | TA

Close to Forillon National Park. A 5 min walk to all services. This Canadian house knows how to please with the welcome of its owners, its cleanliness, comfort and tranquillity. Documentation and information on our beautiful region attractions are available. Complete breakfast. See you soon!

Rte 132 or 198 to Gaspé. Rue Jacques-Cartier or Rue de la Reine to the cathedral where Rue Mgr Leblanc begins.

B&B
GÎTE «LA CANADIENNE»

Hélène Pelletier and
Denis Bériault
201, Mgr. Leblanc, C.P. 2-2
Gaspé G4X 1S3
tel/fax (418) 368-3806

B&B	
single	$45
double	$55
triple	$65
child	$10

Open: June 1 to July 31

Number of rooms	5
rooms with private bath	5
rooms in semi-basement	5

Activities: 🏛 ⛴ 🤿 ⚜ 🚶

16. GASPÉ

F A ⊗ P 🚗 R.1

Less than 30 minutes from Forillon Park, downtown, 3-story house, close to one hundred years old, with great view of Baie de Gaspé. Walking distance from restaurants and museum, promenade, cathedral, marina. Cosy rooms and lounge, period decor and ambiance await you. Refined breakfasts to soft music.

From Percé, after the bridge, continue straight ahead to the first traffic lights. From Forillon, turn right at the first traffic lights. From Murdochville, turn left at the first traffic lights. Everyone: turn left at the 2nd traffic lights and drive 100 metres.

B&B
LES PETITS MATINS
COUETTE-CAFÉ

Noëlline Couture and
Guy Papillon
129, de la Reine,
Gaspé G4X 1T5
(418) 368-1370

B&B	
single	$50-60
double	$50-60
triple	$75

VS MC

Open year round

Number of rooms	3
rooms with sink	1
shared wc	1
shared bathrooms	1

Activities: 🏛 ⛴ 🚶 🎿

17. HOPE TOWN, PASPÉBIAC

F E ⊗ P 🚗 R5 TA

Join us in the comfort of our home, a large, beautiful typical Gaspé house facing the sea, where an unforgettable stay awaits you. The memory of our 30-hectare estate and the hike to Cabane au Canada, by a salmon river, will stay with you. Provincial Excellence Grand Prize 1995-96.

From Québec, Hwy 20 East, Rte 132 East to Hopetown. 4 km from «Automobiles Roland Roussy» turn left. Or from Percé, Rte 132 West to Hope Town.

B&B
LA CLÉ DES CHAMPS

Jo-Anne Guimond and
Bernard Gauthier
254, Route 132
Hope Town, Paspébiac
G0C 2K0
tél/fax (418) 752-3113
toll free 1-800-693-3113

B&B	
single	$40
double	$50
triple	$65
quad.	$75
child	$10

Open year round

Number of rooms	3
shared wc	1
shared bathrooms	1

Activities: ⛴ 🚶 🚴

18. LA MARTRE

F E ⊗ P 🚗 R.5

Far from the noise of the 132, cheerful ancestral home, perched on a hill overlooking the St-Laurent and the picturesque village of La Martre. Lighthouse, interpretation centre, archaeological digs, beach, trails, forest walks, annex for meditation and picnics. Near Parc de la Gaspésie. Snowmobiling trail, 1 km. We speak German.

From Montréal or Québec City, Hwy 20 E. and Rte 132 E. 25 km east of Ste-Anne-des-Monts, 25 km west of Mont St-Pierre. At lighthouse, Rue de l'Église, right on Rue des Écoliers, 300 metres.

B&B
GÎTE L'ÉCUME DE MER

Andréa Neu
21, rue des Écoliers
La Martre G0E 2H0
tel/fax (418) 288-5274
ecmer@globetrotter.qc.ca

B&B	
single	$45
double	$55
triple	$70
child	$10

Reduced rates: 10 %, for 3 nights and more
Open: May 15 to Oct. 15

Number of rooms	4
shared bathrooms	2

Activities: 🚶 🚴 🎿

19. LES BOULES

F e 🦽 🏠 P 🚗 ✕ TA

Come enjoy our cosy inn, snuggle under a warm duvet with a good book. Near Métis/Mer, away from the 132, by the sea. Healthy delicious food, European ambiance, and very cheerful. Come along! Jardins de Métis package. Kayak. Family-sized rooms in adjacent annex.

At Gaspésie entrance, 35 km before Matane, 10 km after Jardins de Métis, left on Rte de Métis-sur-Mer, drive 6 km, opposite the church, by the river.

INN
AUBERGE DU GRAND FLEUVE

Marie-José Fradette and
Raynald Pay
47, Principale, C.P. 99
Les Boules G0J 1S0
tel/fax (418) 936-3332

	B&B
single	$40-60-70
double	$50-60-70
triple	$70-80
quad.	$80-90
child	$5

Taxes extra VS MC IT

Open: May 1 to Oct. 15

Number of rooms	9
rooms with sink	3
rooms with private bath	6
shared wc	2
shared bathrooms	2

Activities: 🍲 🚣 🎣 🚲 🐎

20. LES BOULES

F E 🚫 🐕 P R.3 TA

Near Jardins de Métis, we offer you a warm welcome in a spacious house located in a small, picturesque village by the sea. Golf course 2 km away; 3 km from a seafood restaurant. This part of the country is a must-see!

From Québec City: Aut 20 Est, Rte 132 Est. 15 minutes past St-Flavie, after the Golf Boule Rock, go down toward the sea. At the church, turn left.

B&B
GÎTE AUX CAYOUX

Huguette, Gaétan,
Johanne Cayouette
80, rue Principale, C.P. 129
Les Boules G0J 1S0
(418) 936-3842

	B&B
single	$35
double	$45-55
child	$10 15

Open: May 1 to Oct. 1

Number of rooms	3
shared wc	1
shared bathrooms	2

Activities: 🏛 🍲 🎣 🚣 🐎

21. LES BOULES

F E P 🚗 ✕ TA

Open year round. Near the Jardins de Métis, our inn is licensed and offers refined cuisine. Choose the beauty of nature and the quietness of the countryside. Warm reception, copious breakfasts. Meet the innkeeper, who has lots of tales to tell and activities. Packages available.

Between Rimouski and Matane, following Rte 132, 10 km from Jardins de Métis, after blue tourist sign, inland via Rte McNider, 4 km, turn on 5e Rang to the red-roofed inn.

INN
L'AUBERGE
«UNE FERME EN GASPÉSIE»

Pierre Dufort
1175, 5e Rang
Les Boules G0J 1S0
tel/fax (418) 936-3544

	B&B
single	$40
double	$60
triple	$70
quad.	$80
child	$10

Taxes extra VS MC

Reduced rates: Sep. 1 to July 1
Open year round

Number of rooms	6
shared bathrooms	3

Activities: 🎣 🚶 🐎 🛷 🐎

22. MATANE

F ⊗ P 🚗 R.5 TA

Former site of the Fraser seigneury, where the Rivière Matane joins the St-Laurent River. Take advantage of the calm and the fresh river air, near downtown Matane. Friendly, comfortable atmosphere. Sink in every room. Non-smoker B&B. Gaspésie Excellence Prize 1994-95.

From Québec City, Hwy 20 East, Rte 132 East. At Matane, Avenue du Phare, after the Tim Horton Donuts, right on Rue Druilette, at the 148, welcome and parking.

INN
AUBERGE LA SEIGNEURIE

Raymonde and Guy Fortin
621, rue St-Jérôme
Matane G4W 3M9
(418) 562-0021
1-877-783-4466 (toll free)
fax (418) 562-4455
seigneurie.home.ml.org

B&B	
single	$40-50
double	$60-70
triple	$75-85
quad.	$90-100
child	$10

Taxes extra VS MC AM

Reduced rates: Sep. 15 to June 15
Open year round

Number of rooms	10
rooms with sink	8
rooms with private bath	2
shared wc	1
shared bathrooms	3

Activities: 🏛 🍂 ⚜ ♻ 🏃

23. MATANE

F E ⊗ P 🚗 R.5 TA

Located right by the sea, our B&B offers an exceptional view! You will be treated to a warm welcome, a comfortable bed, a refined and lavish breakfast as well as soft and relaxing music. Excellent restaurants in the vicinity. One kilometre from the town centre and the ferry.

On Route 132 in Matane, second house west of the lighthouse (Matane's Tourist Information Centre).

B&B
GÎTE DU PHARE

Josée Landry and
Gilles Blais
984, du Phare Ouest
Matane G4W 3M6
(418) 562-6606
fax (418) 562-8876
studpass@globetrotter.qc.ca

B&B	
single	$40-50
double	$50-60
triple	$70
quad.	$80
child	$10

VS MC

Open year round

Number of rooms	4
rooms with sink	2
shared bathrooms	2

Activities: ⚓ ⚜ 🚣 ⛷ 🏃

24. MATANE, PETIT-MATANE

F e 〰 P 🚗 🐕 R2 TA

Restful place by the sea. Typical Gaspésie house, a comfortable place to relax in a spa (whirlpool bath) set up in a sunroom with a view of the sea. Relax while watching the sun set into the horizon or benefit from the sea air while strolling the river bank. Massotherapy packages upon reservation.

2 km east of Matane, leave Rte 132, take "Chemin de la grève" which follows the St-Laurent River. A few houses from the church you have arrived. 8 km from the Matane ferry and 6 km from the bus-stop.

B&B
LE CHANT DES MARÉES

Marie-Louise Marchand
633, chemin de la Grève,
C.P. 169
Petit-Matane G0J 1Y0
(418) 562-9552

B&B	
single	$35-45
double	$50-60
triple	$65
quad.	$80
child	$0-15

Reduced rates: with reservation from Oct. 1 to June 15
Open year round

Number of rooms	3
shared wc	2
shared bathrooms	1

Activities: 🏛 🚲 ⚜ 🚣 🏃

25. MATANE, ST-LÉANDRE   F E ⊘ ⌂ P R14 TA

In the mountains 15 min. from Matane, a fine home with ancestral old-manor decor where lace and antiques recall the past. Poetry and culture by the fireside in homage to Émile Nelligan. Gardens and vegetable patches, gay mornings and gourmet food. Guided walk to the falls with Golden Retriever. Natural spa, visit to the Windmill. Hospitality '97 Regional Grand Prize.

Rte 132, between Ste-Flavie and Matane, to St-Ulric south toward St-Léandre. On paved road, follow the 6 blue "Gîte Le Jardin de Givre" tourist signposts.

B&B
LE JARDIN DE GIVRE

Ginette Couture and
Gérald Tremblay,
3263, route du Peintre
Matane, St-Léandre G0J 2V0
tel/fax (418) 737-4411
www.bbcanada.com/866.html
bbran@globetrotter.qc.ca

B&B	
single	$40-50
double	$50-55-60
triple	$65
quad.	$80
child	$0-10

Taxes extra VS

Open year round

Number of rooms	5
rooms with private bath	1
shared bathrooms	2

Activities: 🏛 🚣 🏃 🚲 🐴

---

26. MATANE, ST-LUC   F E P 🚗 🐕 R8 TA

Gaspésie Excellence Prize 1997-98. At 200 m. in altitude, away from Rte. 132, 5 min. from Matane. View over the river and the region. Newly built house, therapeutic bath, hearty breakfast, European coffee, near salmon pass, Matane/Baie-Comeau/Godbout ferry. Winter sports, beaver pond: 8 km, maple grove: 20 km. Mini-cruise. Introduction to winter sports.
In Matane, opposite Jean Coutu, Ave. Jacques-Cartier to lights, left on Ave. St-Rédempteur, continue for about 7 km. Watch for blue "Gîte Le Panorama 1 km" signpost, continue for 100 m., left on Ch. Lebel, 700 m.

B&B
LE PANORAMA

Marie-Jeanne and Hector Fortin
23, chemin Lebel
St-Luc-de-Matane G0J 2X0
tel/fax (418) 562-1100

B&B	
single	$35
double	$50
triple	$70
quad.	$80
child	$10-15

VS

Open year round

Number of rooms	3
rooms in semi-basement	1
shared bathrooms	2

Activities: 🏃 🚣 🎿 🛷 🐴

---

27. MATANE, ST-RENÉ   F e ♿ 🍽 P R10 TA

Goat farm located halfway between Matane and Amqui, by the road that led to the village of St-Nil, closed in the 1970s. Enjoy an array of outdoor activities while enjoying the natural surroundings. Stay in the den of the settler who left his mark at the summits of these mountains... Your hosts await you.
Farm stay p 37.

From Matane: take the Rte 195 South. At the St-René church, drive 5.5 km and turn left on Route 10e and 11e Rang, then continue for 6.2 km. Welcome to the Gîte des Sommets.

B&B
GÎTE DES SOMMETS

Marie-Hélène Mercier and
Louis-Philippe Bédard
161, Route 10e and 11e Rang
Saint-René-de-Matane G0J 3E0
(418) 224-3497
jeani@globetrotter.net

	B&B	MAP
single	$30	$37
double	$45	$59
triple	$65	$86
child	$12	$17

Open year round

Number of rooms	3
shared bathrooms	2

Activities: 🏛 🏃 🎿 🏃

28. MATANE, ST-ULRIC

F e P R5 TA

In Matane, see fishers at work, stock up on shrimp and visit the salmon run. In St-Ulric, take in the river's fresh air, watch superb sunsets and the wind turbines, unique in Canada. Savour home-made jams, admire our magnificent vegetables and flowers garden, all different every year (winner of many prizes). Rooms with sinks. Welcome all.

From Montréal, Hwy 20 East, Rte 132 East. We are 45 km east of Ste-Flavie and 18 km west of Matane. Or from Gaspé, Rte 132 North. From Matane, drive 18 km on Rte 132.

B&B
CHEZ NICOLE

Nicole and René Dubé
3371, Route 132,
St-Ulric-de-Matane
Matane G0J 3H0
tel/fax (418) 737-4896

B&B	
single	$35
double	$45-50
triple	$55
quad.	$65
child	$10

Open year round

Number of rooms	3
rooms with sink	3
shared wc	1
shared bathrooms	1

Activities: 🦪 🍴 🎿 🛷 🎿

29. MONT-JOLI

F e P 🛏 🐕 R2 TA

Our house, located on a plateau 2 km from Mont-Joli and 7 km from Ste-Flavie, offers a magnificent view of the river. Just minutes from the Jardins de Métis, the Atlantic Salmon Interpretation Centre and good restaurants. Lodging in winter with skiing right nearby. We'll be waiting with a hearty breakfast and traditional accordion music.

From Québec City, Hwy 20 East, Rte 132 East. Drive 2 km from Mont-Joli. Or from the Vallée de la Matapédia, our home is located before Mont-Joli, 5 min from the shopping centre.

B&B
GÎTE BELLEVUE

Nicole and Émilien Cimon
2332, rue Principale,
route 132
Mont-Joli G5H 3N6
(418) 775-2402

B&B	
single	$40
double	$50
triple	$65
quad.	$75
child	$10

Reduced rates: Sep. 1 to May 31
Open year round

Number of rooms	3
shared bathrooms	2

Activities: 🏛 🏖 🍴 🎿 🚲

30. MONT-JOLI

F P 🛏 R1

Come share in the calm of the countryside and the history surrounding the first schoolhouse of the region without going much out of your way. Warm welcome and splendid view of the St-Laurent from the hills. Enjoy the grandiose sunsets in a unique decor and atmosphere.

From Québec City, Hwy 20 East, Rte 132 East. In Ste-Flavie take 132 East to Mont-Joli for 7 km until St-Joseph-de-Lepage. Right before the church, 2nd house on the right.

B&B
GÎTE LA VIEILLE ÉCOLE

Jeannine Migneault
90, du Lac
Mont-Joli, G5H 3P2
(418) 775-3504
fax (418) 739-3343

B&B	
single	$40
double	$50
triple	$65
quad.	$75
child	$10

Reduced rates: Sep. 1 to May 31
Open year round

Number of rooms	2
shared bathrooms	1
rooms with sink	1

Activities: 🏛 🦪 🏖 🍴 🎿

B&Bs AND INNS

31. NEWPORT

F | e | Ⓢ | ⛵ | P | 🚗 | R.4 | TA

A B&B to discover! Once the estate of a wealthy merchant, the property includes the most beautiful beach in the township. Old-fashioned charm, enchanting decor and cosy comfort. Breakfast is a treat! Tucked between Percé and Bonaventure, this is an ideal place for a longer stay. Perfect for quiet nights and days filled with discovery. A memory to cherish. **Advertisement end of this region.**

From Québec City, Hwy 20 East, Rte 132 East to Newport, 1 km west of the church. House located on the seaside, facing a rest area.

B&B
AUBERGE LES DEUX ÎLOTS

Guylaine Michel and
André Lambert
207, Route 132, C.P. 223
Newport G0C 2A0
(418) 777-2801
fax (418) 777-4719

B&B	
single	$40-55
double	$50-65
triple	$75-80
quad.	$90-95
child	$5-10

Taxes extra VS

Reduced rates: Sep. 1 to June 30
Open year round

Number of rooms	5
rooms with private bath	2
shared wc	1
shared bathrooms	1

Activities: 🏛 ⚜ 🚶 🏇 🏊

32. NEW RICHMOND

F | E | P | 🚗 | R.5 | TA

Experience the atmosphere of a cosy Victorian and its exceptional view of Baie-des-Chaleurs. A large veranda looks out at the sea and the mountains. Spacious and comfortable rooms. The seashore is accessible!

From Québec City, Hwy 20 East, Rte 132 East to New Richmond. At the intersection of Rte 299, turn right, drive 5 km to Boul. Perron. Or from Percé, once in New Richmond, turn left on Boul. Perron.

B&B
AUBERGE L'ÉTOILE DE MER

Diane Bourdages and
Jacques Veillette
256, Perron ouest
New Richmond G0C 2B0
(418) 392-6246
www.bbcanada.com/3134.html
etoilebb@globetrotter.net

B&B	
single	$40
double	$55-60
triple	$70-75
quad.	$80-85
child	$10

Taxes extra VS

Open year round

Number of rooms	5
rooms with private bath	1
shared bathrooms	2

Activities: 🏛 ⛵ ⚜ 🚶 🚴

33. NEW RICHMOND

F | e | Ⓢ | 🚗 | P | R1 | TA

Ancestral house surrounded by flowers, nestled in a peaceful spot in the heart Baie-des-Chaleurs. Your jovial and sociable hostess serves hearty breakfasts and brightens up your stay with suggestions of things to do in the maritime environment. Sailboat outings, hikes, everything possible to make your stay here an unforgettable one.

From Québec City: Hwy 20 East, Rte 132 Est to New Richmond. Right at 3rd flashing light on Ch. St-Edgar, 1.7 km, left on Ave. Leblanc, 150 m. From Percé: Rte 132, left at 1st flashing light on Ch. St-Edgar, 1.7 km.

B&B
GÎTE DE LA MAISON LEVESQUE

Vyola A. Levesque
180, Avenue Leblanc
New-Richmond G0C 2B0
(418) 392-5267
toll free 1-888-405-5267
fax (418) 392-6948
blaster@globetrotter.qc.ca
www.agricotours.qc.ca

B&B	
single	$30
double	$45-50
triple	$65
child	$5-10

Reduced rates: Sep. 1 to May 31
Open year round

Number of rooms	3
shared wc	2
shared bathrooms	2

Activities: 🐚 ⚜ 🚶 🚴 🏇

34. NEW RICHMOND

| F | E |  | P | R2 | TA |

Amidst beautiful white birch on the Baie-des-Chaleurs, our cottage awaits you with a warm welcome. Wooded paths, access to the beach and peaceful surroundings are yours to enjoy.

From Québec City, Hwy 20 East, Rte 132 East to New Richmond. At the intersection of Rte 299, turn right, drive 3.5 km to Rue de la Plage and turn right. Or from Percé, turn left at same intersection.

B&B
GÎTE «LES BOULEAUX»

Patricia Fallu and
Charles Gauthier
142, de la Plage
New Richmond G0C 2B0
(418) 392-4111
fax (418) 392-6048

B&B	
single	$40
double	$45-60
triple	$60-75
quad.	$85
child	$5-10

VS

Open year round

Number of rooms	4
rooms with sink	3
rooms in basement	2
shared bathrooms	2

Activities:

---

35. NEW RICHMOND

| F | P | R2.8 |

We are located in an attractive little corner of New-Richmond. Relaxation, serenity, home-made breakfasts. The sea and the mountains are also on the menu. Fishing, hiking, cultural and outdoor activities. Our house is your house. I will be waiting for you.

From Québec City, Hwy 20 East, Rte 132 East to New Richmond. Take Chemin Cyr and Boul. Perron East, turn left, drive 2 km. Or from Percé, Boul. Perron, drive 0.4 km and turn right.

B&B
LA RELÂCHE

Émilienne Bourdages
108, Bellevue, C.P. 36
New Richmond (Cap-Noir)
G0C 1C0
(418) 392-6749

B&B	
single	$30
double	$40-45
child	$10

Open year round

Number of rooms	3
shared bathrooms	2

Activities:

---

36. PERCÉ

| F | e |  | P | R.1 |

"La Rêvasse" is a dream come true. Why else visit Percé? Oh yes, the rock... The advantage of the B&B at the rock is that it is accessible at both low and high tides. Plus, it is inhabited by very friendly people... Thanks for the Percé welcome!' *Sébastien Bret (Lyon-France)* Guided tours of the region available.

From Québec City, Hwy 20 East, Rte 132 East to Percé. Near the Palais de Justice, take Rue St-Michel to #16 on the right. House set back from road.

B&B
À LA RÊVASSE

Brenda Cain and
William Lambert
16, St-Michel, C.P. 281
Percé G0C 2L0
tel/fax (418) 782-2102
(418) 782-2980
revasse@globetrotter.net

B&B	
single	$40-45
double	$50-55
triple	$70
quad.	$85
child	$10

Open: May 1 to Oct. 15

Number of rooms	4
rooms with sink	3
shared bathrooms	2

Activities:

B&Bs AND INNS

37. PERCÉ

F E P 🚗 🦮 R.5 TA

We are located in the centre of the village, behind the church. Everything is very quiet, especially at night. Spacious solarium, large rooms, home-made breakfasts. Here you will be able to park the car, relax and go for a walk. Everything is within reach: Île Bonaventure, Percé rock, mountains, restaurants, boutiques. We are from Percé, live hear year-round and can help you plan your activities.

Rte 132 East to the village of Percé. Take rue du Cap Barré to the last house (# 44), with the grey-blue wood siding.

B&B
GÎTE DU MONT STE-ANNE

Ginette Gagné and Michel Méthot
44, Cap Barré
Percé GOC 2L0
tel/fax (418) 782-2739

B&B	
single	$45
double	$55
triple	$70
child	$15

VS

Reduced rates: June 1to June 24 and Sep.15 to Oct. 15
Open: June 1 to Oct. 15

Number of rooms	8
rooms with sink	4
rooms in basement	2
shared bathrooms	2

Activities: 🏛 ⚓ 🐚 ⚲ 🚶

38. PERCÉ

F E 🚫 P R.1 TA

We invite you to discover the charms of an ancestral house and of a rustic barn, right in the heart of Percé. We offer you: beautiful cozy rooms, nourishing breakfasts, lounge with fireplace, reading corner, solarium, terrace and balconies. Tennis court nearby. 5 min walk from the Percé Rock. **Country Home p 138.**

From Québec City, Hwy 20 East, Rte 132 East. In the village centre, facing court house, next to the sea.

INN
LA MAISON ROUGE

Stéphanie Grégoire and Jean-Baptiste Silla
125, Route 132 Ouest
Percé GOC 2L0
(418) 782-2227

B&B	
single	$48
double	$60-67
triple	$75-82
quad.	$90-97
child	$15

Taxes extra VS

Open: June 1 to Sep. 30

Number of rooms	10
shared bathrooms	4

Activities: 🏛 ⚓ 🐚 ⚲ 🚶

39. PERCÉ, STE-THÉRÈSE

F e P 🐕 R1.5 TA

Enjoy a stay in this picturesque fishing village. To better serve our guests, we offer them a choice between relaxing idleness and package deals, including whale-watching excursions, a guided tour of Percé, deep-sea fishing, a tour of Île Bonaventure. Package rates available upon request.

15 min from Percé, Rte 132 W. In Ste-Thérèse, you will see the windmill mid-way between the pier and church; facing the Bria restaurant.

B&B
GÎTE DU MOULIN À VENT

Jeannine Desbois
247, Route 132, C.P. 10
Ste-Thérèse-de-Gaspé
Percé-Ste-Thérèse
GOC 3B0
(418) 385-4922
tel/fax (418) 385-3103

B&B	
single	$35
double	$50
child	$10

Open: May 1 to Sep. 30

Number of rooms	3
shared bathrooms	2

Activities: 🏛 ⚓ 🐚 🚶 🚲

40. PETITE-VALLÉE

F e 🏠 P 🚗 ✕ R5 TA

On a long headland, set back from Route 132 and one hour (70 km) from Forillon Park, our centenary house opens its doors to offer you a family welcome and traditional cuisine, featuring fish and seafood. New glassed-in dining-room with superb sea view. 20th anniversary surprise! **Country home p 135. See colour photos.**

From Québec, Hwy 20 East, Rte 132 East to Petite-Vallée. At the entrance to the village, after the "Coukerie", take the first street on the left. At the fork, stay left.

INN
LA MAISON LEBREUX

Denise Lebreux
2, rue Longue Pointe,
Petite-Vallée GOE 1Y0
(418) 393-2662
tel/fax (418) 393-3105

	B&B	PAM
single	$40-45	$55-60
double	$50-60	$80-90
triple	$65	$110
quad.	$80	$140
child	$10	$20

Taxes extra VS IT MC

Open year round

Number of rooms	8
rooms with sink	4
shared bathrooms	3

Activities: 🦞 ⛵ 👤 🚤 🏃

41. ST-ALEXIS-DE-MATAPÉDIA

F E 🏠 ⊗ P 🚗 R1.5 TA

Enjoy a singular stay on natural plateaus. Original house. Vast woodlands, trails, large heated in-ground pool under a dome. Activities, local history. Around: vistas, salmon fishing, river canoeing, ski-doo, Fort Listuguj Circa 1760 historical site. Very warm welcome.

85 km from Carleton. Enter Matapédia, cross bridge, turn right twd St-Alexis, 10 km. From stop, straight for, 1.4 km. 100 km from Amqui, St-Alexis bridge, via St-Benoît, 10 km.

B&B
AUX BOIS D'AVIGNON

Laura Chouinard
171, Rustico Nord
St-Alexis-de-Matapédia
GOJ 2E0
(418) 299-2537
tel/fax (418) 299-2111
boisdavi@globetrotter.qc.ca

B&B	
single	$44
double	$52
triple	$60
quad	$70
child	$9

Taxes extra

Reduced rates: Oct. 1 to June 1
Open year round

Number of rooms	3
shared bathrooms	2

Activities: 👤 🚴 🚤 🎣 🏃

42. ST-OMER

F ⊗ P 🚗 R1 TA

Our home is your home. Small village between sea and mountains, with 1,300 residents, 10 min from Carleton. Quiet house ringed by trees, 91 m from Route 132; patio, porch, backyard, parking. 5 min from the beach, café, snackbars, 20 min from Parc Miguasha, salmon fishing. Restful rooms. Good breakfast. A true Gaspé welcome awaits you.

From Québec City, Hwy 20 East and Rte 132 East to St-Omer. 1.5 km after Aux Flots Bleus campground. From Percé, 1 km from St-Omer church.

B&B
GÎTE LE ROITELET

Lucina Quinn and
Maurice Leblanc
108, route St-Louis
St-Omer GOC 2Z0
(418) 364-7436
fax (418) 364-6049

B&B	
single	$35-40
double	$50-55
triple	$65-70.50
quad.	$10-15

VS

Reduced rates: Sep. 1 to June 30
Open year round

Number of rooms	5
shared bathrooms	2

Activities: 🦞 🍴 👤 🚤 🏃

B&Bs AND INNS

43. STE-ANGÈLE-DE-MÉRICI

F E P R.5 TA

Located in the heart of the Métis river basin in a small "back-country" village, the ideal place for those touring the Gaspésie. Your stay here will be among your loveliest holiday memories. Right near river salmon and trout fishing. 10 to 20 km from golf course, Atlantic Salmon Interpretation Centre, Jardins de Métis, the river and the airport. In-ground pool on site.

From Québec City: Hwy 20, Rte 132 East. In Ste-Flavie, eastward, 12 km past Mont-Joli. In the village of Ste-Angèle, right on Boul.-de-la-Vallée, next to the church hall.

B&B
LA GUIMONTIÈRE

Jeanne-Mance Guimont
515, av. Bernard Levesque
Ste-Angèle-de-Mérici G0J 2H0
(418) 775-5542

B&B	
single	$40
double	$60
triple	$80
quad.	$100
child	$15

Reduced rates: Sep. 1 to May 31
Open year round

Number of rooms	3
shared bathrooms	1

Activities:

44. STE-ANNE-DES-MONTS

F e P R1 TA

Why Ste-Anne-des-Monts? Well, of course to discover the magnificent Parc de la Gaspésie, Mont Albert and Mont Jacques Cartier. Golf, Explorama, and a warm welcome from the locals. 10% reductions for stays of three days or more. Rooms in the basement have separate entrance.

From Québec City, Hwy 20 East, Rte 132 East to Ste-Anne-des-Monts. Turn left before the bridge. At the stop sign turn left on 1st Avenue. Beige brick house, 3rd on left.

B&B
CHEZ MARTHE-ANGÈLE

Marthe-Angèle Lepage
268, 1re Avenue Ouest,
C.P. 3159
Ste-Anne-des-Monts G0E 2G0
tel/fax (418) 763-2692

B&B	
single	$33-35
double	$48-50
triple	$65-07
quad.	$80
child	$7-12

Open year round

Number of rooms	5
rooms with sink	3
rooms in basement	3
shared bathrooms	3

Activities:

45. STE-ANNE-DES-MONTS

F E P R3 TA

Sept. 2, 1998
"Dear Julie,
Our experience with you has truly enriched our journey. You have shared your home with us in every sense, and your extreme warmth and generosity will always be remembered as the highlight of our visit to the Gaspé. The breakfast alone was worth the trip! We look forward to sharing your passions, good and kindness again!" (Clients)

From Rimouski: Rte 132 Est. 6.7 km past the Cap-Chat church. Ste-Anne-des-Monts. White house with red roof.

B&B
GÎTE LES 2 COLOMBES

Julie Paquet
996, boul. Ste-Anne-Ouest,
C.P. 572
Ste-Anne-des-Monts G0E 2G0
(418) 763-3756

B&B	
single	$35
double	$50
triple	$75
child	$10

Reduced rates: Oct. 1 to May 31
Open year round

Number of rooms	4
rooms with sink	1
shared wc	1
shared bathrooms	2

Activities:

46. STE-ANNE-DES-MONTS

F | e | P | 🛏 | 🐕 | R1 | TA

What past guests have enjoyed in our home: our chatty breakfasts of home-made pancakes, bread and jams; a beautiful and calm location; close proximity to all attractions, but far from traffic; clean and comfortable rooms. Our guests tell us our welcome makes them feel like they're with family.

From Québec City, Hwy 20 East, Rte 132 East, at the intersection of Rte 299 (Rte du Parc) drive 1 km, turn left onto the 5e Rue Est. If you're on 1e Avenue (Explorama, église) drive twd Gaspé, we're 1 km away, on the right.

B&B
SOUS LA BONNE ÉTOILE

Denis Béchard
30, 5ᵉ Rue Est, C.P. 1132
Ste-Anne-des-Monts
G0E 2G0
tel/fax (418) 763-3402

B&B	
single	$40
double	$50
triple	$65
quad.	$80
child	$5-15

VS

Reduced rates: Nov. 1 to Apr. 30
Open year round

Number of rooms	4
rooms with sink	1
rooms in semi-basement	4
shared bathrooms	2

Activities: 🏛 👤 🚶 🎿 ⛷

47. STE-ANNE-DES-MONTS, TOURELLE

F | E | P | 🚗 | R.5

At the heart of the Gaspé peninsula, outdoor terrace from which to admire marine mammals, superb sunsets and fishing village. Discover Parc de la Gaspésie, Mont Albert, Mont Jacques-Cartier, Explorama, walking by the river. One room with private bathroom with whirlpool tub. Copious breakfast. 10% reduction for 3 nights or more. Welcome.

From Québec City, Hwy 20 East, Rte 132 East to Tourelle. From the rest area, drive 0.2 km, turn left, white house.

B&B
AU COURANT DE LA MER

Bibiane Miville and
Rino Cloutier
3, Belvédère, C.P. 191
Tourelle G0E 2J0
tel/fax (418) 763-5440
For reservation only:
1-800-230-6709
from 5 pm to 11 pm

B&B	
single	$35-50
double	$50-60
triple	$65
quad.	$75
child	$7-12

VS

Open: Mar. 1 to Nov. 30

Number of rooms	5
rooms with private bath	1
shared bathrooms	3
rooms with sink	1
rooms in basement	1

Activities: 🏛 🦆 🚲 👤 🏇

48. STE-ANNE-DES-MONTS, TOURELLE

E | e | 🚫 | P | R4 | TA

10 minutes from Ste-Anne-des-Monts. Skiing, excursion, don't miss the Parc de la Gaspésie! Sample some delicious apple crepes while admiring the sea from our flowery terrasse. Enjoy the intimacy and the rustica and romantic ambiance of our home.

From Québec City, Hwy 20 East Located on Rte 132. 1 hour from Matane. 11 km from Tim Horton's in Ste-Anne-des-Monts. 3.5 km east of Tourelle church.

B&B
GÎTE DE LA NOUVELLE-FRANCE

Danielle Martin and
Jean-Guy Brisebois
203, boul. Perron Est
Ste-Anne-des-Monts, Tourelle
G0E 2J0
(418) 763-3338

B&B	
single	$45
double	$50-55
triple	$65-70
child	$10

Taxes extra VS

Reduced rates: Jan. 1 to Apr. 30: packages for groups of skiers
Open year round

Number of rooms	4
rooms with private bath	4

Activities: 🏛 🚲 👤 ⛷

49. STE-ANNE-DES-MONTS, TOURELLE

`F` `e` `⛴` `P` `🐕` `R3.5` `TA`

Welcome to our house at the foot of a lovely mountain by the "sea". You can walk along the shore to Tourelle and watch the fishermen in the harbour. Our breakfasts, complete with crepes and a selection of home-made preserves, go over big with guests - as does our Gaspé-style table talk. You'll feel right at home in our house.

From Québec City: Hwy 20 East, Rte 132 East to Tourelle. Drive 2 km past the church (we are located 8 min from the intersection of the 299 - Parc de la Gaspésie Sainte-Anne-des-Monts).

B&B
GÎTE DE LA TOUR

Elise Dupuis and
Pierre Paul Labrie
151, boul. Perron Est C.P. 183
Tourelle G0E 2J0
tel/fax (418) 763-2802

B&B	
single	$35
double	$50
triple	$60
child	$5-10

VS

Reduced rates: Apr., May, Oct., Dec.
Open: Apr. 1 to Dec. 15

Number of rooms	3
shared bathrooms	2

Activities: 🏛 ⚜ 🎣 🛷 🐟

50. STE-ANNE-DES-MONTS, TOURELLE

`F` `E` `🏊` `P` `🚗` `R.5` `TA`

We offer three comfortable rooms, relaxing family ambiance, exceptional setting, fishing village, superb sea views and sunsets. 30 kilometres from Parc de la Gaspésie, a veritable sea mountains. The only place in Québec where caribou, white-tailed deer and moose co-habit. Come dream with us.

From Montréal, Hwy 20 E., Rte 132 E. to Tourelle. From Ste-Anne-des-Monts, at junction of Rte 299 (Rte du Parc), 4 km on Rte 132 E. twd Gaspé. On Rte 132, on the right.

B&B
GÎTE DU PIONNIER
DE TOURELLE

Doris Therrien
87, boul. Perron Ouest,
C.P. 157
Tourelle G0E 2J0
(418) 763-7254

B&B	
single	$35
double	$45
triple	$60
quad.	$75
child	$10

Reduced rates: Oct. 1 to May 31
Open year round

Number of rooms	3
shared wc	1
shared bathrooms	1

Activities: 🏛 ⚜ 🎣 🛷 🎿

51. STE-FLAVIE

`F` `e` `🚭` `🏊` `P` `🚗` `R.1` `TA`

A relaxing place for a break by the sea in a setting of rare beauty! Vast grounds, partly wooded. Recharge your batteries in facilities near waterfalls along a creek. Jardins de Métis, 5 km; art centre, 0.7 km; golf course, 12 km; snowmobiling, 6 km. Large family-sized room available.

From Québec City, Hwy 20 East, Rte 132 East to Ste-Flavie. Drive to 571 Route de la Mer.

B&B
AUX CHUTES

Nicole R. and Jocelyn Bélisle
571, route de la Mer,
Ste-Flavie G0J 2L0
(418) 775-9432
fax (418) 775-5747
www.bbcanada.
com/1866.html

B&B	
single	$38-45
double	$45-65
triple	$55-75
quad.	$70-85
child	$10

Reduced rates: Oct. 15 to Apr.15
Open year round

Number of rooms	5
rooms with sink	1
shared bathrooms	2

Activities: 🏛 🐚 ⚓ ⚜ 🚤

52. STE-FLAVIE

F E 🚫 P 🚗 R.2

Come and experience traditional Gaspé hospitality in an ancestral home rich with the echoes of four generations of the same family. Magnificent sunsets over the St-Laurent will cast a spell. 6 km from the famous Métis gardens and just a few steps from excellent restaurants.

Take Rte 132 East twd Gaspé, 24 km beyond Rimouski, and 0.4 km beyond the tourist information centre of Ste-Flavie.

B&B
LA MARÉE BLEUE

Jacqueline Paquet and
Peter Innis
411, route-de-la-Mer
Ste-Flavie G0J 2L0
(418) 775-7801
innisp@ri.cgocable.ca

B&B	
single	$50
double	$55
child	$10

VS IT

Reduced rates: Sep. 15 to June 15
Open year round

Number of rooms	4
shared bathrooms	2

Activities: 🏛 🍴 🐎 🎣 🚲

53. STE-FLAVIE

F e P 🚗 🐕 R1 TA

I await you by the river at the gateway to the Gaspé region amongst the charm and comfort of a wooden house. Here, the day starts with the sound of waves lapping on the shore, warms up with the pleasant company and comes to a close with the colourful spectacle of the sunset.

From Québec City, Hwy 20 East, Rte 132 East to Ste-Flavie. 5 km past the church, driving east along the shore. Or from Gaspé, Rte 132 West. 60 km from Matane.

B&B
LA QUÉBÉCOISE

Cécile Wedge
705, de la Mer, route 132 Est
Ste-Flavie G0J 2L0
(418) 775-2898
(418) 775-3209
fax (418) 775-9793

B&B	
single	$40
double	$50-55

Reduced rates: Oct. 1 to May 31
Open year round

Number of rooms	3
shared wc	1
shared bathrooms	1

Activities: 🏛 🍴 ⛵ 🎣 🏃

B&Bs AND INNS

54. CAP-CHAT

F | E | �car | P | 🏊 | R.3 | M.3

My dream home is right on the beach and I would be even happier to share it with you. For a dream vacation, I offer charming little cottages with the musk of real wood and the salt air wafting in from the open sea. I will share these great moments with you. You will be treated to sunsets, passing boats and whales in the peace of the countryside. **Inn p 117, no 4.**

From Québec City: Hwy 20 East, Rte 132 East to Cap-Chat. At the west entrance to Cap-Chat, 3 km from the windmill and 2 km from the Centre d'Interprétation du Vent and de la Mer, on your right.

COUNTRY HOME
LA PETITE NORMANDIE

Jean Ouellet
239 B, Notre-Dame Ouest,
rte 132
Cap-Chat GOJ 1E0
tel/fax (418) 786-5751
www.bbcanada.com/323.html

No. houses	3
No. rooms	1-2
No. people	2-6
WEEK-SUMMER	$350-900
DAY-SUMMER	$50-130

VS MC IT

Reduced rates: Sep. 15 to June 30
Open: May 15 to Oct. 31

Activities: 🏛 🐾 🚶 🐎 🎿

---

55. CAP-D'ESPOIR, PERCÉ

F | e | ♿ | P | 🏊 | R5 | M.5 | TA

Come relax on the beach and be lulled to sleep by the sound of the waves. Share stories by the fire on the beach. Three pleasantly fitted-out cottages (one on ground floor, one upstairs) with a view of Ile Bonaventure are available. 10 minutes from a great attraction: Percé. Welcome.

From Québec City, Hwy 20 E., Rte 132 E., located 12 km west of Percé. Look up and you will see Ile Bonaventure.

COUNTRY HOME
CHALETS DE LA PLAGE

Jason Pitre
mailing address:
1233, Principale, C.P. 26
Val-d'Espoir G0C 3G0
(418) 782-2181
fax (418) 782-5214

No. houses	3
No. rooms	2
No. people	4-8
WEEK-SUMMER	$600-650
DAY-SUMMER	$100

Reduced rates: May 1 to June 23, Sep. 1 to Oct. 31
Open: May 1 to Oct. 31

Activities: 🏛 🚤 ⛵ 🚶

---

56. PERCÉ

F | E | 🚫 | P | 🏊 | R1 | M1

La Maison Laberge is a typical Gaspé house located on Cap Mont-Joli. The house affords magnificent panoramas of the ledge known as the Trois Sœurs, which overlooks Cap Barré. To the east, the massive wall that is the Rocher Percé can be seen rising up behind Cap Mont-Joli. **B&B in Bas-St-Laurent section, p 57 no 28.**

From Québec City: Hwy 20 East, Rte 132 East. Located above the village on a dead end road, on the cap Mont-Joli, on the ocean side.

COUNTRY HOME
LA MAISON LABERGE

Bertrand Daraiche and
Thérèse Ng Wai
232, Route 132 Est
Percé G0C 2L0
(418) 782-2816
(514) 393-1417
fax (514) 393-9444
www.total.net/~chq
chq@total.net

No. houses	1
No. rooms	2
No. people	6
WEEK-SUMMER	$700
DAY-SUMMER	$125

Open: June 1 to Sep.30

Activities: 🏛 🚤 ⛵ 🐾 🚲

57. PETITE-VALLÉE

F e P R5 M1

On a long headland, set back from Route 132 and one hour (70 km) from Forillon Park, our centenary house opens its doors to offer you a family welcome and traditional cuisine, featuring fish and seafood. New glassed-in dining-room with superb sea view. 20th anniversary surprise! **Inn p 129. See colour photos.**

From Québec, Hwy 20 East, Rte 132 East to Petite-Vallée. At the entrance to the village, after the "Coukerie", take the first street on the left. At the fork, stay left.

COUNTRY HOME
LA MAISON LEBREUX

Denise Lebreux
2, Longue Pointe
Petite-Vallée G0E 1Y0
(418) 393-2662
tel/fax (418) 393-3105

No. houses	4
No. rooms	1-2
No. people	2-4
WEEK-SUMMER	$525
WEEK-WINTER	$400
DAY-SUMMER	$80
DAY-WINTER	$60

Taxes extra MC VS IT

Reduced rates: Sep. 16 to May 14
Open year round

Activities:

---

58. ST-ALEXIS-DE-MATAPÉDIA

F E P R1 M4 TA

Why not holiday in Gaspésie on a family-run dairy farm? Enjoy an exciting, edifying stay: fully equipped house, animals, forest and four families of Acadian descent. Stream fishing, swimming, canoeing, cycling, packages available. Guided farm tour, small game hunting, X-country skiing, sugar shack, camping.

From Rimouski, Rte 132 E., 160 km. After St-Alexis bridge, 5 km, Rang St-Benoît. From Pointe-à-la-Croix, to Matapédia after the bridge. Right, 16 km, right on Rang St-Benoît.

COUNTRY HOME
LA P'TITE MAISON
DES LEBLANC

René Leblanc
153 A, St-Benoit
St-Alexis-de-Matapédia
G0J 2E0
(418) 299-2106
tel/fax (418) 299-2443

No. houses	1
No. rooms	3
No. people	6-8
WEEK-SUMMER	$400-500
WEEK-WINTER	$300-400
W/E-SUMMER	$80-100
W/E-WINTER	$60-85
DAY-SUMMER	$30-50
DAY-WINTER	$25-40

Reduced rates: Oct. 15 to May 15
Open year round

Activities:

FARM ACTIVITIES

Farm stay:

COUNTRY HOMES

ÎLES-DE-LA-MADELEINE

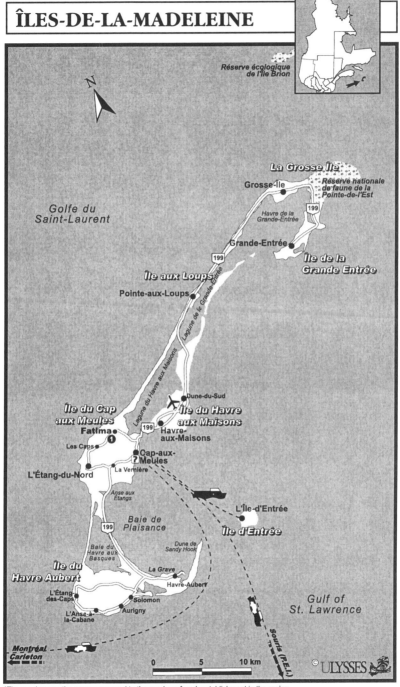

Réserve écologique
de l'Île Brion

La Grosse Île

Grosse-Île

Réserve nationale
de faune de la
Pointe-de-l'Est

Golfe du
Saint-Laurent

Havre de la
Grande-Entrée

199

Grande-Entrée

199

Île de la
Grande Entrée

Île aux Loups

Pointe-aux-Loups

Lagune de la Grande-Entrée

Lagune du Havre aux Maisons

Dune-du-Sud

Île du Cap
aux Meules

Île du Havre
aux Maisons

Fatima

199

Havre-
aux-Maisons

Les Caps

L'Étang-du-Nord

Cap-aux-
Meules

La Vernière

Anse aux
Étangs

L'Île-d'Entrée

Baie de
Plaisance

199

Île d'Entrée

Baie du
Havre aux
Basques

Dune de
Sandy Hook

Île du
Havre Aubert

La Grave

L'Étang-
des-Caps

Havre-Aubert

Solomon

L'Anse-à-
la-Cabane

Aurigny

Gulf of
St. Lawrence

Souris (P.E.I.)

Montréal
Carleton

0   5   10 km

© ULYSSES

*The numbers on the map correspond to the number of each establishment in the region.

1. FATIMA

F e 🚫 🚗 P R1.5

Take advantage of a real "Made-linot" family's hospitality. Wooded area, calm, near amenities, in a residential neighbourhood of the island of Cap-aux-Meules. Generous breakfast, comfortable rooms, 1 km from the beach. Friendly atmosphere and warm welcome. Non-smokers only.

From the ferry, Rte 199 East, Chemin Marconi to Chemin les Caps. In Fatima, near the church take Chemin de l'Hôpital. Turn left on Chemin Thorne.

GÎTE

Blandine and Thomas Thorne
56, chemin E. Thorne
Fatima G0B 1G0
(418) 986-3006
ilesdelamadeleine.com/
b + b/index.htm

B&B	
single	$40
double	$45
triple	$55
child	$10

Open : May 1 to Nov. 30

Number of rooms	3
shared bathrooms	1
shared wc	1

Activities: 🦆 ⛵ 🐟 🚲 🐎

B&Bs AND INNS

LANAUDIÈRE

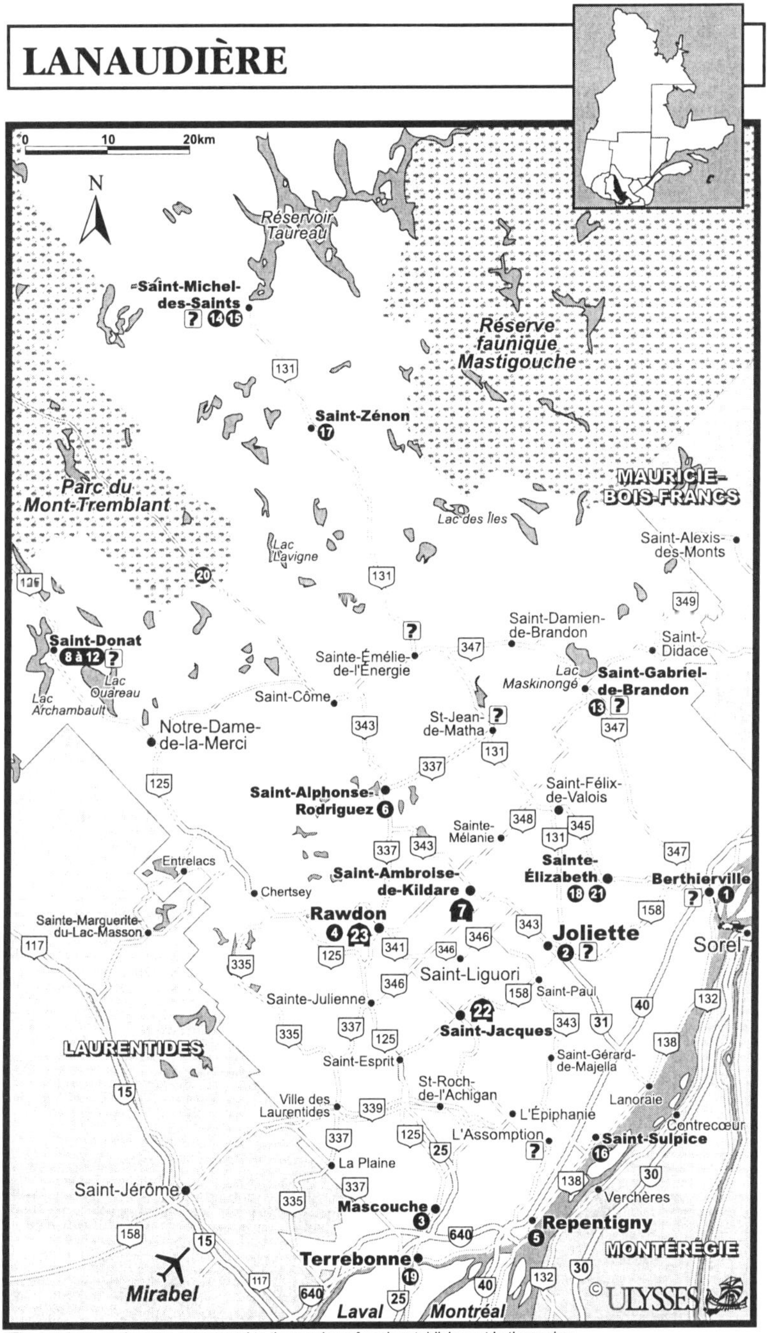

0 10 20km
N
Réservoir Taureau
Saint-Michel-des-Saints
14 15
Réserve faunique Mastigouche
131
Saint-Zénon
17
Parc du Mont-Tremblant
MAURICIE-BOIS-FRANCS
Lac des Îles
Saint-Alexis-des-Monts
Lac Lavigne
20
131
125
349
Saint-Damien-de-Brandon
Saint-Donat
8 à 12
Sainte-Émélie-de-l'Énergie
347
Saint-Didace
Lac Ouareau
Lac Archambault
Lac Maskinongé
Saint-Gabriel-de-Brandon
13
Saint-Côme
343
St-Jean-de-Matha
347
Notre-Dame-de-la-Merci
131
337
125
Saint-Alphonse-Rodriguez
6
Saint-Félix-de-Valois
348
345
Sainte-Mélanie
131
337
343
347
Entrelacs
Saint-Ambroise-de-Kildare
Sainte-Élizabeth
18 21
Berthierville
1
Chertsey
7
Rawdon
4 23
158
Sainte-Marguerite-du-Lac-Masson
343
346
Joliette
2
117
125
341
346
Sorel
335
Saint-Liguori
346
158
Saint-Paul
Sainte-Julienne
22
40
132
335
337
125
Saint-Jacques
343
31
LAURENTIDES
138
Saint-Esprit
Saint-Gérard-de-Majella
15
St-Roch-de-l'Achigan
Lanoraie
Ville des Laurentides
339
L'Épiphanie
Contrecœur
337
125
L'Assomption
Saint-Sulpice
25
16
La Plaine
138
30
337
Verchères
Saint-Jérôme
335
Mascouche
3
640
Repentigny
5
158
15
MONTÉRÉGIE
Terrebonne
19
30
117
40
132
Mirabel
640
25
Laval
Montréal
© ULYSSES

*The numbers on the map correspond to the number of each establishment in the region.

1. BERTHIERVILLE F E ✗ P R2 TA

This elegant Victorian house from 1888 offers you a warm welcome. Sylvie greets you with her little sweet treats that will introduce you to the region's culinary secrets. Make the most of this pied-à-terre and enhance your stay with many activities: music, nature, art and culture will convince you to stay more than a day. Impressive breakfast.

From Montréal: Hwy 40 East, toward Berthier, Exit 144. Rte 158 East to 138 East. Drive 1.5 km, turn left just past the bridge, 3rd house on the right.

B&B
MANOIR LATOURELLE

Sylvie Couture, Roxane,
Colette and Jules Rémillard
120, rivière Bayonne Nord
Berthierville J0K 1A0
(450) 836-1129
toll free 1-877-836-1129
fax (450) 836-2365
valremi@autray.net

B&B	
single	$45
double	$60
triple	$80
quad.	$100
child	$15

Taxes extra VS IT

Open year round

Number of rooms	4
shared bathrooms	2

Activities: 🏛 ⚓ ⛵ 🚶 🚲

---

2. JOLIETTE F e 🚗 P ✗ R.5 TA

Lanaudière Excellence Prize 1997-98. Enjoy comfort, human warmth, breakfast, the terrace, flowery garden and the soul of this hundred-year-old house. Located near the town centre, the amphitheatre, art museum, golf courses, bike paths, skating rink or boating on the river. Bikes available.

From Montréal or Québec city, Hwy 40, Exit 122 to Joliette. In Joliette, left on Rue Salaberry (facing the tourist office) to Boul Base de Roc, turn left.

B&B
GÎTE AUX P'TITS OISEAUX

Céline Coutu
722, boul. Base de Roc
Joliette J6E 5P7
(450) 752-1401
fax (450) 759-7836

B&B	
single	$40
double	$50
triple	$75
quad.	$100
child	$10

VS

Open year round

Number of rooms	4
rooms with private bath	1
rooms in basement	1
shared bathrooms	1

Activities: 🏛 ⚓ 🚶 🚲

---

3. MASCOUCHE F e ♿ 🚭 P R3 TA

30 min from downtown Montréal and Mirabel. Large sunny house in the country, surrounded by fields and greenery. Nearby: horseback riding, snowmobile trails. Parking. Warm and courteous welcome. Welcome to La Maison des Érables.

From Québec City, Hwy 40, Hwy 640 West and 25 North. From Montréal, Hwy 15 North, 440 East, 25 North. From Mirabel, Hwy 15 South, 640 East, 25 North. Exit 34, left on St-Henri, 1.5 km.

B&B
LA MAISON DES ÉRABLES

Marie-Paule and Claude Potvin
2124, boul. St-Henri
Mascouche J7K 3C3
(450) 966-9508

B&B	
single	$40
double	$45
triple	$65
quad.	$85
child	$10

Open year round

Number of rooms	3
rooms with sink	3
shared wc	1
shared bathrooms	2

Activities:

4. RAWDON

F | E | 🚗 | P | R.1 | TA

A memorable stay in this Victorian house is offered to wilderness lovers, history buffs, skiers and golfers alike. Enjoy the mansard roofed bedrooms, the 5-course breakfast on the gallery or in the garden, and a guide for your cultural, gastronomic or sporting activities. My goal is your enjoyment! Mimi. Lanaudière Excellence Prize 1995-96.

From Montréal, Hwy 25 N. In St-Esprit take Rte 125 N. In Ste-Julienne take Rte 337 N. to Rawdon (Rue Queen is the main street). Or from Mirabel, Hwy 15 N., exit Rte 158 E. to Ville des Laurentides, then Rte 337 N... From Dorval, Hwy 40

B&B
GÎTE DU CATALPA

Micheline Trudel
3730, rue Queen
Rawdon J0K 1S0
(450) 834-5253
www.did-dftg.com/
catalpa/index.htm
lucienb@francomedia.qc.ca

B&B	
single	$35-50
double	$50-65
triple	$75-90
quad.	$100-115
child	$10

Taxes extra VS

Open year round

Number of rooms	5
rooms with private bath	1
shared bathrooms	2

Activities: 🛶 🧍 🏇 🚲 🎿

---

5. REPENTIGNY

F | E | 🚗 | 🐕 | P | 🚤 | R.5 | TA

Large modern house nestled in a maple grove, near the majestic St-Laurent river. 30 min from Mirabel and Dorval airport. 15 min from the Olympic Stadium and Biodôme. Inground pool, fireplace. Exceptional hospitality, and heavenly breakfasts. Groups of 12 people. **See colour photos.**

Mirabel: Hwy 15 South, 640 East twd Repentigny. Left on Boul. l'Assomption, right on Rue Perreault, left on Rue Gaudreault. Dorval: 520 East, 40 East, Charlemagne 96 East Exit... 138, Claude David, Boul. l'Assomption...

B&B
LA VILLA DES FLEURS

Denise Cloutier
45, rue Gaudreault
Repentigny J6A 1M3
(450) 654-9209
fax (450) 654-1220

B&B	
single	$30-40-50
double	$40-50-60
triple	$50-60-70
quad	$70-80
child	$10

VS AM

Open year round

Number of rooms	5
rooms with sink	3
rooms with private bath	1
shared bathrooms	2

Activities: 🛶🎿 🏇 🚲 🎿

---

6. ST-ALPHONSE-RODRIGUEZ

F | e | 🚫 | 🐕 | P | R2.5

Perched atop the Promontoire cross, in a relaxing setting, overlooking Lac Pierre, this "Swiss chalet" transports you to heaven. On site: fireplace, books, large plot of land. 500 metres away: beach, canoeing. Nearby: snowmobile trail, skiing, hiking, golf, horseback riding, music festival.

From Montréal: Hwy 40 East, Exit 122 twd Joliette, then Rte 343 North. In St-Alphonse: right at Lac Pierre, left on N.-Dame, past the church, Ch. Lac Pierre North. Drive along Rue Promontoire for 2 km.

B&B
LA PETITE CHARTREUSE

Christiane Merle
771, rue Promontoire
St-Alphonse-Rodriguez
J0K 1W0
(450) 883-3961
www.megacom.net/~latitcha
latitcha@megacom.net

B&B	
single	$35-55
double	$50-70
triple	$65-85
quad.	$100

Open year round

Number of rooms	3
rooms with sink	1
shared bathrooms	2

Activities: 🛶 🧍🧍 🚲 🎿

B&Bs AND INNS

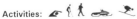

7. ST-AMBROISE-DE-KILDARE

F E P R2 TA

A weekend at school? Why not if it is located on a farm with 400 sheep and offers: rooms with private bathroom, communal kitchen, meeting room, heated in-ground pool and fine cuts of meat. Discover our breeding facilities, our region and wool fleece; we enthusiastically await you. **Country dining p 16.**

From Montréal: Hwy 40 East, Exit 122, Hwy 31 North. Rte 158 West, 1 km, right on Rte 343 North, drive 15 km to St-Ambroise. Left at flashing yellow light on Rang 5, 2 km. Pink-and-white farmhouse on the left!

B&B
BERGERIE DES NEIGES

Desneiges Pepin and
Pierre Juillet
1401, Rang 5
St-Ambroise-de-Kildare
JOK 1C0
tel/fax (450) 756-8395

B&B	
single	$50
double	$65
child	$15

Taxes extra MC

Open year round

Number of rooms	4
rooms with private bath	4

Activities:

8. ST-DONAT

F E P R1 TA

Charm, warmth and comfort await you at this Canadian house right on Lac Archambault, across from the village and a 5 minute's walk via Parc des Pionniers. Private beach, fishing dock, pedal boat, canoe and bike supplied. Motor-boat rental. Mt-Tremblant Park: 12 km away; Mt-Garceau: 3 km away; snowmobile trail: 50 metres away; a few metres from cross-country ski trail; golf course: 4 km away.

From Montréal: Hwy 25 North or 15 North, Exit 89 to St-Donat, left on Ave. du Lac, right on Chemin Bilodeau, right on Chemin La Marguerite.

B&B
AU PETIT CHÂTEAU DU LAC

Johanne Bertrand
59, chemin la Marguerite
St-Donat JOT 2C0
(819) 424-4768

B&B	
single	$50-60
double	$55-65

Open: Dec. 1 to Mar. 31 and from May 1 to Oct. 31

Number of rooms	3
shared bathrooms	2

Activities:

9. ST-DONAT

F E P R.3 TA

An enchanting setting for nature lovers. A trail for cross-country skiing in winter and nature walks, lined with wild mushrooms, in summer, 200 metres from B&B. Many packages offered: golf, ski and cruise. Will soon be offering massage services.

1.2 km from the flashing light on the way into St-Donat. At the first stop sign, turn left and keep to the right. Go to the end of the road and you'll see the "Gîte Nuit de Rêve" sign.

B&B
GÎTE NUIT DE RÊVE

Reine Bernatchez
40, Rivard
St-Donat JOT 2C0
(819) 424-5163

B&B	
single	$50-60
double	$60-70
triple	$90

VS

Open year round

Number of rooms	5
shared bathrooms	2

Activities:

10. ST-DONAT

F E P R1 TA

New, very sunny B&B with 5 spacious, soundproof rooms. Surrounded by lakes, 8 kilometres from Mont-Tremblant park. Lovely village with shops, bars and restaurants. Snowmobile paradise. Specials for groups and extended stays. "Meal" packages. Reduced rates for downhill skiing.
Your hosts, *Louise and Jean.*

From Montréal, Rte 125 North or Hwy 15 North, Exit 89, Rte 329 North to St-Donat. At the lights, in the centre of town, turn right on Allard street, 1 km from church.

B&B
HALTE AUX PETITS OISEAUX

Louise Bigras and
Jean L'Espérance
631, Allard
St-Donat JOT 2C0
tel/fax (819) 424-3064

B&B	
single	$45
double	$65
triple	$90
quad.	$115
child	$10

Taxes extra VS MC AM

Reduced rates: Nov., Apr., May
Open year round

Number of rooms	5
rooms with private bath	5

Activities: 🛶 ⚅ 🚶 🛷 🎿

---

11. ST-DONAT

F e 🚗 P R.1 TA

Near many sports: winter and summer, I have 3 rooms for you, tv, sink, all the conveniences. Comfortable house with wrap-around veranda, close to a large clean lake, with clean beach and park for children. Warm welcome.

From Montréal, Hwy 25 and Rte 125 North to St-Donat. Or Hwy 15 North, Exit 89, Rte 329 North to St-Donat. At the flashing light, Rte 125 North. After the traffic light in the centre of town, at the second stop, left on Rue Bellevue.

B&B
LA MAISON ROBIDOUX

Annie Robidoux
284, rue Bellevue
St-Donat JOT 2C0
(819) 424-2379

B&B	
single	$45
double	$60
triple	$75
quad.	$100
child	$10-15

VS MC

Reduced rates: Nov., Apr., May
and more than 2 nights
Open year round

Number of rooms	4
rooms with sink	4
shared wc	1
shared bathrooms	2

Activities: ⚅ 🐎 🛷 🎿 🏃

---

12. ST-DONAT

F e 🚭 🚗 P 🏊 R2 TA

Ten kilometres from Mont-Tremblant park, at the foot of the ski hills, our modern, air-conditioned lakeside B&B boasts one room with queen-size bed and a family suite with private bathroom, fireplace and fridge. On site: fishing, motor-boat rental, pontoon with guide. Discount for 3 nights or more. Looking forward to welcoming you.

From Montréal: Hwy 25 and Rte 125 North to St-Donat or Hwy 15 North, Exit 89, Rte 329 North to St-Donat. At flashing light, Rte 125 North to traffic lights in the centre of the village; right on Rue Allard,

B&B
LA MAISON SUR LE LAC

Line and Denis Boivin
103, chemin Lac Blanc
St-Donat JOT 2C0
(819) 424-5057

B&B	
single	$50
double	$60-65
triple	$80
quad.	$95
child	$0-15

VS

Reduced rates: 3 nights and more
Open year round

Number of rooms	2
rooms with private bath	1
shared bathrooms	2

Activities: 🏊 🛶 ⚅ 🎿

13. ST-GABRIEL-DE-BRANDON

F E 🚫 🐕 🚗 P ⛵ R.3

Andante! Lento... Here everything is music! The gentle touch of the wind off the lake, the warmth of the hearth for peace and quiet, the spa's caresses for relaxation, Princesse's sweet purring, this B&B's special treats for pleasure! Need a little rest? We are waiting for you!

From Montréal: Hwy 40 East, Exit 144, right on Rte 158 for 2 km, right on Rte 347 North for St-Gabriel to 480 Rue Maskinong (Rte 347 North).

B&B
L'ANDANTE

Lise Vézina and
Claude Perrault
480, rue Maskinongé
St-Gabriel-de-Brandon, J0K 2N0
(450) 835-7658
fax (450) 835-0427
l_andante@yahoo.com

B&B	
single	$40
double	$50

Open year round

Number of rooms	2
shared bathrooms	2

Activities: 🦪 🥾 🚲 🛶 🎿

14. ST-MICHEL-DES-SAINTS

F e 🚗 P ⛵ R1 TA

Crowning the summit of Mont-Roberval, this big country house with chapel was once the home of the founder of Saint-Michel-des-Saints. Several lounges, fireplace, piano, sumptuous period decor, panorama over magnificent Lac Toro, forest trails, river and waterfall... A haven of peace near activities.

2 hours from Montréal: Hwy 40, Exit 122, Hwy 31 twd Joliette and Rte 131 North. In Saint-Michel-des-Saints: left at bowling alley onto Provost and right on Laforest to the end.

B&B
LE GÎTE SAINT-MICHEL

Robert Burelle
1090, rue Laforest
St-Michel-des-Saints J0K 3B0
(450) 833-6008
toll free 1-888-843-6008

B&B	
single	$40
double	$60
triple	$80
child	$5-10

Open year round

Number of rooms	5
shared bathrooms	3

Activities: 🥾 🎿 🚶 🎿 🐕

15. ST-MICHEL-DES-SAINTS

F e 🚗 P R5

Prix Excellence Lanaudière 1996-97. Charm of yesteryear, comfort of today. Come experience a vacation in nature where various little pleasures await you. Warm welcome, comfortable rooms. Copious home-made breakfasts garnished with fresh flowers and herbs. Our wish is to embellish your vacation.

From Montréal, Hwy 40 East and Hwy 31 twd Joliette. Rte 131 to St-Michel-des-Saints. 9 km from St-Zénon church. Bus service St-Michel/Joliette/Montréal.

B&B
PETITES PLAISANCES

Simone Rondeau
7451, chemin Brassard,
route 131
St-Michel-des-Saints J0K 3B0
(450) 833-6342
srondeau@satelcom.qc.ca

B&B	
single	$40
double	$55-65
child	$15

Open year round

Number of rooms	3
shared bathrooms	2

Activities: 🥾 🚶 🚲 🛶 🎿

16. ST-SULPICE

F E ⊘ 🐕 🚗 P R4 TA

Over a century old, our house is located on the Chemin du Roi (Route 138), 15 min from the island of Montréal. Enjoy a peaceful stay in a setting filled with flowers and birds. Breakfast is served inside or outside with the majestic St-Laurent as a backdrop.

Hwy 40, Exit 108, twd the 343 South. At the traffic lights, turn right twd Repentigny and drive for 2 km. Or from Québec City, Rte 138 West, 4.4 km from the church of St-Sulpice; or from Montréal, 138 East 1.7 km from Repentigny.

B&B
GÎTE LES BOUCHARD

Suzanne and
Jacques Bouchard
351, Notre-Dame
St-Sulpice J5W 3X3
(450) 589-2010
fax (450) 589-9648

B&B	
single	$40
double	$50

Open: June 1 to Oct. 31

Number of rooms	2
shared bathrooms	2

Activities: 🏛 ⚓ ⛵ 🎿 🚴

---

17. ST-ZÉNON

F e 🚗 P R.1 TA

Discover Matawinie and relax in a century-old house at the heart of the highest village in Québec. Warm welcome, comfortable rooms and generous breakfast. Nature, golf and history lovers will feel at home.

From Montréal, Hwy 40 East and Hwy 31 twd Joliette. Rte 131 twd St-Michel-des-Saints. Our place is located 300 m from church. Bus service Saint-Zénon/Joliette/Montréal.

B&B
AU VENT VERT

Denise and Marcel Plante
6300, rue Principale
St-Zénon J0K 3N0
(450) 884-0169

B&B	
single	$40
double	$50
child	$0-5

Open year round

Number of rooms	2
shared bathrooms	1

Activities: 🎿 🚶 🚴 ✈ 🐕

---

18. STE-ÉLISABETH

F E P R4

One hour from Montréal, a few minutes from Joliette, in a country setting. We welcome travelers from near and far. From here, a 30- to 60- minute drive takes you to the heart of a region of varied landscapes and flavours. A grand welcome and excellent breakfasts. Sampling of maple products.

One hour from Montréal, Hwy 40, exit 122, Hwy 31 and Rte 131 N. At Notre-Dame-de-Lourdes, twd Ste-Elisabeth, drive for 1.5 km.

B&B
CHEZ MARIE-CHRISTINE

Micheline Adam
3120, Du Ruisseau
Ste-Élisabeth J0K 2J0
(450) 759-9336

B&B	
single	$42
double	$57
triple	$77

Open: May to Oct.

Number of rooms	3
shared wc	1
shared bathrooms	1

Activities: 🏛 ⚓ 🏊 🚶 🚴

19. TERREBONNE

F | E | ⊘ | ↔ | P | R.25 | TA

Discover the country in the city. Our house has been designated an historic monument in old Terrebonne. Nearby: historic site, restaurants, parking, hiking, park, river, skating, cinema. 15 min from Montréal. 45 min from airports. We like conversation, history, genealogy, birdwatching, music and.... travelling.

From Montréal, Hwy 25 North, Exit 22E Terrebonne. At the traffic lights, Boul. des Seigneurs, right on Moody, left on St-Louis, to the church. Also accessible from Rte 640.

B&B
MAISON N.T. ROUSSILLE

Paule and Jacques Tremblay
870, St-Louis
Terrebonne J6W 1J9
(450) 964-6016
fax (450) 471-7127
pages.infinit.net/roussill
roussille@videotron.ca

B&B	
single	$45-54
double	$50-60
triple	$70-78
child	$10-12

Open year round

Number of rooms	2
rooms with sink	2
shared wc	1
shared bathrooms	1

Activities: 🏛 🥾 ⛷ 🚶 🚴

B&Bs AND INNS

20. PARC DU MT-TREMBLANT, ST-CÔME

`F` `e` `♿` `P` `🏊` `R10` `M18` `TA`

Our cottages offer the best of both worlds: creature comforts combined with the beauty of a wild lake. Equipped with propane and a bathroom with shower. Boating, hiking trails, canoeing, picnicking, fishing, mountain biking, observation of flora and fauna await you here. Always on site, our caretakers will share their passion for the area with you.

From Montréal, Hwy 25 to Rte 337 twd Rawdon and St-Côme. From town, follow signs to Parc du Mt-Tremblant (secteur de l'Assomption). The reception area is 20 km from St-Côme.

COUNTRY HOME
CENTRE TOURISTIQUE DES
DEUX VALLÉES

Centre Touristique
des Deux-Vallées
C.P. 1169
Saint-Donat J0T 2C0
(819) 424-7012
fax (819) 424-2086

No. houses	4
No. rooms	2-3
No. people	4-8
DAY-SUMMER	$110-125

Taxes extra VS MC

Open: May 14 to Oct. 11

Activities: 🦆 🛶 👤 🚶 🚴

21. STE-ÉLISABETH

`F` `E` `P` `R4` `M7` `TA`

Our country house dating from 1926 is located one hour from Montreal. Two units including a bedroom, living room, kitchen and bathroom. Enjoy our farm products at breakfast and explore our flower gardens and the countryside. Cycling, strolls, snowshoeing, nature/culture and other tours.

From Montréal: Hwy 40, Exit 122, Hwy 31 and Rte 131 North. In Notre-Dame-de-Lourdes: turn right onto Ste-Élizabeth, right on Rue Principale, left on Chemin St-Pierre, left on Grand Rang St-Pierre.

COUNTRY HOME
AU RYTHME DES SAISONS

Pascale Coutu and
Pierre Tremblay
2321, Grand rang St-Pierre
Ste-Élisabeth J0K 2J0
(450) 752-2950
toll free 1-800-711-2021
fax (450) 759-9697
rythme-saisons.qc.ca
maison@rythme-saisons.qc.ca

No. houses	2
No. rooms	1
No. people	2-4
WEEK-SUMMER	$280 /double
WEEK-WINTER	$280 /double
W/E-SUMMER	$100 /double
W/E-WINTER	$100 /double
DAY-SUMMER	$55 /double
DAY-WINTER	$55 /double

Taxes extra

Open: Mid-June to Oct. 31 and mid-Dec. to Mar. 31

Activities: 🏛 👤 🚶 🛥 ⛷

FARM ACTIVITIES

Country dining*:

7 BERGERIE DES NEIGES, St-Ambroise-de-Kildare 16

22 BERGERIE VOYNE, St-Jacques-de-Montcalm 16

Farm excursion:

23 ARCHE DE NOÉ, Rawdon 30

* Registered trademark.

COUNTRY HOMES

LAURENTIDES

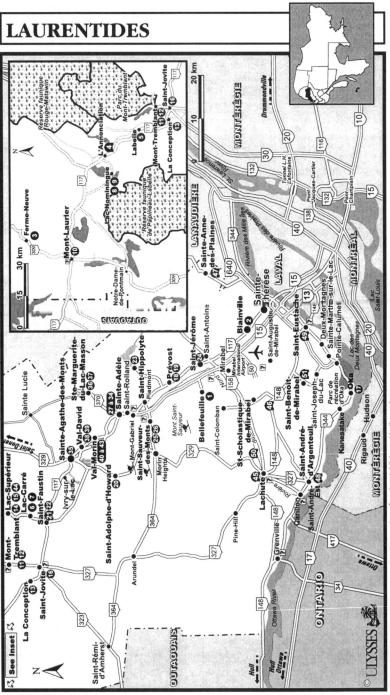

© ULYSSES

1. BELLEFEUILLE

F ⊘ ⌂ ✕ P R12

Panoramic mountain location, halfway between the Montréal airport and Mont Tremblant. Cross-country skiing at your doorstep, forest walks, private lake and healthy breakfasts. We are reserving a warm welcome, tranquillity, intimacy and comfort just for you... massage service available.

From Montréal or Mirabel, Hwy 15 North, Exit 43 West - Bellefeuille. You are on Rue De Martigny, which becomes De la Montagne and Blvd. Lasalette. After the traffic lights and the church, right on Rue St-Camille, drive 4.8 km.

B&B
FLEURS DES BOIS

Monique F. Morin
and Rémi Gagnon
1331, rue St-Camille, R.R. #2
Bellefeuille JOR 1A0
(450) 438-7624

B&B	
single	$40-45
double	$55-60
triple	$85
child	$15

Open: Jan. 5 to Dec.15

Number of rooms	5
rooms with private bath	2
shared wc	2
shared bathroom	1

Activities: ⚓ ⛵ 🚲 🏊 🏃

2. BLAINVILLE

F e P 🛏 ✕ R1 TA

15 min from Mirabel, to fight the inconveniences of jet lag, we offer you the comfort and quietness of our home. At the foot of the Laurentides and 30 min from Montréal it is a pleasant stop for cyclists. Biking, skiing and walking trails nearby.

From Mirabel, Hwy 15 South, Exit 31 twd St-Janvier. Right Rte 117, 3 km. Right Rue Notre-Dame, left Rue J. Desrosiers. Or from Montréal, Hwy 15 North, Exit 25. Left Rte 117 for 3 km, left 98th Ave.

B&B
LE GÎTE DU LYS

Francine Beauchemin
1237, Jacques-Desrosiers
Blainville J7C 3B2
(450) 437-4948
fax (450) 437-3658

B&B	
single	$35
double	$45-55
triple	$75
quad.	$90
child	$15

Open year round

Number of rooms	3
rooms in basement	3
shared bathroom	1

Activities: ⚓ 🚲 🛶 🏊 🏃

3. FERME-NEUVE

F E ✕ P R8 TA

A quiet, cozy house with tremendous charm, artistic woodwork and full of windows. A picture-postcard landscape, 106 acres of fields, forest and a little river. Delicious, lavish cuisine. 20 minutes from the beaches of the Baskatong Reservoir, the devil's mountain and the Windigo Falls.

From Montréal: Hwy 15 North, then Rte 117. In Mont-Laurier: 309 North. In Ferme-Neuve: past the church, left at the ball park, left on Montée Gravel, 8 km.

INN
AUBERGE AU BOIS
D'MON COEUR

Louison Morin
183, rang 4 Gravel
Ferme-Neuve J0W 1C0
(819) 587-3383
(819) 623-7143

	B&B	MAP
single	$40	$55-65
double	$55	$85-105
triple	$60	$105-135
quad.	$65	$125-165
child	$5	$15

Open year round

Number of rooms	4
shared wc	2
shared bathroom	2

Activities: 🏛 🚣 ⚓ ⛵ 🏃

4. L'ANNONCIATION

F e P ☒ R5

We cleared this patch of mountainside land so that our small herd could graze and we could set up house comfortably. Former teachers, your hosts are genuine, unpretentious people who enjoy sharing with their guests the happiness of living according to old-fashioned values. A warm welcome awaits you. **Country Inns p 17 and Farm stays p 38.**

From Montréal: Hwy 15 North and Rte 117 to L'Annonciation. Drive 4.3 km past the hospital, and turn left on Chemin Laliberté. First house on the right. Almond-coloured Canadian-style house.

B&B
LA CLAIRIÈRE DE LA CÔTE

Monique Lanthier and
Yves Bégin
16, chemin Laliberté
L'Annonciation J0T 1T0
(819) 275-2877
fax (819) 275-3363

B&B	
single	$35
double	$50

Open: Dec. 1 to Mar. 31 to
May 1 to Oct. 31

Number of rooms	3
rooms in basement	3
shared wc	2
shared bathroom	1

Activities: ☞ 𝄢 ⚲ ⛷ 🎿

5. LABELLE

F E ⛴ P 🚗 R5

20 min from Mont-Tremblant, close to the linear "Le P'tit Train du Nord" park, our house overlooks Lac Labelle, offering a magnificent view. Warm welcome, princely breakfasts, many activities: beach, canoe, hikes, cross-country skiing, snowshoeing, snowmobiling, packages for cyclists. Enjoy the four seasons...

From Montréal, Hwy 15 North, then 117 North to Labelle. Turn left 3 km after the town at the flashing lights twd Lac Labelle. Follow signs for Domaine Marie Max.

B&B
LA CLOCHE DE VERT

Thérèse and Normand Brunette
1080, chemin Saindon
Lac Labelle
Labelle J0T 1H0
(819) 686-5850
www.angelfire.com/
biz/cloche
clochedevert@bigfoot.com

B&B	
single	$40
double	$55-65
child	$10

Open year round

Number of rooms	3
rooms with sink	2
rooms with private bath	1
shared wc	1
shared bathroom	1

Activities: 𝄢 ⚲ ⛷ 🎿 🏃

6. LAC-CARRÉ

F E P 🐕 R.1 TA

Ten kilometres from St-Jovite and 18 kilometres from Mt-Tremblant, our septuagenarian house is a haven of peace for nature lovers. Fifty metres from the linear park and 1 kilometre from Mont-Blanc, our B&B lets you relax on the beach of the lake, on the terrace or by the fire upon your arrival. Come morning, you will enjoy our now-famous hearty breakfast.

From Montréal, Hwy 15 North and Rte 117 North. After Ste-Agathe drive 18 km. Exit Lac-Carré. At 1st stop sign turn right, drive 1.5 km, right on Rue de La Gare.

B&B
GÎTE DE LA GARE

Isabelle Bourgeault and
Patrick Vandal
362, de La Gare
Lac-Carré
J0T 1J0
(819) 688-6091

B&B	
single	$45
double	$60

Reduced rates: Oct. 1 to Dec. 23,
Jan. 4 to May 31
Open year round

Number of rooms	4
shared bathroom	2

Activities: ☞ 🧍 ⚲ 🎿 🏃

7. LAC-CARRÉ

F E P R.1 TA

"La Licorne", or The Unicorn, symbolizing freedom, invites you to share in its wonders and landscapes. After a day of cycling on the linear park 50 metres away, relax in our garden to the sound of waterfalls or go for a refreshing swim in the lake in front of the B&B. In winter, after skiing, relax in front of a fire. Mt Blanc 1 km away, Tremblant 20 km, good restaurants in St-Jovite 10 km. At km 69.5 of the bike path.

From Montréal, Hwy 15 N. and Rte 117 N. After Ste-Agathe, 20 km, Lac-Carré Exit, at the stop, right for 1 km.

B&B
LA LICORNE

Patricia and Robin
1690, rue Principale
Lac-Carré J0T 1J0
(819) 688-3030
fax (819) 688-5020
www.bbcanada.com/403.html

B&B	
single	$40-50
double	$60-70
triple	$75
quad.	$90

VS

Open: Dec. 1 to Apr. 15,
May 1 to Oct. 31

Number of rooms	4
shared bathroom	2

Activities:

---

8. LAC-NOMININGUE

F E P TA

By the cycling path, skidoo trail and the lake, our inn is the gateway to the Réserve Papineau-Labelle and its nature related activities. We offer guests a delicious cocktail of gastronomy and relaxation: rooms with therapeutic bath, 5-course-dinner menu packages. **See colour photos.**

From Montréal: Hwy 15 North and Rte 117. Past L'Annonciation at the flashing light, Rte 321 South. After 8.8 km, turn right on Ch. des Tilleuls (200 m.). By bike: at Km 141.5 of the P'tit Train du Nord bike path.

INN
AUBERGE-RESTAURANT
«CHEZ IGNACE»

Yolande Louis and
Ignace Denutte
1455, ch. des Tilleuls
Lac-Nominingue J0W 1R0
(819) 278-0689
fax (819) 278-0751
www.laurentides.com

	B&B	MAP
single	$50-60	$65-75
double	$70-80	$110-118
triple	$90	$145
child	$0-5	$5-20

Taxes extra VS MC AM IT

Reduced rates: Mar. 15 to
May 15 and Oct. 15 to Dec. 15
Open year round

Number of rooms	5
shared wc	3
rooms with private bath	5

Activities:

---

9. LAC-NOMININGUE

F E P R1 TA

Centenary manor, ancestral site at the edge of the forest, home cooking straight from our garden. Recommended by F. Trépanier's *Guide des Auberges et Relais de Campagne*, the *Guide Bizier/Nadeau des Meilleures Tables* and *Vélo-Mag* (June 98). Group packages: cycling (1 km of trail), cross-country skiing and canoeing (Papineau-Labelle reserve). **See colour photos and ad end of this region.**

From Montréal, Hwy 15 North and Rte 117 North. After l'Annonciation, at the flashing light take Rte 321 South. Cross Nominingue and turn left on last street, Rue St-Ignace. Inn at top of hill, on right.

INN
LE PROVINCIALAT

P. Seers and G. Petit
2292, Sacré-Coeur
Lac-Nominingue J0W 1R0
tel/fax (819) 278-4928
toll free in Canada
1-877- 278-4928
www.laurentides.com

	B&B	MAP
single	$40	$57.50
double	$60-75	$95-110
triple	$75	$127.50
quad.	$110	$180
child	$15	$27.50

Taxes extra VS MC

Reduced rates: Jan. 10 to Apr. 15
and Nov. 1 to Dec. 15
Open year round

mber of rooms	5
rooms with private bath	1
rooms with sink	2
shared bathroom	2

Activités:

B&Bs AND INNS

10. MONT-LAURIER

F | e | P | R.1 | TA

Memorable stay. Friendly welcome, considerations, cosy bed, lounge at your disposal: chats, reading, soft music, TV. Not to mention the breakfast!!! "As appetizing to the eyes as to the belly." Near the linear park. Welcome to our home with magnificent woodwork.

From Montréal, Hwy 15 N., Rte 117 to Mont-Laurier. We're on Boul A. Paquette which is the extension of Rte 117. The inn is on your right.

B&B
AUBERGE DE LA
MAISON GRENIER

Joane, Dominic and
Gilbert Vincent
335, boul. A. Paquette
Mont-Laurier J9L 1K5
(819) 623-6306
fax (819) 623-5054
dominic.vincent@sympatico.ca

B&B	
single	$35
double	$50
triple	$65
child	$5

Taxes extra VS MC

Open year round

Number of rooms	5
rooms with sink	1
shared bathroom	2

Activities: 🎿 🏃 🚴 ⛷ 🎣

11. MONT-TREMBLANT

F | E | 🚫 | ♿ | P | 🚣 | R.1 | TA

The warmth of a log house within your reach. Ten spacious rooms, each with its own rustic charm to welcome you. Newly built, it boasts a television, therapeutic bath, balcony and a view of magnificent Mont-Tremblant. Lounge with fireplace to warm you in winter, pool to refresh you in summer. Excellent breakfast. Prices higher in winter.

From Montréal: Hwy 15 North, Rte 117 North for 1.5 km. After St-Jovite, turn right on Montée Ryan to Lac Tremblant, turn left toward the village. We are 1 km away on the left.

INN
AUBERGE LA PETITE CACHÉE

Manon Millette and
Normand Chalifour
2681, chemin Principal
C.P. 1009
Mont-Tremblant J0T 1Z0
(819) 425-2654
fax (819) 425-6892

B&B	
single	$55-75
double	$79-110
triple	$104-125
child	$12

Taxes extra VS MC AM IT

Reduced rates: May 1 to June 15,
Oct. 15 to Nov. 15
Open year round

Number of rooms	10
rooms with private bath	10

Activities: 🏛 ⛵ 🚤 🎿 🏃

12. MONT-TREMBLANT

F | A | ♿ | P | 🚤 | 🚣 | 🐕 | R1 | AV

Less than 1 km from the ski resort of Tremblant. Cross-Country skiing and mountain bike trails at our doorstep. Close to the bike paths. Log house, spacious rooms, living room with fireplace. Winter rates $85/double Welcome! **See colour photos.**

From Montréal, Hwy 15 North, Rte 117 North. Pass St-Jovite (2 km) at the yellow flashing light, take montée Ryan on your right until the end (stop). Turn left along the lake, at the stop (Rue Pinoteau) turn left. Le Lupin sign.

INN
AUBERGE LE LUPIN

Sylvie Senécal and
Pierre Lachance
127, Pinoteau
Mont-Tremblant J0T 1Z0
(819) 425-5474
fax (819) 425-6079
www.lelupin.com
lelupin@lelupin.com

B&B	
single	55-75 $
double	72-95 $
triple	109-115 $
child	12 $

Taxes extra VS MC AM ER IT

Reduced rates: May, June (week days) and Oct., Nov. (week days)
Open year round

Number of rooms	9
rooms with private bath	7
shared wc	1
shared bathroom	1

Activities: 🚤 🏃 🚴 ⛷ 🎿

13. MONT-TREMBLANT, LA CONCEPTION

F E 🚭 🏊 P 🚗 🐕 R6 TA

Discover our inn, a peaceful place in the forest by Rivière Rouge, a few minutes from the "P'tit Train du Nord" bike path and the Tremblant ski resort. Cosy and comfortable rooms, lounge with fireplace. Canoes available. Winter rate from $70 double occ. Johanne is an herbalist and Bob a Micmac with a passion for history and traditions. **See colour photos.**

From Montréal, Hwy 15 North, Rte 117 North twd St-Jovite. In La Conception turn right on Chemin des Tulipes. From Ottawa, Rte 323 North twd St-Jovite, Rte 117 North to La Conception, right in Chemin des Tulipes.

INN
L'AUBERGE À LA
CROISÉE DES CHEMINS

Johanne Parent and
Bob Bourdon
4273, chemin des Tulipes
Mt-Tremblant, La Conception
J0T 1M0
tel/fax (819) 686-5289
toll free 1-888-686-5289

B&B	
single	$46-71
double	$65-85
triple	$90-115
child	$10

Taxes extra VS MC IT

Reduced rates: Oct. 15 to Dec. 15 and Apr. 15 to June 15

Open year round

Number of rooms	9
rooms with private bath	7
shared wc	2
shared bathroom	1

Activities: 🏛 ⛷ 🐟 🏹 🐎

14. MONT-TREMBLANT, LAC-SUPÉRIEUR

F E P 🏊 R7 TA

Laurentian Excellence Prize 1996-97. On the edge of a wild 15-hectare forest traversed by a river, our wood house promises cosy nights, musical baths and memorable breakfasts! Ideal spot for visiting Parc du Mt-Tremblant and Mt-Tremblant resort. Welcome to the land of the beaver!

From Montréal, Hwy 15 North, Rte 117 North, Lac-Carré Exit. At the stop turn right drive for 2.3 km. Follow signs for Parc du Mont Tremblant for 5.6 km. Turn left on Chemin Lac-à-L'Équerre, 3.6 km.

B&B
CHEZ NOR-LOU

Louise Lachance and
Normand Sauvé
803, ch. du Lac à L'Équerre
Lac-Supérieur J0T 1J0
(819) 688-3128
www.bbcanada.com/888.html
norlou@intlaurentides.qc.ca

B&B	
single	$40-45
double	$55-65
child	$5-15

VS

Open: May 1 to Oct. 31, Dec. 1 to Mar. 31

Number of rooms	3
shared bathroom	2

Activities: 🐟 🏹 🚴 ⛷ 🎿

15. MONT-TREMBLANT, LAC-SUPÉRIEUR

F E 🐕 🏊 P 🚗 R2.5 TA

At the entrance of the Mont-Tremblant park and on the north side of the mountain is a typical Canadian-style house embraced by nature. Linear park 2.5 km away. Ski, bike and snowmobile rides. Relax in front of the fireplace. Breakfast in a family like environment and share the enthusiasm of your hosts. **See colour photos.**

From Montréal, Hwy 15 North, Rte 117 North, Exit St-Faustin/Lac-Carré. Right at the stop, 2.3 km, follow signs to Parc Mont-Tremblant, drive 2.5 km on Chemin Lac-Supérieur

B&B
GÎTE ET COUVERT
LA MARIE-CHAMPAGNE

Marie-France
and Denis Champagne
654, chemin Lac-Supérieur
Lac-Supérieur J0T 1J0
tel/fax (819) 688-3780

B&B	
single	$40-50
double	$60-70
triple	$75
quad.	$90
child	$15

VS AM

Open: Dec. 1 to Oct. 31

Number of rooms	5
rooms with sink	1
rooms with private bath	2
shared wc	1
shared bathroom	2

Activities: 🐟 🏹 🚴 🛶 ⛷

B&Bs AND INNS

16. MONT-TREMBLANT, ST-JOVITE

F E 🏊 P 🐕 ❌ R3 TA

Secluded within the Laurentian mountains and less than 10 minutes from Mont-Tremblant, Wilde's Heat is a magnificient victorian mansion surronded by beautiful English gardens. Entirely furnished with late 19th century antiques. Wilde's Heath confirms that castle living is alive and well in St-Jovite. Fall asleep in one of our King sire upholstered canape beds and kiss your troubles away... **See colour photos.**

From Mtl: Hwy 15 North which becomes Rte 117 after Ste-Agathe. After St-Jovite, at the viaduct on your left twds Brébeuf, take Rte 323 for 1.6 km, look for the sign "Wilde's Heath B&B".

B&B
LE WILDE'S HEATH B&B

Dorian Grey
268, Route 323
St-Jovite J0T 2H0
(819) 425-6859
fax (819) 425-1197

B&B	
single	$80-100
double	$99-125

VS MC AM IT

Open year round

Number of rooms	4
rooms with private bath	4

Activities: 🚤 ⛵ 🎣 🚴 🎿

---

17. OKA

F e 🚭 🏊 P R.25 TA

A complete change of scenery 40 min from Mirabel, 45 min from Montréal. Complete change of scenery on an enchanting site on a lake and around a pool. Bicycle path. Parc Oka nearby. In summer, water sports and golf are available. In winter, cross-country skiing, ice-fishing, and snowmobile riding.

From Mirabel, Hwy 15 South, exit onto Hwy 640 West to the end. Right on Rte 344 West to Oka, left on Rue Olier. We are on the right, next to the water, 8.5 km from the end of Rte 640 West.

B&B
LA MAISON DUMOULIN

Pierrette Dumoulin
53, rue St-Sulpice, C.P. 1072
Oka J0N 1E0
(450) 479-6753

B&B	
single	$40-45-50
double	$50-55-60
child	$10

Open year round

Number of rooms	4
shared bathroom	2

Activities: ⛵ 🎣 🚶 🚴 🏃

---

18. PRÉVOST

F E ♿ P 🚗 R.3 TA

Enjoy the fresh air just 20 min from Montréal. In a hundred-year-old house 15 min from Mirabel Airport and 5 min from Saint-Sauveur, an oasis of tranquillity 35 km from Montréal. At the entrance to the Laurentides region between Parc de la Rivière Nord and the Parc Linéaire. Ideal for relaxation, comfort and enjoying some fresh air.

From Montréal, Hwy 15 North, Exit 55, turn right on Rue Morin, which becomes Rue Principale, drive for 1.5 km. Or by "Limocar" bus, get off at Chemin du Lac Echo, in Prévost.

B&B
AUX BERGES FLEURIES

Nicole and Fransois Laroche
1028, Principale
Prévost J0R 1T0
(450) 224-7631
fax (450) 436-5997

B&B	
single	$39
double	$49-59
child	$15

VS MC

Open year round

Number of rooms	4
rooms with sink	3
rooms with private bath	1
shared bathroom	1

Activities: 🎿 🎣 🚶 🚴 🏃

19. PRÉVOST

F E ⊘ P 🚗 R1

5 min from St-Sauveur, adult non-smoking home (fireplaces in living and in dining room, Jacuzzi in the solarium, healthy breakfasts). 1 km from Linear Park (200 km) for biking, snowshoeing and skiing, transportation available. 5 min from downhill skiing, golf, flea market, antiques. Mirabel packages. Hablamos español.

Hwy 15 North, Exit 55. You're on Rue Louis-Morin. Right on rue Morin, cross the bridge. Left on Rue De La Station. 1 km past Rte 117's traffic lights, left on Montée-Sauvage, right on Du Sommet, right on De La Voie Lactée.

B&B
CHEZ MADELEINE ET PIERRE

Madeleine Sévigny
and Pierre Lavigne
1460, Voie Lactée, C.P. 92
Prévost J0R 1T0
(450) 224-4628
fax (450) 224-7457
pdaignau@marasuca.com

B&B	
single	$40
double	$50-60

Reduced rates: -10% for stays of 3 nights or more
Open: June 1 to Oct. 15

Number of rooms	2
rooms with private bath	1
shared wc	1
shared bathroom	1

Activities: 🏛 🖐 🚲 🐎 🏃

---

20. ST-ADOLPHE-D'HOWARD

F E ⊘ P 🚗 R4 TA

Enter the tower, smell the cedar, you're in. Welcome in this peaceful house nestled in the mountains right on the lake. Relax in front of a fireplace. Spacious and lovingly decorated rooms await you for a special treat. As for breakfast? WoW! L'Aube Douce: forget about the daily stress.

From Montréal, Hwy 15 N., Exit 60, Rte 364 W., up to Rte 329 N. Drive 10 km turn left at Montée Lac Louise. Drive 1.5 km then turn right on Gais Lurons. Make a left at the stop sign.

B&B
AUBE DOUCE

Michèle Ménard and
Gilles Meilleur
22, chemin de la Québécoise
St-Adolphe-d'Howard J0T 2B0
(819) 327-5048
fax (819) 327-5254
www.bbcanada.com/
2767.html

B&B	
single	$50
double	$60-80
triple	$80-105
child	$0-10

Reduced rates: Nov.1 to Dec. 15
Apr. 1 to May 15
Open year round

Number of rooms	4
rooms with private bath	4

Activities: 🖐 🚐 🚲 ⛷ 🏃

---

21. ST-FAUSTIN

F E 🐕 ⊘ 🏊 P 🚗 ✕ R8

This sheep farm was built with our own hands, along with the surrounding beauty. Lovely rooms are annexed to the barn's calmness. Home cooked meals are served by the stone fireplace, in our log house. Mt-Tremblant at 20 km, "Parc Linéaire" at 7 km. Families are welcome in this homey type of place! **Farm stay p 38.**

From Montréal, Hwy 15 North. In St-Faustin, 2 km after Mt-Blanc, left on Chemin la Sauvagine for 7 km. From St-Jovite, Rte 327 South twd Arundel for 2 km. Left on Chemin Paquette for 6 km.

B&B
FERME DE LA
BUTTE MAGIQUE

Diane, Maud
and children
1724, chemin de la Sauvagine
St-Faustin J0T 2G0
(819) 425-5688

	B&B	MAP
single	$38	$55
double	$60	$90
triple	$80	$110
child	$20	$28

Open year round

Number of rooms	3
shared wc	1
shared bathroom	1

Activities: 🏛 🧍 🚲 ⛵ 🏃

B&Bs AND INNS

22. ST-FAUSTIN

F | E |  ... P | TA

A former general store, our ancestral house has a welcoming spirit as do its hosts. You will enjoy meals on the terrace in summer and by the fireside in winter. Family-size rooms available and studio. One kilometre from the lake and the P'tit Train du Nord Linear Park. 15 minutes from Tremblant. Facing Mont Blanc. Ski and bike packages. Two-star hotel. **Ad end of this region.**

From Montréal or Mirabel Airport, Hwy 15 North to St-Jérome. Continue to Ste-Agathe, Rte 117, 16 km. Take the St-Faustin/Lac-Carré exit and follow the blue signs. We're in front of the church.

INN
LA BONNE ADRESSE

Odette Bélanger and
Jean-Marie Noël
1196, rue de la Pisciculture
St-Faustin J0T 2G0
(819) 688-6422
toll free 1-877-688-6422
fax (819) 688-5052
www.laurentides.com

	B&B	MAP
single	$50	$68
double	$68-90	$103-125
triple	$88-105	$140-157.⁵⁰
quad.	$108-120	$180-190
child	$15	$25

Taxes extra VS

Open: May 15 to Oct. 15
Dec. 1 to Apr. 15

Number of rooms	7
rooms with private bath	3
shared bathroom	2

Activities:

---

23. ST-HIPPOLYTE

F | E | P | ... | R4 | TA

Facing the lake, in the mountains rife with lush flora. Imagine the scene at dusk when the sun paints its canvas! Dining room with terrace, unparalleled view. Innovative, lavish fine cuisine. Discover edible flowers. Charming, comfortable rooms. Private beach, grade-A water. Rowboats. Rest assured. 1st prize Villages Fleuris. A true paradise! **See colour photos.**

1hr from Montréal, Hwy 15 N., Exit 45 twd St-Hippolyte, left at 1st light for 16 km to Rte 333 N. Turn left at the church, drive 4 km, keep to the right, inn is 300 metres further.

INN
AUBERGE LAC DU PIN ROUGE

Nicole Bouffard and
Yvan Trottier
81, chemin Lac-du-Pin-Rouge
St-Hippolyte J8A 3J3
(450) 563-2790
from May 15 :
outside of Mtl
toll free 1-800-427-0840

	B&B	MAP
single	$51-75	$84-108
double	$65-85	$129-151
triple	$88-114	$175-208
child	$20	à la carte

Taxes extra VS MC

Reduced rates: stays of 2 nights or more
Open: May 15 to Oct. 15

Number of rooms	6
rooms with private bath	4
rooms with sink	2
shared wc	3
shared bathroom	3

Activities:

---

24. ST-JÉRÔME

F | E | ... | R.3 | TA

Ten min from Mirabel airport and 30 min from Dorval, generous and considerate hospitality *à la québécoise*. Nice ambience, gourmet breakfast. Gérard, a history professor, is proud to tell you about his Québec! Located at 100 metres from the bicycle path "Le P'tit train du Nord". **Advertisement end of this region.**

Hwy 15 North, Exit 43 East twd downtown. After the bridge, right on Rue Labelle. At the lights, left on Rue du Palais (cathedral), left on Melançon street, first light. B&B is 1 block away on the left.

B&B
L'ÉTAPE CHEZ MARIE-THÉRÈSE
ET GÉRARD LEMAY

Marie-Thérèse and
Gérard Lemay
430, rue Melançon
St-Jérôme J7Z 4K4
(450) 438-1043

	B&B
single	$40
double	$55
triple	$75
child	$15

Reduced rates: Nov.1 to Mar. 31
Open year round

Number of rooms	3
shared wc	1
shared bathroom	2

Activities:

25. ST-SAUVEUR-DES-MONTS

F | E |  | P | R2

Winner of the *Grand Prix du Tourisme Laurentides*: welcome and customer service 1997. Facing ski hills, 2 km from town. Enchanting decor, tranquillity, attention and discretion. Heated pool, central air conditioning, flowered terrace, 2 rms with fireplaces, including one semi-basement suite. Many recreation/tourist activities nearby. But above all relaxation, comfort and a warm welcome. Gourmet breakfast.

From Montréal, Hwy 15 N. left at Exit 60, at Rte 364 W. turn right, 3rd set of lights, left on Rue Principale, 2 km.

INN

AUBERGE SOUS L'ÉDREDON

Carmelle Huppé and
Andrée Cloutier
777, Principale
St-Sauveur-des-Monts
J0R 1R2
(450) 227-3131

B&B	
single	$55-80
double	$70-95
triple	$100-110
child	$10-15

Taxes extra VS MC

Reduced rates: Apr., May, Nov., and 10 % 3 nights and more
Open year round

Number of rooms	7
rooms with private bath	5
rooms in semi-basement	1
shared bathroom	1

Activities:

---

26. ST-SAUVEUR-DES-MONTS

F | E |  | P | TA

Old-charm house in the heart of a scenic village; cosy nest, hearth. View of ski runs. Flowery garden, pool, air conditioning. Suite with double whirlpool bath. Facilities for businesspeople, small groups. Packages: ski, dogsled, snowmobile, golf, biking, water slides, summer theatre. Warm ambiance where the little considerations make all the difference.

45 min. from Montréal. Hwy 15 North, left at Exit 60. Right onto Rte 364 West. At 2nd light, right on Rue de la Gare. Left on Rue Principale (0.6 km). Welcome to our B&B!

B&B

«AUX PETITS OISEAUX...»

Mireille and Benny
342, rue Principale
St-Sauveur-des-Monts J0R 1R0
(450) 227-6116
toll free 1-877-227-6116
fax (450) 227-6171
www.laurentides.com
auxpetitsoiseaux@
sympatico.ca

B&B	
single	$50-125
double	$55-150
triple	$75-170
quad.	$110-185
child	$0-20

Taxes extra VS MC AM

Reduced rates: Apr. 12 to May 14 and Nov.
10 % 3 nights and more
Open year round

Number of rooms	4
rooms with private bath	4
rooms in basement	1

Activities:

---

27. STE-ADÈLE

F | E |  | P | R4 | TA

Between Montréal and Mont-Tremblant in the heart of the woods, a haven to dream for. River, cascades, natural pool, wildlife and foot paths. Snowshoeing and X-country skiing at your doorstep. The area abounds with fine restaurants, cinemas, summer theatres and cultural events.

From Montréal, Hwy 15 N., Exit 67. 7 km on Rte 117 N. At "Lac Millette", left on Chemin du Moulin for 2 km. At the green barn, right on Des Engoulevents. Private road, keep left.

B&B

À L'ORÉE DU BOIS

Louise Durivage and
Robert Parizeau
4400, rue des Engoulevents
Ste-Adèle J8B 3J8
(450) 229-5455
www.bbcanada.com/2738.html
www.laurentides.com
aloreedubois@sympatico.ca

B&B	
single	$60
double	$80
triple	$100
child	$20

MC

Reduced rates: 10 % 5 nights and more
Open year round

Number of rooms	4
rooms with sink	4
shared wc	2
shared showers	2

Activities:

B&Bs AND INNS

28. STE-ADÈLE

F E 🚫 🏤 P 🚗 🐕 R.3 TA

Lovely Canadian house in the woodlands offers central air conditioning, comfort and relaxation. Very large family-size room that can accommodate up to 5 people. Incomparable breakfasts. Pool, hiking, cross-country skiing on site. 25 minutes from Mirabel, 50 from Dorval and 45 from Mont-Tremblant. 10% discount for 3 nights or more.

From Montréal or Mirabel Airport, Hwy 15 North, Exit 69, Rte 370 East, for 0.8 km. Facing the "Clef des Champs" restaurant.

B&B
À LA BELLE IDÉE

Suzanne and Jean-François
894, de l'Arbre Sec
Ste-Adèle J8B 1X6
(450) 229-6173
Canada and USA only:
toll free 1-888-221-1313
fax (450) 229-5423
www.bbcanada.com/870.html
la.belle.idee@sympatico.ca

B&B	
single	$40-60
double	$55-75
triple	$75-90
quad.	$105
child	$0-10

Reduced rates: Apr. 1 to June 14
Oct.15 to Dec. 14
Open year round

Number of rooms	4
rooms with private bath	2
shared bathroom	1

Activities: 🛶 🎿 🚲 ⛷ 🎿

29. STE-ADÈLE

F E 🐕 🏤 P 🚗 R6 TA

Our inn is located 3 kilometres from the village, in the heart of the Laurentians. A welcoming house, with its four rooms, two of which boast a private bathroom, awaits you in a restful haven of peace and tranquillity. Parks, footpaths and bike path within reach.

From Montréal, Hwy 15 North, Exit 67, Rte 117 North to the traffic lights. Turn right at Mont-Rolland, Rue St-Joseph. At the stop sign, turn left on Rue Rolland. Drive about 3 km.

B&B
AUBERGE DES SORBIERS B&B

Lise Fournier and
Alain Parpal
4120, rue Rolland
Ste-Adèle J8B 1C7
(450) 229-3929
fax (450) 229-7510
auberge.des.sorbiers
@sympatico.ca

B&B	
single	$35-45
double	$55-65
triple	$70-80
child	$10-15

Taxes extra VS

Open year round

Number of rooms	4
rooms with sink	2
rooms with private bath	2
shared bathroom	1

Activities: 🛶 🎿 🚲 ⛷ 🏃

30. STE-ADÈLE

F E P 🚗 🍽 R.5 TA

We'll welcome you like special company to our private property 5 min from all the activities in the Laurentians. Fireplace, piano, pinball, air conditioning, outdoor spa... everything to help you relax. Copious breakfast. Other meals by reservation

From Montréal or Mirabel, Hwy 15 N., Exit 69 twd Ste-Marguerite, Rte 370. Drive 6 km, or 1.8 km from linear park (bike path), on your right.

INN
AUX PINS DORÉS

Carmen Champagne and
René Tremblay
2251, chemin Pierre-Péladeau
Ste-Adèle J8B 1Z7
(450) 228-4556
1-877-228-4556
fax (450) 228-1881
members.tripod.com/~pins

	B&B	MAP
single	$40-55	$50-65
double	$50-70	$70-90
triple	$85	$115
quad.	$100	$140
child	$0-10	

Reduced rates: 2 nights or more during weeks except summertime and school holidays.

Open year round

Number of rooms	4
rooms with private bath	1
shared bathroom	2

Activities: 🛶 🎿 🚲 ⛷ 🏃

31. STE-ADÈLE

F E ♿ P 🚗 ❌ R.3 TA

In the heart of this romantic town, the Nid Douillet, or cosy nest, offers a warm reception in its country decor. Private bathrooms with therapeutic bathtubs. Many activities nearby: health packages, snowmobiling, skiing, dog sledding, golf, theatre. Shuttle service offered. Generous breakfasts to brighten up your morning.

From Montréal, Hwy 15 N., Exit 67, right at the 4th set of lights, onto Chemin Ste-Marguerite, 3rd bldg on the left. 20 min from Mirabel airport.

INN
AU NID DOUILLET

Andrée Morrissette and Martin Leduc
430, chemin Pierre-Péladeau
Ste-Adèle J8B 1Z4
(450) 229-6939
toll free 1-800-529-6939
fax (450) 229-6651

	B&B	MAP
single	$55-75	$79-99
double	$65-95	$109-149
triple	$75-105	$149-179
quad.	$85-120	$179-199
child	$0-15	$0-30

Taxes extra VS MC AM ER IT

Reduced rates: Apr. 15 to June 1, Oct. 15 to Dec. 15
Open year round

Number of rooms	12
rooms with private bath	12

Activities: 🎿 🚴 🛷 ⛷ 🐕

32. STE-ADÈLE

F e 🚭 🏠 P 🚗 R.5 TA

Our little love nest is tucked away between Montréal and Tremblant, amidst all the cultural and outdoor activities. Total relaxation is guaranteed. Friendly hosts, a night by the fire. In the morning a big breakfast awaits in the solarium, where you can admire the birds, a flowered garden, a stream and a heated pool. Enjoyable days and nights await. Spoil yourself.

From Montréal, Hwy 15 N., Exit 67, Rte 117, Boul Ste-Adèle for 2 km, stone house on the left. 25 min from Mirabel airport.

INN
AUBERGE BONNE NUIT
BONJOUR

Huguette Leblond and Michel Ouellette
1980, boul. Ste-Adèle
Ste-Adèle J8B 1A8
tel/fax (450) 229-7500
toll free 1-888-229-7500
www.bbcanada.com/
1607.html

	B&B
single	$50-60
double	$70-85
triple	$95
quad.	$110
child	$15

Taxes extra VS AM IT

Reduced rates: Apr. 1 to June 1, Nov. 1 to Dec. 1
Open year round

Number of rooms	6
rooms with private bath	4
shared wc	1
shared bathroom	1

Activities: 🎣 🎿 🚴 🛷 ⛷

33. STE-ADÈLE

F E 🚭 🏠 P 🚗 R.5 TA

Located on an enchanted river with natural whirlpools, enjoy our old stone sauna, ext. spa, massages, relaxation pavillion, walking paths and rest areas. A delicious breafast and tastefully decorated rooms await your visit. Adventure, romance, relaxation packages available. Come dream with us! **See colour photos and advertisement end of this region.**

From Montréal, Hwy 15 North Exit 67, Rte 117, Boul Ste-Adèle, drive 3.6 km. Stone house with blue roof, on left. (25 minutes from Mirabel Airport).

INN
AUBERGE ET SPA BEAUX RÊVES

Hannes Lamothe
2310, boul. Ste-Adèle rte 117
Ste-Adèle J8B 2N5
(450) 229-9226
toll free 1-800-279-7679
fax (450) 229-2999
www.beauxreves.com
bienvenue@beauxreves.com

	B&B
single	$60-75
double	$80-95
triple	$95-115
quad.	$95-135
child	$0-20

Taxes extra VS

Open year round

Number of rooms	6
rooms with private bath	6

Activities: 🎿 🚴 🛷 ⛷ 🐕

34. STE-ADÈLE

F E P 🚗 R.9 TA

A Swiss chalet with a panoramic view of the Laurentians; across from water slides and a 6000-km interprovincial snowmobile trail, right near downtown and close to all the regional tourist attractions. Just 30 min to Mt-Tremblant international ski resort.

From Montréal, Hwy 15 N., Exit 67, to the traffic lights, take Boul Ste-Adèle for 3.4 km, on the left across from the "bungee tower". Or Hwy 15 S., Exit 69, turn right on Chemin Ste-Marguerite.

B&B
GÎTE DES AMÉRIQUES

Sara Padilla and Charles Fillion
1724, boul. Ste-Adèle
Ste-Adèle J8B 1A0
tel/fax (450) 229-9042
www.internest.qc.
ca/amerique.html
amerique@citenet.net

B&B	
single	$35
double	$45-55
triple	$65
quad.	$75
child	$10

VS MC

Open year round

Number of rooms	3
rooms with sink	2
shared bathroom	2

Activities: 🍷 . 🎿 🚲 ⛷ 🏃

---

35. STE-AGATHE-DES-MONTS

F E P R1 TA

Imagine a beautiful 100-year-old house where comfort is a living tradition. A fire burning in the hearth, Swedish massages. The colours of the changing seasons. The peaceful contentment of gathering twilight. 1 hour from Montréal, 35 min from Tremblant: 12 rms, including 8 with fireplace and whirlpool bath. **See ad end of this region and colour photos.**

From Montréal, head north on Hwy 15 to Exit 86. Drive north on Rte 117, at 5th lights turn left on Rue Préfontaine, then follow the lakeshore road, Chemin Tour-du-Lac, to number 173.

INN
AUBERGE DE LA TOUR DU LAC

Jean-Léo Legault
173, Tour-du-Lac
Ste-Agathe-des-Monts
J8C 1B7
toll free 1-800-622-1735
(819) 326-4202
fax (819) 326-0341
www.delatour.qc.ca

B&B	
single	$73-103
double	$88-118
child	$15

Taxes extra VS MC AM ER IT

Reduced rates: Apr. and Nov.
Open year round

Number of rooms	12
rooms with private bath	12

Activities: 🍷 🚲 🛥 ⛷ 🏃

---

36. STE-MARGUERITE-DU-LAC-MASSON

F E P 🚗 R4 TA

A few minutes from the village of Ste-Marguerite, come explore the woods surrounding our country-style B&B on foot, by bicycle, on cross-country skis or on snow-shoes, then return to a rustic atmosphere and a seat in front of the fireplace. Enjoy a comfortable sleep and awaken in the morning to a scrumptious breakfast served in your room or in the dining room.

Hwy 15 North, Exit 69, Rte 370 East. Drive about 8 km to the "Les Deux Rose" nursing home, then turn left on Chemin Guénette. Drive 4.5 km; the Auberge Le Campagnard is on your right.

B&B
AUBERGE LE CAMPAGNARD

Dennis Gosselin
145, chemin Guénette
Ste-Marguerite-du-Lac-Masson
J0T 1L0
(450) 228-4739

B&B	
single	$50
double	$65

VS

Open: June 1 to Oct. 31,
Dec. 1 to Apr. 30

Number of rooms	2
shared bathroom	1

Activities: 🛶 🍷 🚲 🐎 🏃

AUBERGE LA MARÉE DOUCE, Pointe-au-Père, Bas-St-Laurent

LE REFUGE FORESTIER, Maison de campagne, St-Alexandre, Kamouraska, Bas-St-Laurent

AUBERGE LA SOLAILLERIE, St-André, Kamouraska, Bas-St-Laurent

UNE FLEUR AU BORD DE L'EAU, Granby, Cantons-de-l'Est

LA BELLE ÉCHAPPÉE, Magog, Cantons-de-l'Est

À LA CHOUETTE, Baie-St-Paul, Charlevoix

AUX PETITS OISEAUX, Baie-St-Paul, Charlevoix

AUBERGE LA MUSE, Baie-St-Paul, Charlevoix

TOURLOGNON, Petite-Rivière-St-François, Chalevoix

CHEZ GERTRUDE, St-Urbain, Charlevoix

LE GÎTE DU DOCTEUR, L'Islet-sur-Mer, Chaudière-Appalaches

Auberge des Glacis

AUBERGE DES GLACIS, St-Eugène-de-l'Islet, Chaudière-Appalaches

LA MAISON DE L'ERMITAGE, St-Jean-Port-Joli, Chaudière-Appalaches

LA P'TITE BALEINE, Bergeronnes, Côte-Nord, Duplessis-Manicouagan

MAISON HOVINGTON, Tadoussac, Côte-Nord, Duplessis-Manicouagan

LA MAISON LEBREUX, Petite-Vallée, Gaspésie

LA VILLA DES FLEURS, Repentigny, Lanaudière

AUBERGE LE PROVINCIALAT, Lac-Nominingue, Laurentides

AUBERGE-RESTAURANT « CHEZ IGNACE », Lac-Nominigue, Laurentides

AUBERGE LE LUPIN, Mont-Tremblant, Laurentides

L'AUBERGE À LA CROISÉE DES CHEMINS, Mont-Tremblant, La Conception, Laurentides

GÎTE ET COUVERT LA MARIE-CHAMPAGNE, Mont-Tremblant, Lac Supérieur, Laurentides

Wilde's heath
B & B

LE WILDE'S HEATH B&B, Mont-Tremblant, St-Jovite, Laurentides

AUBERGE LAC DU PIN ROUGE, St-Hippolyte, Laurentides

AUBERGE ET SPA BEAUX RÊVES, Ste-Adèle, Laurentides

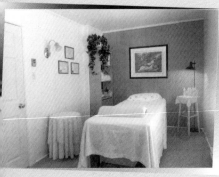

AUBERGE DE LA TOUR DU LAC, Ste-Agathe, Laurentides

LES JARDINS DE LA GARE B&B, Val-Morin, Laurentides

NID D'AMOUR, Val-Morin, Laurentides

Gîte
Le St·Élias
BED & BREAKFAST

PRIX D'EXCELLENCE
RÉGIONAL
D'ACCUEIL
1995-96
AGRICOTOURS

LE ST-ÉLIAS, Batiscan, Mauricie-Bois-Francs

MANOIR BÉCANCOURT, Bécancourt, Mauricie-Bois-Francs

GÎTE DE LA SEIGNEURIE, Louiseville, Mauricie-Bois-Francs

LE CHÂTEAU CRÊTE, Grandes Piles, Mauricie-Bois-Francs

MAISON EMERY JACOB, St-Tite, Mauricie-Bois-Francs

LA MAISON DUCHARME, Chambly, Montérégie

LA SEIGNEURIE DE NEWTON, Table Champêtre, Ste-Justine-de-Newton, Montérégie

LA VICTORIENNE, rue Notre-Dame, Montréal, région de Montréal

À BON MATIN, avenue Argyle, Montréal, région de Montréal

CHEZ PIERRE ET DOMINIQUE, Carré St-Louis, Montréal, région de Montréal

LES JARDINS DE VINOY, Vinoy, St-André-Avelin, Outaouais

MAISON ANCESTRALE THOMASSIN, Beauport, région de Québec

AUBERGE CHEMIN DU ROY, Deschambault, région de Québec

HAYDEN'S WEXFORD HOUSE, rue Champlain, Québec, région de Québec

B&B LA MAISON LESAGE, chemin St-Louis, Québec, région de Québec

B&B LES CORNICHES, chemin St-Louis, Sillery, région de Québec

CHALETS VILLAGE MONT-STE-ANNE, St-Férréol-les-Neiges, région de Québec

AUBERGE PRESBYTÈRE MONT LAC VERT, Hébertville, Saguenay-Lac-St-Jean

AUBERGE LA MAISON LAMY, Métabetchouan, Saguenay-Lac-St-Jean

37. STE-MARGUERITE-DU-LAC-MASSON

F E  P ⊘ ... R1 TA

"The tranquillity of the forest, the beautiful setting, the sun-lit house, the warmth of two hearths, such warm-hearted people, an extra-special breakfast. The place had it all." Here you will find the contentment of a pleasant, informal home. Near St-Sauveur and Ste-Adèle, between Montréal and Mont Tremblant.

Two km. from the "Bistrot Champlain". From Montréal, Hwy 15 North, Exit 69. Rte 370, 10,5 km. After the cemetery and Sommet Vert, left on Lupin. Left on Rue Des Rapides, to the end of the street.

B&B
GÎTE DU LIÈVRE

Chantal Belisle and
Patrice Richard
34, Place du Lièvre
Ste-Marguerite-du-Lac-Masson
J0T 1L0
tel/fax (450) 228-4131
toll free Mtl (514) 823-4582
pages.citenet.net/
users/ctmx0131
gite_du_lievre@citenet.net

B&B	
single	$55
double	$65
triple	$80
quad.	$95
child	$10-15

Open: Dec. 1 to Oct. 31

Number of rooms	3
rooms with private bath	1
shared bathrooms	1

Activities:

---

38. VAL-DAVID

F e  P R.5

In the heart of the Laurentians, we welcome you into a warm family setting. Rustic house, fireplace, screened porch, log-style first floor. Across from the linear park for cycling, cross-country skiing or to simply enjoy the town's charm.

From Montréal, Hwy 15 North, Exit 76, Rte 117 North. Past the sign, "Bienvenue Val-David", first traffic lights, turn right on Rue de L'Église. Turn right on Rue de la Sapinière, two blocks away.

B&B
LA CHAUMIÈRE AUX
MARGUERITES

Fabienne and Marc Girard
and their daughter Jéromine
1267, rue de la Sapinière
Val-David J0T 2N0
(819) 322-2043

B&B	
single	$50
double	$60
child	$0-10

VS

Reduced rates: 2 nights and more
Open year round

Number of rooms	2
shared bathrooms	1

Activities:

---

39. VAL-DAVID

F e 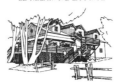 P ... ✗ TA

Old-station-style inn on the summer bike path/winter ski trail (*"P'tit train du nord"*). Terrace on the Rivière du Nord. Ideal for lovers. Rooms on the river or trail. Transport to anywhere on the path (15-passenger minibus). Treks organized: cross-country ski, snowmobile, dogsled, bike, canoe, visits around Québec. At our restaurant: Québec beers and traditional food.

1 hr from Montréal, Hwy 15 N. or Rte 117 N., Exit 76 Val David, then take the 1st street on the left for 600 m.

INN
LE RELAIS DE LA PISTE

Anne-Marie and
Thierry Chaumont
1430, de l'Académie
Val-David J0T 2N0
(819) 322-2280
fax (819) 322-6658
lerelais@polyinter.com

	B&B	MAP
single	$68	$86
double	$75	$110
triple	$90	$145
quad.	$105	$180
child	$15	$30

Taxes extra VS AM IT

Reduced rates: Oct. 10 to
Oct. 31, Mar. 1 to Mar. 31
Open year round

Number of rooms	6
rooms with private bath	6

Activities:

40. VAL-MORIN

F E P 🚗 R.5 TA

Laurentides Excellence Prize 1997-98. A cosy nest where you can relax in private. Lounge around the fire in the living room with its great view. Easy access to the bike path (1 km), cross-country and downhill skiing. Close to Val-David, Ste-Adèle, St-Sauveur and Mt-Tremblant (30 min). We can meet you at the airport, 40 km to Mirabel, 75 km to Dorval.

From Montréal or Mirabel, Hwy 15 North, Exit 76 (Val-Morin). Rte 117, for 0.5 km, turn right on Curé-Corbeil, to the end 1.5 km, then turn right on Rue Morin, 0.5 km.

B&B
LA «CHANT'OISEAU»

Martine and Marc Sabourin
5760, rue Morin
Val-Morin J0T 2R0
(819) 322-6660

B&B	
single	$40
double	$55
triple	$75
child	$10-15

Reduced rates: Oct. 15 to Dec.15, Fev. 1 to May 15
10% 2 nights and more
Open year round

Number of rooms	3
shared bathrooms	1

Activities: 🏊 🚶 🚲 🏊 🎿

---

41. VAL-MORIN

F E ♿ 🚭 🏊 🚗 ✖ P TA

In the heart of the Laurentians, we welcome you into a warm family setting. Rustic house, fireplace, screened porch, log-style first floor. Across from the linear park for cycling, cross-country skiing or to simply enjoy the town's charm.

From Montréal, Hwy 15 North, Exit 76, Rte 117 North. Past the sign, "Bienvenue Val-David", first traffic lights, turn right on Rue de L'Église. Turn right on Rue de la Sapinière, two blocks away.

B&B
LES FLORETTES

Micheline Boutin and
Jacques Allard
1803, de la Gare
Val-Morin J0T 2R0
(819) 322-7614
fax (819) 322-3029
escapade@polyinter.com

B&B	
single	$45
double	$65
child	$16

Taxes extra VS MC

Open year round

Number of rooms	5
shared wc	1
shared bathrooms	2

Activities: 🏊 🚶 🚲 🏊 🎿

---

42. VAL-MORIN

F E 🚭 P 🚗 🐕 R2 🏊 TA

Discover a piece of Laurentian heritage in this former General Store and Post Office. The 2-acre property lies alongside "Parc Linéaire" and Lake Raymond. Bikes, canoes and pedalboats free. Relax on one of the porches in front of the lake, an ideal retreat from which to past the time. Come enjoy our 5-course breakfast and exquisite hospitality. Gift certificate. **See ad end of this region and colour photos.**

From Mtl: Hwy 15 N., Exit 76. Drive 0.5 km on Rte 117 N., then right on Curé-Corbeil to the end. Right on Rue Morin, 0.5 km, left on 8e Avenue, then 7e Avenue and go all the way to the end.

B&B
LES JARDINS DE LA GARE B&B

Françoise and Alain
1790, 7e Avenue
Val-Morin J0T 2R0
tel/fax (819) 322-5559
toll free 1-888-322-4273
http://pages.infinit.net/
racetr/jardin.html

B&B	
single	$50
double	$70
child	$15

Taxes extra VS IT

Reduced rates: Oct. 15 to Dec. 15, Mar. 15 to May 1
Open year round

Number of rooms	5
rooms with sink	2
shared wc	1
shared bathroomss	2

Activities: 🏛 🛶 🏊 🚲 🎿

43. VAL-MORIN

F E  P R2 TA

Between Montréal and Tremblant, discover paradise on a beautiful lake surrounded by mountains. In summer, take a deep breath while canoeing on the lake with the loons. In winter, relax by our impressive fireplace facing a magnificient view. Directly on Far Hills trails. 3.7 km from Linear Park. **See colour photos.**

Hwy 15 North, Exit 76, Rte 117 North. Follow signs Far Hills for 6.3 km. At stop sign for Chemin Far Hills Inn, go straight ahead for 1.4 km. Turn right twd Lac Lasalle then left on CUL-DE-SAC.

B&B
NID D'AMOUR

Lise and Camil Bourque
6455, chemin du Lac Lasalle
Val-Morin J0T 2R0
tel/fax (819) 322-6379
toll free 1-888- 4321-NID
nidamour@hotmail.com

	B&B
single	$70-90-100-120
double	$70-90-100-120

VS

Reduced rates: during the week from Oct. 15 to June 15
Open year round
(except during the Christmas Holidays)

Number of rooms	4
rooms with private bath	4

Activities:

For your Comfort

ALL OUR ESTABLISHMENTS ARE INSPECTED REGULARLY BY THE FEDERATION

Seal of «Quality Control»

AGRICOTOURS

44. LAC-SUPÉRIEUR, MONT-TREMBLANT

F E ♿ P R.9 M.4

Hypnotized by the wind in the trees and an unforgetfull view of the mountains. This carefully decorated home (1930) offers relaxation by the fireplace or access to nature ; beach, lake, river. 7 min. from our two largest sites station and parc du Mont-Tremblant. A few steps away : hiking trail, biking, cross-country skiing and three beautiful studios wich will also charm you.

Hwy 15 North, Rte 117 North, St-Faustin Exit. Right at stop sign, 2.3 km, follow Mont-Tremblant Park and ski resort signs, continue for 9.5 km.

COUNTRY HOME
LE VENT DU NORD

Géraldine and Jean Christie
1954, ch. du Lac Supérieur
Lac-Supérieur JOT 1P0
(819) 688-6140
fax (819) 688-3196

No. houses	4
No. rooms	1-4
No. people	1-10
WEEK-SUMMER	$350-930
WEEK-WINTER	$455-2450
W/E-SUMMER	$150-550
W/E-WINTER	$150-700

Taxes extra VS IT

Open year round

Activities: 🛶 👤 ⛷ 🎿 🏃

FARM ACTIVITIES

* Registered Trademark.

LAVAL

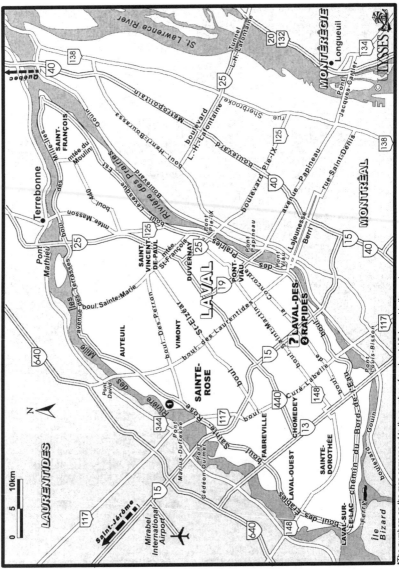

1. LAVAL

F E 🚭 🛏 P 🏠 R1 TA

Welcome to the village of Vieux Ste-Rose in Laval, 30 minutes from Montréal and the Laurentides. We have had guests from 27 countries stay with us. Even businesspeople will feel like they are on vacation here, chatting away over breakfast before the Mille-Îles wildlife sanctuary. See you soon!

Hwy 15 (North or South), Exit 16, right on Boul. Ste-Rose, 2.5 km to Rue des Patriotes (Vieux Ste-Rose restaurant on the corner). Turn left, continue for 0.9 km.

B&B
GÎTE DU BORD DE L'EAU

Louise Trudeau
495, rue des Patriotes
Laval H7L 2L9
(450) 625-3785
fax (450) 625-8235

B&B	
single	$45
double	$60
triple	$80
quad.	$100
child	$5-10-15

Open year round

Number of rooms	1
rooms with private bath	1

Activities: 🏛 ⛴ 🚣 🎣 🏃

2. LAVAL

F e 🚭 P 🏠 🐕 R.75 TA

Old comfortable farmhouse. Located 3 km from Montréal. Henri-Bourassa Métro station (we'll pick you up from there). Warm welcome, hearty breakfast done to your liking. Children welcome. Pool and patio with flowers. 15% reduction after 7 consecutive nights. Taxes included.

From Montréal, Hwy 15 North, Exit 7 Boul. des Prairies East. Or from Mirabel, Hwy 15 South, Exit 7 Boul. des Prairies East. Turn left on Boul. Bon Pasteur, the 13th street heading east.

B&B
L'ABRI DU TEMPS

Marguerite and Raoul St-Jean
2, boul. Bon Pasteur
Laval-des-Rapides
H7N 3P9
tel/fax (450) 663-5094

B&B	
single	$47
double	$57
child	$15

Reduced rates : Nov. 1 to May 1
Open year round

Number of rooms	3
shared bathrooms	2

Activities: 🏛 🚣 🎣 🚶 🚲

B&Bs AND INNS

MAURICIE—BOIS-FRANCS

*The numbers on the map correspond to the number of each establishment in the region.

1. BATISCAN

F E  P R2 TA

An enchanting B&B by the St-Laurent River, on the Chemin du Roy, awaits you. A stone's throw from a superb, unknown beach, near Parc de la Batiscan, less than 40 minutes from Parc de la Mauricie, Village du Bûcheron, Cité de l'énergie, Forges du Saint-Maurice. Winter activities: snowshoeing, dogsledding, snowmobiling, ice fishing. **See colour photos.**

Between Montréal and Québec City, Hwy 40, Batiscan Exit, twd Rte 361 South, Rte 138 West. 4 km from the highway.

B&B
LE ST-ÉLIAS

Monique Bernier
951, Principale rte 138
Batiscan G0X 1A0
(418) 362-2712
fax (418) 362-2081
www.bbcanada.com/886.html
monique.bernier@cgocable.ca

	B&B	PAM
single	$45-50	$60-65
double	$55-60	$85-90

VS MC

Reduced rates : 3 nights and more
Open: Jan. 15 to Oct. 31

Number of rooms	4
shared wc	1
shared bathrooms	2

Activities: 🏛 🦆 🛶 🛥 🚶

2. BÉCANCOUR

F E ✖ P TA

We are renowned for our welcome, our food and our B&B inside a sumptuous victorian house. We serve: ostrich, buffalo, caribou, venison, duck, rabbit, beef, seafood and perch. Refined local cuisine. Right nearby: canoeing, tennis, horseback riding, snowmobiling, swimming, fishing, tourist attractions. **See colour photos.**

From Montréal or Québec City: Hwy 40. In Trois-Rivières: cross the Laviolette bridge, Rte 132 East. Bécancour Exit. Rue Nicolas Perrot. We are next to the church.

INN
MANOIR BÉCANCOURT

Yvon Beaulieu
3255, Nicolas Perrot
Bécancour G0X 1B0
(819) 294-9068
fax (819) 294-9060

	B&B	PAM
single	$35	$50
double	$50	$80
child	$15	$30

Taxes extra VS MC

Open year round

Number of rooms	5
shared wc	4
shared bathrooms	2

Activities: 🏛 🦆 🛥 🚶 🚲

3. DESCHAILLONS-SUR-SAINT-LAURENT

F E P R.5 TA

La Petite Diligence brings the beautiful romances of times past to life. Come explore the St-Laurent, its spectacular landscapes and singular promontories. Let yourselves be won over by its vivacity, and lulled by its fabulous sunsets. The river, our roots, our history. Come take a look!

Rte 132 skirts the river's south shore halfway between the Québec City and Trois-Rivières bridges. From Hwy 20, Exit 253, Rte 265 North to the river; left, about 1 km.

B&B
LA PETITE DILIGENCE

Claire Duhamel
1545, Marie-Victorin, C.P. 26
Deschaillons-sur-Saint-Laurent
G0S 1G0
(819) 292-3119
(819) 292-3106
fax (819) 292-2925

	B&B
single	$30
double	$40

Open year round

Number of rooms	2
shared bathrooms	1

Activities: 🚶 🚲 🐎 🛥 🏃

B&Bs AND INNS

4. DRUMMONDVILLE

F | E | 🚭 | 🚗 | P | ⛵ | R1 | TA

"Experience the house from long ago, where both roses and children grow. Our "small" family (11) welcomes you to its table set with home-made bread and jams, fresh eggs, juice and aromatic coffee. Make yourself at home!

Halfway between Montréal and Québec City, between Sherbrooke and Trois-Rivières. Exit 175 off Hwy 20 to Drummondville (Boul. Lemire Sud), 300 m from Hwy 20.

B&B
LE GÎTE DES ROSES

Diane and Denis Lampron
215, boul. Lemire, R.R. #6
Drummondville J2C 7X2
(819) 474-4587
fax (819) 474-1500
rose.qc.ca/gite
gite@rose.qc.ca

B&B	
single	$40
double	$55
triple	$65
quad.	$75
child	$10

Open year round
closed from Aug. 1 to Aug. 15

Number of rooms	3
shared bathrooms	3

Activities: 🏛 🐚 ⛵ 🎿 🚴

5. DRUMMONDVILLE

F | E | ♿ | 🚗 | 🐕 | P | R5 | TA

A continually well-kept B&B by the St-François River awaits you. Surrounded by woodlands, greenery and flowers, near a brook. Quiet nights. Complete, refined breakfast on the spot or in the house next door, on the same property. We are 12 minutes from the town centre. Meals upon request.

Hwy 20, Exit 55 twd Sherbrooke, then Rte 139 Exit towards St-Nicéphore. Go through the village and continue to the airport near the river. Turn right and drive 1.2 km.

B&B
MAISON LA COULÉE

Beldora and Daniel Roy
4890, boul. Allard
Drummondville J2B 6V3
(819) 477-4359
fax (819) 477-0672
www.quebecweb.com/
lacoulee/
daniel.roy@dr.cgocable.ca

B&B	
single	$35-45
double	$55-80
triple	$80
child	$10

Open year round

Number of rooms	5
rooms with private bath	1
shared bathrooms	3

Activities: 🏛 🐚 ⛵ 🎿 🚴

6. DRUMMONDVILLE, ST-CYRILLE

F | e | 🚭 | P | 🐕 | R3 | TA

L'Oasis is located between Montréal and Québec City, 5 km from Drummondville. A non-smoking and welcoming B&B surrounded by vast spaces, trees, flowers and water garden with air conditioning. Healthy and copious breakfasts home-made products. To see: Village Québécois d'Antan, world folklore festival (July), Festival des cultures. Also bike path and skiing near by.

Hwy 20, Exit 185. Drive 2 km to the church, right on Rte 122 for 1 km.

B&B
L'OASIS

Johanna Beier Putzke
3500, Route 122
St-Cyrille-de-Wendover
J1Z 1C3
(819) 397-2917

B&B	
single	$40
double	$50-55
child	$5-10

Reduced rates : Oct. 1 to May 1
Open year round

Number of rooms	2
rooms with sink	1
shared bathrooms	1

Activities: 🐚 🎿 🚴 🐎 🏃

7. DRUMMONDVILLE, ST-GERMAIN

F E ⊘ 🚗 P 🐕 R6 TA

Old-time charm, a gentle way of life. Large 1916 country house, secluded, surrounded by vast flowered areas. Gourmet breakfast in the solarium: bread, pancakes, French toast and home-made jam. Village Québécois d'Antan and its cross-country skiing trails, "La Campagnarde" bike path, Folklore Festival (early July), Ulverton wool mill, Upton theatre and Drummondville. Welcome to the heart of Québec.

From Québec City, Hwy 20, Exit 166, left on the 10e Rang, to Rte 239 North. From Montréal, Hwy 20 Exit 166, right on the 10e Rang, to Rte 239 North, for 3 km.

B&B
LE MADAWASKA

Juliette Levasseur
644, Route 239 Nord
St-Germain J0C 1K0
(819) 395-4318

B&B	
single	$40
double	$55
triple	$65
child	$10

Reduced rates : Jan. to Mar.
Open year round

Number of rooms	3
shared bathrooms	2

Activities: 🏛 🐚 ⚲ 🚲 🎿

8. DURHAM-SUD

F E ⊘ P 🛶 🐕 R5 TA

Our sixth-generation farm warmly invites you to share in its peace and beauty by walking the fields and woods, stopping at the river or enjoying the numerous other outdoor activities.

From Hwy 20, Exit 147, Rte 116 East to Durham-Sud. From flashing light another 2 km on Rte 116, left on Mooney Rd, 3 km. From Hwy 55 Exit 88, Rte 116 West 12 km, right on Mooney Rd, 3 km.

B&B
LA SIXIÈME GÉNÉRATION

Heather Lunan and
Norman Carson
415, chemin Mooney
Durham-Sud J0H 2C0
(819) 858-2539
fax (819) 858-2001

B&B	
single	$40-45
double	$55-60
triple	$75
quad	$90
child	$0-10

Taxes extra

Open : June 1 to Oct. 31

Number of rooms	3
shared wc	1
shared bathrooms	1

Activities: 🏛 ⚲ 🚲 🛷 🎿

9. GRANDE-ANSE

F E ✖ 🚗 P 🛶 R17 TA

This haven of peace has belonged to Mrs. Anne "the queen of Mauricie" McCormick's since 1918. On the shores of the St-Maurice, the site is the ideal setting to relive this great lady's history, with wide expanses inviting you to relax, have fun and get a good dose of fresh air. Afterwards, there are adventures and anecdotes to relate inside. Tailor-made adventure packages. Family-size suites. **Country home p 184, no 39.**

We are located in Grande-Anse, right on Rte 155, 1.5 hours north of Trois-Rivières, 20 minutes south of La Tuque. Halfway between Lac St-Jean and Montreal.

B&B
MAISON GOYETTE

Domaine McCormick
3970, Route 155 Sud
Grande-Anse G0X 2C0
(819) 676-3388
fax (819) 676-3297

	B&B	MAP
single	$40	$50
double	$55	$80
child	$10	$15

Taxes extra VS MC

Reduced rates: for 6 or more people
Open year round

Number of rooms	2
shared bathrooms	2

Activities: 🛶 🚶 🛷 🎿 🐎

B&Bs AND INNS

10. GRAND-MÈRE

F E 🐾 🐕 P R.1

Come as you are and relive a page of history with us, in large and comfortable rooms. Our lovely Victorian house, having painstakingly preserved its attractive features stands proudly and majestically 20 minutes from Cité de l'Énergie and from the National Park, 5 minutes from the Grand-Mère golf course.

From Québec City: Hwy 40 West, Exit 220 twd Grand-Mère, 0.5 km from the bridge. From Montréal: Hwy 40 East, Hwy 55 North, Exit 223, go all the way down 5e Ave. Circle the park and turn on to 3e Ave.

B&B
GÎTE LA BELLE AU
BOIS DORMANT

Valérie, Lucie,
Pierre and Pierrot Dumont
20, 3ᵉ Avenue
Grand-Mère G9T 2T3
(819) 538-6489
(819) 533-2572

B&B	
single	$50-70
double	$55-75
child	$10

Open year round

Number of rooms	3
shared bathrooms	1
shared wc	1
rooms with private bath	1

Activities: 🛶 🏃 🚲 ⛷ 🎿

11. GRANDES-PILES

F e ♿ 🍽 🚗 P 🏊 TA

"Le Bôme, some Mauricie balm to bask in". Snug inside an ancestral home, you will discover a friendly inn with cozy, comfortable rooms during your stay. The French-Italian-flavoured cuisine is a must. The singular landscape of mountains scored by the St-Maurice river will draw you to its National Park. This 3-star inn boasts a spa, sauna and tennis court.

Halfway between Montréal and Québec City. Hwy 40 to Trois-Rivières, Hwy 55 North and Rte 155 twd La Tuque. Lac St-Jean, 10 km past Grand-Mère, follow roadsigns to the inn.

INN
AUBERGE-LE-BÔME

Matilde Mossa and
Jean-Claude Coydon
720, 2ᵉ Avenue
Grandes-Piles G0X 1H0
toll free 1-800- 538-2805
(819) 538- 2805
fax (819) 538-5879
www.auberge-le-bome.qc.ca
auberge-le-bome@
infoteck.qc.ca

	B&B	PAM
single	$80-115	$115-150
double	$85-120	$150-170
triple	$95-130	$205-245
child	$10	$25

Taxes extra VS MC IT

Open year round

Number of rooms	10
rooms with private bath	10

Activities: 🛶 🏃 🚤 🎿 🐎

12. GRANDES-PILES

F e 🚗 P 🏊 R.1 TA

Perched between the Rivière St-Maurice and the mountains, Château Crête, the jewel of the Mauricie, is ideal for those who love wild open spaces. What awaits: Mauricie National Park and its many activities; lumberjack village; Village d'Émilie; Cité de l'Énergie; all that and more... see you soon! **See colour photos.**

Halfway between Montréal and Québec City by Hwy 40, then 55 N., 155 twd la Tuque and Lac St-Jean. We are less than 60 km from Trois-Rivières. Happy driving. Visit our internet site.

INN
LE CHÂTEAU CRÊTE

Micheline Bardor
740, 4ᵉ Avenue
Grandes-Piles G0X 1H0
(819) 538-8389
toll free 1-888-538-8389
fax (819) 538-7323
www3.sympatico.ca/
chateau_crete

B&B	
single	$45-65
double	$60-80
triple	$75
quad.	$90

Taxes extra

Open year round

Number of rooms	7
rooms with private bath	2
rooms with sink	3
rooms in basement	3
shared wc	3
shared bathrooms	1

Activities: 🏛 🚣 🛶 🏇 🎿

13. HÉROUXVILLE

F | ♿ | ✗ | P | 🚗 | ⛵ | R2

A stop at our B&B will give you a chance to catch your breath. We also offer farm stays that allow you to experience the joys our everyday lives. Landscaped exterior, pool, biking, games, fireplace and interesting attractions. B&B in a farmhouse next to the main house. Air conditioned house. **Farm stay p 38.**

From Montréal, Hwy 40 East. At Trois-Rivières, Hwy 55 North. At the end of Hwy 55, Exit Rte 153 North. At Hérouxville, cross the railway and drive 2 km.

B&B
FERME LES SEMAILLES

Lise Richer and François Naud
1480, rang Saint-Pierre
Hérouxville GOX 1J0
(418) 365-5590
(418) 365-5190

	B&B	MAP
single	$20	$28
double	$40	$56
child	$12	$15

Open year round

Number of rooms	5
shared bathrooms	2

Activities: 🚣 ⛵ 🏃 🐎 ⛷

14. HÉROUXVILLE

F | E | 🚗 | 🐕 | P | R5 | TA

A warm B&B located near Parc de la Mauricie between Montréal and Lac St-Jean. Come relax by the fire and sample grilled marshmallows. Family ambiance where it is pleasant to share our traditions with you. Prix Excellence Mauricie-Bois-Francs 1994-95. **Country house p 184.**

Halfway between Québec City and Montréal by Hwy 20 or 40, take Hwy 55 N. via Trois-Rivières. At the end of Hwy 55, Exit Rte 153 N. At Hérouxville, at the flashing light, street beside the church.

B&B
MAISON TRUDEL

Nicole Jubinville
and Yves Trudel
543, Goulet
Hérouxville GOX 1J0
(418) 365-7624
fax (418) 365-7041
www.bbcanada.com/408.html
maison-trudel-quebec
@concepta.com

	B&B
single	$40
double	$50
triple	$75
child	$10

Open year round

Number of rooms	4
shared bathrooms	3

Activities: 🎣 🚶 🐎 ⛷

15. LOUISEVILLE

F | e | 🚗 | ✗ | P | R1 | TA

Comfortable, peaceful Victorian farmhouse (1880) in a shaded and flowered park. A romantic trip back in time. Quality and harmony, it has been called "a corner of paradise..." 10 km from Ste-Ursule waterfalls, Lac St-Pierre. Dine on the farm (5 courses) with reservations. **Farm Stay p 38, country-style dining p 21, country home p 184 and Farm Excursion p 32.** See colour photos.

From Montréal or Québec City, Hwy 40, Exit 166. Rte 138 East, drive 2.4 km to Rte 348 West. Left twd St-Ursule, drive 1.5 km, 1st road on the right, 1st house tucked behind the trees.

B&B
LE GÎTE DE LA SEIGNEURIE

Michel Gilbert
480, chemin du Golf
Louiseville J5V 2L4
tel/fax (819) 228-8224

	B&B	MAP
single	$45-70	$65-90
double	$60-90	$100-130
triple	$85	$145
quad.	$100	$180
child	$20	$30

Taxes extra

Open year round

Number of rooms	5
rooms with sink	2
rooms with private bath	1
shared bathrooms	2

Activities: 🏛 🚶 🎣 🚶 🚴

16. LOUISEVILLE

`F` `E` ⊘ ⅱ 🚗 `P` 🐕 `TA`

The Carrefour is not only a prestigious B&B but also one of the most cultural in Québec. Our Queen-Anne house is the only official historic one in the village. Sumptuously furnished and decorated, it offers the utmost in comfort. Each of its four rooms is more opulent than the next. Discover its garden, as well.

From Montréal or Québec, Hwy 40, Exit 166 or 174 to Rte 138 twd downtown Louiseville. Corner Rte 349 and 138.

B&B
GÎTE DU CARREFOUR

Réal-Maurice Beauregard
11, av. St-Laurent Ouest
Louiseville J5V 1J3
tel/fax (819) 228-4932
www.quebecreservation.com

B&B	
single	$45
double	$55

Open year round

Number of rooms	4
shared wc	1
shared bathrooms	3

Activities: 🏛 ⛴ 🚶 🚲 🐎

---

17. LOUISEVILLE

`F` `e` `P` `R2`

Old-fashioned charm and modern comforts. The magnificent ancestral house, set on an immense property bordered by flowers and trees, reveals its flavourful cuisine and beauty secrets. Three carefully decorated rooms offer comfort and tranquillity. One hour from Montréal, a peaceful oasis.

From Montréal, Hwy 40, Exit 166. Rte 138 E. for 3.5 km. Rte 349, Rue Notre-Dame N. for 1 km. From Québec City, Hwy 40, Exit 174. Rte 138 W., for 4.9 km, Rte 349, Rue Notre-Dame N., for 1 km.

B&B
LA MAISON DE L'ANCÊTRE

Julienne Leblanc
491, Notre-Dame Nord
Louiseville J5V 1X9
(819) 228-8195

B&B	
single	$40-45
double	$45-50
triple	$60-65
child	$10

Open year round

Number of rooms	3
shared bathrooms	1
shared wc	1

Activities: 🚶 🚶 🚲 ⛴ 🐎

---

18. NOTRE-DAME-DE-HAM

`F` `E` 🐕 🚗 `P` `R5` `TA`

Fairytale house in a little village in the heart of the Appalachians, where Morpheus, the god of sleep and dreams warmly welcomes you to his magical little wooden home. The river, the trout, the falls invite you as I await you in the privacy of my own home.

Hwy 20: Jean-Lesage twd Québec city, Exit 210. In Victoriaville: twd the Laurier museum or S.Q. Boul. Laurier South (Rte 161 South). Notre-Dame-De-Ham 26 km.

B&B
LA MAISON DE MORPHÉE

Madeleine Codère
23, Principale
Notre-Dame-de-Ham, G0P 1C0
tel/fax (819) 344-5476

B&B	
single	$45
double	$55-65
child	$12

Taxes extra

Open year round

Number of rooms	3
rooms with private bath	1
shared bathrooms	1

Activities: 🏛 🍽 🚶 🚲

19. NOTRE-DAME-DE-HAM

F E 🚫 ♿ P 🐕 R7 TA

The Appalachians please and, above all, surprise those in search of new horizons. Mr. Pierre Dupont of the Enjeux show, on Radio-Canada, gave our cuisine the highest rating and his spouse is of the same opinion! Our special attraction: fly and light rod-and-reel fishing; each site has a limited capacity. Our B&B is set up in such a way as to respects the environment and the beauty of the site.

Hwy 20 Jean-Lesage twd Québec City. Exit 210. In Victoriaville, follow directions to Laurier Museum or S.Q., take Boul. Laurier South, 161 S. At 26 km to Notre-Dame-de-Ham.

B&B
LE GÎTE J.D. TROTTIER

Jeanne D. Trottier
37, rue Principale
Notre-Dame-de-Ham G0P 1C0
tel/fax (819) 344-5640
jdarc@boisfrancs.qc.ca

B&B	
single	$40
double	$55
triple	$70
child	$12

VS MC

Open year round

Number of rooms	3
shared bathrooms	2

Activities: 🏛 ⚲ 🎣 🚲 🎿

---

20. ST-MATHIEU-DU-PARC

F E P 🐕 R5 TA

Welcome to our haven of peace and harmony. 7 km from Parc de la Mauricie. You're invited to l'Herbarium, a picturesque residence, enchanting and grandiose decor, amidst lakes, mountains, flower gardens. Friendly welcome, relaxing atmosphere, delicious breakfast. Picnics and hiking on site.

From Montréal, Hwy 40 East, Hwy 55 North, Exit 217. Rte 351 North, 12 km. Right on Ch. St-François, 4 km. Left on Ch. Principal, 1 km. Right on Ch. St-Paul, 0.5 km.

B&B
L'HERBARIUM

Anne-Marie Groleau
1950, chemin St-Paul
St-Mathieu-du-Parc G0X 1N0
(819) 532-2461

B&B	
single	$40
double	$55-65
triple	$75
child	$10

Open year round

Number of rooms	3
shared wc	1
shared bathrooms	1

Activities: 🧍 ⛷ 🎣 🚲 🎿

---

21. ST-PIERRE-LES-BECQUETS

F E P 🛶 🐕 R1

Come live according to the rhythm of the tides, the life of the river, the country and a village that takes the time to welcome you. We offer you rest and comfort in a welcoming home with unique vistas. Heated pool in season. Unforgettable sunrises and sunsets.

From Montréal Hwy 40 East. In Trois-Rivières, Laviolette Bridge, Hwy 30 East which becomes Rte 132 East, to St-Pierre. Or from Québec City bridge twd Nicolet, Rte 132 West to St-Pierre.

B&B
LA MAISON SUR LE FLEUVE

Suzanne Chartrand
and Jacques Lefebvre
136, Marie-Victorin
St-Pierre-les-Becquets
G0X 2Z0
(819) 263-2761
fax (819) 375-2512

B&B	
single	$35
double	$50
child	$5-15

Open year round

Number of rooms	3
shared wc	1
shared bathrooms	1

Activities: 🎣 🚲 🐎 🛷 🎿

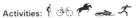

B&Bs AND INNS

22. ST-STANISLAS-DE-CHAMPLAIN

F | e | P | R8 | TA

Set in a rural environment, the Gîte du Vagabond will live up to your expectations, with its 4 ancestral rooms and incredible breakfast. Our local attractions, hikes, horseback riding and water sports less than an hour away will add to your stay. Come wander with us, we await you.

On the north bank of the St-Laurent, halfway between Québec City and Montréal, on Rte 352 twd St-Stanislas. Pass the church and continue for 8 km toward St-Adelphe.

B&B
LE GÎTE DU VAGABOND

Isabelle Germain
444, rg de la Rivière
Batiscan Sud-Ouest
St-Stanislas-de-Champlain
G0X 3E0
(418) 328-3653
(418) 289-3742

B&B	
single	$25
double	$50

Taxes extra

Open year round

Number of rooms	4
shared bathrooms	2

Activities: 🚣 🚶 🏇 🏃

---

23. ST-TITE

F | e | 🚫 | 🐕 | 🚗 | P | 🏊 | R.03 | TA

At Lucie's,
Spontaneous personal welcome,
Intimate family ambiance,
Player piano as melodious,
Hot bread, well-stocked table,
All year round,
Dreamy attractions,
Bikes in the shed, refreshing pool,
In St-Tite: original Western village,
A stay in a little corner of paradise,
Near Parc de la Mauricie,
On the road to Lac St-Jean...
Heaven on earth!
See colour photos
From Québec City or Montréal: Hwy 40. At Trois-Rivières, take Hwy 55 North and exit 153 north. At St-Tite, at the "caisse populaire", turn left and drive 500 metres.

B&B
MAISON EMERY JACOB

Lucie Verret and Réal Trépanier
211, Notre-Dame
St-Tite G0X 3H0
(418) 365-5532
fax (418) 365-3957

B&B	
single	$40
double	$50
triple	$75
child	$10

VS AM

Reduced rates : Nov. 1 to Apr. 1
Open year round

Number of rooms	3
shared wc	1
shared bathrooms	1

Activities: 🚴 🎣 🛷 🏃 🐎

---

24. STE-ANNE-DE-LA-PÉRADE

F | E | ✖ | P | TA

On the Chemin du Roy, between "smelt" river and the forgotten *"marigotte"*, the timeless old Manoir Dauth offers a world of delightful packages: fishing, snowmobiling, dogsledding, sightseeing, croquet, cycling, mouthwatering cuisine and sweet dreams in a canopy bed.

Between Montréal (2 hours) and Québec City (1 hour) on Chemin du Roy (Rte 138), 100 m from the church. Via Hwy 40, Exit 236, right at 1st stop, left at 2nd stop, then go 200 m.

INN
AUBERGE DU
MANOIR DAUTH

Lise Garceau and
Yvan Turgeon
21, boul. de Lanaudière
C.P. 111
Ste-Anne-de-la-Pérade
G0X 2J0
tel/fax (418) 325-3432

	B&B	PAM
single	$40	$53
double	$52-62	$78-88
triple	$64-74	$103-113
quad.	$76-86	$128-138
child	$10	$17

Taxes extra VS MC ER IT AM

Open year round

Number of rooms	5
rooms with private bath	1
shared wc	2
shared bathrooms	2

Activities: 🏛 🚴 🛷 🏃 🐎

25. STE-ANNE-DE-LA-PÉRADE

F e 🐕 ✕ 🚗 P R1 TA

Ancestral house where time has stopped. Stay in a historic monument; documents and furniture (1702-1998). Part of the Heritage Tour. Magnificent French garden. Tommy-cod fishing is one way to enhance your stay. Step back in time in our museum-house.

On the Chemin du Roy, Rte 138, 2 hours from Montréal, 1 hour from Québec City, via Hwy 40, Exit 236, 2 km east of the church.

INN
L'ARRÊT DU TEMPS

Serge Gervais
965, boul. de Lanaudière
Chemin du Roy
Ste-Anne-de-la-Pérade
G0X 2J0
(418) 325-3590

B&B	
single	$40-45
double	$50-55
triple	$65-70

Taxes extra VS MC

Open year round

Number of rooms	3
shared wc	1
shared bathrooms	1

Activities: 🏛 ⚲ 🚲 🛶 🏃

26. STE-ÉLIZABETH-DE-WARWICK

F e 🚗 P ✕ R6 TA

Enjoy the relaxing wide expanses and the quiet countryside. Kitchen garden, orchard and flower gardens surround our home. For more action less than 6 kilometres away, bike along the country road (110 km) or enjoy yourselves at the Grands-Chênes theatre in Kingsey Falls. Tempted? Pack your bags, we await you! Packages: cycling, canoeing, theatre.

Hwy 20, Exit 210. Rte 955 to St-Albert, follow signs for Warwick, turn right on 4e Rang (6 km). After the village of Ste-Élizabeth, left on Rte Mondoux, drive 1.5 km.

B&B
LE PETIT BALUCHON

Marie-France, Daniel and
Jean-René Dumas
305, route Mondoux
Ste-Élizabeth-de-Warwick
J0A 1M0
(819) 358-2406

	B&B	PAM
single	$40	$55
double	$58	$88
child	$5-10	$10-20

Taxes extra

Open year round

Number of rooms	5
shared bathrooms	2

Activities: 🏛 ⚲ ⚲ 🚲 🐎

27. STE-GENEVIÈVE-DE-BATISCAN

F E 🚭 P 🚗 🐕 R1.5

On Rivière Batiscan, right near "Chemin du Roy" Rte 138, experience the warm, intimate atmosphere of our ancestral home (large beds, whirlpool). Learn about raising angora goats. Walk through pastures to our blueberry patch. Close to Parc de la Batiscan.

Between Montréal and Québec City, Hwy 40, Exit 229 twd Ste-Geneviève-de-Batiscan, Rte 361 N. for 4.2 km. After the N.P. Massicotte bridge, turn right on Rue Principale for 0.5 km. From Rte 138, Exit 361 N...

B&B
LA MARIE-JEANNE

Marie Auger and Alfred Pellerin
241, Principale, C.P. 84
Ste-Geneviève-de-Batiscan
G0X 2R0
(418) 362-2337

B&B	
single	$45
double	$55
child	$15

Open year round

Number of rooms	2
shared bathrooms	2

Activities: 🏛 🐾 ⚲ 🚶 🚲

B&Bs AND INNS

28. SHAWINIGAN SUD

F | e | 🚗 | P | R4 | TA

At the gate of the Cité de l'Énergie, the country in the city. Four rooms overlooking the St-Maurice: calm nights, tantalizing breakfast. Writer Adrienne Choquette once lived here; her words echo through Time. Pleasant old-fashioned decor; always pleasant and warm.

From Montréal or Québec City, Hwy 40. At Trois-Rivières, Hwy 55 N. Exit 211 twd Cité de l'Énergie, Rte 157. After bridges, right at the overpass Boul. du Capitaine. At the end, before the hill, go left on Ch. St-Laurent.

B&B
LE TEMPS DES VILLAGES

Reynald Roberge
155, chemin Saint-Laurent
Shawinigan Sud G9P 1B6
tel/fax (819) 536-3487

B&B	
single	$50-60
double	$60-70
child	$10

Open year round

Number of rooms	4
shared wc	1
shared bathrooms	1

Activities: 🏛 ⛵ 🚶 🏊 🎿

29. SHAWINIGAN SUD

F | E | 🐕 | 🚗 | P | 🏊 | R1 | TA

Pamper yourselves at two artists' cozy place of refuge. Retire to your suite, born out of a dream. Behold the Cité de l'Énergie, enjoy the National Park. Private living room with fireplace, bathrooms with shower or whirlpool bath, garden with pool, breakfast on terrace, the only thing missing... is you.

From Trois-Rivières: Hwy 55 North, Exit 211 twd Cité de l'Énergie. After 2 bridges, right at 104th St. Exit. Go up hill to hospital. Left on Lacoursière (119th). Right on Adrienne-Choquette; right on Albert-Dufresne.

B&B
LES P'TITS POMMIERS

Michelle Fortin and
Jean-Louis Gagnon
2295, Albert-Dufresne
Shawinigan Sud G9P 4Y6
(819) 537-0158
fax (819) 537-4839
www.destinationquebec.com/
ftpdocs/pommiers/
pommiers.html
pommiers@caramail.com

B&B	
single	$40
double	$50

Open year round

Number of rooms	3
rooms in semi-basement	3
shared bathrooms	2

Activities: ⛵ 🚶 🚲 🏊 🎿

30. TINGWICK

F | e | 🍴 | 🚗 | P | 🏊 | R7 | TA

Enjoy the ambiance, hospitality and pleasures of yesteryear on our 27-acre farm. Animals, brook, large organic gardens, woodstove, heated outdoor spa. Food made from fresh farm products. Near a cycling path; theatre packages. Welcome to our little paradise! **Farm stay p 39.**

From Montréal or Québec City, Hwy 20, Exit 210, Rte 955 South twd St-Albert, to the end. Turn right. After 1 km, turn left twd Warwick, continue straight to Tingwick. At the stop, continue straight for 4 km. Turn left on Rang 7, drive 3.4 km.

B&B
LES DOUCES HEURES D'ANTAN

Francine Gareau
and Claude Barabé
703, Rang 7
Tingwick J0A 1L0
(819) 359-2813
fax (819) 359-3229
www.login.net/dhdantan
dhdantan@login.net

B&B	
single	$40
double	$55
triple	$70
child	$10

Taxes extra VS

Open year round

Number of rooms	4
rooms with sink	3
shared bathrooms	2

Activities: 🦆 ⛷ ⛵ 🚲 🐎

31. TROIS-RIVIÈRES

F E ⊗ ✕ P TA

Our beautiful Victorian inn is nestled in the centre of town, on the way into historic Trois-Rivières, on a secluded, shady street. Rich oak woodwork, bevelled doors, gilding and lovely moulding, handed down from the old aristocracy. The elegant dining room, with its lustrous chandelier, lacework and old lamps is open to the public. Parking and air conditioning.

Hwy 40 Exit Trois-Rivières downtown. To Notre-Dame. Left on Rue Radisson (on your left). You'll see two big black awnings.

INN
AUBERGE DU BOURG

Monic and Jean-Marc Beaudoin
172, Radisson
Trois-Rivières G9A 2C3
(819) 373-2265
(819) 379-9198

	B&B	PAM
single	$50-70	$65-85
double	$60-80	$90-110

Taxes extra VS MC AM IT

Open year round

Number of rooms	4
rooms with sink	2
rooms with private bath	2
shared wc	2
shared bathrooms	1

Activities: ⚓ ⸙ 🚶 🚲 ⛵

---

32. TROIS-RIVIÈRES

F ⊗ 🚗 P R1

Family heritage. Over 120 years old, but looking good with my big flower gardens, kitchen garden and hen house. The city has come closer, with its many restaurants, cafés and tourist attractions. Nearby, Forges St-Maurice, Mauricie National Park, Cité de l'Énergie. A stone's throw from the university.

From Québec City: Hwy 40 West, Exit 199 for the town centre, right on Ste-Marguerite, 2 km. From Montréal: Hwy 40 East, Exit 199. Left at 2nd light onto Ste-Marguerite, 2 km.

B&B
CHEZ GRAND'PAPA BEAU

Carmen and Yvon Beaudry
3305, rue Ste-Marguerite
Trois-Rivières G8Z 1X1
(819) 693-0385
grandpapa_beau@altavista.net

B&B	
single	$40
double	$50
triple	$60
quad.	$70
child	$0-10

VS

Reduced rates : Nov. 1 to May 1
Open year round

Number of rooms	3
shared bathrooms	2

Activities: 🏛 🍷 ⸙ 🚲 🏃

---

33. TROIS-RIVIÈRES

F E ⊗ 🚗 P 🐕 R.1 TA

Located in the heart of downtown and just moments from old Trois-Rivières. Former nunnery with county decor, mansard-style rooms. Come and relax by the water and one of the terraces. Massage and outdoor packages available. Parking.

From Montréal, Hwy 40 East, Exit Trois-Rivières Centre-Ville. At the traffic lights, turn right, at the next traffic lights, turn left. Drive 0.4 km to Rue Bonaventure, and drive 0.4 km.

B&B
GÎTE DU PETIT COUVENT

Maryse Bergeron et
Martin Gagnon
466, Bonaventure
Trois-Rivières G9A 2B4
(819) 379-4384
toll free 1-800-582-4384
fax (819) 371-2430

B&B	
single	$45
double	$55-60
triple	$70
quad.	$85
child	$5-15

Open year round

Number of rooms	3
rooms with sink	3
shared wc	1
shared bathrooms	1

Activities: 🏛 ⚓ 🚣 ⸙ 🚲

B&Bs AND INNS

34. TROIS-RIVIÈRES

F E ⊗ 🚲 P ⛵ R.3 TA

Hundred-year-old house in the heart of the old, historic part of the city, facing the majestic St-Laurent River. Abundance of campanulas on the property. Outdoor hot tub. Children welcome. Sweet treats await you. Gargantuan breakfast and friendly welcome. A galaxy of activities nearby.

Hwy 40, downtown exit. Take Rue St-Georges to the end, turn left on Notre-Dame, right on Rue Des Casernes and left on Des Ursulines.

B&B
GÎTE LA CAMPANULE

Kostas Grusudis and
Bertrand Dubé
634, Des Ursulines
Trois-Rivières G9A 5B4
(819) 373-1133
kg@infoteck.qc.ca

B&B	
single	$47
double	$58
child	$0-10

VS

Open year round

Number of rooms	3
shared bathrooms	1

Activities: 🏛 🍷 ⛵ 🚣 🎿

35. TROIS-RIVIÈRES

F E 🚲 P ⛵ R.1 TA

A must on the shores of the St-Laurent. Comfort, safety in an upscale decor. Gardens, pool and air conditioning. Renowned for its welcome and gastronomic breakfast. If reserving all 4 rooms, good deal for family get-togethers or with friends. One French guide commented: "In short, an excellent place for the price".

From Hwy 55, Exit Notre-Dame, to Rte 138 East, drive about 1 km. At McDonald's, turn right on Rue Garceau. Right on Rue Notre-Dame, 5th house on the left.

B&B
GÎTE SAINT-LAURENT

Yolande and René Bronsard
4551, Notre-Dame
Trois-Rivières Ouest G9A 4Z4
tel/fax (819) 378-3533
www.bbcanada.com/
2101.html
rene.bronsard@sympatico.ca

B&B	
single	$45
double	$60

Open year round

Number of rooms	4
rooms with sink	4
shared wc	1
shared bathrooms	1

Activities: 🚣 ⛵ 🎿 🚴 🛷

36. TROIS-RIVIÈRES

F e 🚗 P R.7 TA

Warm, English-style house located in Old Trois-Rivières. Parking, air conditioning, terrace, fireplace. A stone's throw from town centre, harbour park, restaurants, museum. Near Mauricie National Park, Cité de l'Énergie, Forges St-Maurice, saphouse. Children welcome.

Hwy 40, Exit 201, Boul. des Chenaux south, right, 1.6 km. Right on Rte 138 West or St-Maurice, drive 0.8 km. At the 4th traffic lights, at the church left on Rue St-Francois-Xavier, drive 0.7 km.

B&B
MAISON WICKENDEN

Lydia Marghem
467, St-François-Xavier
Trois-Rivières G9A 1R1
tel/fax (819) 375-6219

B&B	
single	$35-45
double	$45-55
triple	$65
quad.	$75
child	$0-10

VS

Reduced rates : Nov. 1 to May 1
Open year round

Number of rooms	3
shared wc	1
shared bathrooms	1

Activities: 🏛 🚣 ⛵ 🎿 🚴

37. TROIS-RIVIÈRES, POINTE-DU-LAC

F E 🚗 P 🏊 🐕 R1.6 TA

10 km from old Trois-Rivières and its waterfront park, enchanting site right on the shores of the St. Lawrence River and Lac St-Pierre. Large garden, in-ground pool, picnic tables, B.B.Q. Calm and restful, close to all the sites you'll want to discover. Generous breakfast. Discount: 3 days or more. English, German, Italian, Spanish spoken. Flight packages available. **See ad end of this region.**

From Montréal (130 km), Hwy 40 E., Exit 187. Rte 138 E., 7 km. From Mirabel, Hwy 15 S., 640 E., 40 E. From Québec City (130 km) Hwy 40 W. and 55 S., Exit Notre-Dame, Rte 138 W., 5 km.

B&B
GÎTE BAIE-JOLIE

Barbara and Jacques Piccinelli
711, Notre Dame, route 138
Pointe-du-Lac G0X 1Z0
tel/fax (819) 377-3056
www.becquee.qc.ca/baiejolie

B&B	
single	$35
double	$55-60
triple	$70-75
quad.	$90
child	$10

Reduced rates : Oct.15 to May 31
Open : Dec. 1 to Oct. 31

Number of rooms	3
rooms with private bath	3

Activities: 🚣 ⛷ 🎣 🏃 🐎

38. TROIS-RIVIÈRES, POINTE-DU-LAC

F e 🚭 🏊 🚗 P R2

Excellence Prize Mauricie-Bois-Francs 1997-98. Are you seeking rest and tranquillity? At our lovely Canadian-style house we guarantee a relaxing time in a cosy atmosphere! Treat yourself to a generous, varied, fine quality breakfast. Go for a refreshing swim any time of the year in the indoor pool and enjoy a therapeutic bath. Air conditioning.

Montréal, Hwy 40 East, Exit 187, then Rte 138 East for 7 km. Turn left on Rue des Saules to the end. From Québec City, Hwy 40 West, then Hwy 55 South, Notre-Dame Exit, Route 138 West for 5 km, then turn right on Rue des Saules to the end.

B&B
SOLEIL LEVANT

Léonie Lavoie and
Yves Pilon
300, av. des Saules
Pointe-du-Lac G0X 1Z0
(819) 377-1571
fax (819) 377-1292

B&B	
single	$40-45
double	$60-65
triple	$80
child	$15

Reduced rates : Nov. 1 to Mar. 31
Open year round

Number of rooms	3
shared bathrooms	2

Activities: 🏛 🍷 🚣 🎣 🏊

B&Bs AND INNS

39. GRANDE-ANSE

F E P R17 M13 TA

The estate has been Mrs. Anne said "the queen of Mauricie" McCormick's haven of peace since 1918. On the St-Maurice, the site is the ideal setting to relive this great lady's history, with wide expanses inviting you to relax, have fun and get a good dose of fresh air. Afterwards, there are adventures and anecdotes to relate inside. Tailor-made adventure packages. Family-size suites. **B&B p 173, no 9.**

We are located in Grande-Anse, right on Rte 155, 1.5 hours north of Trois-Rivières, 20 minutes south of La Tuque. Halfway between Lac St-Jean and Montréal.

COUNTRY HOUSE
MAISON PAUL-ÉMILE

Domaine McCormick
3970, Route 155 Sud
Grande-Anse G0X 2C0
(819) 676-3388
fax (819) 676-3297

No. houses	1
No. rooms	2
No. people	36206
WEEK_SUMMER	$500
WEEK-WINTER	$500
W/E-SUMMER	$250
W/E-WINTER	$250

Taxes extra VS MC

Open year round

Activities:

40. HÉROUXVILLE

F E P R5 M1 TA

Heart of the Mauricie. From 1883, the house has kept its old-fashioned cachet, rooms have period decor. Right in town, perfect for relaxation and calm. Close to Mauricie National Park, wild fishing, horseback riding, cycling, all winter sports. Backwoods cabin also available in the Upper Mauricie. **B&B p 175.**

Halfway between Québec City and Montréal by Hwy 20 or 40, take Hwy 55 N. via Trois-Rivières. At the end of Hwy 55, Exit Rte 153 N. At Hérouxville, at the flashing light, street beside the church.

COUNTRY HOUSE
MAISON TRUDEL

Nicole Jubinville and
Yves Trudel
543, Goulet
Hérouxville G0X 1J0
(418) 365-7624
fax (418) 365-7041
www.bbcanada.com/408.html
maison-trudel-quebec
@concepta.com

No. houses	1
No. rooms	6
No. people	14
WEEK-SUMMER	$600
WEEK-WINTER	$600
W/E-SUMMER	$300
W/E-WINTER	$300
DAY-SUMMER	$150
DAY-WINTER	$150

VS

Open year round

Activities:

41. LOUISEVILLE

F e R1 M1.5 TA

Ancestral house on the farm's property. Enjoy the beautiful mature gardens (4 acres), once spring arrives. Ideal place to get into gardening or learn more. Gardening library. All-season guided excursions: hiking, canoeing, fishing, biking, snowshoeing, dogsledding... Ste-Ursule waterfalls, Lac St-Pierre. **Farm Stay p 38, B&B p 175, Country-style Dining p 21 and Farm Excursion p 32. See ad end of this region.**

From Montréal or from Québec City, Hwy 40, Exit 166. Rte 138 East, drive 2.4 km to Rte 348 West. Turn left twd Ste-Ursule for 1.5 km. 1st road on the right, 1st house, under the trees.

COUNTRY HOUSE
LA MAISON DU JARDINIER

Michel Gilbert
480, chemin du Golf
Louiseville J5V 2L4
tel/fax (819) 228-8224

No. houses	1
No. rooms	3
No. people	4
WEEK-SUMMER	$400
WEEK-WINTER	$400
DAY-WINTER	$100

Taxes extra

Open year round

Activities:

42. PRINCEVILLE

F e 🏇 🚗 P R3 M3

Heidi and her grandfather knew about the richness of wide expanses, the beauty of nature. The peace and comfort of "Paradis d'Émy" also makes us embrace nature again. A stone's throw from the farm are the pleasures of skiing, golfing, cycling, snowmobiling. This cozy paradise is a dream come true!

Between Québec City and Montréal. Hwy 20, Exit 235, for Princeville. Rte 263 South. Drive 15 km, turn left on Rang 7 East. From Rte 116 in Princeville, take the 263 North, 3 km, first right onto Rang 7 East.

COUNTRY HOME
AU PARADIS D'ÉMY

Joceline Desfossés and
Normand Jutras
7, Rang 7 Est
Princeville G6L 4C2
(819) 364-2840
fax (819) 362-8449
www.pearle.net/
~pcboss/emy.htm
pcboss@pearle.net

No. houses	1
No. rooms	3
No. people	2-16
WEEK-SUMMER	$350-700
WEEK-WINTER	$350-700
W/E-SUMMER	$120-220
W/E-WINTER	$120-220
DAY-SUMMER	$60-110
DAY-WINTER	$60-110

Taxes extra

Open year round

Activities: 🦆 🐄 🏃 🐎

43. ST-PIERRE-BAPTISTE

F e ♿ 🏇 P 🛶 R6 M6

Lovely house in the Appalachian foothills: natural wood and brick interior. During the cold season, a crackling fire awaits you. Hand-woven bedding and rugs. All necessary cooking equipment, 2 bathrooms. On the farm: trails, cross-country skiing, small animals. Nearby: snowmobile trails, swimming at the falls.

From Montréal Hwy 20, Exit 228, from Québec City, Exit 253 to Thetford Mines. Drive 11 km past Plessisville, turn left St-Pierre-Baptiste for 4 km. Left at the church 100 m, then right on Route Roy; drive 5 km. Right Gîte Domaine des Pins.

COUNTRY HOME
DOMAINE DES PINS

Danielle Pelletier and
Yvon Gingras
2108, rang Scott
St-Pierre-Baptiste G0P 1K0
(418) 453-2088
fax (418) 453-2760
www.domaine.qc.ca

No. houses	1
No rooms	5
No. people	2-16
WEEK-SUMMER	$300-450
WEEK-WINTER	$350-500
W/E-SUMMER	$200-300
W/E-WINTER	$300-350
DAY-SUMMER	$125
DAY-WINTER	$150

Taxes extra

Open year round

Activities: 🏛 🦆 🐄 🏃 🛶

FARM ACTIVITIES

Farm stay:

*Country-style dining *:*

Farm excursions:

* Registered trademark.

COUNTRY HOMES

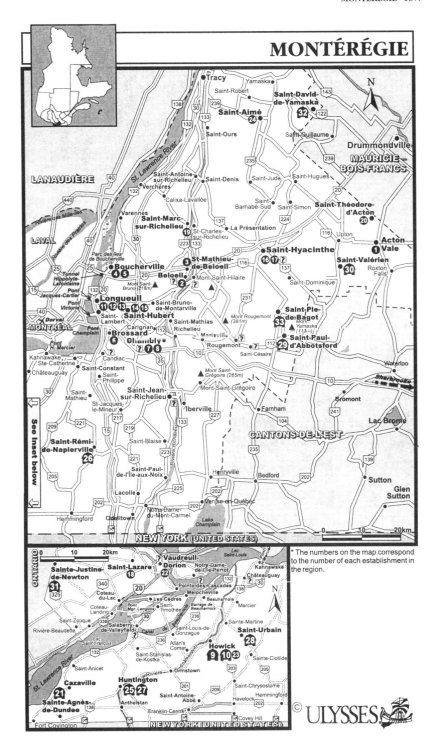

* The numbers on the map correspond to the number of each establishment in the region.

© ULYSSES

1. ACTON VALE

F E 🚫 P 🛏 🐕 ✕ R2 TA

Between Montréal and Québec City, in cycling country, 2 km from "La Campagnarde" path, 8 km from La Dame de Cœur theatre, across from a golf course, what more could you ask for! Breakfast on the veranda. Take advantage of golf and cycling packages. It's about the simple pleasure in welcoming people from far and wide.

Hwy 20, Exit 147, right on Rte 116 for 17 km, you have arrived. Or, Hwy 55, Rtes 139 and 116. All these roads lead you here. Remember: across from the golf course.

B&B
AUBERGE AUX P'TITS OIGNONS

Denise Morin and
Jacques McCaughan
1011, Route 116 Ouest
Acton Vale J0H 1A0
(450) 549-5116
fax (450) 549-6116
www.bbcanada.com/
1086.html
auberge@ntic.qc.ca

B&B	
single	$35-45
double	$50-60
triple	$65-75
quad.	$80
child	$10

VS MC

Open year round

Number of rooms	4
rooms with private bath	1
rooms in basement	3
shared wc	1
shared bathrooms	2

Activities: 🦪 𝄽 🚲 ⛵ 🏃

2. BELOEIL

F E 🚫 P R.3 TA

The Richelieu valley will win you over... 20 minutes from Montréal, stop and enjoy the peace and cozy charm of our ancestral home (1846) on the banks of the Rivière Richelieu, in the heart of Old Beloeil. Admire the beauty of Mont St-Hilaire. Copious breakfast; lace, china and silver.

Hwy 20, Exit 112, Rte 223 South, for 4 km. House next to presbytery and church. Or from Rte 116, Rte 223 North, 1 km.

B&B
BEAUX BRUNELLES

Iris Mason and
Jacques Blanchet
1030, rue Richelieu
Beloeil J3G 4R2
(450) 467-4700
(450) 464-2717
fax (450) 467-4668
www.bbcanada.com/652.html
beauxbrunelles@convitech.ca

B&B	
single	$45
double	$60
triple	$75
child	$0-10

Open year round

Number of rooms	5
shared bathrooms	2

Activities: 🏛 🦪 𝄽 🏃 🚲

3. BELOEIL, ST-MATHIEU

F E 🛏 R5 P TA

Twenty minutes from Montreal. Climb Mt-St-Hilaire, ski Mont St-Bruno; a stone's throw from 2 summer theatres. In the country, 6 kilometres from Old Beloeil. Boasting spacious rooms, our (1905 ancestral) house beneath the trees awaits you. Variety of breakfast served in the warmth of our kitchen graced with a wood-burning stove.

From Montréal or Québec City, Hwy 20, Exit 109. On Rue St-Jean-Baptiste go north twd St-Mathieu-de-Belœil, drive for 1 km. Right on first street Ruisseau Sud for 3.8 km.

B&B
LA MAISON DU GAZEBO

Monique and
Georges Blanchard
2054, Ruisseau Sud
St-Mathieu-de-Beloeil J3G 2C9
(450) 464-2430
fax (450) 464-4541
www.bbcanada.com/
2349.html
gazebo@zoo.net

B&B	
single	$40
double	$55
triple	$70
child	$10

Open year round

Number of rooms	3
shared wc	1
shared bathrooms	1

Activities: 🏛 🦪 𝄽 🐎 🏃

4. BOUCHERVILLE

F E P R1 TA

Located near the old village on the St-Laurent, Highways 132, 20 and 30, restaurants and shops, this air-conditioned B&B offers spacious rooms, a huge kitchen, view on equipped terrace and in-ground pool. Package: 4th night free. Free for children 10 and under. Hearty breakfast, Bilingual.

From Montréal: L.-H. Lafontaine tunnel, Hwy 20, Exit 92, left on Boul. Montagne (or right from Québec City). Drive 3 km, cross Boul. Montarville, drive 1 km, left on Étienne-Brûlé, right on Duluth.

B&B
CHEZ FLEUR DO

Doris Hupé
919, rue Duluth
Boucherville J4B 6Y5
(450) 449-5659

B&B	
single	$38-48
double	$48-58
triple	$58-68
quad.	$78
child	$10

Reduced rates: Sep. 1 to Dec. 20 and Jan. 10 to Apr. 20
Open year round

Number of rooms	2
shared wc	1
shared bathrooms	2

Activities:

5. BOUCHERVILLE

F E P R.5 TA

Just 15 min from the sights of Montréal. Friendly atmosphere, we like to chat with people. Bicycles and tandems available for free; bike paths; bus to the Métro. Generous breakfasts, air conditioning and a small souvenir for everyone.

From Montréal by Louis-H. Lafontaine tunnel or from Québec City, Hwy 20, Exit 90: twd Varennes. Rte 132 East Exit 18: Montarville. Turn left to Boul. Fort St-Louis, turn left and drive 1.2 km.

B&B
LE RELAIS DES ÎLES PERCÉES

Colette and Raymond LeBlanc
85, des Îles Percées
Boucherville J4B 2P1
tel/fax (450) 655-3342
www.total.net/~lerelais/bb_en_ligne.htm
lerelais@total.net

B&B	
single	$40
double	$55
triple	$70
child	$10

VS

Open year round

Number of rooms	3
rooms in basement	2
shared bathrooms	2

Activities:

6. BROSSARD

F E P R.5

Business or pleasure, for a single night or more, partake of our classic breakfast to the sound of music. Terrace and garden brightened by birdsong, flowery pool. Spacious room (1 to 5 people). Period furniture; 15 minutes from downtown, casino, Old Montreal. Corporate rates (November to April). Speciality: Alexandre Legrand's crepes.

From Montréal, Mirabel, Dorval: Hwy 15 South, Champlain bridge, Exit 8-0 Taschereau-La Prairie, left on Rome, right on Niagara. From Québec City, Hwy 20, Exit 90 La Prairie-USA, Exit 53, Boul. Rome to Niagara, go right.

B&B
AU JARDIN D'ALEXANDRE

Diane and Jean-Marie Caissie
8135, Niagara
Brossard J4Y 2G2
(450) 445-2200
fax (450) 445-1244
www.bbcanada.com/2462.html
b.bjardinsalex@videotron.ca

B&B	
single	$37
double	$50-55
triple	$65
quad.	$80
child	$10

Reduced rates: Nov. 1 to Apr. 30, 4 nights for the price of 3
Open year round

Number of rooms	1
shared bathrooms	1

Activities:

7. CHAMBLY

F | e | P | 🚗 | R.2 | TA

20 min from Montréal, Victorian house from 1914 with magnificent woodwork, period mouldings, fireplace and French doors. Breakfast on the veranda with a view of the mountains rising out of the water. Boat dock. Close to all the city's services and activities. Dinner by reservation. Air conditionned.

From Montréal, Hwy 10, Exit 22, Boul Fréchette to the end. Follow directions. Beside St-Joseph church.

B&B
AUBERGE L'AIR DU TEMPS

Lucie Chrétien and
Daniel Desgagné
124, Martel
Chambly J3L 1V3
(450) 658-1642
toll free 1-888-658-1642
fax (450) 658-2830

B&B	
single	$55
double	$65-75
triple	$95
quad.	$115

Taxes extra VS

Reduced rates: sunday to thursday from Oct. 16 to Dec. 14
Jan. 6 to Apr. 20
Open: year round except Nov.

Number of rooms	5
rooms with private bath	5

Activities: 🐚 ⛵ 🎣 🚴 🏇

8. CHAMBLY

F | E | 🏊 | P | 🚗 | R.5 | TA

This former Fort Chambly officers' barracks (1812) has been transformed into a luxurious manor offering panoramic views, comfort and ambiance. Make it your base for visiting Montréal (20 min) and Montérégie after a gourmet breakfast, before returning for some lounging by the pool or by the fire. The murmur of the rapids will rock you to sleep. Rated 3 diamonds by the AAA (CAA). **See colour photos.**

Hwy 10 (Exit 22), Rte 112 or Rte 223, then follow the signs for Fort Chambly. The Maison Ducharme is next to the guardhouse.

B&B
LA MAISON DUCHARME

Danielle Deland and
Edouard Bonaldo
10, de Richelieu
Chambly J3L 2B9
(450) 447-1220
fax (450) 447-1018

B&B	
single	$90-105
double	$100-115
triple	$120-135
quad.	$140-155
child	$20

Taxes extra VS MC

Reduced rates: Oct. 15 to Dec. 17 and Jan. 4 to May 15
Open year round

Number of rooms	4
rooms with private bath	4

Activities: 🚶 🎣 🚴 🏊 🏃

9. HOWICK

F | E | ✖ | 🚗 | P | 🏊 | R.5 | TA

Welcome to our century-old house situated in the country-side. Feed the animals, swim, cycle, canoe, fish and finally relax around an evening campfire by the river. Visit our antique shop where we also recycle wood, doors and windows into reproductions on antique furniture. **Farm stay p 39 and country home p 196.**

30 km from Montréal. From Mercier bridge, Rte 138 West, then Rte 203 to Riverfield (about 9 km). At the church, turn right on Rang des Écossais and cross the bridge; we are on the left.

B&B
AUBERGE LA CHAUMIÈRE

Patricia Rae and
Suzanne Chéné
1071, rang Des Écossais
Howick (Riverfield) J0S 1G0
(450) 825-0702
info@lachaumiere.qc.ca

	B&B	MAP
single	$35	$53
double	$50	$86
child	$10	$25

VS

Reduced rates: Nov. 1 to Apr. 30
Open year round

Number of rooms	4
shared bathrooms	2

Activities: 🎣 🚴 🏇 🏃 🐴

10. HOWICK

f E  P R3

Welcome to our 150-acre 5th-generation dairy farm. Enjoy feeding small animals, campfire, take a hay ride, cycle or relax by our inground pool. Non-smokers please. A delicious home-baked breakfast is served! We have been receiving guests for more than 11 years. **Farm Stay p 39.**

From Montréal, Hwy 20 West, Mercier bridge, Rte 138 West. Rte 203 to Howick (about 40 km). Cross the bridge, turn left on Rue Lambton. Take English River Road and drive 2 km.

B&B
HAZELBRAE FARM

Gloria and John Peddie
1650, English River Road
Howick J0S 1G0
(450) 825-2390

B&B	
single	$30
double	$50
child	$5-9

Open year round

Number of rooms	3
rooms with private bath	1
shared wc	1
shared bathrooms	2

Activities: 🏛 🛶 ⛷ 🚲 🏃

---

11. LONGUEUIL

F e  P R1 TA

On the South Shore, 10 minutes from downtown Montreal, on a quiet street near the metro in the heart of Old Longueuil, a welcoming house invites you to come relax in a warm ambiance. Come as you are and enjoy its charming rooms and good breakfast.

From Montréal: Jacques-Cartier bridge, keep left, Rte 132 or Hwy 20 Exit directly on the right, Rue St-Charles Exit or Rte 132 Exit 8, Rue St-Charles right on Quinn at the Esso. 500 m. along Ste-Élizabeth, on the left.

B&B
GÎTE LA BRUNANTE

Louise Bélisle
480, Ste-Elisabeth
Longueuil J4H 1K4
(450) 442-7691

B&B	
single	$35
double	$45-55
triple	$55-65
child	$0

Open year round

Number of rooms	2
rooms with sink	1
shared wc	1
shared bathrooms	1

Activities: 🚤 ⛷ 🏃 🚲 🏃

---

12. LONGUEUIL

F e 🐕 P R1 TA

La Maison de Madame Dufour is a friendly place in a peaceful area near downtown Montréal. Come stay in a cozy setting and soak up the tranquil atmosphere. Relax in our three living rooms. Savour a delicious breakfast of crepes or eggs served on a bed of onions. An oasis of peace that will provide you with wonderful memories. See you soon! Your host, *Gaby.*

From Montréal or Québec City: Route 132, Exit Roland-Therrien. Drive about 4 km to Rue Desormeaux; turn left and continue to Berthelet.

B&B
LA MAISON DE
MADAME DUFOUR

Gaby Dufour
1260, Berthelet
Longueuil J4M 1G3
(450) 448-6531

B&B	
single	$75
double	$85
child	$25

MC

Reduced rates: Nov. to May
Open year round

Number of rooms	5
rooms in basement	2
shared bathrooms	3

Activities: 🏛 🍷 🚤 🏃 🚲

B&Bs AND INNS

13. LONGUEUIL

F e ♿ 🚗 🐕 R.2 TA

Come take advantage of a poetic ambience in a warm century-old house in the heart of old Longueuil. Succulent breakfasts served on the terrace in the summer. Close to downtown Montréal by Métro or the ferry. Reductions for stays of 3 nights and more.

From Montréal, Jacques-Cartier Bridge, keep left, Exit Rte 132 or Hwy 20 immediately right, Exit Rue St-Charles. Or from Rte 132, Exit 8. Rue St-Charles and right on Rue St-Jean. Located behind Longueuil Town Hall.

B&B
LE REFUGE DU POÈTE

Louise Vézina
320, rue Longueuil
Longueuil J4H 1H4
(450) 442-3688

B&B	
single	$45-50
double	$50-60
triple	$60-70
child	$10

Reduced rates: 3 nights and more
Open year round

Number of rooms	2
rooms with sink	1
rooms with private bath	1
shared bathrooms	2

Activities: 🏛 ⚓ ♨ 🚲 🏃

14. ST-HUBERT

F e P 🚗 R.5 TA

Excellence Prize Montérégie 1997-98. 7 km south of Montréal, easy access to major highways. Great place to get away. All the activities of Montréal on your doorstep. Biodôme, festivals, Gilles Villeneuve racetrack, etc. Wake up to our regional specialties and breads. Looking forward to your visit.

From Montréal, Hwy 20 East to Hwy 30 West or Hwy 10 East to Hwy 30 Exit 115. Rte 112 West (Boul. Cousineau) for 3.7 km, left on Rue Prince Charles, right on Rue Primot, left on Rue Latour.

B&B
AUX DEUX LUCARNES

Ginette and
Jean-Marie Laplante
3310, Latour
St-Hubert J3Y 4V9
(450) 656-1224
fax (450) 656-0851
www.bbcanada.com/
2345.html
auxdeuxlucarnes@
sympatico.ca

B&B	
single	$40
double	$55
child	$0-10

Reduced rates: Oct. 15 to Apr. 15, also for long stays
Open year round

Number of rooms	4
rooms with sink	3
rooms with private bath	1
shared bathrooms	2

Activities: 🍴 ⛄ 🎿 🚲 🏃

15. ST-HUBERT

F e ⃠ P R.75

A base for all your activities in Montérégie: cycling, golfing, Parc Safari, cruise, summer theatre, festival, museum, etc. For a short or long stay, it will be our pleasure to welcome you to the quietness of the suburbs. Right near Montréal, a few kilometres from the highways. Simple & quiet ambiance.

From Montréal via the Champlain bridge, Boul. Milan to Brossard, change to Gaétan Boucher in St-Hubert, left on Normand, right on Harding. In Québec City, via Hwy 10, 20, 30.

B&B
CHEZ GRAND-MAMAN
JACQUELINE

Jacqueline Castonguay
4545, Harding
Saint-Hubert J3Y 2K5
(450) 676-8667

B&B	
single	$35
double	$45
triple	$55
quad.	$65
child	$0-5

Open year round

Number of rooms	1
rooms with private bath	1
rooms in basement	1
shared bathrooms	1

Activities: 🏛 ⚓ 🚲 ⛷ 🏃

16. ST-HYACINTHE

F E ⊘ ⛴ P 🚗 🐕 R.2 TA

Montérégie Excellence Prize 1996-97. An English garden hidden in the heart of the town. 1 km from the convention centre and agriculture campus. In summertime the spa, the plant and water gardens offer complete relaxation. Antiques, paintings and books will warm you up in winter. Scrumptious home-made breakfasts on the menu. Come and share our house! Montérégie Excellence Prize 1996-97.

From Montréal or Québec City, Hwy 20, Exit 130. Boul Laframboise to the arch. Rue Bourdages turn right, Rue Bourassa turn right, Rue Raymond, turn left.

B&B
LE JARDIN CACHÉ

Carmen and Bernard Avard
2465, avenue Raymond
St-Hyacinthe J2S 5W4
(450) 773-2231

B&B	
single	$40-50
double	$55-65

Taxes extra VS MC

Reduced rates: corporate rates and Oct. 1 to May 31
Open year round

Number of rooms	3
shared bathrooms	2

Activities: 🍷 🎿 🎣 🚴 🐎

17. ST-HYACINTHE

F E ⊘ P 🚗 R.8 TA

Let yourselves be pampered in our warm and peaceful nest, located in a quiet neighbourhood. Romantic decor. Delicious breakfast in the solarium. Rest area filled with birdsong near the water garden and amidst flowers. Little considerations guaranteed. Golf, horseback riding, canoeing and pedal boating only a 5-minute drive away.

Hwy 20, Exit 123, twd St-Hyacinthe, drive 7 km. Turn right at the 1st lights (Boul. Laurier). Left at the 2nd lights (Dieppe). 2nd street turn right.

B&B
LE NID FLEURI

Suzanne and Gilles Cournoyer
5985, Garnier
St-Hyacinthe J2S 2E8
(450) 773-0750

B&B	
single	$40-50
double	$50-60

VS

Reduced rates: Sep. 1 to Dec. 1 and Apr. 1 to May 31. Corporate rates.
Open: Apr. 1 to Dec 1

Number of rooms	3
shared wc	1
shared bathrooms	1

Activities: 🍷 🎿 🎣 🚴 🐎

18. ST-LAZARE-DE-VAUDREUIL

F E ⊘ P 🚗 R1 🍴 TA

20 min from Dorval airport with Montréal at your doorstep, on the way to Ottawa and Niagara Falls. Enjoy the nature on our little, country-style farm. Unforgettable visit, quality, comfort, gourmet food. Packages available: yoga, re-energizing cocooning, etc. New: cycling stopover.

Hwy 20 and/or Hwy 40, Exit 22; to St-Lazare, then turn left on Chemin Ste-Angélique and look for #2565.

B&B
HALTE DE RESSOURCEMENT

Lise Bisson
2565, ch Ste-Angélique
St-Lazare-de-Vaudreuil
J7T 2K6
(514) 990-7825
fax (450) 455-1786
ressourcement@hotmail.com

	B&B	MAP
single	$50-70	$65-85
double	$60-80	$90-110
triple	$80-100	$125-145
quad.	$100-120	$160-180
child	$10-15	$20-25

MC AM

Open year round

Number of rooms	5
rooms with private bath	1
shared bathrooms	3
rooms with sink	2

Activities: 🍷 ⛵ 🎿 🚴 ⛷

B&Bs AND INNS

19. ST-MARC-SUR-RICHELIEU
F E P R.25 TA

The enchantment begins by following the Richelieu River and the small country roads, continues in the theatres, restaurants and art galleries, and ends in the warm ambiance of our house. We offer guests three spacious rooms with private bathroom and a most delicious breakfast. You'll be back...

Take Exit 112 off Hwy 20 and follow the 223 North.

B&B
LE VIREVENT

Johanne Jeannotte
511, rue Richelieu
Saint-Marc-sur-Richelieu
JOL 2E0
(450) 584-3618
www.generation.net/
~neige/virevent/virevent.htm
neige@generation.net

B&B	
single	$35-55
double	$55-75
triple	$65-85
quad.	$75-95

Open year round

Number of rooms	3
rooms with private bath	3

Activities: 🏛 🦆 🚲 🐎 ⛷

---

20. ST-THÉODORE-D'ACTON
F e P ✗ R8

This little château has a drive lined with pine trees and is surrounded by vines, a vegetable garden, a rock wall adorned with perennials and a small cottage. Memorable breakfasts, table d'hôte with pork in the spotlight (braised pork in season). Fondues, a variety of traditional Swiss raclettes, home-made products. The perfect place for receptions. Bike path. Golf and theatre packages.

From Montréal: Hwy 20 East, Exit 147, Rte 116 East to Acton Vale, Rte 139 North, for 8 km past the town, then turn left on 8e Rang and left at the second lot; a drive lined with pine trees leads to the inn.

INN
LE CLOS DES ROCHES

Louise and Denis Levasseur
1313, 8e Rang, route 139
St-Théodore-d'Acton JOH 1Z0
(450) 546-4107
toll free 1-888-546-4107
fax (450) 546-1148

B&B	
single	$45
double	$60
child	$10

VS MC

Open year round

Number of rooms	4
shared bathrooms	2

Activities: 🦆 🍴 🚲 ⛷ 🎿

---

21. STE-AGNÈS-DE-DUNDEE
F e 🚗 ✗ ✗ P R10 TA

Peaceful country setting, flowering gardens, roomy house, columns and balconies reminiscent of Louisiana. 15 km: Dundee border to New York, 5 km: Lac St-François wildlife reserve and Droulers archeological site (prehistoric Iroquois village), borrow a bike, golf, lake, waterskiing, snowmobiling. Lunch and dinner specials by reservation. Looking forward to your visit! **Farm Stay p 39.**

Rte 132 from Valleyfield to Cazaville, left on Montée Cazaville to Ch. Ridge, turn right, 8th house on the left.

B&B
LE GÎTE CHEZ MIMI

Émilienne Marlier
5891, chemin Ridge
Ste-Agnès JOS 1L0
(450) 264-4115

B&B	
single	$35
double	$45
triple	$60
quad.	$75
child	$10

Taxes extra VS MC

Open year round

Number of rooms	3
rooms with sink	2
shared bathrooms	1

Activities: 🚣 🍴 🚲 🐎 ⛷

22. VAUDREUIL-DORION

F e 🐕 ⛵ P R1 TA

Our B&B offers a superb view of Lac des Deux-Montagnes and its sailboats. Nearby: shopping centre, restaurant and museum. Come lounge around our pool and patio or rest in the relaxation room of our veranda. A generous breakfast served with home-made goods will complete your stay. We look forward to welcoming you.

From Montréal, Hwy 40 West, Exit 35, at the traffic lights right on Rue St-Charles, 1 km. At the convenience store turn right on Chemin de L'Anse, 0.4 km. 3rd house on left.

B&B
GÎTE DE L'ANSE

Denise and Gilles Angell
154, chemin de l'Anse
Vaudreuil-Dorion J7V 8P3
(450) 424-0693

B&B	
single	$45
double	$55-65
child	$5-10

Open: May 1 to Oct. 31

Number of rooms	2
shared bathrooms	2

Activities: 🏛 ♣ 🏊 🚶 🚲

B&Bs AND INNS

23. HOWICK

F E 🚗 P 🏊 R.5 M6 TA

Small chalet suitable for a pleasant family farm stay. Antique reproduction shop onsite, camfire by the river, canoeing, swimming, biking. **Farm stay p 39 and B&B p 190.**

30 km from Montréal. From Mercier bridge, Rte 138 West, then Rte 203 to Riverfield (about 9 km). At the church, turn right on Rang des Écossais and cross the bridge; we are on the left.

COUNTRY HOME
AUBERGE LA CHAUMIÈRE

Patricia Rae and
Suzanne Chéné
1071, rang des Écossais
Howick (Riverfield) J0S 1G0
(450) 825-0702
info@lachaumiere.qc.ca

No. houses	1
No. rooms	4
No. people	6
WEEK-SUMMER	$450
W/E-SUMMER	$200
DAY-SUMMER	$100

VS

Open: June 1 to Sep. 30

Activities: 🎣 🚲 🎯 🏃 🐎

24. ST-AIMÉ

F E P R1 M2 TA

One hour from Montréal. House in farming country. Comfort, fire in the hearth. By the Yamaska river. Canoe. 20 minutes from Odanak Indian reservation, Sorel Islands cruise, Gibelotte and Western festivals. Admire Canada geese and snow geese. Golfing, skidooing, Cyclo-Québec path at our door.

From Montréal: Hwy 20 twd St-Hyacinthe, Exit 130 North, right at 3rd light onto the 235 North. Massueville left on Royale, 2 km. From Sorel: 132 East, before Yamaska bridge right on Rang Bord de l'Eau, 8 km.

COUNTRY HOME
MAISON BOIS-MENU

Nicole Larocque and
Gaétan Boismenu
387, rang Bord de l'Eau
St-Aimé (Massueville) J0G 1K0
(450) 788-2466
tel/fax (450) 788-2937

No. houses	1
No. rooms	4
No. people	8
WEEK-SUMMER	$350
WEEK-WINTER	$350
W/E-SUMMER	$160
W/E-WINTER	$160
DAY-SUMMER	$100
DAY-WINTER	$100

Open year round

Activities: 🏛 🍂 ⛷ 🚣 🎣

FARM ACTIVITIES

Farm stays:

Country-style dining*:

Farm excursions:

*Registered trademark.

MONTRÉAL

ISLAND OF MONTRÉAL

MONTRÉAL

*The numbers on the map correspond to the number of each establishment in the region.

1. LACHINE

`F` `e` `⊗` `⌂` `✗` `P` `🚃` `R2` `TA`

Tourists or businesspeople, we offer you tranquillity only 20 minutes from Montréal and 10 minutes from the Dorval Airport. The cycling path on our doorstep leads to Old Montréal, running past many historic and tourist attractions. "Surprise" breakfast for stamina, pool for fitness.

From Montréal, 20 W., Exit 58, left on 55ᵉ Ave. Straight to Victoria. Turn left then take 1st right, 53ᵉ Ave to the river. Left to 50ᵉ Ave and left at the 1st dead end.

B&B
LES LORRAINS

Viviane and Jean-Paul Mineur
21, 50ᵉ Avenue
Lachine H8T 2T4
(514) 634-0884
www.bbcanada.
com/2677.html
lorrains@aei.ca

B&B	
single	$50
double	$60
child	$10

Reduced rates: 10% 4 nights and more
Open year round

Number of rooms	1
shared bathroom	1

Activities: 🏛 ⛵ 🚶 🚲 🏃

---

2. MONTRÉAL

`F` `E` `P` `R.1` `TA`

Right downtown, a charming sunny house with fireplaces, a garden and terraces. All our rooms have a private bathroom. Suites with whirlpools or fireplaces. Southern decor and relaxed atmosphere, young courteous hosts. Access to a separate kitchen. Private parking. 50 m from the metro. **See colour photos.**

From Ville-Marie Hwy (720 E.), Rue Guy Exit. Right at 1st lights onto René-Lévesque to Guy (2nd lights). Right on Guy (south), 1st left (after Days Inn). Lucien-L'Allier metro.

B&B
À BON MATIN

1393, av. Argyle
Montréal H3G 1V5
(514) 931-9167
toll free 1-800-588-5280
fax (514) 931-1621
www.bonsmatins.com

B&B	
single	$70-110
double	$75-115
triple	$85-125
quad.	$95-135
child	$10

Taxes extra VS MC AM ER IT

Open year round

Number of rooms	5
rooms with private bath	5

Activities: 🏛 🍷 ⛵ 🚣 🚲

---

3. MONTRÉAL

`F` `e` `P` `R.1`

Historic Victorian house with a private garden facing a cosy park. 3 min walk from Métro, 5 min drive from downtown and old Montréal. Outdoor market and many antique dealers in the area. Free private parking and easy access from highway. Bicycles available. Charming and friendly.

From east or west, take Atwater exit on Ville-Marie expressway (720). Take St-Antoine (one way) until you meet Rue Agnès. It's one block past "Impérial Tobacco" building, turn left.

B&B
À BONHEUR D'OCCASION

Francine Maurice
846, rue Agnès
Montréal H4C 2P8
tel/fax (514) 935-5898
www.bbcanada.com/526.html

B&B	
single	$45-50-55
double	$65-70-75
triple	$85-90
child	$5-10

Taxes extra

Reduced rates: Nov. 1 to Dec. 15, Jan. 15 to Apr. 15
Open year round

Number of rooms	4
shared bathroom	2

Activities: 🏛 🚣 🚣 🚶 🚲

B&Bs AND INNS

4. MONTRÉAL

F e ⊘ R.2

Discount on local calls for 2 nights or more! The next best thing to home. Steps from Berri-UQAM metro, bus terminal, old port, museums, restaurants. Ancestral home, roof-top terrace, huge rooms, good breakfasts. Low-season: extended-stay rates, living room, equipped kitchen. See you soon...

From the terminus: walk one street to the east. By Métro: Berri-UQAM, exit Place Dupuis. By car: Hwy Ville-Marie (720), Berri Exit, right on Ontario, right on St-André, right on de Maisonneuve, right on St-Christophe.

B&B
À L'ADRESSE DU CENTRE-VILLE

Huguette Boileau, Nathalie Messier and Robert Groleau
1673, St-Christophe
Montréal H2L 3W7
(514) 528-9516
fax (514) 879-3236
www.bbcanada.com/
657.html
augite@mailcity.com

B&B	
single	$50
double	$65
triple	$85
child	$15

Reduced rates: Nov. 1 to Mar. 31
Open year round

Number of rooms	4
shared bathroom	2

Activities: 🏛 🍴 ⛵ 🧍 🚲

5. MONTRÉAL

F e 🛥 P R.1 TA

Located in a residential neighbourhood, on a quiet street, we offer a warm welcome, family atmosphere and copious breakfast. Free parking, flowered terrace, pool and t.v. in room. Near services (0.1 km), buses, Crémazie Métro, highways, bicycle path and olympic pool (0.8 km).

Easy access from Dorval and Mirabel airports. Hwy 40 East, Exit 73 - Ave. Christophe-Colomb, north 1 km to Rue Legendre. Turn right and drive 0.2 km to Ave. André-Grasset, turn left. First street turn right. First house on the right.

B&B
À LA BELLE VIE

Camille and Lorraine Grondin
1408, Jacques Lemaistre
Montréal H2M 2C1
(514) 381-5778
fax (514) 381-3966

B&B	
single	$45-50
double	$55-60

Open year round

Number of rooms	2
shared bathroom	1

Activities: ⛵ 🚣 🧍 🚲

6. MONTRÉAL

F E ⊘ 🚗 R.2 TA

A park and a flowery garden surround a B&B offering an incomparable welcome. Easy parking. Here will you find everything a B&B has to offer: comfort, discrete environment, varied breakfasts, information. Everything to make your stay a memorable one... when one has a lucky star!

From the Jacques-Cartier bridge, Boul. de Lorimier North right on Boul. St-Joseph. Left on 3rd street, Messier, left on Rue Laurier, right on Rue de Bordeaux. From the North, Rue Papineau South, left on Boul. St-Joseph, left on Rue Bordeaux at the traffic lights.

B&B
À LA BONNE ÉTOILE

Louise Lemire and Christian Guéric
5193, rue de Bordeaux
Montréal H2H 2A6
(514) 525-1698
www.bbcanada.com/
1947.html

B&B	
single	$45
double	$60
triple	$75
quad.	$90

Open year round

Number of rooms	2
shared bathroom	1

Activities: 🏛 🍴 ⛵ 🚣 🚲

7. MONTRÉAL

F | E | 🐕 | R.1

Simple comfort in a grand old house 2 minutes walking distance from the metro, restaurants, cultural and entertaining activities. Warm welcome, very good and lively breakfast, spacious rooms, 10% off for stays of 5 days or more. Parking available.

From the airports: take the shuttle to the Voyageur bus terminal. Métro Mont-Royal, go right until St-Hubert. By car: Rue Sherbrooke, East to St-Hubert, heading North.

B&B
À LA DORMANCE

Chantal Savoye
and Eddy Lessard
4425, St-Hubert
Montréal H2J 2X1
(514) 529-0179
fax (514) 529-1079
dormance@microtec.net

B&B	
single	$50
double	$70
triple	$85
child	$0-10

Reduced rates: 10% 5 nights and more
Open year round

Number of rooms	5
shared wc	1
shared bathroom	2

Activities: 🏛 ⤳ 🦮 🧍 🚲

---

8. MONTRÉAL

F | E | 🐕 | P | R.1 | TA

Meet colourful Montrealer Denis and Sacha (gentle canine public-relations director). Facing the Olympic Park. Cosy, roomy, hospitable; super breakfast. Clean as a whistle. Free parking. Near the metro. 10 min. from downtown. Winner of the Chamber of Commerce's "Self-Employed Entrepreneur '98" award. Recipient of the "Fleurir Montréal '98" award.

From Dorval, 520 E., 40 E., Exit 76, Boul Pie-IX S., 4 km. From Mirabel, 15 S., 40 E., Exit 76, Boul Pie-IX S., 4 km. From downtown, east on Sherbrooke, right (south) on Boul. Pie-IX.

B&B
AU GÎTE OLYMPIQUE

Denis Boulianne
2752, boul.Pie-IX
Montréal H1V 2E9
(514) 254-5423
toll free (CAN and USA)
1-888-254-5423
fax (514) 254-4753
www.dsuper.net/~olympic
olympic@dsuper.net

B&B	
single	$50-65
double	$65-85
triple	$00-100
child	$10

Taxes extra VS MC AM

Reduced rates: Nov. 1 to Dec. 23, Jan. 2 to Apr. 30
Open year round

Number of rooms	5
rooms with private bath	3
rooms with sink	2
shared bathroom	1
rooms in semi-basement	3

Activities: 🏛 ⤳ 🧍 🚲

---

9. MONTRÉAL

F | E | 🚫 | P | R.1 | TA

Victorian house. Quiet street facing magnificent Square St-Louis (downtown). View of the park or on the Mont-Royal. We love arts and sciences. Rooms with private bathroom. Honoured for quality reception: Montréal Excellence Prize 1994-95. "My personal B&B favourite" W.A. Davis, Boston Globe, 1997. Also see Linda Kay's "Romantic Days & Nights in Montréal".

Métro Sherbrooke, Rigaud Exit (3 min), cross the park to reach Ave. Laval. By car: Rue Sherbrooke, north on St-Denis left on Ave. des Pins, left again on Laval.

B&B
AUX PORTES DE LA NUIT

3496, av. Laval
Montréal H2X 3C8
(514) 848-0833
www.bbcanada.com/807.html

B&B	
single	$60-75
double	$70-85
triple	$85-100
quad.	$110-135
child	$30

Number of rooms	3
rooms with private bath	3

Activities: 🏛 🍷 ⤳ 🧍 🚲

B&Bs AND INNS

10. MONTRÉAL

F E [no smoking] R.1 TA

Amiable hostess creates a friendly ambience for visitors. Excellent information. Fine, varied Québec breakfasts, we'll create a menu for you! A calm spot downtown, close to Berri metro and bus terminal. For private bathroom, see Maison Grégoire, no 29. Special rates during summer 5 nights and more. Monthly rates during winter: 400 $ and +. **City home p 209.**

Hwy 720: twd downtown. Exit 6 Vieux-Port-Vieux-Montréal-St-Laurent-Berri, twd Berri. Turn left on Rue Berri, right on Boul René-Lévesque, left on Rue Wolfe. From airport: bus to Voyageur Terminal, 4 min taxi ride.

B&B
BED & BREAKFAST GRÉGOIRE

Christine Grégoire
1766, rue Wolfe
Montréal H2L 3J8
(514) 524-8086
toll free (Can and USA):
1-888-524-8086
w3.arobas.net/~cgregoir
cgregoire@arobas.net

B&B	
single	$55-60
double	$70-75
triple	$85-90
quad.	$110
child	$15

VS

Reduced rates: Nov. 1 to Apr. 30
Open year round

Number of rooms	2
shared bathroom	1

Activities:

11. MONTRÉAL

F E [no smoking] P R.1 TA

Huge breakfasts and a jovial atmosphere in a relaxing decor. Close to old Montréal, just 2 steps from Rue St-Denis and all the festival sites. Métro and bus are less than 5 min from our lovely Victorian residence overlooking Lafontaine park.

Near the Jacques-Cartier bridge on Sherbrooke East. Métro Sherbrooke or bus 24.

B&B
CHAGRI

Eve Bettez
1268, Sherbrooke Est
Montréal H2L 1M1
tel/fax (514) 524-1691
www.colba.net/~chagri/
chagri@colba.net

B&B	
single	$55-60
double	$65-70
triple	$75-80
quad.	$100
child	$10

Open year round

Number of rooms	3
shared wc	1
shared bathroom	1

Activities:

12. MONTRÉAL

F E P R.5 TA

Our old house facing Lafontaine park and surrounded by greenery has been entirely renovated; Botanical Gardens, Olympic Park and summer theatres are nearby. Copious breakfast, cosy and modern comfort, whirlpool bath. Refined atmosphere, original works of art. An oasis of peace and tranquillity. Private parking.

From Dorval, twd Montréal Hwy 40 E., Exit Papineau S., drive 5 km. From Métro Papineau, bus #45 N., 2nd stop after Sherbrooke.

B&B
CHEZ FRANÇOIS

François Baillergeau
4031, Papineau
Montréal H2K 4K2
(514) 239-4638
fax (514) 596-2961

B&B	
single	$60-65
double	$75-95
triple	$90-110
child	$5-10

Taxes extra VS

Open year round

Number of rooms	5
rooms with private bath	3
rooms with sink	1
shared bathroom	1

Activities:

13. MONTRÉAL

F E 🚫 R.1 TA

Square Saint-Louis is the peace of the countryside downtown. Everything is within walking distance: museums, exhibitions, restaurants, shopping, Old Montréal, etc. After a long day, relax in the park filled with birdsong. At breakfast, we eat, chat, laugh and start all over again! **See colour photos.**

From Dorval: Hwy 20 East, then Hwy 720 East, Boul. St-Laurent North Exit. Continue for 1 km, then right on Ave. des Pins, right on Ave. Laval, left on St-Louis square. Or Sherbrooke metro station, Rigaud exit.

B&B
CHEZ PIERRE ET DOMINIQUE

Dominique Bousquet
and Pierre Bilodeau
271, Carré St-Louis
Montréal H2X 1A3
(514) 286-0307
www.pierdom.qc.ca
info@pierdom.qc.ca

B&B	
single	$40-55
double	$70-80
triple	$85-95
quad.	$110
child	$10

Open year round

Number of rooms	3
rooms with sink	1
shared wc	1
shared bathroom	1

Activities: 🏛 ⛵ 🚶 🚴 🤾

---

14. MONTRÉAL

F E R.1 TA

Get a taste of Montréal in one of its most spectacular homes: a traditional Québécois house (1865) offering 19th-century ambience in the heart of the city. This home base is in a neighbourhood both authentic and 'hip'. Come experience Montréal at Côteau St-Louis: we'll show you its rhythms and colours.

St-Hubert to Boucher (between St-Joseph and Rosemont), west to Berri (2 streets). On the left. By Métro: Laurier station, Laurier Exit. Turn left on Berri.

B&B
COTEAU ST-LOUIS

Valérie and Daniel
5210, rue Berri
Montréal H2J 2S5
(514) 495-1681
pages.infinit.net/bbslouis
bbslouis@videotron.ca

B&B	
single	$50
double	$68-73
triple	$93
quad.	$98
child	$5-10

Open year round

Number of rooms	3
shared bathroom	1

Activities: 🏛  🚶 🚴

---

15. MONTRÉAL

F E 🐕 P R.1 TA

Opulent house in the heart of cultural French Montréal. A few min away from downtown and Old Montréal boutiques and restaurants, but also from the Biodome, the Olympic Stadium and the Botanical Garden. Feel at home with your hosts: her an actor/singer and him director of professional tennis tournaments.

From Québec City or the US, Jacques-Cartier bridge to Rue Sherbrooke, straight, 1.5 km on Rue de Lorimier. From Dorval, Hwy 520 E. and 40 E., Exit Papineau S., 6.3 km, left on Rachel, left on de Lorimier, 0.4 km.

B&B
ENTRE RACHEL ET
MARIE-ANNE

Andrée Racine and
Eugène Lapierre
4234, de Lorimier
Montréal H2H 2B1
tel/fax (514) 523-0366
www.bbcanada.com/2405.html
elapierre@tenniscanada.com

B&B	
single	$50
double	$65
triple	$80
quad.	$95
child	$15
Taxes extra	

Open year round

Number of rooms	3
rooms with sink	1
shared wc	2
shared bathroom	1

Activities: 🏛   ⛵ 🚴

16. MONTRÉAL

F | e | R.1 | TA

Soothed by the stately trees lining the quiet street, right by a lively avenue of shops and restaurants sure to delight strollers, near the metro to explore the city, our B&B offers an ambiance where time stands still, to fully enjoy a comfortable stay and savour the morning's lavish breakfasts.

From the Jacques-Cartier bridge, Rue de Lormier. Left on Sherbrooke Est. Right on Émile-Duployé. Left on Rachel Est. Right on Boyer. From Mont-Royal metro station, right to the exit. Right on Boyer.

B&B
GÎTE LA CINQUIÈME SAISON

Jean-Yves Goupil
4396, rue Boyer
Montréal H2J 3E1
(514) 522-6439
fax (514) 522-6192
www.bbcanada.com/
1952.html

B&B	
single	$55
double	$65
child	$0-10

Reduced rates: Nov. 1 to Apr. 30
Open year round

Number of rooms	5
shared wc	1
shared bathroom	1
shared showers	1

Activities: 🏛 🐚 ⛵ 🚣 🚴

17. MONTRÉAL

F | e | R.5 | TA

In the city centre! Parking available. Residential neighborhood, close to all services and festivals. Pleasant rooms with TV, radio and phone, close to Palais des Congrès, museums, hospitals, universities and to a shopping mall. Full breakfast. "An excellent address" according to our guests. See you soon!

Métro Place-des-Arts, Jeanne-Mance Exit, bus 80, get off at 2nd stop and walk to the right. By car: from downtown 4 streets west of Boul St-Laurent and 1 street north of Sherbrooke, between Milton and Prince-Arthur.

B&B
GÎTE TOURISTIQUE
ET APPARTEMENTS
DU CENTRE-VILLE

Bruno Bernard
3523, Jeanne-Mance
Montréal H2X 2K2
(514) 845-0431
fax (514) 845-0262
www3.sympatico.ca/app
app@sympatico.ca

B&B	
single	$50-55
double	$65-75
triple	$85

Taxes extra VS MC AM

Open year round

Number of rooms	3
shared wc	1
shared bathroom	1

Activities: 🏛 🚣 🧍 🚴 ⛷

18. MONTRÉAL

F | E | 🐕 | P | R.1 | TA

In the heart of the city, the peacefulness of the country. Located at the foot of a tree-lined stairway, come admire the house's interior architecture, skylights, fireplace and antique furniture. Comfortable bedrooms. As for the garden, several terraces look out onto English gardens and the wooded and flowered alley. Private parking.

Métro Berri, Voyageur terminal. By car: Aut. Ville-Marie (720) Exit Berri. Turn left on Berri, right on Rue Ontario East, 2nd street on left. Or Jacques-Cartier bridge, to Sherbrooke, turn left at 1st traffic lights, Rue Ontario for 1 km, turn right.

B&B
LA MAISON CACHÉE

Yvette Beigbeder
2121, St-Christophe
Montréal H2L 3X1
(514) 522-4451
fax (514) 522-1870
www.cam.org/
~mcachee/index.html
mcachee@cam.org

B&B	
single	$65-75
double	$70-80

VS MC

Open year round

Number of rooms	3
shared bathroom	1

Activities: 🏛 🐚 🚣 🚴 ⛷

19. MONTRÉAL

F e R.1 TA

A few min from the Old Montréal market, St-Denis and Ste-Catherine, the yellow house right in the midst of Montréal's cultural, social and tourist activities. This ancestral house's unique character and tranquillity will add to your stay. Good advice on activities, restaurants, entertainment.

Hwy 20, Rte 132, Jacques-Cartier bridge twd Rue Sherbrooke, left on Ontario, drive 1.2 km, right on St-Hubert.

B&B
LA MAISON JAUNE

Sylvain Binette and François Legault
2017, St-Hubert
Montréal H2L 3Z6
(514) 524-8851

B&B	
single	$45-55
double	$65
triple	$80
quad.	$95
child	$10

Taxes extra

Reduced rates: Nov. to May
Open year round

Number of rooms	5
shared wc	2
shared bathroom	2

Activities: 🏛 🍴 ⚓ 🚣 🚲

20. MONTRÉAL

F e 🚭 🐕 R.3 TA

Built for veterans in 1948, La Petite Maison Peyrot has a quiet, family ambiance. Marie-Claire and Gérard welcome you here. You will be served a delicious breakfast on the terrace among the flowers. Our house is small, but our hearts are big. Every guest who comes leaves as a friend.

Hwy 40, Viau South Exit. Drive 1 kilometre and turn right on St-Zotique, then right on 25e Avenue.

B&B
LA PETITE MAISON PEYROT

Marie-Claire and Gérard Peyrot
6822, 25e Avenue
Montréal H1T 3L9
(514) 721-3010

B&B	
single	$50
double	$60
child	$10

Reduced rates: Nov. to May
Open year round

Number of rooms	3
shared bathroom	1

Activities: 🏛 🍴 👥 🚶 🚲

21. MONTRÉAL

F E 🚭 🏊 P R1 TA

Montréal Region Excellence Prize 1996-97. 25 min from downtown on the banks of the St. Lawrence, this home built in 1900, home to three generations of notaries, will charm you with its gardens, flowers and in-ground pool. Generous breakfast on the terrace. The country in the city. Private parking. Children welcome. **See colour photos.**

From Mirabel, Hwy 15 S., Hwy 40 E. From Dorval, Hwy 40 E. Exit 87 Tricentenaire South to Notre-Dame, turn right, 200 metres. Hwy 20 Exit Pont-tunnel L.-H.-Lafontaine, 1st Exit on east, head south, east on Rue Notre-Dame.

B&B
LA VICTORIENNE

Aimée and Julien Roy
12560, rue Notre-Dame Est
Montréal H1B 2Z1
(514) 645-8328
fax (514) 255-3493

B&B	
single	$35
double	$50
triple	$65
child	$0-5

Open: May 1 to Oct. 15

Number of rooms	3
rooms with sink	1
shared bathroom	2

Activities: ⚓ 🚣 👥 🚶 🚲

22. MONTRÉAL

| F | E | 🚭 | P | R.2 | TA |

Right near a vast park, our large and sunny room with private entrance and parking awaits you. It provides easy access to expressways and airports while offering you a guaranteed haven of peace with healthy breakfasts and private garden. Come enjoy the metropolis in a warm and intimate ambiance.

From Dorval: 520 East, Hwy 40 East, Exit 73 Ave. Papineau North. From Mirabel: Hwy 15 South, 440 East, 19 South, Ave. Papineau South. We are 0.6 km east of Ave. Papineau, via Prieur (two blocks south of Gouin Blvd.).

B&B
LE CLOS DES ÉPINETTES

Diane Teolis and Léo Lavergne
10358, Parthenais, app. 1
Montréal H2B 2L7
(514) 382-0737

B&B	
single	$50
double	$60
triple	$80
quad.	$90
child	$5-10

Open year round

Number of rooms	1
rooms with private bath	1
rooms in basement	1

Activities: 🏛 ⚲ 🏃 🚴 🎿

23. MONTRÉAL

| F | E | R1 | TA |

Lovely Victorian house (marble fireplace) a stone's throw from festival sites, restaurants, museums, shops. Quiet and centrally located historic district. Relaxed ambiance with a soothing decor, home-made jams and rooms tempting one to take a nap. Friendly young hosts respectful of everyone's space. Make yourselves at home!

From Mirabel or Toronto: Hwy 40 East, St-Denis Exit, 6 km. Right on Des Pins, right on Laval. From Québec City: Hwy 20, Rte 132, J.-Cartier bridge, left on Sherbrooke, right on St-Denis, left on Des Pins, right on Laval.

B&B
LE ZÈBRE

Jean-François Pépin and
Éric Fourlanty
3767, avenue Laval
Montréal H2W 2H8
(514) 844-9868
fax (514) 844-4665
www.bbcanada.com/2729.html
lezebre@mlink.net

B&B	
single	$50
double	$65
triple	$80
Taxes extra	

Open year round

Number of rooms	3
shared bathroom	2

Activities: 🏛 ⚲ 🛶 🐟 🚴

24. MONTRÉAL

| F | E | 🚭 | 🏊 | R1 | TA |

This is the place for comfort and a warm welcome at a low price. Close to the Olympic tower, L'Assomption metro and 10 min from the botanical garden. Breakfasts are made with fresh, quality ingredients and you can have as much as you like. Pool, bikes available, free laundry.

From Mirabel Hwy 40 East, Boul. Lacordaire South Exit. Drive down to Boul. Rosemont and turn right, continue to Rue Lemay (2nd street, turn right). From Dorval, Hwy 520 East to Hwy 40 East...

B&B
«LE 6400»
COUETTE ET CAFÉ
BED & BREAKFAST

Lise and Jean-Pierre Durand
6400, rue Lemay
Montréal H1T 2L5
(514) 259-6400
www.agricotours.qc.ca

B&B	
single	$35-45
double	$55-65

Reduced rates: Nov. 1 to May 31
Open year round

Number of rooms	2
shared bathroom	1

Activities: 🛶 🐟 ⚲ 🏃 🚴

25. MONTRÉAL

F | E | ⊗ | 🐾 | P | R.1

In the heart of the Latin Quarter (restaurants-nightclubs-theatres-boutiques). Easy parking. Garden, hammocks. Quiet, safe street. 2 min from Métro. Near the bike path, international events: Jazz Festival, Just For Laughs, World Film Festival. 6-person suite. Superb lovers' suite. Family or group rooms (2 to 6 people).

Airports: Voyageur bus terminus: Métro Mont-Royal. By Car: twd downtown. Berri is parallel to St-Denis (2 streets to the east). 4272 Berri is between Mont-Royal and Rachel.

B&B
SHÉZELLES

Lucie Dextras and
Lyne St-Amand
4272, Berri
Montréal H2J 2P8
(514) 849-8694
cell. (514) 943-2526
fax (514) 528-8290
shez.masq@sympatico.ca

B&B	
single	$40-85
double	$60-100

Open year round

Number of rooms	3
rooms with private bath	1
shared bathroom	1

Activities: 🏛 🦆 ⚓ 🛶 🚲

---

26. MONTRÉAL, NOTRE-DAME-DE-GRÂCE

F | E | ⊗ | P | R.25 | TA

Montréal Excellence Prize 1997-98. Picturesque Victorian manor offers luxurious rooms, total comfort, and the warmth of antique furnishings. Only steps from the cafés and shops of Monkland Village, near Decarie Hwy leading to Dorval Airport and straight to the downtown core, near the Villa-Maria metro station with its easy access to the "underground city". Free parking. **See photo back cover/inside flap.**

Decarie Hwy, Côte-St-Luc/Queen Mary Exit, head west on Côte-St-Luc to Somerled, left on Somerled to Havard, turn right on Harvard, our home is located on the corner of Somerled and Harvard in N.D.G.

B&B
MANOIR HARVARD

Robert and Lyne Bertrand
4805, avenue Harvard
Notre-Dame-de-Grâce,
Montréal H3X 3P1
(514) 488-3570
fax (514) 369-5778
www.bbcanada.com/1963.html
alrc@sympatico.ca

B&B	
single	$75-85
double	$85-95
triple	$105
child	$10

Taxes extra VS MC ER IT

Open year round
Reduced rates: Nov. 1 to May 1

Number of rooms	5
rooms with private bath	5

Activities: 🏛 🛶 🚶 🏃 🚲

---

27. PIERREFONDS

F | E | ⊗ | P | 🛏 | R.1 | TA

Air-conditioned, renovated ranch house in west-end Montréal, close to Dorval airport, accessible from downtown via Rtes 40 or 20. Free off the street parking. Cozy bedrooms, spacious meeting rooms, piano, fireplaces, screened veranda, well kept grounds. Healty & hearty breakfast. A restful place to return to.

Coming from Dorval Airport: travel on Hwy 20 West (7 km) until Boul Saint-Jean (Exit 50 N.); proceed on St-Jean for 7km, then left on Boul Pierrefonds (1.4 km), turn left again at Rue Paiement.

B&B
GÎTE MAISON JACQUES

Micheline and Fernand Jacques
4444, rue Paiement
Pierrefonds H9H 2S7
(514) 696-2450
fax (514) 696-2564
www.maisonjacques.qc.ca
gite.maison.jacques
@sympatico.ca

B&B	
single	$37-43
double	$53-58
triple	$78-81
child	$6-12

MC AM VS

Open: Jan. 29 to Nov. 30

Number of rooms	3
rooms with private bath	2
rooms in basement	1
shared bathroom	1

Activities: 🏛 🚶 🏃 🐎 🛷

B&Bs AND INNS

28. VERDUN

F | E | 🚭 | P | R.7 | TA

Peaceful oasis 10 minutes from downtown (museums, festivals, theatre), right near the magnificent Parc des Berges (cycling, hiking, rafting, rollerblading) on the St-Laurent river. Private entrance and parking. Ideal location for quick access to airports and local tourism. Discount on stay of 4 nights or more.

From Dorval: Hwy 20 East, Hwy 15 South. From the south, Champlain bridge to 15 North, La Vérendrye Exit, turn left at 5th light onto Stéphens, left on Beurling and left on Rolland.

B&B
PACANE ET POTIRON
CAFÉ COUETTE

Nathalie Ménard and
Jean-Pierre Bernier
1430, Rolland
Verdun H4H 2G6
(514) 769-8315
jpb_nm@hotmail.com

B&B	
single	$50-70
double	$70-95
child	$15

VS MC

Reduced rates: Oct. 15 to Dec. 10 and Jan. 15 to Apr. 15
Open year round

Number of rooms	2
shared bathroom	1

Activities: 🛶 🚣 🧍 ⛷ 🏃

29. MONTRÉAL

F E ⊘ P R.1 M.1 TA

Nice, big 4-room apartment in "Off Broadway" downtown Montréal. For vacations, business or study. Private entrance, phone, jacuzzi, stove, fridge, microwave oven, TV, patio door, terrace, garden. View of the city, trees and sky. Safe, quiet and comfortable. Laundry and meals on request. **B&B p 202.**

Downtown-bound Hwy 720, Old Port-Old Montréal-St-Laurent-Berri Exit 6 for Berri. Left on Berri, right on Boul. René-Lévesque, left on Rue Wolfe. 4-minute taxi ride from Voyageur bus terminus.

CITY HOME
MAISON GRÉGOIRE

Christine Grégoire
1766, rue Wolfe
Montréal H2L 3J8
(514) 524-8086
toll free (Can and USA)
1-888-524-8086
w3.arobas.net/~cgregoir
cgregoire@arobas.net

No. houses	1
No. rooms	2
No. people	1-6
WEEK-SUMMER	$480-780
WEEK-WINTER	$340-520
W/E-SUMMER	$230-375
W/E-WINTER	$200-310
DAY-SUMMER	$115-185
DAY-WINTER	$100-160

VS ER

Reduced rates: Nov.1 to Apr. 30
Open year round

Activities: 🏛 ⚓ 🚶 🚴 ⚔

---

30. ST-LAURENT

F E ⊘ 🚗 R.4 M.2 TA

Lovely 3 1/2 (living room, kitchen, bathroom). Very roomy, quiet, fully equipped, phone, cable TV, stereo. Residential district, near Marcel Laurin city park, Raymond Bourque arena, shopping centres, 5 min. from Côte-Vertu metro, 15 min. from downtown Montréal, 10 min. from Dorval airport. Access to garden, laundry. Parking. Personalized welcome.

Reach Hwy 40, Exit 67 (Marcel Laurin North), drive about 1.5 km. Turn left on Place Thimens. At the stop sign, turn left on Alexis-Nihon, right on Hufford and left on Sigouin.

CITY HOME
STUDIO MARHABA

Assia and Ammar Sassi
2265, Sigouin
St-Laurent H4R 1L6
(514) 335-7931
(514) 744-9732
fax (514) 335-2177

No. houses	1
No. rooms	1
No. people	1-3
WEEK-SUMMER	$350-500
WEEK-WINTER	$250-350
W/E-SUMMER	$100-180
W/E-WINTER	$60-140
DAY-SUMMER	$60-100
DAY-WINTER	$40-80

MC IT

Reduced rates: Nov.1 to Apr. 30
Open year round

Activities: 🏛 ⚓ 🚶 🚴 ⚔

CITY HOMES

Hochelaga-Maisonneuve *It's Montréal at heart!*

Only 15 minutes from Downtown by metro or car, **Hochelaga-Maisonneuve** is a unique section of the city.

Home to the **Tower of Montréal**, the tallest inclined tower in the world, it also boasts the **Olympic Stadium**, the **Botanical Gardens**, the **Insectarium**, the **Biodôme**, and, we must not forget **Maurice "Rocket" Richard's Universe**, a museum devoted to one of the greatest players for the Montréal Canadiens hockey team.

Hochelaga-Maisonneuve is also...

HERITAGE A unique and faithful reflection of the life of an industrial city of the early 20th century, with impressive heritage buildings such as the **Très-Saint-Nom-de-Jésus** Church which has a famous **Casavant organ**, one of the most powerful in North America, and numerous **Beaux-Arts style buildings** such as the **Morgan Baths** and the **Maisonneuve Market**.

VOYAGE IN TIME Thanks to our **animated tour** (theatre and music) called **"In the steps of La Bolduc"** which offers an original way to discover the major attractions of the neighbourhood and to learn all about the life and work of one of Québec's most celebrated singers of the Pre-War period.

AGREEABLE STROLL Along **typical Montréal streets** either in the company of one of our guides or by yourself, with stops in our café-restaurants from time to time.

DISCOVERY A cultural life which is both intense and varied. On the **Market Place** in the summer months, shows, concerts, Sunday brunches and activities for the whole family are on the program.

PLEASURE The smells and atmosphere of a traditional market at the **Maisonneuve Public Market**, shopping on **Promenade Ontario**, and experiencing the warm hospitality of one of our bed & breakfasts.

Tourisme Hochelaga-Maisonneuve *welcomes you!*

Information **(514) 256-4636**
Web Site **www.tourismemaisonneuve.qc.ca**

OUTAOUAIS

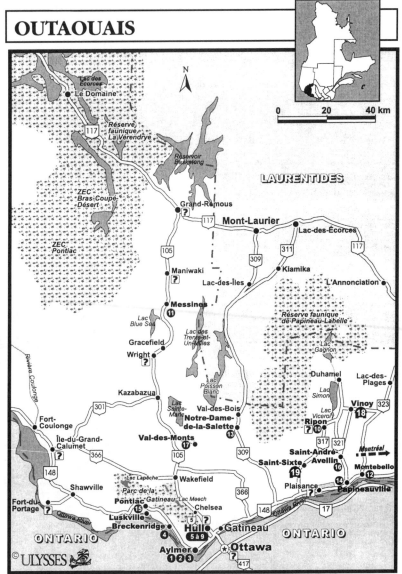

N

| 0 | 20 | 40 km |

Lac des Écorces

Le Domaine

117

Réserve faunique
La Vérendrye

Réservoir
Baskatong

ZEC
Bras-Coupé-
Désert

LAURENTIDES

ZEC
Pontiac

Grand-Remous **?**

117 Mont-Laurier

Lac-des-Écorces

105 311 117

309

Maniwaki **?**

Kiamika

Lac-des-Îles

L'Annonciation

Messines **11**

Réserve faunique
de Papineau-Labelle

Lac
Blue Sea

Gracefield

Lac des
Trente-et-
Un-Milles

Lac
Gagnon

Wright **?**

Kazabazua

Lac
Poisson
Blanc

Duhamel

Lac-des-
Plages

Rivière Coulonge

Lac
Sainte-
Marie

Val-des-Bois

Lac
Simon

Lac
Viceroy

Vinoy
18

323

301

Notre-Dame-
de-la-Salette **13**

Ripon **10 ?**

Fort-
Coulonge

Île-du-Grand-
Calumet **?**

366

Val-des-Monts **17**

105

309

Saint-André-
Avellin **16**

317 321

Montréal

Montebello **12**

148

Saint-Sixte
19

Plaisance **?**

Papineauville **14**

Shawville

Lac Lapêche

Parc de la
Gatineau

Wakefield

366

17

Fort-du-
Portage **?**

Lac Meech

Pontiac **15**

Chelsea

148

Ottawa River

Luskville
Breckenridge **4**

Hull **5 ? 5 à 9**

Gatineau

ONTARIO

ONTARIO

Aylmer **1 2 3**

★ Ottawa **?**

417

© ULYSSES

*The numbers on the map correspond to the number of each establishment in the region.

1. AYLMER

F E ⊘ P R1

10 min from Ottawa/Hull. Artist home, 3 spacious rooms, 1 with balcony. Enjoy fine breakfast on terrace surrounded by trees and flowers by trees and flowers, or in a dining room aglowed with morning light. Peacefull environnement close to everything: ski, golf, parks, beaches, bike paths, museums. Air conditionning.

Via Ottawa, Hwy 417, exit 123: Island Park Dr. to Champlain Bridge, After bridge, left on Aylmer Rd. (148). Pass 3rd traffic lights, turn left on Lakeview (no 32).

B&B
GÎTE ENCHANTÉ

Rita Rodrigue
32, Lakeview
Aylmer J9H 2A1
(819) 682-0695

B&B	
single	$50-60-70
double	$55-65-75
triple	$65-75-85
child	$10

Reduced rates: Oct. 15 to Apr.30
Open year round

Number of rooms	3
shared wc	1
shared bathrooms	1
rooms in basement	1

Activities: 🏛 ⛵ 🚶 🚲 🎿

2. AYLMER

F E ⊘ 🚌 🚗 P R.5

B&B with surrounded by magnificent woodlands. Healthy breakfast served on a large terrace around the pool and relaxation packages. Near the Aylmer marina, Gatineau Park, cycling paths, footpaths, golf courses, Hull and Ottawa tourist attractions. Computerized office and shuttle service available. Bike shed, private parking lot.

Hwy 417 West, Exit 123, Island Park Drive (2 km) cross Champlain bridge, at 2nd light left on Ch. Aylmer (6 km), right on Wilfrid Lavigne (1 km) cross Aut McConnell Laramée, 2nd street on right (cul-de-sac).

B&B
L'ÉQUINESSENCE

Joanne Tessier and
Hélène Tremblay
120, avenue Des Ormes
Aylmer J9J 1S9
(819) 685-3555
toll free 1-888-909-1061
fax (819) 684-2424
equinessence@sprint.ca

B&B	
single	$45-55
double	$70-80
child	$20

VS IT

Open year round

Number of rooms	2
rooms with private bath	1
rooms in basement	1
shared bathrooms	1

Activities: 🚶 🚶 🚲 🎿 🎿

3. AYLMER

F E P ⊘ R1

Provincial Excellence Prize 1996-97. A few minutes from Ottawa/Hull, this charming residence is referred to by many guests as "their home away from home". A warm welcome, comfortable rooms, attention to details and great breakfasts are a winning combination. Close to bike and ski trails, golfing, Gatineau Park. Air conditionning and private parking.

From Montréal, Hwy 417, in Ottawa Exit 123 (Island Park Drive) follow Island Park, cross Champlain Bridge to 148 West sign, left, drive 2 km. From Hull, 3 km west of the Hull/Aylmer border

B&B
L'ESCAPADE GÎTE

Lise and Rhéal Charron
912, chemin d'Aylmer
Aylmer J9H 5T8
(819) 772-2388
fax (819) 772-4354

B&B	
single	$45-55
double	$60-70
child	$10

VS MC

Open year round

Number of rooms	3
rooms with sink	2
shared wc	1
shared bathrooms	1

Activities: 🏛 🚶 🚲 🎿 🎿

B&Bs AND INNS

4. AYLMER, BRECKENRIDGE

F | E | ⊘ | P | R1 | TA

Our split-level home offers you comfort, tranquillity and a warm welcome. Take the time to enjoy nature in the magnificent woods bordering the Outaouais River. 20 min to the Parliament and Ottawa's other tourist attractions. Bicycle storage available. Generous breakfast.

From Montréal, Hwy 417, in Ottawa Exit 123 (Island Park Drive) follow Island Park, cross Champlain Bridge to 148 West sign. From the Aylmer city hall, right on Eardley Street for 5 km. Left on Terry Fox twd the river, right on Cedarvale.

B&B
MAISON BON REPOS

Denyse and Guy Bergeron
37, Cedarvale, Breckenridge
Aylmer, Pontiac
J0X 2G0
(819) 682-1498
tel/fax (819) 684-6821
www.inexpress.
net/~dbergero/
dbergero@inexpress.net

B&B	
single	$40-45
double	$50-55
child	$10

Open year round

Number of rooms	3
rooms with private bath	2
shared bathrooms	1

Activities: 🚣 ⛷ 🚶 🚴 🎿

5. HULL

F | E | ⊘ | P | 🚗 | R1 | TA

Come experience Outaouais hospitality at its best, in a peaceful area right near downtown Hull, Ottawa and Parc de la Gatineau. Unforgettable breakfasts served in a solarium looking out onto a rose garden... or a blanket of snow. A place for people of all different ages and all different cultures! Se habla español!

From the Queensway, Exit Nicholas, Hull to the Hwy 5 North, Mont-Bleu Exit. Turn right on Boul. Riel to Normandie. From Montréal, via the 148 West, take the 5 North and follow the directions above.

B&B
AU NORMANDIE

Colette and Guy Claveau
67, rue de la Normandie
Hull J8Z 1N6
tel/fax (819) 595-2191
www.bbcanada.com/
1024.html
claveau@admin.uottawa.ca

B&B	
single	$50-55
double	$60-65
triple	$75
quad.	$85
child	$10

VS

Open year round

Number of rooms	3
rooms in basement	1
rooms with private bath	1
shared bathrooms	1

Activities: 🏛 ⛷ 🚶 🚴 🎿

6. HULL

F | P | R1 | TA

An invitation to relax in a calm spot, near Gatineau Park, bike paths and walking trails. Country charm in the city. Warm welcome. Comfortable rooms and delicious breakfasts. Living room with fireplace, piano and TV. A few min from Ottawa, the casino and museums. Make yourself at home.

From Queensway, Nicholas Exit twd Hull and Hwy 5 N.; Mt-Bleu Exit. Right on Boul. Mt-Bleu, on the hill go left. Take Rue des Bouleaux, turns into des Ormes. From Mtl, Rte 148, Hwy 5 N... as above.

B&B
AU PIGNON SUR LE PARC

Fernande Béchard-Brazeau
63, des Ormes
Hull J8Y 6K6
(819) 777-5559
fax (819) 777-0597
brazeau-a@sympatico.ca

B&B	
single	$45
double	$55
triple	$80
quad.	$100
child	$10-15

Open year round

Number of rooms	3
rooms in basement	1
shared bathrooms	2

Activities: 🏛 ⛷ 🚶 🚴 🏃

7. HULL

F | E | ⊗ | P | 🚗 R2 | TA

Relaxing ambiance, 2 minutes from Gatineau Park, cycling paths, footpaths; 8 minutes from Hull/Ottawa centre (museums); near the casino. Attentive service. Finely decorated, air-conditioned house. Delicious breakfast on the terrace looking out on a golf course, in the country; living room with fireplace. Parking included. Welcome.

From Montréal, Rte 148 W. to Hull, then Hwy 5 N., Exit 8, right on Boul. Hautes Plaines E., left on Du Contrefort and right on Du Versant. From Ottawa, Hwy 417, Exit Mann, then King Edward twd Hull; MacDonald-Cartier Bridge, Hwy 5 N......

B&B
AU VERSANT
DE LA MONTAGNE

Ghyslaine Vézina
19, du Versant
Hull J8Z 2T8
(819) 776-3760
fax (613) 569-2356
auversant@sympatico.ca

B&B	
single	$45-50
double	$55-60
triple	$75
child	$5-10

VS

Open year round

Number of rooms	3
rooms in semi-basement	1
shared bathrooms	2

Activities: 🏛 🚶 🧍 🚴 🏃

8. HULL

F | e | ⊗ | 🐕 | P | R.5

Welcoming Victorian house, lovingly decorated. A few minute's walk to Ottawa, Parliament, museums, Rideau Canal, etc. Access to bicycles and to the nicest bike paths. Casino 5 min away by car. Private parking, copious breakfast. Recommended by La Presse, in Dec. '94 and August '97.

From Montréal, Rte 148 then 550. Exit Hull West, Exit Boul Maisonneuve, left on Verdun, left on Champlain. Or from Montréal, Hwy 417, Exit Mann (becomes King Edouard), Cartier McDonald bridge Exit Boul Maisonneuve.

B&B
COUETTE ET CROISSANT

Anne Picard Allard
330, rue Champlain
Hull J8X 3S2
(819) 771-2200

B&B	
single	$50-55
double	$60-65

VS

Open: Jan. 31 to Oct. 31

Number of rooms	3
rooms with private bath	1
rooms in basement	1
shared bathrooms	2

Activities: 🏛 🍎 ⛴ 🚴 🏃

9. HULL

F | E | ⊗ | 🐕 | P | R1 | TA

By Gatineau Park, a few minutes from downtown Hull and Ottawa. Welcome to our home with modern-classical decor and family ambiance. You will enjoy comfort, quiet and hearty breakfasts while abandoning yourselves to tourist activities such as: museums, outdoors, etc. See you soon! Families welcome.

From Ottawa or Rte 148 via Montréal, take Hwy 5 North, St-Raymond Exit toward Rte 148 West, right on Ch. Pink, left on Des Peupliers, left on Atmosphère, right on Astrolabe.

B&B
MANOIR DES CÈDRES

Christiane and Yvon Charron
5, rue de l'Astrolabe # 1
Hull J9A 2W1
(819) 778-7276
fax (819) 778-6502

B&B	
single	$55
double	$65
triple	$80
quad.	$95
child	$10

Open year round

Number of rooms	2
shared wc	1
rooms in basement	2
shared bathrooms	1

Activities: 🏛 🚶 🧍 🚴 🏃

B&Bs AND INNS

10. LAC-VICEROI (CANTON DE RIPON)

F E ⌂ P ⇄ ✗ R5 TA

Stately residence with turrets, antique furniture, family and gastronomic cooking. Free access to our summer theatre. Other free activities: fishing, canoe, swim in our private lake or river, dog sleds, two snowmobiles, cross-country ski trail and equipment, snowshoes. Nearby: at special rates, horseback riding, seaplane tours, camping in a camper in a wildlife reserve, golf.

From Montréal, Rte 148 West. From Ottawa-Hull, Hwy 50 and Rte 148 East. In Papineauville, Rte 321 North for 27 km. At the four-way intersection, turn left, Rte 317. After the bridge, right Chemin des Guides, drive 1.6 km, on the right.

B&B
CHÂTEAU ÉPI D'OR

Claire and Charles Dussault
15, chemin Périard
Canton de Ripon (Lac-Viceroi)
J0V 1V0
(819) 428-7120

	B&B	MAP
single	$40	$47.⁵⁰
double	$50	$65
triple	$65	$87.⁵⁰
child	$10	$17.⁵⁰

Taxes extra VS MC

Open year round

Number of rooms	5
rooms with private bath	4
rooms with private wc	1
rooms with wc and shower in basement	1

Activities: ● ⚓ ⇆ 🎿 🐕

---

11. MESSINES

F E ⊘ ♿ P ✗ TA

Located in a peaceful, enchanting setting in Haute-Gatineau, our inn has a tranquil atmosphere that will envelop you in a pleasant sense of well-being. The fine cuisine served in our restaurant is among the best in the Outaouais. Golf, horseback riding, downhill and cross-country skiing, etc.

From Ottawa/Hull, take Hwy 5 North and Rte 105 twd Maniwaki. Turn left at the flashing light in Messines. From Montréal, Hwy 15 North, Rte 117 North in St-Jovite to Grand-Remous. Turn left on Rte 105 South, to Maniwaki...

INN
MAISON LA CRÉMAILLÈRE

Andrée and André Dompierre
24, chemin de la Montagne
Messines J0X 2J0
(819) 465-2202
fax (819) 465-5368

B&B	
single	$50
double	$65

Taxes extra VS MC IT

Open year round

Number of rooms	2
shared wc	1
shared bathrooms	1

Activities: ⚓ 🕺 🚲 🐎 ⇆

---

12. MONTEBELLO

F E ⊘ ⌂ P R1 TA

Let yourself be seduced by the enchanting decor, warm reception and creature comforts of the spacious rooms. Prestigious house. 45-acre property 3km from Châteacu Montebello. Foyer. In-ground pool, canoeing, pedal-boating. Health packages, fishing, sea kayaking, dog-sledding... a dream vacation!

From Montréal: Ottawa-Hull-bound Aut 40 Ouest; Hawkesbury Exit, Rte 148 Ouest, 2 km before Montebello. From Ottawa-Hull: Aut 50 and Rte 148 Est to Montebello; 2 km east of the village.

B&B
JARDINS DE RÊVES

Michelle Lachance
1190, Côte du Front
Montebello J0V 1L0
(819) 423-1188
fax (819) 423-2084
jardins.reves@orbit.qc.ca

B&B	
single	$65
double	$85
triple	$100
quad.	$115
child	$15

Taxes extra VS MC IT

Open year round

Number of rooms	5
rooms with private bath	5

Activities: 🧍 🚲 🐎 ⇆ 🎿

13. NOTRE-DAME-DE-LA-SALETTE

`F` `E` `X` `P` `R.5` `TA`

Looking for peace and tranquillity? That is just what our B&B offers. Located by a river surrounded by mountains. Our farm animals graze on our 9-acre park. Your hostess is a nurse. Chef Georges treats guests to excellent meals. Liquor license. Skidoo rental. Meals upon reservation.

2.5 hours from Montréal, take Hwy 40 West twd Ottawa-Hull; take the Hawksbury Exit to Cumberland. Take the ferry at traffic light then Rte 309 twd Buckingham. After 27 km, cross the bridge.

B&B
DOMAINE DE LA MAISON BLANCHE

Doreen Desjardins and
Jean-Georges Burda
C.P. 185
Notre-Dame de la Salette
J0X 2L0
(819) 766-2529
fax (819) 766-2572
impactmrk.com/mb

	B&B
single	$50
double	$60
triple	$75

Taxes extra VS

Open year round

Number of rooms	4
shared wc	1
shared bathrooms	2

Activities: 🦪 ⛵ 🎣 🚶 🛷

14. PAPINEAUVILLE, MONTEBELLO

`F` `E` `P` `R.5` `TA`

Our 150-year-old house will charm you. Peaceful environement. Just 5 km from Chateau Montebello, 65 km from Hull/Ottawa. Home-made jams, outdoor pool. Nearby you will find: golf, horseback riding, rafting, cross-country skiing, ice- fishing. Golf packages available.

Halfway between Montréal and Hull-Ottawa by Rte 148. From Montréal to Papineauville, right on Rue Joseph Lucien Malo at the corner with the Ultramar garage.

B&B
À L'ORÉE DU MOULIN

Suzanne Lacasse
170, Joseph Lucien Malo
Papineauville (Montebello)
J0V 1R0
tel/fax (819) 427-8534
www.bbcanada.com/
128.html

	B&B
single	$45
double	$60
triple	$85
child	$15

VS

Open year round

Number of rooms	4
shared bathrooms	2

Activities: 🏛 🍷 🎣 🐎 🏃

15. PONTIAC, LUSKVILLE

`F` `E` `⃠` `♿` `🐕` `P` `R2` `TA`

Outaouais Excellence Prize 1997-98. Large one-story log house, impressive stone fireplace. Pine grove, 25 kilometres from Ottawa, near Gatineau Park. On site: old forge; cycling, snowshoeing, canoeing; reflexology, Reiki. Paddle down Ottawa River in a canoe while singing to the rhythm of the oars.

From Hull, Ch de la Montagne N. After 17.5 km, right on Ch. Crégheur, 2nd house on the right. From Ottawa, cross a bridge, take the 148 W., 16.5 km after Aylmer, take Ch. Crégheur, 1.5 km.

B&B
AU CHARME
DE LA MONTAGNE

Thérèse André and
Armand Ducharme
368, chemin Crégheur
Pontiac (Luskville) J0X 2G0
(819) 455-9158
fax (819) 455-2706

	B&B
single	$45-55
double	$50-60
triple	$60-70
quad.	$70-80
child	$10

VS

Open year round

Number of rooms	3
shared bathrooms	2

Activities: 🛶 ⛵ 🚶 🐎 🛷

B&Bs AND INNS

16. ST-ANDRÉ-AVELLIN

F E P R.5 TA

Hundred-year-old house on the heritage tour in the historic heart of the village. Victorian period furniture. 4 cosy romantic rooms. Solarium. Restaurants, shops, attractions and services close by. The charm and simplicity of days gone by... Friendly welcome.

From Montréal, Rte 148 West or from Ottawa-Hull Hwy 50 and Rte 148 East to Papineauville. Rte 321 North, 12 km. In St-André-Avellin, turn left in front of the church, grey-stone house on the left.

B&B
L'ANCESTRALE

Ginette Louisseize
and Bertin Mailloux
19, rue St-André
St-André-Avellin J0V 1W0
(819) 983-3232
fax (819) 983-3466

B&B	
single	$45
double	$60

Taxes extra

Open year round

Number of rooms	5
rooms in basement	1
rooms with private bath	2
shared wc	2
shared bathrooms	1

Activities: 🦪 ⛴ 🎿 🚴 🏃

17. VAL-DES-MONTS

F e 🚫 P 🏊 R2

Country B&B near lakes, forests and wide expanses, 25 kilometres from Hull-Ottawa. Nearby: fish breeding, saphouse, skidoo trails (rentals available) and cross-country skiing, cycling paths, Laflèche cave. On site: bee-keeping, pool, recreation canoes.

From Montréal, Rte 148 W. or from Ottawa/Hull, Hwy 50 twd Montréal, Exit Boul. Lorrain, 10.5 km on Rte 366 N., left on Rue École (at the dépanneur), go for 1 km, right on Prud'homme.

B&B
AUX PETITS OISEAUX

Gaétane and Laurent Rousseau
6, Prud'homme
Val-des-Monts J8N 7C2
(819) 671-2513
www.cyberus.ca/
~rousseau/gite
rousseau@cyberus.ca

B&B	
single	$45
double	$55
child	$10

Open year round

Number of rooms	2
rooms with sink	1
shared bathrooms	2

Activities: 🎿 🏃 🚴 🚣 🏃

18. VINOY, CHÉNÉVILLE

F E P 🚗 ❌ TA

In a wooded valley stream-laced, a retreat where period decor revives old memories while creating new ones and time is measured by the passing of the seasons. A farmyard enchants children, cosy corners invite lovers' whispers, nature's bounty nurtures the camaraderie old friends. Taste each season at its peak, from strawberry summers to wonderland winters. Outaouais Excellence Prize 1995-96. **Farm Stay p 40. See colour photos.**

From Montréal, Rte 148 West. From Ottawa/Hull, Hwy 50, Rte 148 East to Papineauville. North on Rte 321. 12 km from St-André-Avellin, right on montée Vinoy.

INN
LES JARDINS DE VINOY

Suzanne Benoit and
André Chagnon
497, Montée Vinoy Ouest
Vinoy (St-André-Avellin)
J0V 1W0
(819) 428-3774
fax (819) 428-1877
a.chagnon@orbit.qc.ca

	B&B	MAP
single	$45-60	$63-78
double	$60-75	$96-111
triple	$70-85	$124-139
quad.	$80-95	$152-167
child	$10	$19

Taxes extra VS MC

Reduced rates: Sep. 6 to June 22
Open year round

Number of rooms	5
rooms with private bath	2
shared wc	1
shared bathrooms	1

Activities: ⛴ 🚴 🐎 🏃 🐎

FARM ACTIVITIES

Farm stay:

18 LES JARDINS DE VINOY, Vinoy, Chénéville 40

Country-style dining*:

19 FERME CAVALIER, St-Sixte 26

* Registered trademark.

Looking for Quality

ALL OUR ESTABLISHMENTS
ARE INSPECTED REGULARLY
BY THE FEDERATION

Seal of «Quality Control»

QUÉBEC CITY REGION

*The numbers on the map correspond to the number of each establishment in the region.

1. BEAUPORT

| F | e | P | R.5 | TA |

Panoramic view: St. Lawrence River, Île d'Orléans, Parc Montmorency. All you have to do is cross the street to discover the charms of Parc de la Chute Montmorency with its picnic sites, trails and manor, etc... 10 km from old Québec City and 4 km from Île d'Orléans. Between Mont-Ste-Anne and Stoneham.

From Montréal, twd Ste-Anne-de-Beaupré, Exit 322, turn left, drive 2.3 km. Corner Royale and Avenue Larue. Or from the Côte-Nord, twd Montréal, exit 322, etc... (facing Manoir Montmorency).

B&B
EN HAUT DE LA CHUTE
MONTMORENCY

Gisèle and Bertrand Tremblay
2515, avenue Royale
Beauport G1C 1S2
tel/fax (418) 666-4755
gisele@oricom.ca

B&B	
single	$37
double	$55-65
triple	$70-80
child	$10

Open year round

Number of rooms	3
rooms with private bath	1
rooms with sink	2
rooms in basement	2
shared wc	2
shared bathrooms	1

Activities: 🏛 ⚲ ⚓ 🚶 🚲

2. BEAUPORT

| F | e | 🚫 | ✕ | P | R.3 | TA |

Ancestral house in Old Beauport. Near the Montmorency Falls, Île d'Orléans, the Old City (5 minutes) and Mont-Sainte-Anne (30 minutes). The master chef invites you to partake of a hearty breakfast, table d'hôte delicacies in an art-gallery-like decor.

Hwy 40 twd Ste-Anne-de-Beaupré. Seigneuriale South Exit, right on Ave. Royale. From Old Québec: Hwy Dufferin, Exit François-de-Laval, right on Ave. Royale.

B&B
LA MAISON DUFRESNE

France Collin and Michel Nigen
505, avenue Royale
Beauport G1E 1Y3
(418) 666-4004
(418) 261-6713
fax (418) 663-0119
www.mlink.net/~dufresne
dufresne@mlink.net

	B&B	MAP
single	$50	$67.50
double	$65	$100
triple	$77	$130
child	$5	$10

Taxes extra VS MC

Open year round

Number of rooms	3
rooms with sink	3
shared wc	1
shared bathrooms	1

Activities: 🏛 ⚲ ⚓ 🎿 🏃

3. BEAUPORT

| F | e | P | 🚫 | R1 | TA |

Hike the country in the city. The Maison Latouche dates back to 1791 and is located 10 min from old Québec City and close to the Chutes Montmorency. Stunning view of the majestic St-Laurent and Île d'Orléans. Decor of yesteryear, warm welcome, generous breakfast. What sets our B&B apart is its tranquillity and the discretion of your hosts.

From Montréal, Hwy 40 East or from the Côte-Nord, Hwy 40 West; Boul. Des Chutes Exit (322), left at the traffic lights, left on Rue St-Jean-Baptiste (Esso), right on Ave. Royale.

B&B
LA MAISON LATOUCHE (1791)

Raymonde Mailloux and
Pierre St-Hilaire
2031, avenue Royale
Beauport G1C 1N7
(418) 821-9333
www.bbcanada.com/
1009.html

B&B	
single	$45
double	$58
triple	$70
quad.	$85
child	$5-10

Open year round

Number of rooms	4
shared wc	1
shared bathrooms	2

Activities: 🏊 ⚓ 🚲 🎿 🏃

B&B's AND INNS

4. BEAUPORT

F E ⊗ ♿ 🚗 P 🏊 R.2

Built in 1875, the Manoir Vallée will take you back to the warmth and ambiance of the past. Located 5 minutes from the Old City and the Montmorency Falls. Relax in our large rooms with stone walls and romantic decor. You will appreciate our old-time breakfasts. Relaxing living room, suite with kitchen.

From Montréal: Hwy 40 East or from North Shore, rue Labelle Exit, go down to Royale, turn right, 10th house, opposite the "Ultramar".

B&B
LE MANOIR VALLEE

Francine Huot and Kevin Strassburg, Carlos and Rosalee 907, avenue Royale Beauport G1E 1Z9 **(418) 660-3855** (418) 666-5421 kevenstr@total.net

B&B	
single	$45-65
double	$55-75
triple	$65-85
quad.	$80-105
child	$10

Taxes extra VS MC

Open: May 1 to Oct. 31

Number of rooms	4
rooms with private bath	4

Activities: 🏛 🍴 🚣 🎿 🚲

5. BEAUPORT

F E P 🏔 ⊗ R.5 TA

Québec Excellence Prize 1997-98. You'll find us on the oldest road in Québec, 10 min from Old Québec, 1 km from Montmorency Falls park, and 30 min from Mt Ste-Anne. Come relax in our outdoor pool or lounge in the large garden. Free parking and what delicious breakfasts! **See colour photos.**

From Montréal, Hwy 40 East, from the Côte-Nord, Hwy 40 West, Exit 322. From Québec City, Hwy 440, Exit 29, then Exit 322, left on Boul. Des Chutes, left at the Esso station, right on Ave. Royale, drive 0.5 km.

B&B
MAISON ANCESTRALE THOMASSIN

Madeleine Guay 2161, avenue Royale Beauport G1C 1N9 **(418) 663-6067** fax (418) 660-8616

B&B	
single	$45
double	$60
triple	$75
quad.	$90
child	$10

Reduced rates: Nov. 1 to April 30
Open year round

Number of rooms	4
shared bathrooms	2

Activities: 🍴 🚣 🎿 🚲 ⛷

6. BOISCHATEL

F e ⊗ P 🚗 R.2 TA

Large Canadian house in the heart of all the attractions in the Québec City area. 300 metres from the Montmorency falls, opposite Île d'Orléans. 10 minutes from Old Québec City. Fax and Internet service on site. Theatre package, whale-watching excursion reservations. Storage for bikes and skis. Free parking lot.

From Montréal, Hwy 20 E. or Hwy 40 E. twd Ste-Anne-de-Beaupré. Left at Côte-de-l'Église, Boischatel Exit, 1.6 km after Chutes Montmorency (at 1st traffic lights). Head up the hill, left on Ave. Royale, 0.6 km.

B&B
AU GÎTE DE LA CHUTE

Claire and Jean-Guy Bédard 5143, avenue Royale Boischatel G0A 1H0 tel/fax (418) 822-3789 www.franco.ca/chute 5143gite@clic.net

B&B	
single	$40-45
double	$50-60
child	$15

Reduced rates: Nov. 1 to April 30
Open year round

Number of rooms	5
rooms in basement	3
shared wc	1
shared bathrooms	2

Activities: 🍴 🚣 ⛷ 🚲 ⛷

7. BOISCHATEL

F | e | 🚗 | P | R2

Ten minutes from Quebec City, "Le Refuge du Voyageur" offers an exceptional view of the city, the St-Laurent River, the Pont de l'Île bridge and Île d'Orléans. Rustic decor, spacious rooms with balcony and a family-size suite with kitchenette.

From Québec City: Hwy Dufferin-Montmorency East, Boischatel Exit. Côte de l'église, to Ave. Royale. One minute's drive, on your right.

B&B
LE REFUGE DU VOYAGEUR

Raynald Vézina
5516, avenue Royale
Boischatel G0A 1H0
(418) 822-2589

B&B	
single	$30-40
double	$60-70
triple	$75-85
quad.	$90-100

Reduced rates : Nov. 1 to June 1
Open year round

Number of rooms	2
rooms with private bath	2

Activities: 🏛 🖖 🚴 🎿 🏃

8. CAP-ROUGE

F | E | P | 🚭 | 🚗 | R1 | TA

15 min from Old Québec, close to the bridges, English-style cottage (1991) B&B. Peaceful and welcoming, with parking, terrace and flower gardens. Nearby: marina, paths along the rivers, art galleries, restaurants, shopping centres. Generous breakfast served by your hosts.

Hwy 20, after the bridges, Exit 133, right on Ch. St-Louis, to the end (3 min), Louis-Francœur is to the right. Or Hwy 40 Duplessis Hwy Exit Ch. Ste-Foy. Go right, to Louis-Francœur (3 min).

B&B
GÎTE LA JOLIE ROCHELLE

Huguette Couture and
Martin Larochelle
1450, Louis-Francœur
Cap-Rouge (Pointe-Ste-Foy)
G1Y 1N6
(418) 653-4326

B&B	
single	$50
double	$60
child	$10-15

Reduced rates : Oct. 1 to June 1
Open year round

Number of rooms	3
shared wc	1
shared bathrooms	1

Activities: 🏛 🛶 🎿 🏃 🚴

9. CAP-ROUGE

F | e | P | 🚭 | R.5 | TA

Large, comfortable house in residential neighbourhood, quiet, restful. 15 km from old Québec City. Varied, home-made, all-you-can-eat breakfast. Living room, flower garden and parking. Near a golf course, marina, footpath near the river, great shopping centre. Welcome!

From Montréal, Hwy 20 East, Pierre-Laporte bridge, Exit Ch. St-Louis W. Rue Francœur, left on Chemin Ste-Foy, Rue St-Félix, right on Rue du Golf. From Rte 138 twd Cap-Rouge.

B&B
L'HYDRANGÉE BLEUE

Yvan Denis
1451, du Golf
Cap-Rouge G1Y 2T6
(418) 657-5609

B&B	
single	$40-50
double	$50-60
triple	$65-75
quad.	$80-90
child	$10

Open year round

Number of rooms	2
rooms with private bath	1
shared bathrooms	1
rooms in basement	1

Activities: 🏛 🖖 🛶 🎣 🏃

10. CAP-ROUGE

F E P ⊘ R.5

The Feeney house is 200 years old, close to the river and the village. Enjoy the friendly ambiance around the fireplace. Old village, extraordinary history, water park and long beaches along the St-Laurent allow for pleasant and relaxing walks. Meet some of the local "Carougeois", visit the studios of artists, potters, sculptors.

From Montréal, Hwy 20 East, Pierre-Laporte bridge Exit Hwy Duplessis, Exit Chemin Ste-Foy twd Cap-Rouge. Go down the hill, follow the river, Rue St-Félix is after the stop sign, white and green house, parking on Rue du Tracel.

B&B
LA MAISON FEENEY

André Létourneau
4352, St-Félix
Cap-Rouge G1Y 3A5
(418) 651-3970
maisonfeeney@sympatico.ca

B&B	
single	$45
double	$58
triple	$75
quad.	$90
child	$12

Open year round

Number of rooms	3
rooms with sink	2
shared wc	1
shared bathrooms	1

Activities: 🏛 ⅄ 🚲 🎿 🏃

11. CAP-TOURMENTE, MONT-STE-ANNE

F E ⊘ 🐕 P 🏊 R1 TA

In the heart of Cap-Tourmente, 12 min from Mont Ste-Anne (view of the slopes), house with 5 rooms with private bathrooms. Lodging also in the hosts' house (right next to the B&B) where breakfast is served. On site: outdoor pool, hiking or cross-country skiing to the falls and the sugar shack. **Country home p 243.**

From Québec City, Henri IV Hwy N., twd 40 E., Ste-Anne-de-Beaupré, Rte 138 E., twd St-Joachim, Cap-Tourmente.

B&B
GÎTE DE L'OIE DES NEIGES

Gisèle Perron
390, ch. du Cap Tourmente
St-Joachim G0A 3X0
(418) 827-5153
tel/fax (418) 827-2246
www.bbcanada.com/
2690.html
melifre@total.net

B&B	
single	$45
double	$75
triple	$100
quad.	$125
child	$15

VS

Open year round

Number of rooms	5
rooms with private bath	5

Activities: 🏊 ⅄ 🏃 🎿 🏃

12. CHARLESBOURG

F E ⊘ P R.25

Health B&B located near all tourist attractions and sports activities. Ten minutes from the Old City and open-air centres. Warm ambiance, soothing music. Enjoy an authentic, nutritious health-food breakfast. Free: regular or herbal tea, snack.

From P.-Laporte bridge twd Chicoutimi, 40 East, 73 North for 13 km, Junction 175, Exit 313, left, 4 km, Jean-Talon Exit, right at 1st light to Henri-Bourassa, right, 0.25 km, corner 94e Rue West.

B&B
LE GÎTE DU NATUROPATHE

France Villeneuve and
François Létourneau
9385, boul. Henri-Bourassa
Charlesbourg, G1G 4E5
(418) 624-2328
fax (418) 624-9836

B&B	
single	$35
double	$55
triple	$75
child	$10

Taxes extra

Open year round

Number of rooms	2
shared bathrooms	1

Activities: 🏛 🚣 🏃 🚲 🎿

13. CHÂTEAU-RICHER

F E P ☒ R2 TA

The warm welcome of a small inn, an ancestral house restored to its original style, only 15 minutes from the centre of Québec City, facing Île d'Orléans, and 20 minutes from Mont- Ste-Anne. Hablamos español.

Rte 138 E. Twd Ste-Anne-de-Beaupré, after the Île d'Orléans bridge, left on Rte du Petit-Pré, right on Ave. Royale, 9 km after Chutes Montmorency.

INN
AUBERGE DU PETIT PRÉ

Ginette Dion and Yvon Boyer
7126, avenue Royale
Château-Richer G0A 1N0
(418) 824-3852
fax (418) 824-3098

B&B	
single	$50-60
double	$60-70
triple	$85
quad.	$100
child	$15

Taxes extra VS MC AM IT

Open year round

Number of rooms	4
shared wc	1
shared bathrooms	2

Activities: 🏛 ⚘ 🚲 🛶 🎿

---

14. CHÂTEAU-RICHER

F E ⊘ P ☒ TA

Between Mont Ste-Anne and Québec City, in the heart of the Beaupré region, treat yourself to an incomparable stay at our home, along with delicious meals from the Baker restaurant. You will find all the charm of a country home.

East of Québec City, Rte 138 East. To Ste-Anne-de-Beaupré. 18.5 km from the Montmorency falls. Watch for "Baker" on the roof of the restaurant.

INN
BAKER

Gaston Cloutier
8790, avenue Royale
Château-Richer G0A 1N0
(418) 824-4478
(418) 824-4852
fax (418) 824-4412
www.auberge-baker.qc.ca
gcloutier@auberge-baker.qc.ca

	B&B	MAP
single	$59-85	$90-115
double	$65-89	$124-150
triple	$80-104	$170-195
quad.	$95-120	$215-245
child	$10	$32

Taxes extra VS MC AM ER IT

Reduced rates : Apr. 6 to June 23 and Oct. 11 to Dec. 22
Open year round

Number of rooms	6
rooms with sink	4
rooms with private bath	2
shared bathrooms	2

Activities: 🛶 ⚘ 🛷 🎿 🏃

---

15. CHÂTEAU-RICHER

F E P ☒ TA

Fifteen minutes from Old Québec City and 10 minutes from Mont-Ste-Anne, stay in a magnificent Victorian house (1868). Hearty home-made breakfast with exceptional view over the river and Île d'Orléans. Large lounge with fireplace. Exquisite, cosy rooms furnished in the old style. Dinner with reservations. Delicious French cuisine. We speak German.

From Québec City, Rte 138 East. Drive 15 km past the Île d'Orléans bridge. In Château-Richer, left at the traffic lights on Rue Dick, right on Ave. Royale, left on Côte Ste-Achillée, drive 100 feet, left on Rue Pichette.

INN
LE PETIT SÉJOUR

Pascal Steffan,
Christiane and Anne-Marie
394, Pichette
Château-Richer G0A 1N0
tel/fax (418) 824-3654

	B&B	MAP
single	$50	$75
double	$60-85	$110-135
triple	$85-100	$160-175
quad.	$100-115	$200-215
child	$15	$30

Taxes extra VS MC

Reduced rates : Apr. 15 to June 15, Oct. 15 to Dec. 1
Open year round

Number of rooms	5
rooms with private bath	1
shared wc	1
shared bathrooms	2

Activities: 🏛 🛶 ⚘ 🎿 🏃

16. DESCHAMBAULT

F E P R4 TA

With the St-Laurent, the falls and Rivière Belisle at its feet, this large hundred-year-old Victorian, nick-named "the little château", will transport you back in time with flowers, lace and a decor from days gone by. Evening meal of creative and meticulously prepared meals. Snowmobiling, sleigh rides, cross-country skiing, ice-fishing. **See colour photos.**

From Montréal or Québec City, Hwy 40 "Félix Leclerc", Exit 254, drive 1.6 km to the river. Turn left onto Rte 138 (Chemin du Roy), drive 2 km. Turn left at the Auberge "Chemin du Roy" sign, Rue St-Laurent.

INN
AUBERGE CHEMIN DU ROY

Francine Bouthat and Gilles Laberge
106, rue St-Laurent
Deschambault G0A 1S0
(418) 286-6958
toll free 1-800-933-7040

	B&B	MAP
single	$54-89	$74-109
double	$64-99	$104-139
triple	$79-114	$139-174
quad.	$124	$204
child	$10	$20-30

Taxes extra VS MC

Open year round

Number of rooms	8
rooms with sink	2
rooms with private bath	6
shared wc	2
shared bathrooms	2

Activities: 🏛 🛶 🎿 🚲 🎿

17. ÎLE D'ORLÉANS, ST-FRANÇOIS

F E P R2 TA

30 min from old Québec City. We invite you to the great outdoors... B&B 300 metres from road, on 14 hectares of woods and fields. Pan-oramic view of the Laurentides and the St-Laurent River. Country break-fast. Rooms with balcony or private terrace. Spring and fall: see snow geese. Welcome! Witamy! Willkommen!

From Québec City, Rte 138, Hwy 40 or Hwy 440 twd Ste-Anne-de-Beaupré, Exit Île d'Orléans. After the bridge at the traffic lights, turn left, 21 km. 112A is soon after the blue sign "Peche à la truite", on the right.

B&B
LA MAISON BLEUE DE L'ÎLE

Zofia Sroka and Jacques Côté
112A, chemin Royal
St-François, Île d'Orléans
G0A 3S0
(418) 829-2572

B&B	
single	$45
double	$65
triple	$95
quad.	$115
child	$15-20

VS

Open year round

Number of rooms	3
shared bathrooms	2

Activities: 🏛 🍂 🎿 🚲 🎿

18. ÎLE D'ORLÉANS, ST-JEAN

F e P R.1 TA

We are 25 minutes from Québec City, in an ancestral home very close to the river, and near muse-ums, theatres, handicraft bou-tiques, art galleries, and restau-rants. Friendly atmosphere and hearty breakfast. We will do every-thing we can to make your stay a pleasant one. Welcome to Île d'Orléans.

From Québec City, Rte 440 East twd Ste-Anne-de-Beaupré, Île d'Orléans Exit. At the traffic lights, go straight ahead for 20 km. House on the right, corner of Chemin du Quai.

B&B
B&B DU QUAI

Rita and Grégoire Roux
1686, chemin Royal
Saint-Jean, Île d'Orléans
G0A 3W0
(418) 829-2278

B&B	
single	$35
double	$45-50
triple	$70
quad.	$90
child	$5-10

Reduced rates : May 1 to June 15, Oct.1 to Oct. 31
Open : May 1 to Oct. 31

Number of rooms	3
shared bathrooms	2

Activities: 🏛 🍂 🛶 🎿 🚲

19. ÎLE D'ORLÉANS, ST-JEAN

F | E | X | P | R.5 | TA

Ancestral home, where calm and tranquillity are the most important things. View of the river. Bedrooms with natural wood and sinks. Twenty minutes from Québec City. Close to first seigneury on Île d'Orléans. Generous breakfast, served in our little restaurant in the summer. A gem of a discovery!

From Québec City, Rte 440 East twd Ste-Anne-de-Beaupré, Exit Île d'Orléans. At the traffic lights, straight for 17.7 km. Turn left on first street after the Manoir Mauvide de Genest, at the top of the hill, 1st green and white house.

B&B
LA MAISON SUR LA CÔTE

Hélène and Pierre Morissette
1477, chemin Royal
St-Jean, Île d'Orléans
G0A 3W0
(418) 829-2971
fax (418) 829-0991

B&B	
single	$50
double	$55
triple	$75

MC

Open : Apr. 1 to Oct. 31

Number of rooms	4
rooms with sink	4
shared bathrooms	2

Activities: 🏛 🍷 ⛵ 🚣 🚴

20. ÎLE D'ORLÉANS, ST-JEAN

F | E | P | 🏊 | 🚭 | R4 | TA

25 min from old Québec City, 20 min from Montmorency falls, you will appreciate the calm of our B&B located 300 m from the road, near the river. Our full and hearty home-made breakfast will please all tastes and appetites. Wherever you come from, you will be warmly welcomed. Hoping to see you soon.

From Québec, Hwy 40 or 440 east twd Ste-Anne de Beaupré, Île d'Orléans Exit. At traffic lights, head straight to St-Laurent and St-Jean. Chemin des Lièges is located on your right, 2.4 km past St-Jean's church along the river.

B&B
LE GIRON DE L'ISLE

Lucie and Gérard Lambert
120, chemin des Lièges
St-Jean, Île d'Orléans
G0A 3W0
(418) 829-0985
toll free 1-888-280-6636
fax (418) 829-1059
www.total.net/~giron
giron@iname.com

B&B	
single	$45
double	$55

VS MC

Reduced rates : Oct. 15 to Dec. 15 and from Jan. 15 to Apr. 30
Open year round
with reservations Oct. 15 to Apr. 30

Number of rooms	3
shared bathrooms	2

Activities: 🍷 🎿 🚴 🐎 🏃

21. ÎLE D'ORLÉANS, ST-JEAN

F | E | P | 🚭 | 🐕 | R.5 | TA

If you're looking for a peaceful and comfortable place, our 18th-century replica of an old farm house, situated on a cliff, is awaiting you. Your hosts: Yolande, Claude and Canelle the cat.

From Québec City, Rte 138 East twd Ste-Anne-de-Beaupré, Île d'Orléans Exit. After the bridge straight ahead for 17.5 km. At the B&B sign, turn left, the house is on your right on the cliff.

B&B
LE MAS DE L'ISLE

Yolande and Claude Dumesnil
1155, chemin Royal
St-Jean, Île d'Orléans
G0A 3W0
tel/fax (418) 829-1213
www.bbcanada.com/382.html
www.otc.cuq.qc.ca

B&B	
single	$55
double	$60
triple	$90
quad.	$115
child	$20

VS

Reduced rates : $10 discount per room from Oct. 1to Apr. 30
Open year round

Number of rooms	3
shared bathrooms	2

Activities: 🏛 🎿 🚴 🐎 🏃

B&B's AND INNS

22. ÎLE D'ORLÉANS, ST-LAURENT

F | e | P | R.4

A charming flowery house on the St-Laurent River where hospitality and a family ambiance have pride of place. Tranquillity and rest are guaranteed; you will sleep to the soothing sounds of the waves and wind. A hearty breakfast rounds off your stopover at La Nuitée. Non-smoking B&B.

From Québec City: Hwy 40 East twd Ste-Anne-de-Beaupré, Île d'Orléans Exit. After the bridge, at traffic light, continue straight ahead for 11 km. House overlooking the river.

B&B
À LA NUITÉE

Réjeanne and Michel Galibois
925, chemin Royal
St-Laurent, Île d'Orléans
G0A 3Z0
(418) 829-3969
fax (418) 829-0185

B&B	
single	$55-60-65
double	$55-60-65
triple	$75-80-95
quad.	$115
child	$15-20

Open year round

Number of rooms	3
rooms with sink	1
shared bathrooms	2

Activities: 🏛 ⚓ ⚜ 🚲 🏃

23. ÎLE D'ORLÉANS, ST-LAURENT

F | E | P | 🚫 | R.5

By the shores of the St-Laurent River on a vast property far from the road, surrounded by trees and flowers, a large, peaceful house invites rest. All rooms have a view of the river. Complete breakfast. Your hosts' desire: that you feel at home "Aux Capucines" and that you experience the beauty of Île d'Orléans.

From Québec City, Hwy 40 East twd Ste-Anne-de-Beaupré, Exit Île d'Orléans. After the bridge at the traffic lights, straight for 12 km. House on river side.

B&B
AUX CAPUCINES
SUR LE BORD DE L'EAU

Mariette and
Jean-Marc Bouffard
625, chemin Royal
St-Laurent de l'Île d'Orléans
G0A 3Z0
(418) 829-3017
www.bbcanada.
com/2689.html
jmmb@globetrotter.net

B&B	
single	$50-55
double	$60-65

Open year round

Number of rooms	3
shared bathrooms	1

Activities: ⚓ ⛵ ⚜ 🏃 🚲

24. ÎLE D'ORLÉANS, ST-LAURENT

F | e | 🚫 | P | R.5 | TA

The St-Laurent at your feet! Between the rhythm of the waves breaking on the beach and the silent force of the rising tide, we offer an interlude of peace and rest. Air conditioned. Appetizing breakfast, welcome worthy of our most honoured traditions... Off-season rates for 2 nights or more.

From Québec City, Hwy 440 East twd Ste-Anne-de-Beaupré, Île d'Orléans Exit. After the bridge, at the traffic lights, go straight for 11 km. House on the right.

B&B
GÎTE «EAU VIVE»

Micheline and Michel Turgeon
909, chemin Royal
St-Laurent de l'Île d'Orléans
G0A 3Z0
(418) 829-3270
michelineturgeon@hotmail.com

B&B	
single	$50-60
double	$55-65
triple	$80-85
child	$10-15

Reduced rates : 2 nights or more Jan. 1 to Apr. 30 and during Nov.
Open : Jan. 1 to Nov. 30

Number of rooms	3
rooms with private bath	1
shared bathrooms	1

Activities: 🏛 ⚓ ⚜ 🚲 🏃

25. ÎLE D'ORLÉANS, ST-LAURENT

F | e | P | 🚗 | 🏊 R1 TA

Come drop anchor at our hundred-year-old house, right in the heart of town, on the river a few steps away from the marina. The horizon is constantly changing and the landscape transforms with the rhythm of the tide. Library with 2,500 books, reading room, heated pool.

From Québec City, Hwy 40 E. or 440 E. twd Ste-Anne-de-Beaupré, Exit 325 Île d'Orléans. After the bridge, at the lights, go straight for 8 km. About 0.2 km after the church, house on the riverside.

B&B
LA CHAUMIÈRE DU NOTAIRE

June and Jacques Bouffard
1449, chemin Royal
St-Laurent, Île d'Orléans
G0A 3Z0
(418) 828-2180
fax (418) 653-1023

B&B	
single	$60-70
double	$70-80
child	$10

Open: Jan. 1 to Mar. 31,
May 1 to Oct. 31

Number of rooms	2
rooms with private bath	2

Activities: 〜 🛶 🎿 🏃

---

26. ÎLE D'ORLÉANS, ST-LAURENT

F | e | P R3 TA

Steps from the St Lawrence, on an island perfect for dreaming and relaxing, our house tells its own tales with its creaking floors that have seen their fair share of jigs and revelry. You'll be treated to a big breakfast, served with a smile and great hospitality. Snowmobiling packages.

Hwy 40 or 440 E., twd Ste-Anne-de-Beaupré, Île d'Orléans Exit. Straight for 7 km. House on the left, "red door".

B&B
LA VIEILLE MAISON FRADET

Lyse Demers
1584, chemin Royal
St-Laurent, Île d'Orléans
G0A 3Z0
tel/fax (418) 828-9501
pages.infinit.net/fradet

B&B	
single	$55
double	$60-80
triple	$85-100
quad.	$120
child	$15-20

VS
Reduced rates: Sep. 1 to May 31
Open year round

Number of rooms	3
rooms with sink	1
rooms with private bath	2
shared wc	1
shared bathroom	1

Activities: 🍴 🎿 🛷 🏃 🐎

---

27. ÎLE D'ORLÉANS, ST-PIERRE

F | e | P R1 TA

Located near the Pont de l'Île, our B&B is only 10 min east of Québec City, 5 min from the Chutes Montmorency, and 20 min from Ste-Anne-de-Beaupré. With us, comfort, spotlessness, intimacy and generous breakfasts are guaranteed! Bike and motorcycle storage. One room with private entrance. "Crépuscule" is also the explosion of brilliant fall colours. Welcome.

From Québec City, Hwy 40 East or 440 East, twd Ste-Anne-de-Beaupré, Exit 325 Île d'Orléans. At the traffic lights at top of the hill, straight for about 1 km. B&B on left.

B&B
CRÉPUSCULE

Louise Hamel
863, rue Prévost
St-Pierre-de-l'Île, Île d'Orléans
G0A 4E0
(418) 828-9425

B&B	
single	$50
double	$60
triple	$75
quad.	$90
child	$10

Reduced rates: Nov. 1 to Apr. 30
Open year round

Number of rooms	3
rooms with private bath	3

Activities: 🎿 🏛 🍴 🛷

28. ÎLE D'ORLÉANS, ST-PIERRE

F e 🚫 P R1 TA

Welcome to the B&B "Bel Horizon", the gateway to Île d'Orléans, only 15 min from Québec City. Nature, comfort, intimacy, complete breakfast. Comfortable rooms, view of the river, facing Chutes Montmorency. 2 rooms on ground-floor with private bathroom, first floor family suite (6 people) with living-room and private bathroom. 10% off for 3 rooms or 4 nights. Reserve now!

At entrance to Québec City take Rte 440 or Hwy 40 East twd Ste-Anne-de-Beaupré. Drive about 35 km, Exit 325 Île d'Orléans. At the top of the hill, at the traffic lights, turn right and drive about 1 km.

B&B
GÎTE «BEL HORIZON»

Yvandte and Paul-Émile Vézina
402, chemin Royal
St-Pierre, Île d'Orléans
G0A 4E0
(418) 828-9207
fax (418) 828-2618
www.destinationquebec.com

B&B	
single	$45-60
double	$50-70
triple	$75
quad.	$90-100
child	$15

Reduced rates: Feb. 1 to May 31
Open: Feb. 1 to Nov. 1

Number of rooms	3
rooms with private bath	3

Activities: 🏛 ● ⛵ 🚶 🚴

29. ÎLE D'ORLÉANS, ST-PIERRE

F E P ✕ TA

A house with over 200 years of history... is cosy comfort where antique furniture and dried flowers encourage calm and relaxation. Come share authentic and refined country cooking in the intimacy of the dining room. Relax by the fire in the living room or in the garden near the farmyard.

From Québec City: Aut 40 or 440 East toward Ste-Anne-de-Beaupré, Ile d'Orléans Exit. Left at the traffic light. At the village exit, on the left side of the road.

INN
L'AUBERGE SUR LES PENDANTS

Chantale Vigneault and
Jean-Christophe L'Allier
1463, chemin Royal
St-Pierre, Île d'Orléans
G0A 4E0
(418) 828-1139

	B&B	MAP
single	$50	$72
double	$60	$104
triple	$75	$141
quad.	$90	$178
child	$5-10	$11-21

Taxes extra VS *MC IT*

Open year round

Number of rooms	5
shared bathroom	2

Activities: ● 🚶 🚴 ⛵ 🎿

30. ÎLE D'ORLÉANS, ST-PIERRE

F E 🐕 🚗 P R.5

Situated in one of the most beautiful spots on Île d'Orléans, nestled in a vineyard, our ancestral house offers you a "rendez-vous" with history. Guests will be offered a visit to the vineyard and free wine tasting. Three renovated rooms combining comfort and an intimate ambiance. Outstanding breakfasts!

Located at the Île d'Orléans entrance, left at the traffic light, drive 2 km, just before the village of Saint-Pierre.

B&B
LA MAISON DU VIGNOBLE

Lise Roy
1071, chemin Royal
St-Pierre, Île d'Orléans
G0A 4E0
(418) 828-9562

B&B	
single	$45-60
double	$55-80
triple	$65-90
quad.	$110
child	$10

VS MC

Open year round

Number of rooms	3
rooms with private bath	1
shared bathroom	2

Activities: 🏛 ● 🚶 🚴 🎿

31. ÎLE D'ORLÉANS, STE-FAMILLE

F E P R.5 TA

The wind has carried us to all the continents and we've brought back the scents, great life experiences, a different way of doing things and the desire to share. Hundred-year-old house, adjoining shop, view of the river and the Laurentians, walking path, cycling, X-country skiing, snowshoeing, picnic baskets. We speak Japanese.

From Québec City, Rte 440 E. twd Ste-Anne-de-Beaupré, Île d'Orléans Exit. After the bridge, go left at the lights, straight for 13 km. House with the blue roof on the left.

B&B
AU TOIT BLEU

Loulou and Iris Germain
3879, chemin Royal
Ste-Famille, Île d'Orléans
G0A 3P0
(418) 829-1078
fax (418) 829-3052

B&B	
single	$40-55
double	$55-65
triple	$80
quad.	$95
child	$10

VS AM

Reduced rates: Oct. 1 to May 31
Open year round

Number of rooms	3
shared bathroom	2

Activities: 🏊 🎿 🚲 🚣 🏃

---

32. ÎLE D'ORLÉANS, STE-PÉTRONILLE

F E P ♿ R.5

Enchanting setting on magical Île d'Orléans. Come discover the art of living in harmony with the past in our home, amidst a century and a half of history. The magnificent view of the majestic St. Lawrence and a visit to the Chutes Montmorency will leave you with unforgettable memories. To top it all off, we offer generous breakfasts and hospitality worthy of the finest establishments; a wonderful stay awaits you.

From Québec City: Rte 138 and Hwy 40 or 440 twd St-Anne-de-Beaupré, Île d'Orléans Exit. Turn right at the traffic lights after the bridge and continue for 3.5 km.

B&B
LE 91 DU BOUT DE L'ÎLE

Jeanne Trottier
91, chemin Royal,
ch. du Bout de l'Île
Ste-Pétronille, Île d'Orléans
G0A 4C0
(418) 828-2678

B&B	
single	$45-50
double	$55-60
triple	$80
child	$10-15

Reduced rates: Nov. 1 to Apr. 1
Open year round

Number of rooms	4
rooms with sink	2
shared bathroom	2

Activities: 🏛 🏊 🎿 🏂 🏃

---

33. L'ANGE-GARDIEN

F E 🚭 P R1.5 TA

You'll be welcomed into a 200-year-old ancestral home with picturesque view of Île d'Orléans. 4 charming rooms await you. A superb stone fireplace creates a warm ambiance. Located 5 min from Montmorency falls, 20 min from Mont Ste-Anne and 10 min from old Québec City.

From Montréal, Hwy 20, Pierre-Laporte bridge, to Ste-Anne-de-Beaupré. Rte 138, turn left at 2nd traffic lights. In L'Ange Gardien, right at the stop sign on Ave Royale. Drive 1.5 km. Or from Hwy 40 twd Ste-Anne-de-Beaupré...

B&B
AUBERGE AUX TOURNESOLS

Éric Van Campenhout
6757, avenue Royale
L'Ange-Gardien G0A 2K0
(418) 822-3273

B&B	
single	$50
double	$60

Open: year round except for Nov.

Number of rooms	4
shared bathroom	2

Activities: 🏛 🏊 🎿 🏂 🏃

B&Bs AND INNS

34. MONT-STE-ANNE, ST-FERRÉOL

F E P ☒ TA

Nature lovers : get a good dose of energy in complete peace and tranquillity. Spacious, rustic inn. Living room with fireplace. Private bathroom. To visit and experience: whale-watching cruise, waterfalls, wildlife reserve, museum... packages available. Spend your vacation in pleasant company!

At Mont-Ste-Anne. 30 minutes from Québec City: Rte 138, twd Ste-Anne-de-Beaupré Exit 360 East (St-Ferréol). Drive 4 km. From Tadoussac: Rte 138 West, twd Québec City, Exit 360 East (St-Ferréol).

AUBERGE
AUBERGE FERRÉOL

Nathalie and Jean-François 1930, boul. des Neiges St-Ferréol-Les-Neiges G0A 3R0
(418) 826-9999
toll free 1-888-826-9999
fax (418) 826-0047
www.quebecweb.
com/aubergeferreol

B&B	
single	$60
double	$65
triple	$78
quad.	$91
child	$5

Taxes extra VS MC AM IT

Reduced rates: April 1 to June 15, Sep. 7 to Dec. 15
Open year round

Number of rooms	9
rooms with private bath	9

Activities: 🛶 ⛷ 🎿 🐎

35. MONT-STE-ANNE, ST-FERRÉOL

F E 🚭 P 🚗 R1 TA

5 min from Mt Ste-Anne, 30 min from Québec City, discover the calm and comfort of soundproof rooms, twin or queen-size beds, sinks, suites, living room with fireplace. Magnificent scenic view. Nearby: Sept Chutes (falls), Grand Canyon, Cap Tourmente, skiing, cycling, golf, walking trails, snowmobiling, horseback riding, dogsledding. Ski package.

From Québec City, Rte 138 East, drive 40 km. At Beaupré, to Mont-Ste-Anne, Rte 360, 10 km. Or from Baie-St-Paul, Rte 138 West, drive 30 km, take Rte 360 to St-Ferréol. After the 7 Chutes, drive 3 km. Near the church.

B&B
LES AROLLES

Claire Boutet and Gilles Dumas 3489, av. Royale, route 360
St-Ferréol-les-Neiges
G0A 3R0
tel/fax (418) 826-2136

B&B	
single	$45
double	$60-75
child	$0-15

VS MC

Open year round

Number of rooms	5
rooms with sink	3
rooms with private bath	1
shared bathroom	2

Activities: 🚴 🏊 🎿

36. NEUVILLE

F e 🚭 ♿ P 🏊 R2 TA

All the charm of the country 15 minutes from Québec City. View of the St Lawrence, the perfect spot. Large property, woods, terrace with inground pool. Generous breakfast served on the terrace or in the dining room. Living room with TV, pool room. Bikes available. Large parking lot.

From Montréal, Hwy 40 East, Exit 281 Neuville, Rte 138 East, for 6 km. From Québec City, Hwy 40 West, Exit 298, Rte 138 West, 10.4 km.

B&B
LE GÎTE DE NEUVILLE

Louise Côté and Ernest Germain 173, Route 138
Neuville G0A 2R0
(418) 876-3779
(418) 876-3060
fax (418) 876-3780

B&B	
single	$40
double	$50-60

Open year round

Number of rooms	3
shared wc	2
shared bathroom	1

Activities: 🏊 ⛷ 🚴 🛶

37. NEUVILLE

F E P ⊘ R1 TA

15 min from Québec City, in one of the prettiest villages in Québec, discover many ancestral houses. Stunning view of the St. Lawrence. Relax on the terrace, in the sunroom or near the fireplace. Air conditioned. Nearby: marina, antiques, theatre and dogsledding. Guides tours of the village and church. Bikes available.

From Montréal or Québec City: Hwy 40, Exit 285, to Neuville (Route 138); drive 3 km.

B&B
MAISON DUBUC

Madeleine and Antoine Dubuc
421, rue des Érables
Neuville G0A 2R0
tel/fax (418) 876-2573
www.bbcanada.
com/2687.html

B&B	
single	$40
double	$55
enfant	$10

Open: Dec. 1 to Mar. 31,
May 1 to Oct. 31

Number of rooms	2
shared bathroom	1

Activities: 🏛 ⛵ 🎣 🚲 🛶

---

38. QUÉBEC

F e P ⊘ R.8

Cosy house built in 1930, near the Musée du Québec; you'll admire the river and greenery of the Plains of Abraham as you walk towards the old city. Exquisite breakfast, served in the flowery garden or the dining room. We'll chat about art and the history of our beautiful city. Free parking.

Hwy 20, Pierre-Laporte bridge, Boul. Laurier to downtown. 7.9 km from the bridge, turn on Avenue Murray. Or from Hwy 40, Avenue St-Sacrement South, left on Chemin St-Louis, drive 1.3 km..

B&B
À LA CAMPAGNE EN VILLE

Marie Archambault
1160, avenue Murray
Québec G1S 3B6
(418) 683-6638

B&B	
single	$55
double	$65
child	$15

Reduced rates: 4 nights or more
Open year round

Number of rooms	2
shared wc	1
shared bathroom	1

Activities: 🏛 ⛵ 🎣 🚲 🎿

---

39. QUÉBEC

F E ⊘ P R.5 TA

Discover enchantment in this beautiful, turn-of-the-century Tudor-style home, near national parks and Vieux-Québec. Top-quality lodging under a gabled roof. Private parking, sheltered in winter months. Office and internet computer facilities upon request. Discrete, personal attention to travellers' needs.

From Montréal, Hwy 20 East to Québec City. After the Pierre-Laporte bridge, follow Boul. Laurier to old Québec. Turn left onto Ave. Moncton at the Plains of Abraham.

B&B
À LA MAISON TUDOR

J. Cecil Kilfoil
1037, avenue Moncton
Québec (QC) G1S 2Y9
(418) 686-1033
fax (418) 686-6066
www.clic.net/~ckilfoil
ckilfoil@clic.net

B&B	
single	$60-85
double	$70-85
triple	$85-105
quad.	$125
child	$15

Taxes extra VS MC ER

Reduced rates: Oct. 15 to Dec18
and Jan. 5 to June 22
Open year round

Number of rooms	2
shared wc	1
shared bathroom	1

Activities: 🏛 🎣 🚲 🛶 🎿

40. QUÉBEC

F E ♿ P ⊘ R.1 TA

Right in the heart of Québec City, come enjoy the comfort of our English-style residence. Steps from the Plains of Abraham, the Musée du Québec, restaurants and terraces. Generous home-made breakfast. All welcome. Free parking.

Hwy 20, Pierre-Laporte bridge, Boul. Laurier Exit, continue for 8 km, left on Rue Cartier, to 2nd street, Aberdeen, turn left. Or Hwy 40, Av St-Sacrement S., left on Ch. Ste-Foy, right on Rue Cartier to Aberdeen, right.

B&B
AU BALUCHON

Caroline Fitzmorris
206, rue Aberdeen
Québec G1R 2C8
(418) 649-0146
fax (418) 647-2621

B&B	
single	$50-55
double	$65-70
triple	$80-85
quad.	$100-110
child	$15

Open year round

Number of rooms	2
shared bathroom	1

Activities: 🏛 ⛵ 🚲 🧍 🏃

---

41. QUÉBEC

F e 🐕 🛏 P R.25

In the heart of the marvellous Montcalm district, near the Plains of Abraham, a stone's throw from Rue Cartier, with restaurants, cafés and shops, "Au Maric" offers you a warm welcome. Quiet and comfortable rooms. Lavish breakfast with music.

Aut 20, Pierre-Laporte bridge, Boul. Laurier twd downtown. Turn left on Ave. Des érables, after crossing Chemin Ste-Foy or Aut 40, right on l'Aqueduc.

B&B
AU MARIC

Micheline Rioux
470, des Franciscains
Québec G1S 2R1
(418) 688-9341

B&B	
single	$55
double	$65
triple	$80

Open: May 1 to Oct. 31

Number of rooms	2
shared bathroom	1

Activities: 🏛 ⛵ 🚲 ⛷ 🏃

---

42. QUÉBEC

F E P 🛏 ⊘ 🐕 R1 TA

Located at the entrance to Old Québec City, a neighbourhood with European charm, restaurants, cafés and boutiques. Located just 2 min from the Plains of Abraham and the Museum of Québec. Old Québec City is a 10-min walk away. Gourmet breakfast and free parking.

Hwy 20, Pierre-Laporte bridge, Boul. Laurier to downtown (Grande-Allée). 8.7 km after the bridge, turn on Cartier, then left on Saunders. Or Hwy 40, Boul. Charest East, right on St-Sacrement South, left on Chemin Ste-Foy, right on Rue Cartier, right on Saunders.

B&B
AUX TROIS BALCONS

Chantal Javaux and
Paul Simard
130, Saunders
Québec G1R 2E3
(418) 525-5611
fax (418) 529-6227
chantaljavaux@sympatico.ca

B&B	
single	$55-65
double	$70-80
triple	$85-100
quad.	$105
child	$10
Taxes extra VS MC	

Open year round

Number of rooms	4
rooms with private bath	3
shared bathroom	1

Activities: 🏛 ⛵ 🚲 ⛷ 🏃

43. QUÉBEC

F | E | ⊗ | 🐾 | 🚗 | R.1

Vacation at L'Heure Douce in old Québec City, close to the convention centre and all services. Ancestral house with comfortable rooms. Dining room reserved for guests. Panoramic view and balcony where you'll relax with a drink and watch the sun go down. Québécois, continental and vegetarian breakfast. We'll give you some good suggestions.

Hwy 20, Pierre-Laporte bridge, Boul. Laurier Exit, Rue Cartier, left, right on Chemin Ste-Foy, left on St-Augustin to Richelieu. Hwy 40, Boul. Charest, right on Langelier to St-Olivier, left, right on Ste-Geneviève. Next corner.

B&B
ACCUEIL B&B L'HEURE DOUCE

Diane Dumont
704, Richelieu
Québec G1R 1K7
tél/fax (418) 649-1935
www.bbcanada.
com/2695.html
jacques.gagne1@sympatico.ca

B&B	
single	$50-55
double	$60-65
triple	$75-85
quad.	$100-110
child	$15

VS

Reduced rates: week or month stay and from Feb. 15 to Mar. 30
Open year round

Number of rooms	3
shared bathroom	2

Activities: 🏛 ⚓ 🚲 🤽 🐎

44. QUÉBEC

F | E | ⊗ | P | 🚗 | R.1 | TA

Stone house dating from 1848, 200 m from the walls of the old city and the convention centre (Centre des Congrès). Lively family atmosphere full of surprises. Garden in summer, a crackling fire in winter, old-fashioned character, cosy, indoor greenery, excellent music and copious breakfasts complete with a serving of helpful tourist advice. Parking.

Hwy 40: Charest East, right at the St-Vallier turn-off. Drive up Côte d'Abraham, and at the top turn right on Richelieu. Hwy 20: Pierre-Laporte bridge, Boul. Laurier to Cartier, turn left, turn right on Ste-Foy, left on St-Augustin and left on Richelieu.

B&B
B&B À L'AUGUSTINE

Caroline Collet and Kamal Elhaji
775, Richelieu
Québec G1R 1K8
tel/fax (418) 648-1072
www.oricom.ca/augustine/
bb.html
carocol@oricom.ca

B&B	
single	$50
double	$65
triple	$80
child	$10

Reduced rates: Nov. 1 to Jan. 31 and Feb. 20 to Apr. 30
Open year round

Number of rooms	3
shared bathroom	2

Activities:
🏛 ⚓ 🚲 ⛷ 🤽

45. QUÉBEC

F | E | R.1 | TA

Magnificent Victorian home just steps from old Québec City in the heart of the Faubourg St-Jean-Baptiste: historic, artistic and early settlement district. I am a professional artist. Large, comfortable rooms. 2 rooms with private bath, two double beds and fridge. One room with private but separate bathroom, good ventilation. Copious breakfast.

Boul. Laurier to Québec City. After the parliament, Aut. Dufferin to the left, right on Rue St-Jean. Left at the first traffic lights, Rue d'Aiguillon. Cross Dufferin again to Côte St-Geneviève.

B&B
B&B CHEZ PIERRE

Pierre Côté
636, rue d'Aiguillon
Québec G1R 1M5
(418) 522-2173

B&B	
single	$55-65
double	$65-85
triple	$85-100
quad.	$110-130
child	$15

Taxes extra VS MC

Reduced rates: Feb. 1 to May 31
Open: Dec. 1 to Oct. 31

Number of rooms	3
rooms with private bath	3

Activities: 🏛 ⚓ 🚣 🚲 🏃

46. QUÉBEC

`F` `e` `R.3` `TA`

On a quiet street in the heart of the Old City, a stone's throw from Château Frontenac and the river. Fully renovated hundred-year-old house. Clean and comfortable rooms. Breakfast in the Victorian dining room served by your young Quebec hosts mindful of your well-being.

Hwy 20, Laporte bridge, Boul. Laurier Exit, twd Vieux-Québec. After the Porte St-Louis, 1st street on the right, left on Ste-Geneviève and left on Rue Des Grisons.

B&B
B&B DES GRISONS

Claudine Desbois and Jocelyn Santerre
1, rue des Grisons
Québec G1R 4M6
(418) 694-1461
(418) 694-9204
bbcanada.com/2608.html
jsanterr@videotron.ca

B&B	
single	$55
double	$65-75
triple	$95
child	$15

MC

Reduced rates: Nov. 1 to Feb. 1 and Mar. 15 to May 15
Open year round

Number of rooms	3
shared bathroom	2

Activities: 🏛 🍵 ⛵ 🚲 ⛷

47. QUÉBEC

`F` `E` `🚫` `P` `R1` `TA`

Warm house located on a quiet street near services, restaurants, university, hospitals, shopping centres, 5 minutes from the Old City. Family ambiance, opportunities for great conversations! Facilities for children. Healthy breakfast served in our dining room. Storage for skis and bikes.

Hwy 20, Pierre-Laporte bridge, downtown Québec City twd Boul. Laurier. Past Université Laval, turn left on Ave. Des Gouverneurs, left on Boul. René Lévesque, left on Madeleine-de-Verchères.

B&B
B&B LA BEDONDAINE

Sylvie and Gaétan Tessier
912, Madeleine-de-Verchères
Québec G1S 4K7
(418) 681-0783

B&B	
single	$40-45
double	$50-60
child	$10

Reduced rates: Sep. 1 to May 31
Open year round

Number of rooms	2
rooms with private bath	4
rooms in basement	1
shared wc	1
shared bathroom	1

Activities: 🏛 👤 🚲 🏊 🎿

48. QUÉBEC

`F` `e` `🚫` `P` `R1`

Near the Plains of Abraham, Old Quebec, museums and major places of interest, in a lovely residential district; spacious rooms with distinctive style, large living room with fireplace; work room available on request for businesspeople. **See colour photos.**

Hwy 20, Pierre-Laporte bridge, Boul. Laurier, Chemin St-Louis to Ave. des Laurentides (7.8 km). Or Aut 40, right on St-Sacrement, left on Chemin St-Louis to Ave. des Laurentides (1.2 km).

B&B
B&B MAISON LESAGE

Jean-Luc Lesage and Yves Ruel
760, chemin St-Louis
Québec G1S 1C3
(418) 682-9959
bbmaisonlesageyr@
videotron.ca

B&B	
single	$62
double	$73

VS

Open year round

Number of rooms	3
shared wc	3
shared bathroom	1

Activities: 🏛 👤 🚲 🏊 🎿

49. QUÉBEC

F E P 🚗 🐕 R.1 TA

Regional winner of Québec Tourism Grand Prizes for hospitality and customer service (1995); come enjoy unparalleled accommodations in a Victorian house aptly named the "Château St-Pascal". We are located downtown, a few minutes from old Québec City and its many interesting sights. Pool room, shop and table d'hôte upon reservation.

Hwy 20 Pierre Laporte bridge, or hwy 40, twd Ste-Anne-de-Beaupré, Exit 316. At Henri-Bourassa, turn left. Drive 1 km (5 traffic lights). Turn left on Chemin de la Canardière at 1720.

B&B
CHEZ MONSIEUR GILLES²

Gilles Clavet
1720, chemin de la Canardière
Québec G1J 2E3
(418) 821-8778
fax (418) 821-8776

B&B	
single	$55-65
double	$65-75
triple	$80-90
quad.	$10

Taxes extra VS ER

Open year round

Number of rooms	5
rooms with sink	2
rooms with private bath	3
shared wc	2
shared bathrooms	1

Activities: 🏛 ⛵ 🎿 🚴 ⛷

50. QUÉBEC

F E 🚭 ♿ 🚗 P 🍴 TA

A unique experience in an old mansion in Québec city. It is a perfect rendez-vous with the one you love. Our rooms have private bathrooms and fine bed linen. Also our dining room is open to the public from 11 am to 10 pm with Belgian delights and more than 100 Belgian beers. Just 3 km away from the Jean Lesage international airport. Hope to see you soon. A cycling path passes through the domain.

Hwy 20, P.-Laporte bridge. Hwy 40 take Henry IV twd Ste-Anne-de-Beaupré, through Aut. de la Capitale Exit. 1st Exit 308, Masson-l'Ormiere. Left on Masson. At Les Saules terminus, right on Michelet.

INN
DOUCEURS BELGES

Lise Gill and Gilbert Chevalier
4335, Michelet
Québec G1P 1N6
(418) 871-1126
fax (418) 871-6319
www.oricom.
ca/douceursbelges/
douceursbelges@altavista.net

	B&B	PAM
single	$70-80	$95-105
double	$80-90	$130-140

Taxes extra VS MC AM ER IT

Reduced rates : Oct. 15 to Dec. 15 and Mar. 15 to May 15
Open year round

Number of rooms	2
rooms with private bath	2

Activities: 🏛 🍷 🎿 🚴 ⛷

51. QUÉBEC

F E 🚭 🚗 R1 TA

Magnificent Irish house from 1832, view of the St Lawrence, in historical Old Québec, 10 min walk from main attractions. Generous and unbeatable breakfast served in stone and wood decor with fireplace. Quiet street. Nearby: skiing, snowmobiling, dogsledding. Reduced rates for families and groups. **See colour photos.**

When entering Québec City, Hwy 20, Pierre-Laporte bridge, Exit 132 Boul Champlain, left at 6th set of lights Rue Champlain (1 km, turn left at the Québec-Lévis ferry exit).

B&B
HAYDEN'S WEXFORD HOUSE

Jean and Loulou
450, rue Champlain
Québec G1K 4J3
(418) 524-0524
(418) 524-0525
fax (418) 648-8995
www.bbcanada.com/384.html
www.otc.cuq.qc.ca
haydenwexfordhouse@
videotron.net

B&B	
single	$65-95
double	$80-105
triple	$145
quad.	$160
Enfant	$15

Taxes extra VS MC

Open year round

Number of rooms	4
rooms with private bath	1
shared wc	3
shared bathrooms	2

Activities: 🏛 ⛵ 🚣 🚴 ⛷

B&Bs AND INNS

52. QUÉBEC

F e 🐕 P R.5 TA

Charming house with view of the river located in a historic district, near the Plains of Abraham, Place Royale, renowned places of interest and restaurants. Opposite a park, public pool, cycling path. Very lovely and comfortable rooms, canopy beds, balcony, free parking, flowery courtyard and lavish breakfasts indoors or outdoors.

Hwy 20, Pierre-Laporte bridge, Exit 132, Boul. Champlain, left at 6th traffic light onto Rue Champlain, at the foot of the Cap-Blanc stairway. 1 km, then left of the Québec City-Lévis ferry (opposite the park).

B&B
L'ANSE DES MÈRES

Linda Pelchat
553, rue Champlain
Québec G1K 4J4
tel/fax (418) 649-8553
www.anse-des-meres.qc.ca

B&B	
single	$50-85
double	$65-100
triple	$100-115
quad.	$130
5-6 people	$140-150

Taxes extra VS AM

Reduced rates : Nov. 1 to Feb. 1 and Feb. 20 to Mar. 15
Open year round

Number of rooms	3
shared wc	1
shared bathrooms	1

Activities: 🏛 🍂 ⛵ 🦮 🚴

53. QUÉBEC

F e 🚭 🐕 🚗 P R4 TA

French artist's home located in "Upper Town" and in the cultural heart of Québec City. Personalised welcome, cosiness, relaxation, tranquillity and security. Special meals (for diabetics). Two cats. Near most tourist attractions, shops, boutiques, restaurants.

Chemin Ste-Foy to "Vieux Québec". Turn left on Rue Désy street. La Coule Douce is on Dolbeau street, 2nd street on your left.

B&B
LA COULE DOUCE

Michel Champagne
473, rue Dolbeau
Québec G1S 2R6
(418) 527-2940
fax (418) 527-0288
pages.infinit.net/hotel/
quebec.html
ntherio@videotron.ca

B&B	
single	$55
double	$65
triple	$100
quad.	$125
child	$25

Open year round

Number of rooms	2
shared bathrooms	1

Activities: 🏛 🍂 ⛵ 🚴 🎿

54. QUÉBEC

F A 🚗 R1 AV

Stay in a historic monument 2 min from old Québec City: an old schoolhouse transformed into a comfortable residence where the past is everpresent. Breakfast is served in the garden or by the fire. Try engraving in our studio and uncover the secrets of silkscreen art. Close to everything, the train station and buses. Our secret garden is yours to discover...

Boul. Laurier to Québec City. After the parliament, turn left on Honoré-Mercier then Aut. Dufferin East, Exit 22. At the 1st traffic lights turn left, continue to the end and turn left. Turn left on the 3rd street.

B&B
LE JARDIN SECRET

André Lemieux
and Yves Dumaresq
699 and 701, 3e Rue
Québec G1J 2V5
(418) 640-7321
tel/fax (418) 529-5587

B&B	
single	$45-55
double	$60-70
child	$10-15

VS

Open: Feb. 1 to Nov. 30

Number of rooms	2
rooms with private bath	1
shared bathrooms	1

Activities: 🏛 🧍 ⛵ 🚴 🎿

55. QUÉBEC, STE-FOY

F E 🚫 P 🚗 R.5 TA

Ten minutes from Old Quebec City, quiet residential district, access to highways. Warm ambiance, comfortable rooms with sink, generous breakfast. Walking distance from Université Laval, big shopping centres, public transport, cinema, restaurants. Free and easy parking.

From Québec City: Hwy 20, take Pierre Laporte bridge, Boul. Laurier, right at 5th light onto Rue Jean Dequen to Rue Lapointe. Hwy 40, take Hwy Duplessis South, Boul. Laurier, right at 5th light.

B&B
LA MAISON LECLERC

Nicole Chabot
and Conrad Leclerc
2613, rue Lapointe
Ste-Foy G1W 3K3
(418) 653-8936
fax (418) 653-5266
www.bbcanada.
com/2693.html
lamaisonleclerc@videotron.ca

B&B	
single	$40
double	$55
child	$0-15

VS MC

Reduced rates : 3 nights and more, and Nov. 1 to May 31
Open year round

Number of rooms	5
rooms with sink	2
rooms in basement	2
shared bathrooms	2

Activities: 🏛 ⛵ ⚲ 🚲 🎿

56. QUÉBEC, STE-FOY

F 🚫 P R.5

House located in the heart of the town of Ste-Foy, 1 km from the Pierre-Laporte bridge. Very close to the largest shopping centres in Québec City, the bus terminal, the post office, banks, hospitals. Chilean-style breakfast available. We speak Spanish very well.

After the Pierre-Laporte bridge towards downtown Québec City, Boul. Laurier Exit. At the 2nd traffic lights, turn left. Right on Rue Légaré, and right again on the next street.

B&B
MAISON DINA

Dina Saéz-Velozo
2850, rue Fontaine
Ste-Foy G1V 2H8
(418) 652-1013

B&B	
single	$40
double	$50
child	$12

Open : June 1 to Nov. 30

Number of rooms	3
rooms in basement	2
shared bathrooms	2

Activities: 🏛 🍴 ⛵ ✈ 🚲

57. QUÉBEC, STE-FOY

F e P 🚗 R.1 TA

Canadian-style house located in a calm residential neighborhood, near services, shopping centre, public transport and expressways. 5 min from the airport and Université Laval. 15 min from old Québec City. Warm atmosphere, comfortable rooms, central air conditioning system. Welcome. Québec City Region Excellence Prize 94-95.

From Montréal, Hwy 20 East to Québec City, Pierre-Laporte bridge, Boul. Laurier Exit. At the 1st traffic lights, turn right on Rue Lavigerie, at the 3rd street, right on Rue de la Seine.

B&B

Monique and André
Saint-Aubin
3045, rue de la Seine
Ste-Foy G1W 1H8
(418) 658-0685
fax (418) 658-8466
www.qbc.clic.net/
~staubin

B&B	
single	$40-45
double	$50-60
triple	$70-80
child	$10

Reduced rates : Nov. 1 to May 31
Open year round

Number of rooms	3
shared bathrooms	3

Activities: 🏛 🍴 ⛵ 🎿 🏃

B&Bs AND INNS

58. QUÉBEC, SILLERY

F E P ⊗ R.2 TA

White, English-style house dating back to the 1930s surrounded by hundred-year-old trees. Exceptional neighbourhood. Fireplace, terrace, large rooms, king and queen-size beds. Varied, home-made breakfast. Nearby: Université de Laval, Plains of Abraham, old Québec City and just steps from Cataraqui. Welcome. **See colour photos.**

Hwy 20, Pierre-Laporte Bridge, Boul Laurier to Québec City. 3.8 km from bridge right on Rue Maguire. Right on Ch. St-Louis. Hwy 40, Boul. Duplessis South Exit to Boul. Laurier...

B&B
B&B LES CORNICHES

Francine C. DuSault
2052, chemin St-Louis
Sillery, Québec G1T 1P4
(418) 681-9318
fax (418) 681-4028

B&B	
single	$55
double	$65-75
triple	$90
child	$15

VS

Open year round

Number of rooms	3
rooms with private bath	1
shared bathrooms	2

Activities: 🏛 ⛴ 🚶 🚲 🎿

59. ST-ADOLPHE-DE-STONEHAM

F e P 🏊 ⊗ R7

Near Jacques-Cartier Park, our farm offers you: walking trails, river, lake with wriggling trout, bountiful greenery and rock gardens, small-scale maple grove and many small animals. Lunch with home-made and farm products awaits you at this separated B&B from our house.

From Québec City, Hwy 73 N., twd Chicoutimi. At the intersection with 175 N. (After Exit 167 - Stoneham) drive 7 km to the sign for St-Adolphe. Right on rue St-Edmond and drive 3 km.

B&B
AUBERGE DE LA FERME
ST-ADOLPHE

Jocelyne Couillard and
George Legendre
1035, rue St-Edmond
St-Adolphe-de-Stoneham
G0A 4P0
(418) 848-2879
fax (418) 848-6949
www.qbc.clic.net/
~geleg/auberge/
geleg@qbc.clic.net

B&B	
single	$45
double	$55
child	$10-15

Taxes extra

Open year round

Number of rooms	3
shared bathrooms	2

Activities: 🚶 🏃 🐎 🎿 🏃

60. ST-GABRIEL-DE-VALCARTIER

F E 🐕 🚗 P 🏊 R8 TA

Large country house, in an exceptional environment, in the heart of the Jacques-Cartier valley. Romantic ambiance. Fine gourmet country cooking. Dinner on the farm with reservations. Near Jacques-Cartier park, Village Vacances Valcartier. **Farm stay p 40.**

30 minutes from Old Québec. Hwy 73 North, De La Faune Exit, left on Des Érables toward the Huron village, 5 km. Right on Boul. Valcartier, 15 km. Right at the stop sign, Rte 371, then 8 km on 5e Ave.

B&B
LE GÎTE DES EQUERRES

Annette Légaré
171, 5e Avenue
St-Gabriel-de-Valcartier
G0A 4S0
(418) 844-2424
toll-free 1-877-844-2424
fax (418) 844-1607
www.auxancienscanadiens.
qc.ca/gite.html

B&B	
single	$55-60
double	$70-80

VS MC

Open year round

Number of rooms	3
rooms with private bath	3

Activities: 🚶 🚲 ⛴ 🎿 🏃

61. ST-RAYMOND

F E ⊘ ♿ ✕ P R.2 TA

Lovely, turn-of-the-century brick house surrounded by equally charming neighbours. A short bike ride away from the cycling path, three strides from nature (canoeing, hiking, skidooing, skiing, gliding...). Colours, local flavours and exotic aromas mingle here. Prices include taxes.

Hwy 40, Rte 365 North, at 1st light in the village turn right, a little past the church. By Bike: St-Raymond Exit on the path, follow road toward downtown. By snowmobile: via trail 365.

INN
LA VOISINE

Odile Pelletier and
Denis Baribault
443, Saint-Joseph
C.P. 448
Saint-Raymond G0A 4G0
(418) 337-4139
fax (418) 337-3109
odilep@hotmail.com

	B&B	PAM
single	$45-55	$58-68
double	$60-70	$85-95
triple	$75-85	$113-123
child	$15	$24

VS MC IT

Open year round

Number of rooms	5
rooms with sink	4
rooms with private bath	1
shared wc	1
shared bathrooms	2

Activities: 🎣 🚶 🚲 🛷 🐕

62. ST-RAYMOND

F E ⊘ P R3 TA

See, smell and taste the difference in the quietness of the countryside; access to cycling path, skidoo trail and the river. Get back in touch with your inner self by getting some fresh air, taking part in merry encounters and sharing a breakfast of fresh home-made products. Welcome to our home.

From Montréal or Québec City: Hwy 40, twd Pont-Rouge/St-Raymond Exit 281, Rte 365 for about 25 km. After Côte Joyeuse, Rue St-Pierre, 1st street on left, straight toward Chute Panet, 4 km.

B&B
SENS SAINT-RAYMOND NID

Christine Robert and
Louis Vallée
570, ch. Chute Panet, Rte 354
St-Raymond G0A 4G0
(418) 337-1430

	B&B
single	$30
double	$45-60
child	$0-15

Open year round

Number of rooms	3
rooms with sink	1
shared wc	2
shared bathrooms	1

Activities: 🎣 🚲 🛷 ⛷ 🎿

63. STE-ANNE-DE-BEAUPRÉ

F e P ⊘ R1 TA

Pretty country house (1909) located 10 min from Mont Ste-Anne and 20 min from Québec City. Nearby: Cap Tourmente, Grand Canyon, Sept-Chutes. Generous breakfast served in the sun-room with view of the river. Cosy bedrooms decorated with care. Fireplace in living room. Ski and mountain-bike packages at Mont Ste-Anne and Le Massif. Small farm: goats, rabbits...

From Québec City, Rte 138 East to Ste-Anne-de-Beaupré. Beyond Château-Richer, after the Écomusée du Miel, turn left on Rue Paré. At the end, Ave. Royale, turn right.

B&B
LA MAISON D'ULYSSE

Carole Trottier and
Raymond Allard
9140, av. Royale
Ste-Anne-de-Beaupré G0A 3C0
(418) 827-8224

	B&B
single	$45
double	$60-65
triple	$75
child	$0-15

VS MC

Reduced rates : 3 nights and more
Open year round

Number of rooms	4
rooms with sink	2
rooms with private bath	1
shared bathrooms	2

Activities: 🏛 🚶 ⛷ 🎿 🐕

B&Bs AND INNS

64. STONEHAM

F e P R5 TA

20 minutes from Québec City, in the mountains, relive the charming era of little inns when travellers spent the evening telling tales in front of a stone fireplace. Enjoy a night in one of our romantic rooms until it's time for breakfast. Closest B&B to Parc de la Jacques-Cartier.

From Québec City, Hwy 73 N. twd Chicoutimi. At the intersection with 175 N. (after Exit 167 - Stoneham) drive 7 km to the sign for St-Adolphe. Right on St-Edmond, drive 1.7 km.

B&B
AUBERGE LA SAUVAGINE

Francine Beauregard and Pierre Desautels
544, rue St-Edmond
Stoneham G0A 4P0
(418) 848-6128
fax (418) 848-7168
www.clic.net/~sauvagin/
sauvagin@clic.net

B&B	
single	$45-70
double	$55-70
triple	$70-90
quad.	$110
child	$10-20

VS MC

Open year round

Number of rooms	3
rooms with private bath	1
rooms with sink	1
shared wc	1
shared bathrooms	1

Activities: 🚶 🐎 ⛷ 🎿 🐴

65. STONEHAM, ST-ADOLPHE

F E P TA

Overlooking the valley at 1,700 ft. in altitude, our B&B offers a grand view of the Jacques-Cartier mountains. Enjoy Stoneham ski resort, cross-country skiing (Camp Mercier), J.-Cartier Park, rafting, hikes, fall colours. Fine country B&B before Parc des Laurentides. Dinner package Dec. 1 to Mar. 31: 2 nights, 2 dinners, 2 breakfasts for $155/couple.

From Québec City: Hwy 73 twd Chicoutimi. Hwy 73 Nord. Do not get off at Exit 167 (Stoneham), but 7 km farther at St-Adolphe sign. Turn right on Rue St-Edmond and continue for 5 km. Left on Rue Lepire.

B&B
AU SOMMET DES RÊVES

Christine Venditto and Gilles Benoit
25, rue Lepire
Stoneham G0A 4P0
(418) 848-6154
fax (418) 848-8686
www.bbcanada.com/
2042.html

B&B	
single	$45
double	$60
triple	$80
quad.	$100
child	$12

VS MC

Reduced rates : from Apr. 1 to June 30 and Sep.1 to Nov 30 10 $ less per room
Open year round

Number of rooms	3
shared bathrooms	1

Activities: 🚶 🚴 🐎 ⛷ 🏃

66. VILLAGE HURON

F E P R.25 TA

Century-old house where the past mingles with the present. Friendly atmosphere, in which Native art transports guests back in time. Breakfast with a Huron flavour. The Bear, Wolf and Turtle Rooms await you. Located in the heart of the old village of Huron-Wendat, which you can explore and 15 min from Québec City and area ski resorts. Guided tours of historic sites.

From Québec City: Hwy 73 and Hwy 369 to Loretteville. The B&B is located on a street parallel to Boul. Bastien; drive up Rue Gabriel Vincent and you're there.

B&B
LA MAISON AORHENCHE

Line Gros-Louis
90, François Gros-Louis,
C.P. 298
Village Huron G0A 4V0
(418) 847-0646
fax (418) 847-4527

B&B	
single	$55-65
double	$65-75
triple	$85
quad.	$110
child	$15

Open year round

Number of rooms	3
rooms with private bath	1
shared bathrooms	1

Activities: 🏛 🚶 🚶 🚴 🐎

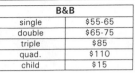

67. CAP-TOURMENTE, MONT-STE-ANNE

F E P R1 M7 TA

In the heart of Cap-Tourmente, 12 min from Mont Ste-Anne (view of the slopes). House with five guestrooms with private baths, kitchen with dishwasher, family room, small sitting room with cable TV, washer and dryer, pool table in the basement. Covered pool in the warm weather, hiking, cross-country skiing and mountain biking (visit the falls and the sugar shack). Also: skiing, golf, horseback riding, etc. **B&B p 224.**

From Québec City, Aut. Henri IV North, to 40 East Ste-Anne-de-Beaupré, Rte 138 East, twd St-Joachim, Cap-Tourmente.

COUNTRY HOME
L'OIE DES NEIGES

Gisèle Perron
390, ch. du Cap Tourmente
St-Joachim G0A 3X0
(418) 827-5153
tel/fax (418) 827-2246
www.bbcanada.com/2690.html
melifre@total.net

No. houses	1
No. rooms	5
No. people	4-16
WEEK-SUMMER	$795-1200
WEEK-WINTER	$795-1200
W/E-SUMMER	$550-650
W/E-WINTER	$550-650
DAY-SUMMER	$350-450
DAY-WINTER	$350-450

VS

Open year round

Activities:

68. MONT-STE -ANNE, ST-FERRÉOL

F E P R.5 M.5 TA

Savour the tranquillity of our lovely country homes, ancestral or recent, 30 min from downtown Québec City, at the edge of Charlevoix. Dreamy, legendary spot, in a small typical Québécois town. Houses are well equipped and can comfortably accommodate 4 to 30 people, and even up to 50! We are nestled at the foot of Mt Ste-Anne, a year-round internationally renown resort. **See colour photos and advertisement end of this region.**

1 km after Mt Ste-Anne, as you enter the small town of St-Ferréol-les-Neiges.

COUNTRY HOME
CHALETS-VILLAGE
MONT-STE-ANNE

Marie Flynn and Gilles Éthier
C.P. 275
Ste-Anne-de-Beaupré G0A 3C0
tel/fax (418) 650-2030
toll free 1-800-461-2030
Visit us on the Internet:
www.chalets-village.qc.ca

No. house	8
No. rooms	2-8
No. people	4-30
WEEK-SUMMER	$525-2200
WEEK-WINTER	$500-4700
W/E-SUMMER	$195-1200
W/E-WINTER	$225-1700

Taxes extra VS MC

Reduced rates : spring and fall
Open year round

Activities:

69. QUÉBEC

F E P R.01 M.01 TA

For business or pleasure, the Maison Calou, in the shadow of Château Frontenac, invites you to the cosy comfort of its fully equipped, 3 or 4-room suites with parking. Explore the history so close at hand (typical streets, museums, churches) and the present (restaurants, shows, shops, street performers). Monthly rental available. **Country house p 244, no 71.**

Hwy 20, Laporte bridge, Boul. Laurier Exit twd Old Québec City. After the St-Louis gate, 4th street, go left. Parking at the back.

MAISON DE VILLE
MAISON CHALOU

Mariette Poirier and
Jean Dreyer
40, des Jardins
Québec G1R 4L7
(418) 628-9913
(418) 655-6364
jdreyer@riq.qc.ca

No. apartments	1
No. rooms	1
No. people	2-4
WEEK-SUMMER	$350-400
WEEK-WINTER	$350-400
W/E-SUMMER	$130-140
W/E-WINTER	$130-140
DAY-SUMMER	$75-85
DAY-WINTER	$75-85

Open year round

Activities:

COUNTRY AND CITY HOMES

70. QUÉBEC

F E 🚫 🐕 P R.01 M.2 TA

CITY HOUSE
RÉSIDENCE THIBAUDEAU

A comfortable English-style house with 3 balconies, 2 bathrooms, equipped kitchen and a piano all in the heart of lovely Québec City. Right near the Old City, the Plains of Abraham, Musée du Québec, bustling Rue Cartier and the Grand-Théâtre. Near roads leading to Île d'Orléans, Mont-Ste-Anne. **Country house in Bas-St-Laurent, p 59, no 36.**

On Rue St-Jean near the intersection of Rue Turnbull at the beginning of the St-Jean-Baptiste district. 3 blocks west of Rue Cartier and 7 blocks east of Porte St-Jean, 3 blocks north of Boul. René-Lévesque.

Chantal Brisson and
Serge Thibaudeau
230, rue St-Jean
Québec G1R 1P1
(418) 640-9255
fax (418) 640-0795
www.craph.org/mti
sthibau@globetrotter.net

No. houses	1
No. rooms	3
No. people	6
WEEK-SUMMER	$800
WEEK-WINTER	$800
W/E-SUMMER	$400
W/E-WINTER	$400

Open year round

Activities: 🏛 🦪 🎣 🚶 🚴

71. STONEHAM

F a 🐕 P 🏊 R.25 M4 AV

COUNTRY HOME
LE TEMPS DE VIVRE

On the mountainside, in the heart of the Stoneham ski resort, we invite you to the comfort of a magnificent, fully equipped house. Take the time to live. Ski or snowboard down the slopes; once the snow has melted, enjoy a host of activities on site or in the neighbourhood. Explore the past and present in Old Québec, only 20 minutes away. **City home p 243, no 69.**

Hwy 75 North, Exit 167 (Stoneham). Follow "Station Touristique" signs. At the resort, before the chalet, turn right, turn right at the end, go under the bridge to Chemin Des Skieurs.

Mariette Poirier and
Jean Dreyer
14, chemin Des Skieurs
Stoneham G0A 4P0
(418) 628-9913
(418) 655-6364
jdreyer@sutton.com

No. houses	1
No. rooms	3
No. people	10
WEEK-SUMMER	$1450
WEEK-WINTER	$1800
W/E-SUMMER	$450
W/E-WINTER	$600
DAY-SUMMER	$300-350
DAY-WINTER	$400-500

Reduced rates: Sep. 15 to Dec. 1 and Apr. 15 to June 15
Open year round

Activities: 🏊 🎣 🚶 🐎 🎿

FARM ACTIVITIES

Farm stay:

SAGUENAY–LAC-ST-JEAN

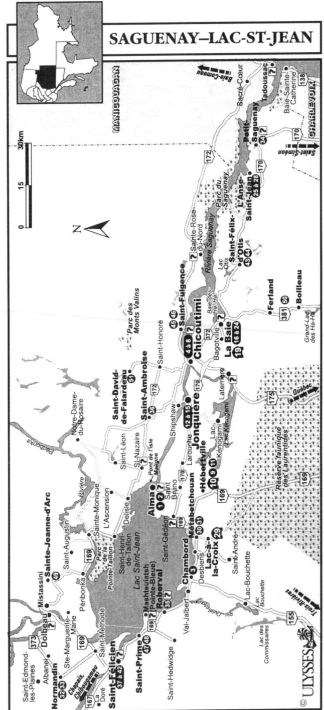

*The numbers on the map correspond to the number of each establishment in the region

1. ALMA

F | e | P | R1.5

It is our pleasure to welcome you. Large property ideal for picnics. Swing set. Bicycle storage. Generous breakfast and good cheer await you. 80 km from the town of La Baie and the St-Félicien zoo (450 species of wild animals) Sport fishers welcome.

From Québec City, Rtes 175 North and 169 to Hébertville. At the exit of Parc des Laurentides, towards Alma. House near the 6e Rang. Or from La Tuque, Rte 155 North, at Chambord, Rte 169 to Alma. Facing the Caravane de Luxe.

B&B
GÎTE DU BLEUET

Georgette and Roland Dufour
3100, Dupont Sud, route 169
Alma G8B 5V2
(418) 662-7017

B&B	
single	$35
double	$45
triple	$60
child	$0-10

Reduced rates: Sep. and Oct.
Open: Apr. 1 to Oct 31

Number of rooms	3
shared wc	2
shared bathrooms	1

Activities:

---

2. ALMA

F | e | ⊘ | P | 🚗 | R9 | TA

Rest in a natural setting where our ducks swim about the pond, where trails, gardens and local plants abound. Treat yourself to an unforgettable getaway in an oasis in the forest just steps from Lac St-Jean, a flowery island of dreams. Generous breakfasts with home-made goods. In winter: skate, cross-country ski, snowshoe, 1.5 km of snowmobile trails. Packages.

From Québec City, Rte 169 North. In Alma, Riv. Pte-Décharge bridge. After the traffic lights, turn left on 3rd street, Melançon. Watch for blue sign for Colonie Notre-Dame, 9 km. From South, 1st street on right after the Carrefour Alma (mall).

B&B
LA RESSOURCE

Paulette Leclerc and
Jean-Guy Fortin
6840, rang Melançon
Alma G8B 5V3
(418) 662-9171
fax (418) 662-1498
www.atrsaglac.
d4m.com/gites/ressource
leclercp@digicom.qc.ca

B&B	
single	$40
double	$50-55
triple	$70
quad.	$85
child	$10

MC

Open year round

Number of rooms	3
rooms with sink	3
shared wc	1
shared bathrooms	1

Activities:

---

3. CHAMBORD

F | E | 🐕 | P | R1.5 | TA

Welcome to our farm house. Enjoy a magnificient view over Lac St-Jean and the calm beach. Listen to the roar of the Val-Jalbert falls only 1 km away, smell the freshly cut hay while resting in hammocks and listening to ghost stories.

From Parc des Laurentides, Rte 169 to Roberval. Pass through Chambord. Drive 5 min. Or from La Tuque, Rtes 155 North and 169 on your left.

B&B
MARTINE ET SERGE

Martine Fortin and
Serge Bouchard
824, Route 169
Chambord G0W 1G0
tel/fax (418) 342-8446

B&B	
single	$35
double	$45
triple	$60
quad.	$70
child	$10

VS MC AM ER IT

Open year round

Number of rooms	4
shared shower rooms	1
shared wc	1
shared bathrooms	1

Activities:

B&Bs AND INNS

4. CHICOUTIMI

F e ⊗ 🐾 🛏 P ♨ R.5 TA

In the kingdom of Saguenay-Lac-St-Jean, you will be dazzled by everything the place has to offer, with its fjord, lavish productions, zoo, museums and legendary hospitality. Welcome to blueberry and maple-syrup country, together we will raise a glass to friendship.

From Québec City: Rte 175 Nord, Chicoutimi, Boul. Talbot. Left on Boul. Université, at Burger King, immediately turn left onto Thérèse Casgrain, then 1st street on the right (Rue Marguerite-Tellier).

B&B
AU FIL DES SAISONS

Murielle Boulé
524, Marguerite-Tellier
Chicoutimi G7H 6C1
(418) 543-1839
fax (418) 693-0163

B&B	
single	$40
double	$50
triple	$65
child	$10

VS

Reduced rates: May 1 to June 15 and from Sep. 15 to Oct. 30
Open: May 1 to Oct. 3

Number of rooms	4
shared bathrooms	2
rooms in basement	2

Activities: 🏛 ⛴ 🛶 🚶 🚴

---

5. CHICOUTIMI

F e 🚗 P R.3 TA

If you enjoy the simple things in life, welcome to our home! You are invited to my house enveloped in flowers with an exceptional view of the Saguenay. Delight in a visit to the greenhouses. Cosy comfort and a delicious breakfast will whet your appetite after a good night's rest. Intimacy, calm and pleasures of long ago. A deserved break.

From Québec City, Rte 175 to Chicoutimi. Boul Talbot, left on Boul Université. Right on Boul St-Paul, at the 2nd traffic lights, left on Rue Price. Next traffic lights, left on Boul Saguenay, 1 km.

B&B
GÎTE AUX MILLE FLEURS

Ghislaine Morin
976, boul. Saguenay Ouest
Chicoutimi G7J 1A5
(418) 545-9256

B&B	
single	$40
double	$50
child	$10

VS

Reduced rates: Oct. 1 to Oct. 15
Open: May 15 to Oct. 15

Number of rooms	3
shared bathrooms	1

Activities: 🐚 ⛴ 🚶 🚴 🐎

---

6. CHICOUTIMI

F e ⊗ P 🐾 R7

Overlooking a majestic fjord, this very quiet B&B is centrally located. It is close to town, with all its attractions and services. The rooms are cosy and the abundant and varied lunches are served in a spacious dining room with panoramic view of the river. Welcome all.

From Québec City, Rte 175 North to Chicoutimi. Right on Boul. Université Est (near the shopping centre), left on Boul. Saguenay and take the first right (after the golf course), Rang St-Martin, drive 6.8 km.

B&B
GÎTE DE LA BERNACHE

Denise Ouellet
3647, rang St-Martin
Chicoutimi G7H 5A7
(418) 549-4960
fax (418) 549-9814

B&B	
single	$40
double	$50
triple	$70
child	$10

Open year round

Number of rooms	4
rooms with sink	3
rooms in basement	1
shared wc	1
shared bathrooms	2

Activities: 🏛 🐚 ⛴ 🚶 🚶

7. CHICOUTIMI

F e 🚫 🚗 P 🐕 R.7 TA

Very cozy. Near downtown Chicoutimi. On the banks of the Rivière Saguenay. Steps away from the old port, the Pulperie, Marjolaine cruises, bike path, the Promenade and the famous white house that survived the flood. Winter: Carnaval, skiing, snowmobiling and ice fishing. Breakfast served in a splendid dining room with a view of the fjord.

From Québec City: Rte 175 to Chicoutimi. Boul Talbot to the end, turn left on Rue Jacques-Cartier. At the 2nd traffic lights (by the hospital), turn right again and head down to Boulevard Saguenay Est (no 782).

B&B
GÎTE DE LA PROMENADE

Lisette Blackburn and Jacques Grenon
782, boul. Saguenay Est
Chicoutimi G7H 1L3
tel/fax (418) 543-9997
www.bbcanada.com/1936.html

B&B	
single	$40
double	$50
triple	$70
quad.	$90
child	$10

Open year round

Number of rooms	3
rooms with sink	3
shared bathrooms	1

Activities: 🚤 🕴 🏃 🚲 🛷

8. CHICOUTIMI

F ♿ P R2 TA

Just east of Chicoutimi on a vast property with a commanding view of the city and the Rivière Saguenay, is a comfortable home away from home. Copious breakfasts. Various services 0.6 km away: bank, pharmacy, convenience store, gas station. Welcome to my home.

From Québec City, Rte 175 North to Chicoutimi. Right on Boul. Université East (near the shopping centre), left on Boul. Saguenay. After the Hôtel Parasol, right on Boul. Renaud. 2nd house on the left.

B&B
LE CHARDONNERET

Claire Tremblay
1253, boul. Renaud
Chicoutimi G7H 3N7
(418) 543-9336

B&B	
single	$35-40
double	$45-50
triple	$70
child	$10

Open: Apr. 1 to Oct. 31

Number of rooms	3
shared bathrooms	2

Activities: 🏛 ♣ 🚤 🕴 🚲

9. HÉBERTVILLE

F e P 🚗 🛶 ❌ TA

Presbytery built in 1917. Historical character and period furniture. Warm reception, intimate dining room, refined cuisine, spacious comfortable and warm rooms with full bathrooms. Conference room, peaceful, calm, inspires creativity. In the heart of the Saguenay-Lac-St-Jean region with its activities. Looking forward to your visit. **See colour photos.**

From Rte 169, (don't go to the town of Hébertville), head twd Mont Lac Vert, 3 km. Across from the municipal campground.

AUBERGE
AUBERGE PRESBYTÈRE
MONT LAC VERT

The Tremblay family
335, rang Lac-Vert
Hébertville G8N 1M1
(418) 344-1548
fax (418) 344-1013

	B&B	MAP
single	$50	$70
double	$65	$130
triple	$90	$180
quad.	$105	$225
child	$10	$20

Taxes extra VS MC AM IT

Reduced rates: Oct. 1 to Nov. 30
Apr. 1 to June 1
Open year round

Number of rooms	6
rooms with private bath	6

Activities: 🚣 🕴 🚲 🛷 ⛷

B&Bs AND INNS

10. HÉBERTVILLE

F 🏠 P 🚗 ✕ R1 TA

B&B on the farm, charming welcome. Perfect location for visiting the entire region. Come share in our family life and visit our dairy farm in the shade of Parc des Laurentides. Children welcome. Pool, beach, mountain biking, skating and roller-blading track, fishing playing field. Downhill and cross-country skiing, ice-fishing, inner-tubes sliding. **Farm stay p 41.**

From Parc des Laurentides, Rte 169. 1st village, Rue St-Isidore.

B&B
FERME CAROLE and
JACQUES MARTEL

Carole and Jacques Martel
474, St-Isidore
Hébertville G8N 1L7
(418) 344-1323

B&B	
single	$35
double	$45
triple	$65
quad.	$90
child	$10

Open year round

Number of rooms	2
shared bathrooms	1

Activities: 🏖 🚴 🎿 🛷 ⛷

11. HÉBERTVILLE

F e 🚗 P 🐕 R4 TA

Visit a part of the country where nature still means adventure. An ancestral house in French-speaking country with a family-size room welcomes you all year round. Nearby museum, cross-country skiing, zoo, etc. Almost midway between whales and zoo, we await you to share pleasant family moments. Freshwater-salmon pond on site and dinner on request.

From Parc des Laurentides, Rte 169, 6 km, twd Roberval.

B&B
GÎTE BELLE-RIVIÈRE

Marie-Alice Bouchard
872, rang Caron, rte 169
Hébertville G8N 1B6
(418) 344-4345
fax (418) 344-1933
bouchard@digicom.qc.ca

B&B	
single	$30
double	$45
triple	$65
quad.	$85
child	$10

Open year round

Number of rooms	4
shared bathrooms	2

Activities: 🛷 🎿 🚴 🛷 ⛷

12. JONQUIÈRE

F e 🚫 🚗 P R.1 TA

Two artists welcome you to their ancestral home. Experience an encounter with art: paintings, studio, films and books. Rooms upstairs painted by artist-hosts and decorated with antiques. Breakfast in your room or in the art studio. A stone's throw from Rivière-aux-Sables. Right near activities. Three-night-plus packages.

From Québec City: Rte 175 Nord. In Chicoutimi: Rte 170 to Jonquière and Boul. Harvey. Turn on St-Dominique. Go up 100 metres to the cinema. Right on Rue Ouellet. Follow the river for 100 metres. Left on 3e Rue.

B&B
GÎTE DE LA MAISON JAUNE

Lyne Proulx and
Maurice Lignières
3973, rue Chesnier
Jonquière G7X 3M2
(418) 695-1457

B&B	
single	$40
double	$50
triple	$65
child	$0-5

Open year round

Number of rooms	3
shared bathrooms	1

Activities: 🏛 🛷 🚴 🛷 🐎

13. JONQUIÈRE

F ⊗ ⛴ P 🚗 R1

Saguenay-Lac-St-Jean Excellence Prize 1995-96 and finalist in 1997-98. 5 min walk from downtown. Soundproof rooms with sinks and TVs. Breakfast in the sunroom with a view of the river. One-of-a-kind aluminum footbridge, private beach, rowboat, pedal boat, fishing, bike path nearby. Rest and tranquillity guaranteed.

From Québec City, Rte 175 and Rte 170, left to Jonquière, drive 11.2 km. Take Boul. Harvey, drive 2.8 km, left on Rue St-Jean-Baptiste, (St-Raphaël parish) drive 1.1 km. Left on Rue des Saules.

B&B
GÎTE DE LA RIVIÈRE
AUX SABLES

Marie and Jean Eudes Girard
4076, des Saules
Jonquière
G8A 2G7
(418) 547-5101
fax (418) 547-6939

B&B	
single	$40
double	$50
triple	$70
quad.	$85
child	$10

Open year round

Number of rooms	4
rooms with sink	4
rooms in basement	4
shared wc	1
shared bathrooms	2

Activities: 🐚 ⛵ 🚣 🎿 🚲

14. JONQUIÈRE

F E ⊗ P 🚗 ⛴ R1 TA

Saguenay-Lac-St-Jean **Excellence Prize 1997-98**. For the great pleasure of serving you. Vast solarium, landscaped exterior and a magnificent in-ground pool encourage relaxation. TV in every room. Right near restaurants, bars, the Cegep and the sports centre.

In downtown Jonquière, at corner of St-Dominique and Harvey, go south to the Irving station, left on Rue des Hirondelles, left on the 1st street, Des Merles.

B&B
LE MERLEAU

Andrée Côté and Léo April
2456, des Merles
Jonquière G7X 8B3
(418) 542-1093
fax (418) 542-1031

B&B	
single	$40
double	$50-55
triple	$70
quad.	$85
child	$10

Reduced rates: Sep. 1 to May 31
Open year round

Number of rooms	5
rooms in basement	2
shared bathrooms	3

Activities: 🎿 🚣 🚲 🐎

15. JONQUIÈRE

F e ⊗ 🐕 ✕ 🚗 P R.5 TA

A moment of rest in the "Mitan", the middle of the trip. Warm welcome in a charming, perfectly comfortable turn-of-the-century house. Picturesque Arvida district near Alcan plant; the Manoir; Pont d'Aluminium; tourist, cultural and sports activities; with the cycling path at its doorstep. Enjoy an original, hearty breakfast.

From Québec City: Rte 175 North. In Chicoutimi: Rte 170 twd Jonquière for 8 km, right on Rue Mellon to the roundabout, drive 3 km, take Boul. Saguenay to Jonquière for about 80 metres. Le Mitan is on the right.

B&B
LE MITAN

Denise F. Blackburn
2840, boul. Saguenay
Jonquière G7S 2H3
(418) 548-7388
fax (418) 548-3415

B&B	
single	$40
double	$55
triple	$70
quad.	$85
child	$15

Open year round

Number of rooms	2
rooms with sink	2
shared bathrooms	1
rooms in basement	2

Activities: 🎿 🚲 🚗 ⛷️

B&Bs AND INNS

16. LA BAIE

`F` `e` `⟷` `P` `⊘` `🐾` `R1`

Located by the water, every room has its own private entrance and balcony, offering a superb view. Walk along the shoreline, watch the tides, discover the artist-host's granite sculptures. Evening beach campfires, for those who so desire. If nature enchants you, one day is not enough. Winter rate: $45 for 2. Ice-fishing and dog-sledding packages.

From the Parc des Laurentides, Rtes 175 North and 170 East to Boul de la Grande-Baie Sud. After the Musée du Fjord drive approx. 5 km. Or from St-Siméon, Rte 170 North. On the water side, a huge granite block marks the entrance.

B&B
À FLEUR DE PIERRE

Colette Létourneau and
Carrol Tremblay
6788, boul. Grande-Baie Sud
La Baie G7B 3P6
(418) 544-3260

B&B	
single	$45-50
double	$55-60
triple	$70-75
quad.	$85
child	$10

Reduced rates: Oct. 1 to May 31
Open year round

Number of rooms	3
rooms with private bath	1
shared bathrooms	1

Activities: 🦪 🏛 ⚓ ⛵ 🚶

17. LA BAIE

`F` `E` `♿` `P` `🚣` `🐕` `R.1` `TA`

Located at the heart of La Baie, on the shore of the Saguenay fjord, a few metres from the Parc Mars promenade. Spacious house offers tranquillity and comfort. Rooms for one, two or four people available. Hearty breakfast. Restaurants nearby. Large garage for some 8 motorbikes or skidoos.

20 km from Chicoutimi. From Québec City, Rtes 175 North and 170 East or Rtes 138 East and 170 West. At the Ville de La Baie, Rue Victoria is parallel to Parc Mars alongside the water.

B&B
À LA MAISON
DU DOCTEUR TANGUAY

Janine Minier and Pierre Lemay
547, rue Victoria
La Baie G7B 3M5
(418) 544-3515

B&B	
single	$40
double	$50
triple	$65
quad.	$80
child	$10

Reduced rates: Jan. 1 to May 1
Open year round

Number of rooms	5
rooms in basement	3
shared bathrooms	2

Activities: ⛵ 🦪 ⚓ 🚲 🚤

18. LA BAIE

`F` `E` `⊘` `P` `⟷` `🚣` `R1` `TA`

15,000 square metres of land right at the edge of the water (*au bord de l'eau*), in town, an outstanding location with a spectacular view, spacious rooms. Here, the "bay" (*baie*) is the sea; it is a vast stretch of salt water, and its 7-metre tides transform the landscape. Five min from the theatre and various activities, but in a world of its own. Hearty breakfasts, homey atmosphere.

From Parc des Laurentides, Rte 175 North, then 170 East to Boul Grande-Baie South. Drive 1.5 km past the Musée du Fjord. Make sure not to drive right past the house; you can't see it from the road!

B&B
AU BORD DE L'EAU

Lyne Fortin and Réjean Ouellet
5208, boul. Grande-Baie Sud
La Baie G7B 3P6
(418) 544-0892
toll free 1-888- 811-0892
rejean.ouellet@sympatico.ca

B&B	
single	$45-70
double	$55-80
triple	$65-90
quad.	$75-100
child	$5

VS MC

Reduced rates: Sep. 1 to
June 15
Open year round

Number of rooms	4
rooms with private bath	2
shared bathrooms	1
rooms in basement	1

Activities: 🦪 ⚓ 🚲 🚤 ⛷

19. LA BAIE

F | e | 🐕 | ⛵ | P | R2

Come live an incredible experience with the Gagné family at the "Chez Grand-Maman" B&B where you will find tranquillity in picturesque surroundings. You'll experience extraordinary things on our farm by the Baie des HA! HA! We will make you feel at home. **Farm stay p 41.**

From Parc des Laurentides, Rtes 175 North and 170 East towards "Ville de la Baie", Rue Bagot. Left on Rue Victoria for about 2 km. Straight ahead, 1st farm, "Alain Gagné".

B&B
CHEZ GRAND-MAMAN

Jacinthe Bouchard and
Alain Gagné
1254, chemin St-Joseph
La Baie G7B 3N9
(418) 544-7396
(418) 697-0517
fax (418) 544-8073

B&B	
single	$35
double	$45
triple	$65
child	$10-12

Open year round

Number of rooms	3
shared bathrooms	2

Activities: 🍃 🏊 🕴 🚲 🎿

20. LA BAIE

F | E | P | 🚗 | ⛵ | R.1 | TA

Saguenay Lac-St-Jean Excellence Prize 1996-97. Warm fellowship and simplicity will make fast friends of us by your departure. Located near the water, the rooms have views of the Baie de HA! HA! Winter and summer activities alike – just short walks away. Cruises, hiking trails, bike paths, marina, ice-fishing. Breakfast in the sunroom. Bikes available. On site: seakayak rental.

From Parc des Laurentides, Rtes 175 N. 170 E. to La Baie. On Rue Bagot straight ahead and left on Rue Victoria, left to Rue Damase-Potvin, left to Rue Simard. B&B facing the bay, welcome!

B&B
GÎTE BELLE-VUE

Monique and Régent Goyette
1442, Simard
La Baie G7B 2X9
(418) 544-4598
fax (418) 544-5861

B&B	
single	$40-55
double	$50-65
triple	$65-80
quad.	$90
child	$15

Reduced rates: Jan. 1 to May 1
Open year round

Number of rooms	5
rooms with sink	2
rooms with private bath	2
shared bathrooms	2

Activities: 🍃 ⛵ 🕴 🚙 🎿

21. LA BAIE

F | 🚗 | P | R2

To rediscover the charm of the countryside of long ago, drop anchor off l'Anse-à-Benjamin. Near all services: theatre, walking trails, marina, skating rink. Pleasant rooms. Enjoy our B&B winter or summer. Outfitter of fishing cabins. Packages available upon request.

From Parc des Laurentides, Rtes 175 North and 170 East to Ville de la Baie, Rue Bagot. Left on Rue Victoria, keep right for 2 km.

B&B
GÎTE DE LA PÊCHE BLANCHE

Laurence Blanchette and
Jean-Claude Simard
1352, route de
l'Anse-à-Benjamin
La Baie G7B 3N9
tel/fax (418) 544-4176

B&B	
single	$40
double	$45
triple	$55
child	$10

Open year round

Number of rooms	4
rooms in basement	3
shared bathrooms	2

Activities: 🍃 🏊 🕴 🚶 🛷

B&Bs AND INNS

22. LA BAIE

`F` `e` `🚗` `P` `R1`

On the heights of the bay, you will find a warm and comfortable B&B, one that has acquired an enviable reputation with tourists over the last 7 years. A magnificent landscaped garden graced with a fountain offers our guests a peaceful spot. Hearty breakfast; bicycles available to guests.

From Parc des Laurentides: Rte 175 Nord and 170 Est toward La Baie. From Rue Bagot, straight ahead to the Caisse Populaire, turn left on Rue des Pins to No. 1273: we await you.

B&B
GÎTE DES PINS

Doris Bolduc and
Freddy Pouliot
1273, rue des Pins
La Baie G7B 3H7
(418) 544-5178

B&B	
single	$40
double	$50
triple	$60
quad.	$70
child	$10

Reduced rates: May 1 to June 15 and Sep. 1 to Oct. 31
Open: May 1 to Oct. 31

Number of rooms	3
rooms in basement	2
shared wc	1
shared bathrooms	1

Activities: 🏛 ⛴ 🎣 🚶 🚴

23. LA BAIE

`F` `e` `♿` `P` `🚗` `R2` `TA`

2 km west of Ville de La Baie and 12 km east of Chicoutimi. You are welcome in our ancestral home. You will enjoy staying with us. We will serve you breakfast with fresh farm products. We will be happy to meet you. Near the "Fabuleuse Histoire du Royaume".

From Parc des Laurentides, Rtes 175 North, and 170 East to Ville de La Baie. At the 2nd traffic lights, straight to Rue Victoria, turn left. Drive 2 km on Victoria which becomes St-Joseph. 2nd house on right after flashing light.

B&B
LA MAISON DES ANCÊTRES

Judith and Germain Simard
1722, chemin St-Joseph
La Baie G7B 3N9
(418) 544-2925
fax (418) 544-8090

B&B	
single	$35
double	$45
triple	$60
child	$10

Open: May 1 to Oct. 31

Number of rooms	4
shared bathrooms	2

Activities: 🏛 🍷 ⛴ 🚶 🚴

24. LA BAIE

`F` `e` `🚫` `P` `🚗` `R4` `TA`

Built in 1875, this farmhouse is one of La Baie's "heritage buildings". Enjoy nature a few minutes from a variety of tourist attractions and activities. Quietness of the countryside and breakfast in a family ambiance. You will relish our raspberry specialties. Families welcome!

From Rte 170, via either Rue Mgr Dufour (4 km), or Rte 381 S., less than 1 km from Rte 381 and from St-Antoine road.

B&B
LA MAISON DUFOUR

Lilianne Gagnon and
Gilles Dufour
4362, chemin St-Jean
La Baie G7B 3P6
(418) 697-0967
fax (418) 697-6749

B&B	
single	$35
double	$50
triple	$65
child	$10

Reduced rates: Oct. 1 to June 1
Open year round

Number of rooms	4
rooms with private wc	1
shared bathrooms	2

Activities: 🏛 ⛴ 🎣 🚶 🛷

25. L'ANSE-ST-JEAN

F E P ☒ TA

A kingdom in the heart of Parc Saguenay. Facing the covered bridge, with a large veranda off the rooms. Big living room with fireplace. Recommended for its game, fish and seafood dishes; 15% off for Inn guests. Direct access to snowmobile trails. Skiing, fjord and ice fishing nearby.

Rte 170 twd L'Anse-St-Jean. Take Rue St-Jean-Baptiste twd the dock. The inn is 0.2 km from the church, facing the covered bridge.

AUBERGE
AUBERGE DES CÉVENNES

Enid Bertrand and
Louis Mario Dufour
294, rue St-Jean-Baptiste
L'Anse-St-Jean G0V 1J0
(418) 272-3180
(418) 272-1202
fax (418) 272-1131

B&B	
single	$55-65
double	$60-70
triple	$85
quad.	$90

Taxes extra VS MC ER IT

Reduced rates: Sep. 11 to Dec. 22 and Jan. 4 to June 20
Open year round

Number of rooms	8
rooms with private bath	8

Activities: 🛶 🏇 ⛷ 🎿

26. L'ANSE-ST-JEAN

F e P R1.5 TA

Cosy Québec-style house echoing the colours of the fjord. Breakfast in the sunroom with river and mountain view. Rest in comfortable rooms, relax and daydream to the sound of the river. Nearby: walking trails, horseback riding, sea kayaking, fjord cruises, mountain biking, salmon fishing. Françoise (the homebody) and François (the sportsman) offer simple hospitality.

From Québec City, via St-Siméon, Rtes 138 E. and 170 to Anse-St-Jean. Via Chicoutimi, Rtes 175, then 170, Rue Principale de l'Anse for 3.5 km.

B&B
LA PANTOUFLARDE

Françoise Potvin and
François Asselin
129, St-Jean-Baptiste
L'Anse-St-Jean G0V 1J0
(418) 272-2182
(418) 545-1099
fax (418) 545-1914

B&B	
single	$40
double	$55
triple	$70
quad.	$85

Open: June 1 to Oct. 31

Number of rooms	3
shared bathrooms	2
rooms with sink	2

Activities: 🛶 🏇 ⛷ 🎿

27. L'ANSE-ST-JEAN

F E P R1.5 TA

"...A beautiful terrace and river behind the B&B is ideal for enjoying a good book, and offers a splendid view of the mountains. Your host offers a friendly welcome into his sunny and spacious home; beautiful rooms will help put your worried behind you. Budget-conscious travellers in search of the utmost in comfort will find it here." A French tourist.

From Québec City via St-Siméon: Rtes 138 East and 170 to Anse St-Jean; via Chicoutimi: Rtes 175 and 170. Take the main street of Anse St-Jean and drive 3.5 km.

B&B
LE GLOBE-TROTTER

Anne Lambert and
André Bouchard
131, St-Jean-Baptiste
L'Anse-St-Jean G0V 1J0
tel/fax (418) 272-2353
bur: (418) 272-2124
www.bbcanada.com/322.html
andreb7@hotmail.com

B&B	
single	$45
double	$55
child	$15

Open: Mar. 1 to Oct. 31

Number of rooms	3
shared bathrooms	2

Activities: 🛶 🚣 🏇 🚲 🐎

B&Bs AND INNS

28. L'ANSE-ST-JEAN

F e P ⛴ 🚭 R.2

Ancestral home caressed by the majestic Saguenay Fjord. Your eyes can't open wide enough to take in all that nature has to offer. The cozy, comfortable rooms bring you back to the turn of the century. Walking trails are at our doorstep. Horseback riding, mini-cruises up the fjord, sea kayaks, mountain bikes, salmon fishing, ski and ice-fishing available.

From Québec City, Rte 175, Parc des Laurentides to Chicoutimi. Or Rte 138 to St-Siméon, Rte 170 to Anse-St-Jean. Rue St-Jean-Baptiste, 8 km to Saguenay Fjord.

B&B
LE NID DE L'ANSE

Suzanne and Ronald Bilodeau
376, St-Jean-Baptiste
L'Anse-St-Jean G0V 1J0
(418) 272-2273
(418) 549-1807
fax (418) 549-9284

B&B	
single	$45
double	$55

Open: Mar. 1 to Oct. 30

Number of rooms	3
shared wc	1
shared bathrooms	1

Activities: 🚤 🛶 🏇 🐎 🎿

29. LAC-À-LA-CROIX

F e 🚗 P R8 TA

Century-old farmhouse where we like to keep up traditions: a toast to friends, home-made meals, cows in their pyjamas in the fall. Well-located for touring the region. Traditional recipes to be shared. Cross-country skiing on the farm and near the mountain. **Farm stay p 41.**

From Parc des Laurentides, Rte 169, 1e Rang on the left before the village of Hébertville. Drive 11 km.

B&B

Céline and Georges Martin
1311, Rang 3
Lac-à-la-Croix G0W 1W0
tel/fax (418) 349-2583

B&B	
single	$28
double	$42
child	$12

Open year round

Number of rooms	3
shared wc	2
shared bathrooms	1

Activities: 🚲 🏊 🎿 🐎

30. MÉTABETCHOUAN

F 🚗 P ⛴ R.5 TA

At Berthe and Jean-Charles's, in a quiet and intimate spot right near the lake. Let yourselves be charmed by the flowers and birds. Five-kilometre-long beach with services and landscaped promenade. Concert at music camp, summer theatre, golf course, horseback riding, cycling path, special breakfasts.

From Parc des Laurentides: Rte 169 twd Roberval. In Métabetchouan: 1st exit, keep turning right.

B&B
AU SOLEIL COUCHANT

Berthe and Jean-Charles Fortin
31-2, rue Foyer du Lac
Métabetchouan G0W 2A0
(418) 349-2138
fax (418) 349-2203

B&B	
single	$40
double	$50
child	$0-10

Open year round

Number of rooms	3
shared wc	1
shared bathrooms	1

Activities: 🚤 🛶 🏇 🐎 🏃

31. MÉTABETCHOUAN

F e P R.4 TA

Majestic turn-of-the-century Victorian house crowned by stately maples. Where uniformity stops to make way for the pleasures of refinement. Large dining room inspired by the charms of the past. Cozy rooms, delicious brunch, music, flowers and little considerations. Nearby: beach and cycling path. **See colour photos.**

From Québec City: Rte 169 North twd Roberval. From La Tuque: Rte 155 to Chambord, turn right heading toward Alma. In Métabetchouan: enter on Rue Principale, near the church opposite the post office.

AUBERGE
AUBERGE LA MAISON LAMY

Lise Girard and Normand Doré
56, rue St-André
Métabetchouan G0W 2A0
(418) 349-3686
toll free 1-888-565-3686
www.bbcanada.com/
2733.html

B&B	
single	$45-60
double	$60-75
triple	$75
quad.	$90
child	$10

Taxes extra VS MC IT

Reduced rates: Sep. 15 to Dec.15 and Jan. 5 to June 15
Open year round

Number of rooms	6
rooms with sink	6
shared bathrooms	3

Activities:

32. NORMANDIN

F e ⊘ 🐕 P R8

"What a joy to find this haven of peace and harmony after a day of travelling." Everything to "recharge your batteries": peace and quiet, wide expanses and beautiful grounds. Personalized breakfasts. Singular decor. You will be greeted like the special guest that you are! Motorcycle garage. Seven minutes from the Grands Jardins.

From Parc des Laurentides: Rte 169 toward Roberval then St-Félicien and St-Méthode. Straight ahead on Rte 373 to Normandin. At traffic light, toward St-Thomas Didyme (8 km).

B&B
LE GÎTE DU PASSERIN

Gaétane Savard and
Philippe Laliberté
2292, St-Cyrille
Normandin G8M 4K5
(418) 274-2170

B&B	
single	$35
double	$50
triple	$65
child	$10-15

Open year round

Number of rooms	3
shared bathrooms	2

Activities:

33. NORMANDIN

F e ⊘ P R4 TA

Let your stomach, your heart or your taste for freedom be your guide; all three will lead you to our spacious country house, which is the perfect place for walks, bike rides, sitting in front of the fire or reading by the water. Guests can also enjoy a visit to the Grands Jardins, an enchanting flower garden located just 4 km away. Our delicious brunch tops it all off.

From Parc des Laurentides, Rte 169 to Roberval, to St-Félicien. In St-Félicien, turn right at the 2nd traffic lights, to St-Méthode/Normandin; at the traffic lights straight ahead for 3 km. Welcome!

B&B
LES GÎTES MAKADAN

Micheline Villeneuve and
Daniel Bergeron
1728, St-Cyrille
Normandin G8M 4K5
(418) 274-2867
www.destinationquebec.
com/ftpdocs/makadan/
makadan.htm
makadan@destination.ca

B&B	
single	$35
double	$50-65
triple	$65-75
quad.	$95
child	$15

VS

Reduced rates: Sep. 30 to May 31
Open year round

Number of rooms	5
rooms with private bath	1
shared bathrooms	2

Activties:

B&Bs AND INNS

34. PETIT-SAGUENAY

F e 🚗 P ✕ R1 TA

In an old rural inn, we have recreated the warm and intimate ambiance of a large country house. Located on a mountainside, facing the salmon river, at the entrance of Parc Saguenay. Cruise tickets: Fjord and whales. Snowbiling.The warmth of the hearth, a meal worthy of our hospitality, receiving you will be a pleasure.

From St-Siméon in the Charlevoix region, take Rte 170 towards Chicoutimi for about 50 km. The inn is located 100 m from the tourist booth, an hour from Tadoussac and Chicoutimi.

INN
AUBERGE LES 2 PIGNONS

Régine Morin
117, route 170
Petit-Saguenay G0V 1N0
(418) 272-3091
fax (418) 272-1125
www.royaume.com/auberge-2-pignons
auberge-2-pignons
@royaume.com

	B&B	MAP
single	$40-50	$57-67
double	$50-70	$67-87
triple	$75-85	$126-136
quad.	$90-100	$158-168
child	$10	$22.50

Taxes extra VS MC ER IT
Reduced rates: Sep. 15 to Dec 15 and Mar. to June 15
Open year round

Number of rooms	8
rooms with sink	1
rooms with private bath	6
shared wc	2
shared bathrooms	2

activities: 🚤 🎣 🚶 🛷 🎿

35. ROBERVAL

F 🚗 P 🏊 R6

Come relax by splendid Lac St-Jean, a veritable inland sea. Take advantage of a well-deserved quiet moment and stretch out on our private beach near the house. It gives us great pleasure to have you as our guests.

From Parc des Laurentides, Rte 169. We are 3.5 km from the Val-Jalbert bridge. Or from La Tuque, Rte 155 to Chambord. Turn left to Roberval, Rte 169, drive 10 km B&B on your left.

B&B
LA MAISON AU TOIT ROUGE

Yolande Lalancette and
Raynald Girard
1345, boul. de l'Anse,
route 169
Roberval G8H 2N1
(418) 275-3290

B&B	
single	$35
double	$45
child	$10

Open: May 15 to Sep. 30

Number of rooms	3
shared bathrooms	2

Activities: 🏛 🛷 🚣 🚶 🚴

36. ST-AMBROISE-DE-CHICOUTIMI

F 🚫 ✕ 🚗 P ✕ R.5 AV

Located at the heart of the Saguenay-Lac-St-Jean region our house is pure country. Garden, barnyard, birds complete the enchanting setting. We offer 2- to 10-day packages in the summer: fishing, blueberry picking, lake tours. In the winter, snowmobiling, dogsledding, skiing, ice-fishing. You'll be happy year round in our home.

Route 172 between Chicoutimi and Alma. Near St-Ambroise take Rte Bégin and drive 3 km on paved road. Turn right on Rang 9 and drive 500 m on gravel road.

B&B
AUX PIGNONS VERTS

Ghislaine Ouellet and
Jean-Claude Villeneuve
925, Rang 9
St-Ambroise-de-Chicoutimi
G7P 2A4
(418) 672-2172
fax (418) 672-6622

	B&B	MAP
single	$45	52.95-64.95
double	$55	70.90-94.90
child	$25	

VS

Open year round

Number of rooms	3
shared bathrooms	2

Activities: 🚶 🚴 🛷 🐕

37. ST-FÉLICIEN

F e ⊗ 🚗 P R.1

Ten metres from the Ashuapmushuan River, and boasting a large terrace. What a joy to meet people from all over the world. Tourist attractions: zoo (6 km), falls (5 km), Val-Jalbert (20 km). Located near the town centre. Come meet us for a pleasant time. Special little considerations await you.

From Parc des Laurentides: Rte 169 twd Roberal to St-Félicien; located opposite "Mets Chinois". From Dolbeau: at 2nd light, left on Sacré-Coeur; located opposite "Mets Chinois".

B&B
À FLEUR D'EAU

Claudette Nadeau and
Paul Hébert
1016, Sacré-Coeur
St-Félicien G8K 1R5
(418) 679-0784

B&B	
single	$35
double	$45-50
triple	$55-60
quad.	$65
child	$10

Reduced rates: Oct. 1 to June 1
Open year round

Number of rooms	5
rooms with private bath	2
shared wc	1
shared bathrooms	3

Activities: 🏛 ⛴ 🚤 🕴 🚴

38. ST-FÉLICIEN

F P R3.5

Rediscover tranquillity in our old farmhouse. Large living room and balcony adjacent to rooms, private exit, outdoor rest corner. A multitude of activities nearby. In the winter, snowmobile excursions with guide possible. A warm welcome awaits you.

From Parc des Laurentides, Rte 169 to Roberval to St-Félicien. At the 1st traffic lights, left on Rue Notre-Dame. Drive 2.5 km. Left on Rang Double South, drive 1 km, farm on the left.

B&B
À LA FERME DALLAIRE

Gisèle Dallaire
678, rang Double Sud
St-Félicien G8K 2N8
(418) 679-0728

B&B	
single	$35
double	$40-45
triple	$65-70
quad.	$75-80
child	$8-15

Reduced rates: Oct. 1 to May 31
Open year round

Number of rooms	3
shared bathrooms	2

Activities: 🐾 🚤 🐎 ⛷ 🎿

39. ST-FÉLICIEN

F e P 🚗 R2

If you like the charm of the country, you'll be enchanted by our surroundings. A warm welcome in a calming and restful atmosphere. A sitting room is at your disposal. Evenings outdoors around the campfire lead to good conversation. Healthy, generous breakfast. 3 km to town, 6 km to the zoo. Reduced rates: September to June.

From Parc des Laurentides, Rte 169 towards Roberval to St-Félicien. At the 1st traffic lights, turn left on Rue Notre-Dame, drive 2.6 km. Right on Rang Double, drive 0.7km.

B&B
À LA FERME HÉBERT

Céline Giroux and
J-Jacques Hébert
1070, rang Double
St-Félicien G8K 2N8
(418) 679-0574

B&B	
single	$35
double	$45
triple	$55
child	$10

Taxes extra

Reduced rates: Sep. 15 to June 15
Open year round

Number of rooms	4
rooms with sink	1
rooms in basement	2
shared bathrooms	2

Activities: 🐾 🚤 🚴 ⛷ 🐎

B&Bs AND INNS

40. ST-FÉLICIEN

F P R2 TA

With my easy smile and the simplicity of the people of the Lac St-Jean region, I've got a warm welcome ready for you. Bedrooms with fans, generous breakfast, relaxing spot, country calm and sitting room with wood-burning stove. We will be happy to have you. Nearby: zoo, water-slides, horseback riding centre.

From Parc des Laurentides, Rte 169 twd Roberval to St-Félicien. At the 1st traffic lights, Rue Notre-Dame left, drive 2.4 km and turn left on Rang Double. Drive 0.8 km.

B&B
AU DOMAINE TREMBLAY

Lucienne and Robert
677, rang Double
St-Félicien G8K 2N8
(418) 679-0169

B&B	
single	$30
double	$40-45
child	$5-15

Reduced rates: Sep. to May 15
Open year round

Number of rooms	4
shared bathrooms	2

Activities: 🦆 🚲 🎿 🐎 ⛷

---

41. ST-FÉLICIEN

F e 🚗 P R.1

Located downtown, near a bus station, and an information centre. A warm welcome awaits you from a retired couple. Breakfast served with home-made bread and jellies. You will learn much about our culture. With pleasure.

From Parc des Laurentides, Rte 169 to Roberval. At St-Félicien, at the 1st traffic lights, left on Notre-Dame. Or from Dolbeau, at the 1st traffic lights, left on Sacré-Coeur and at the 2nd traffic lights, right on Notre-Dame.

B&B
AU JARDIN FLEURI

Thérèse and
Jean-Marie Tremblay
1179, rue Notre-Dame
St-Félicien G8K 1Z7
(418) 679-0287

B&B	
single	$30
double	$40-45
child	$7-12

Open year round

Number of rooms	4
shared bathrooms	2

Activities: 🦆 🎣 🎿 🚶 🏃

---

42. ST-FÉLICIEN

F e P R4 TA

"Chez Denise" you'll discover the hospitality of the people of Lac-St-Jean. Large house located at the heart of tourist activities: zoo, race-car track, car museum (2 km away), drive-in, golf, etc. Fishing possible. It is out pleasure to welcome you.

From Parc des Laurentides, Rte 169 to Roberval, or from La Tuque, Rte 155 to Chambord, turn left to Roberval to St-Félicien. At the 2nd traffic lights turn left, 5 km. From Dolbeau at the 2nd traffic lights, drive 5 km.

B&B
GÎTE CHEZ DENISE

Denise and Louis-Marie Gagnon
1430, rang Double
St-Félicien G8K 2N8
tel/fax (418) 679-1498

B&B	
single	$30
double	$50
child	$7-15

Open year round

Number of rooms	4
shared bathrooms	2

Activities: 🏊 🎣 🎿 🚶 🏃

43. ST-FÉLIX-D'OTIS

F | e | ⊘ | 🚗 | P | 🐕 | ✕ | R1 | TA

Halfway between La Baie and Rivière-Éternité. Small farm in the great outdoors surrounded by a pretty farmyard with animals roaming about, flowers, a large artistic garden. A haven for relaxation and rejuvenation, where life flows with the seasons. Healthy breakfast, home-made bread (bread oven), field berries and fruits. Nearby: Parc Saguenay, *Robe Noire*, *La Fabuleuse*. Air conditioned. **Farm stay p 41.**

From Parc des Laurentides, Rtes 175 N. and 170 E. Or, from St-Siméon, Rte 170 N. twd Chicoutimi.

B&B
GÎTE DE LA BASSE-COUR

Huguette Morin and
Régis Girard
271, rue Principale, route 170
St-Félix-d'Otis G0V 1M0
(418) 544-8766

B&B	
single	$35
double	$45
triple	$65
quad.	$75
child	$5-15

Open year round

Number of rooms	3
shared bathrooms	2

Activities: 🚣 ⛷ 🚶 ⛷

44. ST-FÉLIX-D'OTIS

F | e | 🚗 | P | R1 | TA

The fjord route invites you: Lac Otis, beach, canoeing fishing, kayaking. Backdrop for the film *Black Robe*, the traditions and customs of the Amerindians and the first colonists in an Iroquois village. 15 km from Rivière Éternité; cruises, cliffs, hiking trails, beavers and town of La Baie (Fabuleuse and Jos Maquillon). Copious breakfasts, blueberry crepes; tv, tourist info. Come and chat with us.

From Parc des Laurentides, Rtes 175 North and 170 East. Or from St-Siméon, Rte 170 North towards Chicoutimi.

B&B
MAISON JONCAS

Dorina Joncas
291, rue Principale
Route 170 Est, C.P. 51
St-Félix-d'Otis G0V 1M0
(418) 544-5953

B&B	
single	$30
double	$40-45
triple	$60
quad.	$65
child	$5-8

Open: May 1 to Nov. 1

Number of rooms	2
shared wc	1
shared bathrooms	1

Activities: 🦆 ⛷ 🚣 🚶

45. ST-FULGENCE

F | e | ♿ | P | 🛶 | ✕ | TA

Fairy tales are often set in enchanted forests like this. La Futaie is a wooded, 160-ha property between the Saguenay Fjord and Mont Valin. Do a bit of fishing in our wild lake. We serve ouananiche, fresh-water salmon (Montagnais called them "the little lost ones"), you can even catch your own! In winter: snowmobile base with excursion services.

Between St-Fulgence and St-Rose-du-Nord, 21 km from Dubuc bridge in Chicoutimi and 115 km from Tadoussac.

INN
AUBERGE LA FUTAIE

Jocelyne and Benoît Girard
1061, boul. Tadoussac
St-Fulgence G0V 1S0
tel/fax (418) 674-2581
grap@saglac.qc.ca

B&B	
single	$50-65
double	$60-75
triple	$75-90
quad.	$90-105
child	$10-15

Taxes extra VS MC IT

Open year round

Number of rooms	6
rooms with private bath	1
shared wc	1
shared bathrooms	2

Activities: 🦆 ⛷ 🚶 ⛷ 🛷 🐕

B&Bs AND INNS

46. ST-FULGENCE

F E 🐕 P ✗ 🛶 R8 TA

La Maraîchère du Saguenay our ancestral home, our old barn and our latest addition, a tiny house similar to our old home. Warm and stunning, cosy rooms with antique furnishings. A grandiose fjord and magnificent parks nearby, Mont-Valin, Saguenay and Cap-Jaseux. Activities around: kayak, canoe, hike, dogsled, snowmobile plus all the activities we can organise for you. Dinner available, must reserve ahead of time. See you soon.

From Chicoutimi, 8 km past Dubuc bridge, Rte 172 towards Tadoussac. Turn left 400 m after Esso station.

B&B
LA MARAÎCHÈRE
DU SAGUENAY

Adèle Copeman Langevin
97, boul. Tadoussac
St-Fulgence G0V 1S0
(418) 674-9384
(418) 674-2247
fax (418) 674-1055

B&B	
single	$45
double	$60
triple	$75
quad.	$90

VS MC

Open year round

Number of rooms	5
rooms with private bath	1
shared wc	1
shared bathrooms	2

Activities: 🧍 🚲 🛶 ⛷ 🐎

47. ST-PRIME

F 🐕 P R4 TA

Come pay us a visit. Discover the dairy farm's animals and natural surroundings. Make a date for some relaxation and tranquillity. Warm welcome. Savour an original, generous breakfast. Your trip will make for wonderful memories. Close: Zoo St-Félicien, Cheddar museum, native village, pioneer mill, ghost village, etc.

From Parc des Laurentides, Rte 169 twd Roberval. At St-Prime, across from the church, left on 15e Avenue for 3.3 km, right for 4.1 km.

B&B
GÎTE FERME DU PATURIN

Francine Villeneuve and
Yvan Grenier
1028, Rang 3
St-Prime G8J 1X5
tel/fax (418) 251-2837

B&B	
single	$35-40
double	$50-55
child	$5-12

Open year round

Number of rooms	4
rooms with private bath	1
shared bathrooms	2

Activities: 🏛 🚗 🧍 🚲 🛶

48. ST-PRIME

F P 🐕 🛶 R4 TA

Century-old house on a dairy farm, on one of the prettiest farm roads, surrounded by pretty gardens, waterfalls, pool. If you like the space and tranquillity of the country, you'll feel at home at our house. It will be our pleasure to share special moments with you. Visit the farm. Located amidst all the main tourist attractions of Lac-St-Jean: St-Félicien zoo, Indian and ghost town, cheddar museum, pioneer mills, hydraulic-plane tours, etc.

From Parc des Laurentides, Rte 169 to Roberval. In St-Prime, facing the church, turn left on 15e Ave. Drive 3.3 km, turn right, drive 2 km.

B&B
LA MAISON CAMPAGNARDE

Brigitte Boivin and
Roger Taillon
850, Rang 3
St-Prime G8J 1X3
tel/fax (418) 251-3235

B&B	
single	$35-40
double	$45-55
child	$5-12

Open year round

Number of rooms	4
shared wc	1
shared bathrooms	1

Activities: 🐚 🚗 🧍 🚲 🛶

49. STE-JEANNE-D'ARC

F P R7 TA

Enjoy the peacefulness of a small turn-of-the-century farm amidst the wide expanses of the countryside. We have been warmly welcoming guests for 20 years now. Our breakfasts include: pancakes with blueberry syrup, local-fruit jelly, blueberries, etc. Discover the farm's attractions, a blueberry grove.

From Parc des Laurentides, Rte 169 towards Roberval to Ste-Jeanne-d'Arc. Do not go into the village, but continue on Rte 169 for 7.5 km, turn left towards St-Augustin, drive 0.9 km. At the 1st curve, keep going straight on the gravel road, drive 1.5 km on Route Harvey, turn right.

B&B
FERME HARVEY

Denise Bouchard and
Bertrand Harvey
230, chemin Lapointe
Ste-Jeanne-d'Arc G0W 1E0
(418) 276-2810

B&B	
single	$30
double	$45
triple	$65
child	$5-10

Open year round

Number of rooms	3
shared bathrooms	2

Activities: 🏖 🚲 🧍 ⛷ 🐕

50. FERLAND-ET-BOILLEAU

F e P R30 M30

Welcome to our home! Awe-inspiring site nestled deep in the mountains. Personalized welcome in rustic cottages with all modern conveniences, by a wild lake. Traditional meals. On site: hikes, dogsledding expeditions, skidooing and horseback riding; small farm, teepee, snowshoeing, observation of fauna.

From Québec City (2 h 15): Rte 138 twd Baie-St-Paul, Rte 381 via St-Urbain. In Boilleau: drive 6 km, left on Rang Edmour-Lavoie. From La Baie (25 min): Rte 138 to Ferland. Drive 8 km, right on Rang Edmour-Lavoie.

COUNTRY HOME
GÎTES and AVENTURES DU
LOUP POLAIRE

Lucie Tremblay and
William Antoine
1105, rang Edmour-Lavoie
Ferland-et-Boilleau G0V 1H0
(418) 676-1013
fax (418) 676-1037

No. houses	2
No. rooms	2
No. people	36314
WEEK-SUMMER	$350-450
WEEK-WINTER	$300-400
W/E-SUMMER	$250-300
W/E-WINTER	$200-250
DAY-SUMMER	$30-150
DAY-WINTER	$30-150
Taxes extra	

Open year round

Activities: 🏛 🍷 ⛷ ⛷ 🤸

51. ST-DAVID-DE-FALARDEAU

F E P R3 M3 TA

Come and discover our little paradise on an enchanting and charming site, next to the forest. A magnificent log chalet, fully equipped, facing a little lake and our pack of huskies. Discover our original table d'hôte menu and our winter activities. Sleigh rides, snowmobiling, ice-fishing. Close by: rafting, archery, fishing and swimming. We look forward to welcoming you.

From Québec City, Rte 175 N. In Chicoutimi, take the Dubuc bridge, Rte 172 W. to the "FALARDEAU" sign. In Falardeau, right at the church, right after the corner store, right on the 3rd street, 1.7 km.

COUNTRY HOME
LES CHIENS and GÎTE
DU GRAND NORD

Valérie Nataf and
Frédéric Dorgebray
Lot 18, Lac Durand #2
C.P. 310
St-David-de-Falardeau
G0V 1C0
(418) 673-7717
fax (418)673-4072
www.chiens-gite.qc.ca
clarouche@qc.aira.com

No. houses	1
No. rooms	1
No. people	7
WEEK-SUMMER	$347.75
WEEK-WINTER	$304.28
W/E-SUMMER	$217.35
W/E-WINTER	$217.35
DAY-SUMMER	$17.38
DAY-WINTER	$17.38
Taxes extra	

Open year round

Activities: 🏖 🧍 ⛷ 🎿 🐕

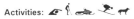

**B&Bs AND INNS
COUNTRY HOME**

FARM ACTIVITIES

Farm stay:

* Registered trademark

—M—

Travel Notes _____

ACCOMMODATION

Your opinion is important for the continued EXCELLENCE of our guide.

In order to continue to improve the network and the quality of the services it offers, please send your comments and suggestions to: Fédération des Agricotours, C.P. 1000 succ., M, Montréal, Québec, H1V 3R2.

Win a free stay !

Each year, Agricotours awards a prize of EXCELLENCE to several of its members. The selection is based on clients' commentary cards, therefore we invite you to fill out the following card to show your appreciation and win the chance of staying at one of our members' establishments for free!

What was your overall experience?

RECEPTION
Friendliness and availability of hosts, special details

_____
_____
_____
_____

YOUR ROOM
Comfort of beds, overall comfort of room, cleanliness, quality of bedding

_____
_____
_____
_____

MEALS
Quality of food, quality of presentation, flexibility of serving times

_____
_____
_____
_____

HOUSE
Comfort, cleanliness, decor, general impression of the site

_____
_____
_____
_____

BATHROOM
Appropriate installation, cleanliness

_____
_____
_____
_____

Comments and suggestions

_____
_____
_____
_____
_____
_____
_____
_____
_____

YOUR OVERALL APPRECIATION
Excellent ☐   Good ☐
Very good ☐   Poor ☐

For our statistics

Was this your first experience with the Agricotours network?

☐ Yes
☐ No   How many times_____

Profession _____

Age

☐ 8-19   ☐ 20-29   ☐ 30-39   ☐ 40-49
☐ 50-59   ☐ 60-69   ☐ 70 and
                              more

YOUR NAME	
YOUR ADDRESS	STREET
	CITY
	COUNTRY POSTAL CODE
NAME OF THE ESTABLISHMENT VISITED	
DATE OF VISIT	
MUNICIPALITY OR REGION	

ACCOMMODATION

Your opinion is important for the continued EXCELLENCE of our guide.

In order to continue to improve the network and the quality of the services it offers, please send your comments and suggestions to: Fédération des Agricotours, C.P. 1000 succ., M, Montréal, Québec, H1V 3R2.

Win a free stay !

Each year, Agricotours awards a prize of EXCELLENCE to several of its members. The selection is based on clients' commentary cards, therefore we invite you to fill out the following card to show your appreciation and win the chance of staying at one of our members' establishements for free!

What was your overall experience?

RECEPTION
Friendliness and availability of hosts, special details

_____

_____

_____

_____

YOUR ROOM
Comfort of beds, overall comfort of room, cleanliness, quality of bedding

_____

_____

_____

_____

MEALS
Quality of food, quality of presentation, flexibility of serving times

_____

_____

_____

_____

HOUSE
Comfort, cleanliness, decor, general impression of the site

_____

_____

_____

_____

BATHROOM
Appropriate installation, cleanliness

_____

_____

_____

_____

Comments and suggestions

_____
_____
_____
_____
_____
_____
_____
_____
_____
_____

YOUR OVERALL APPRECIATION

Excellent ☐   Good ☐

Very good ☐   Poor ☐

For our statistics

Was this your first experience with the Agricotours network?

☐ Yes

☐ No   How many times_____

Profession _____

Age

☐ 8-19   ☐ 20-29   ☐ 30-39   ☐ 40-49

☐ 50-59   ☐ 60-69   ☐ 70 and more

YOUR NAME	
YOUR ADDRESS	STREET
	CITY
	COUNTRY POSTAL CODE
NAME OF THE ESTABLISHMENT VISITED	
DATE OF VISIT	
MUNICIPALITY OR REGION	

Your opinion is important for the continued EXCELLENCE of our guide.

In order to continue to improve the network and the quality of the services it offers, please send your comments and suggestions to: Fédération des Agricotours, C.P. 1000 succ., M, Montréal, Québec, H1V 3R2.

Win a free stay !

Each year, Agricotours awards a prize of EXCELLENCE to several of its members. The selection is based on clients' commentary cards, therefore we invite you to fill out the following card to show your appreciation and win the chance of staying at one of our members' establishments for free!

What was your overall experience?

RECEPTION
Friendliness and availability of hosts, special details

_____
_____
_____
_____

YOUR ROOM
Comfort of beds, overall comfort of room, cleanliness, quality of bedding

_____
_____
_____
_____

MEALS
Quality of food, quality of presentation, flexibility of serving times

_____
_____
_____
_____

HOUSE
Comfort, cleanliness, decor, general impression of the site

_____
_____
_____
_____

BATHROOM
Appropriate installation, cleanliness

_____
_____
_____
_____

Comments and suggestions

_____
_____
_____
_____
_____
_____
_____
_____
_____

YOUR OVERALL APPRECIATION

Excellent ☐   Good ☐
Very good ☐   Poor ☐

For our statistics

Was this your first experience with the Agricotours network?

☐ Yes
☐ No   How many times_____

Profession _____

Age

☐ 8-19   ☐ 20-29   ☐ 30-39   ☐ 40-49
☐ 50-59   ☐ 60-69   ☐ 70 and
                            more

YOUR NAME		
YOUR ADDRESS	STREET	
	CITY	
	COUNTRY	POSTAL CODE
NAME OF THE ESTABLISHMENT VISITED		
DATE OF VISIT		
MUNICIPALITY OR REGION		

COUNTRY DINING

Your opinion is important for the continued EXCELLENCE of our guide.

In order to continue to improve the network and the quality of the services it offers, please send your comments and suggestions to: Fédération des Agricotours, C.P. 1000 succ., M, Montréal, Québec, H1V 3R2.

Win a free stay !

Each year, Agricotours awards a prize of EXCELLENCE to several of its members. The selection is based on clients' commentary cards, therefore we invite you to fill out the following card to show your appreciation and win the chance of staying at one of our members' establishments for free!

What was your overall experience?

	Excellent	Very good	Good	Poor
ACCESSIBILITY, EASY TO FIND				
WELCOME				
-friendliness of hosts	☐	☐	☐	☐
-availability of hosts	☐	☐	☐	☐
THE MEAL				
-quality of the food	☐	☐	☐	☐
-freshness of ingredients	☐	☐	☐	☐
-quality of presentation	☐	☐	☐	☐
-quantity of food served	☐	☐	☐	☐
THE DINING ROOM				
-comfort	☐	☐	☐	☐
-cleanliness	☐	☐	☐	☐
ROOMS IN GENERAL				
-comfort	☐	☐	☐	☐
-cleanliness	☐	☐	☐	☐
OVERALL IMPRESSION				
-exterior of the house	☐	☐	☐	☐
-out-buildings	☐	☐	☐	☐
-fields	☐	☐	☐	☐
-cattle	☐	☐	☐	☐
-garden (in season)	☐	☐	☐	☐
Tour of the area suggested by hosts	☐	☐	☐	☐
Quality-price ratio	☐	☐	☐	☐

Comments and suggestions

YOUR OVERALL APPRECIATION

Excellent ☐   Good ☐

Very good ☐   Poor ☐

For our statistics

Was this your first experience with the Agricotours network?

☐ Yes

☐ No   How many times_____

Profession _____

Age

☐ 8-19   ☐ 20-29   ☐ 30-39   ☐ 40-49

☐ 50-59   ☐ 60-69   ☐ 70 and more

YOUR NAME		
YOUR ADDRESS	STREET	
	CITY	
	COUNTRY	POSTAL CODE
NAME OF THE ESTABLISHMENT VISITED		
DATE OF VISIT		
MUNICIPALITY OR REGION		

Travel Notes _____

ORDER FORM

ULYSSES TRAVEL GUIDES

☐ Atlantic Canada	$24.95 CAN $17.95 US	☐ Lisbon	$18.95 CAN $13.95 US
☐ Bahamas	$24.95 CAN $17.95 US	☐ Louisiana	$29.95 CAN $21.95 US
☐ Beaches of Maine	$12.95 CAN $9.95 US	☐ Martinique	$24.95 CAN $17.95 US
☐ Bed & Breakfasts in Québec	$13.95 CAN $10.95 US	☐ Montréal	$19.95 CAN $14.95 US
☐ Belize	$16.95 CAN $12.95 US	☐ New Orleans	$17.95 CAN $12.95 US
☐ Calgary	$17.95 CAN $12.95 US	☐ New York City	$19.95 CAN $14.95 US
☐ Canada	$29.95 CAN $21.95 US	☐ Nicaragua	$24.95 CAN $16.95 US
☐ Chicago	$19.95 CAN $14.95 US	☐ Ontario	$27.95 CAN $19.95US
☐ Chile	$27.95 CAN $17.95 US	☐ Ottawa	$17.95 CAN $12.95 US
☐ Colombia	$29.95 CAN $21.95 US	☐ Panamá	$24.95 CAN $17.95 US
☐ Costa Rica	$27.95 CAN $19.95 US	☐ Perú	$27.95 CAN $19.95 US
☐ Cuba	$24.95 CAN $17.95 US	☐ Portugal	$24.95 CAN $16.95 US
☐ Dominican Republic	$24.95 CAN $17.95 US	☐ Provence - Côte d'Azur	$29.95 CAN $21.95US
☐ Ecuador and Galapagos Islands	$24.95 CAN $17.95 US	☐ Québec	$29.95 CAN $21.95 US
☐ El Salvador	$22.95 CAN $14.95 US	☐ Québec and Ontario with Via	$9.95 CAN $7.95 US
☐ Guadeloupe	$24.95 CAN $17.95 US	☐ Toronto	$18.95 CAN $13.95 US
☐ Guatemala	$24.95 CAN $17.95 US	☐ Vancouver	$17.95 CAN $12.95 US
☐ Honduras	$24.95 CAN $17.95 US	☐ Washington D.C.	$18.95 CAN $13.95 US
☐ Jamaica	$24.95 CAN $17.95 US	☐ Western Canada	$29.95 CAN $21.95 US

ULYSSES DUE SOUTH

☐ Acapulco	$14.95 CAN $9.95 US	☐ Cartagena (Colombia)	$12.95 CAN $9.95 US
☐ Belize	$16.95 CAN $12.95 US	☐ Cancun Cozumel	$17.95 CAN $12.95 US

ULYSSES DUE SOUTH

☐ Puerto Vallarta	$14.95 CAN $9.95 US	☐ St. Martin and St. Barts	$16.95 CAN $12.95 US

ULYSSES TRAVEL JOURNAL

☐ Ulysses Travel Journal .. $9.95 CAN
(Blue, Red, Green, Yellow, Sextant)
$7.95 US

☐ Ulysses Travel Journal ... $14.95 CAN
(80 Days)
$9.95 US

ULYSSES GREEN ESCAPES

☐ Cycling in France ...... $22.95 CAN
$16.95 US
☐ Cycling in Ontario ...... $22.95 CAN
$16.95 US

☐ Hiking in the .... $19.95 CAN
Northeastern U.S.
$13.95 US
☐ Hiking in Québec ...... $19.95 CAN
$13.95 US

ULYSSES CONVERSATION GUIDES

☐ French for Better Travel .. $9.95 CAN
$6.50 US

☐ Spanish for Better Travel .. $9.95 CAN
in Latin America
$6.50 US

TITLE	QUANTITY	PRICE	TOTAL

Name _____	Sub-total	
Address _____	Postage & Handling	$8.00*
_____	Sub-total	
Payment : ☐ Money Order ☐ Visa ☐ MasterCard	G.S.T. in Canada 7%	
Card Number _____		
Signature _____	TOTAL	

ULYSSES TRAVEL PUBLICATIONS
4176 St-Denis,
Montréal, Québec, H2W 2M5
(514) 843-9447 fax (514) 843-9448
www.ulysses.ca
* $15 for overseas orders

U.S. ORDERS: **GLOBE PEQUOT PRESS**
P.O. Box 833, 6 Business Park Road,
Old Saybrook, CT 06475-0833
1-800-243-0495 fax 1-800-820-2329
www.globe-pequot.com